BIRDS OF THE WORLD

Recommended English Names

REGION CHAIRS

G. Stuart Keith
Christopher Perrins
Nigel Redman
Robert S. Ridgely
Stephen M. Russell
Peter G. Ryan
Richard Schodde

Taxonomic Editor

David B. Donsker

Compiler

Sally Conyne

BIRDS OF THE WORLD
Recommended English Names

FRANK GILL AND MINTURN WRIGHT
on behalf of the International Ornithological Congress

PRINCETON UNIVERSITY PRESS
PRINCETON AND OXFORD

Library of Congress Cataloging-in-Publication Data

Gill, Frank B.
Birds of the world : recommended English names / Frank Gill and Minturn Wright,
on behalf of the International Ornithological Congress.
p. cm.
Includes bibliographical references and index.
ISBN-13: 978-0-691-12827-6 (alk. : paper)
ISBN-10: 0-691-12827-8 (alk. : paper)
1. Birds—Nomenclature (Popular) I. Wright, Minturn T., 1925–   II. International
Ornithological Congress. III. Title.
QL677.G55 2006
598.01′4—dc22   2006041605

British Library Cataloging-in-Publication Data is available
This book has been composed in Baskerville
Printed on acid-free paper. ∞

pup.princeton.edu

Printed in the United States of America

1 3 5 7 9 10 8 6 4 2

Contents

CONTENTS

CONTENTS

BIRDS OF THE WORLD

Recommended English Names

Introduction

"Wisdom begins with putting the right name to a thing" (Old Chinese Proverb)

Most of us refer to birds by their English names, which seem to change too frequently, or be the same for different species on different continents, or vary from list to list. Nearly twenty years ago, the leadership of the International Ornithological Congress (IOC) saw the need for better standardized vernacular names. First came French names (Devillers and Ouellet 1993), then Spanish names (Bernis 1995). English names were especially challenging, taking more than fifteen years to compile.

Our goal—a set of unique English-language names for the extant species of the birds of the world—was easier to state than it was to achieve. The names would conform to a set of rules formulated through a consensus of leading ornithologists worldwide.

When one valued colleague saw our work in progress, he exclaimed, "What a total waste of time!" He was bent on saving the world's oceans and their declining fisheries, both pressing issues. Some colleagues in ornithology expressed similar sentiments when they declined our invitation to participate on one of the committees. "Can't be done," they said. "Isn't that what scientific names are for?" others asserted.

Many others disagreed, committed themselves to participate, and then worked long and hard together for over a decade. Our team view is that an improved and better standardized system of English names based on consensus and a logical set of rules will lead to success in ornithology and the conservation of beleaguered avifaunas worldwide. The proposed names would also increase clear, crisp, and global communication among various stakeholders. These stakeholders include government officials, publishers, and philanthropists, many of whom are not comfortable with or literate in scientific names. Many stakeholders also contribute as amateur ornithologists, not as taxonomists. Global birders need improved standardization and greater simplicity of English names. So does the vital community of conservation biologists. So do the editors of the growing industry of books on the birds of different countries and different families. All stakeholders need to communicate clearly without using hyphens in four different ways and without trying to reconcile the treatment of different names in varied authoritative works.

So, on behalf of the IOC we submit this list of recommended International English names of the extant birds of the world. The members of the IOC Standing Committee on English Names endorse these names and encourage their use by our colleagues in ornithology, and by book publishers, government agencies, checklist committees, and conservation organizations.

Passions about bird names run high. We know that adoption of the names on this list will be strictly voluntary, perhaps piecemeal, and probably slow. The same colleagues who professed no interest in the initiative likely will rush to defend their preferred names of favorite birds. But we truly believe that the list of names recommended here has important strengths, and, if used widely, will promote consistency and authority.

The names are:
- based on rules that simplify and standardize name construction
- selected to involve minimal use of hyphens for group names
- anglicized without glottal stops, accents, and the like
- based on interregional agreement and global consensus, with compromises
- selected with deference to long-established names
- aligned with current, though ever-changing, species taxonomy
- recommended but not mandatory; local adoptions are wholly voluntary
- sponsored and endorsed by the IOC and by committee members

This is not primarily a taxonomic work. Rather, it supplements the third edition (Dickinson 2003) of Howard and Moore's (H&M) Checklist of the Birds of the World. We started with the world list of Sibley and Monroe (1990). In the end, we adopted H&M as the taxonomic reference for this work. We employed H&M's family classification, generic sequences, and assignments to "incertae sedis," with few exceptions and updates. Many changes are forthcoming, informed by DNA-based phylogenetic analyses. Paramount among these will be overhauls of the relationships and classification of the sylvioid "warblers" of Eurasia and Africa. Also informing future editions of this list will be major new works such as Rasmussen and Anderson's *Birds of South Asia: The Ripley Guide* (2005). We adhered to H&M's conservative species taxonomy, unless committee chairs requested otherwise. We accepted species additions to the world list published prior to December 31, 2004, and endorsed by committee chairs.

We offer this list as our recommendations to the communities of ornithologists and their publishers. It is a first edition and a work in progress that will benefit from use, evaluation, and thoughtful feedback. It does not achieve some potentially desirable consistencies, for instance, with respect to using the same group name for all members of a genus (e.g., raven versus crow [*Corvus*], serin versus canary [*Serinus*], tit versus chickadee [*Poecile*]). But it is a major step in the direction of logic and standardization. Some will use it in its entirety, others will pick and choose the parts they like. Still others will reject it, at least initially. We ask only that our colleagues explore its merits and seek out its deficiencies diligently. It has, we believe, depth built on the expertise of some of the best ornithologists of our generation. Each found balance between local traditions and progressive improvements.

The naming of birds is an ongoing work-in-process. New discoveries and new tastes will produce new names. We hope that we have started down the road of progress. We welcome ideas on how to proceed.

HISTORY

The project to standardize the recommended English names of every extant bird species in the world was set in motion at the 1990 meeting of the IOC, which appointed a committee of eminent ornithologists to consider the matter. The late Burt L. Monroe Jr. was named as chair of the committee, and he in turn named eleven well-known ornithologists as committee members.

Monroe created an initial list of all the species and subspecies of birds from the monumental "Distribution and Taxonomy of Birds of the World" authored by himself and Charles Sibley. The project had to have a starting point, and this was a natural one. Monroe and his committee engaged in extended preliminary discussions and debates. Their votes on a series of issues revealed a great deal of disagreement on how birds should be named and what the jurisdiction of the committee should be. The project thus proved to be more difficult and time-consuming than had been expected, and Monroe died before much had been accomplished. The project then went into abeyance.

It was revived in late 1994 by Frank Gill and Walter Bock. Speaking for the IOC, Bock invited Gill to take over the project, which he did early in 1995. Gill asked Minturn Wright, a lawyer by profession and world birder by avocation, to act as recording secretary and organizer of the process the project would follow. Bock named Gill and Wright to act as co-chairs of the committee. Gill then asked each person on Monroe's committee to rejoin the project; most of them did. Gill expanded the committee by the addition of another twelve or thirteen eminent ornithologists, bringing the committee to twenty-eight ornithologists from fourteen countries (see Acknowledgments) plus the co-chairs (Gill and Wright) for a total of thirty. The committee operated through six regional subcommittees, chaired as follows: Palearctic—Christopher Perrins; Nearctic—Stephen M. Russell; Africa—Peter G. Ryan and the late G. Stuart Keith; Neotropics—Robert S.

Ridgely; Oriental Region—Nigel Redman; Australasia—Richard Schodde.

PROCESS AND PRINCIPLES

The creation of the committee and the organization of its process were based on the following principles:

- The committee operated almost exclusively through its six regional sub-committees. The members of each subcommittee were experts on the birds of that region.
- In an effort to resolve many of the problems that had plagued the Monroe committee, the committee adopted at the outset a set of basic rules or principles that would be applied in the selection and spelling of names.
- The project was not to be a vehicle for the wholesale changing of the names of birds but rather an effort to standardize names.
- The subcommittees would strive for consistency, an important aspect of standardization, but if long usage and common sense required inconsistencies the committee would accept them.
- No special consideration would be given to the names on the Sibley-Monroe list, which was selected as the initial working list.
- The project was to standardize the names of full species and would not include subspecies (although the Sibley-Monroe list covered both). This decision was made to give the project a manageable scope. A corollary was that the description of a taxon by Sibley-Monroe as a full species or subspecies would not govern the committee's selection of the taxon. The committee decided early on that as a general rule it was not within its province to make taxonomic decisions, but as the project progressed it became necessary to do so to some extent.
- Similarly, in the course of the work, taxa were noted that did not appear on

the Sibley-Monroe list. Each committee was free to decide whether to add those taxa to the list under the basic principles adopted. Looking ahead, we expect this process to continue for new species (either discovered or split off from existing species).

The process agreed to was as follows:
- The entire list of names was divided among the six subcommittees, each of which took the initiative with respect to the names assigned to it. Two or more committees shared an interest in some widespread species. In most cases, however, it was clear which subcommittee had precedence.
- Each subcommittee came up with its list of names, which often involved compromises and sometimes non-unanimous decisions within the subcommittee.
- Through their chairs, each subcommittee was given the opportunity to comment on the names submitted by the other subcommittees, and while their comments were often accepted, each subcommittee had the final say as to the names on its list in most cases. In those cases where a taxon is substantially present in two or more regions, a general consensus was sought.
- The lists were reviewed by the co-chairs to determine compliance with the basic principles that had been adopted (mentioned above and detailed below). Finally, the co-chairs had the responsibility of ensuring that the six lists were consistent not only with the basic principles but with one another, and of resolving any differences that remained.

The committee's first job was to agree on and frame the basic principles that would govern the selection and spelling of names. It took years of discussion and debate to do so. The following basic rules were adopted:

1. Existing usage would be the predominant guideline. A long-established name

would not be changed just to correct a perceived inaccuracy or misdescription. "Inaccurate" names like Philadelphia Vireo and Dartford Warbler would stand. Names utilizing widespread words like *Warbler* and *Robin* for many groups of unrelated species would not be changed. Names with faulty descriptions of taxa were subject to change if the taxa had had several names, or if the name or the taxon was not widely known (as is notably the case for a number of tropical taxa). On occasion it was hard to draw the line between the importance of retaining a long-used name and the need to correct a misdescription, and some subcommittees drew the line more strictly than others.

2. Local vernacular names would not prevail over established formal names. The committee rejected the many "local" names for species of waterfowl and the names used, for example, by native Jamaicans to describe some of their birds (e.g., Old Man Bird). If a local nickname or vernacular name had been long used as the chief or only name for a taxon, however, the committee retained it (e.g., Go-away Bird, Morepork, Jacky Winter).

3. If a name was offensive to a substantial group of people, it would be changed. Kaffir Rail was an example, as were names using the former name of a certain country or region, such as Ceylon (now Sri Lanka) or Formosa (now Taiwan). The name of a former country was not changed just to reflect a new name if no one was offended by the old name or there was uncertainty about acceptance of the new name, such as Burma instead of Myanmar.

4. Every taxon would have only one recommended International English name throughout the world. The co-chairs consistently rejected suggested compromises that would list alternative names (e.g., Bearded Vulture or Lammergeier, Little Auk or Dovekie). This principle appears obvious and easy to state, but it presented serious problems for members of the Nearctic and Palearctic subcommittees, who favored one or the other of the different names used in Great Britain or the United States for the same taxa.

5. The name of each taxon must be different from the names of all other taxa. This principle generated the corollary that where two or more taxa had basically the same name, modifiers would have to be added to distinguish them. Thus three "Black Ducks" had to be named American, African, and Pacific and two "White Ibises" American and Australian. A related rule that the committee adopted was that the full name of one species should not be included in the longer name of another species, which required modifiers to be added to taxa that for centuries were one-word names like Swallow, Wren, and Robin in Britain. It would also prohibit a pair of names like Black-headed Gull and Great Black-headed Gull.

6. Since the project was undertaken to create a list of recommended English names, the committee adopted the principle that only English words should be used. A name did not have to reflect its taxonomic name, which is usually in either Greek or Latin, but the committee decided that just because a bird's long-standing name was in fact its taxonomic name, it did not have to be changed to an English word. Usage would govern. Thus names like Junco, Vireo, and Rhea have been retained. This is of particular significance in names of tropical birds, many of which are the taxon's generic names (e.g., *Elaenia, Jacana, Dacnis, Attila, Myzomela*). The committee rejected the idea of a wholesale renaming of these taxa, while recognizing that ongoing revisions of bird genera will continue to create odd mismatches. The committee likewise accepted a large number of Spanish words on the basis of long usage (e.g., Doradito, Monjita, Tapaculo) and

even a number of Amerindian ones (e.g., Quetzal, Cacique). These latter two names are now in such wide usage that they appear in the *Oxford English Dictionary*. The committee decided that non-English words that have been in common use for a substantial time have in effect become "English," at least in the absence of any recognized English alternatives.

The most troublesome question was whether to adopt Hawaiian-language names for endemic Hawaiian birds. The spelling of those names with generally unfamiliar accent marks made this an even closer call. In the end the committee decided to follow such authorities as the *New York Times Atlas of the World* (for country names that are included in a species name), the AOU Checklist (7th ed.), and others, and to use anglicized versions of Hawaiian bird names and other established non-English names.

7. Many bird names include the names of persons, often discoverers or eminent ornithologists. Using patronyms in bird names has been popular or unpopular over the years, depending on the tastes or principles of the namers. The committee adopted a neutral stance. There would be no bias for or against patronyms. This had the effect of letting long usage largely govern these names, although the differing tastes and attitudes of the various committee members have played a role.

8. A bird's name may consist of a single word (e.g., Brolga, Killdeer, Twite). The committee rejected the contrary view that every name must have a modifier. Yet it agreed that a taxon could have a two-word name even where it is the only taxon in its group and could therefore potentially have a one-word name (e.g., Kinglet Calyptura, Marvelous Spatuletail). Despite such rare exceptions, we adopted the general principle that brevity and simplicity are virtues and that each name

should be as short as reasonably possible and with rare exceptions never exceed four words, hyphenated or not.

9. If a name includes an island or islands, the word *island* or *islands* will not be included except where the resulting name is misleading (e.g., Pitt Shag and Christmas Frigatebird, but Inaccessible Island Rail).

10. For group names, defined as a word or words that apply to two or more taxa, the committee adopted several basic principles. A group name may be applied to two or more unrelated groups (e.g., Warbler [Parulidae, Sylviidae] and Robin [Turdidae, Petroicidae, *Erithacus*]). A group name can consist of one, two, or more words (e.g., Warbler, Eagle-Owl, Green Pigeon). A single genus may have two or more group names within it (e.g., Duck, Wigeon, Shoveler, and Teal within *Anas*).

PROBLEMS OF SPELLING

The selection of names proved to be easier than agreement on how to spell them. Some spelling problems were simple and readily agreed to by the committees. Briefly, the rules are as follows:

1. Official English names of birds are capitalized, as is the current practice in ornithology (e.g., Yellow-throated Warbler).

2. Patronyms are used in the possessive case (e.g., Smith's, Ross's).

3. Names on this list do not include diacritical marks.

4. There are compromises between British and American spellings in this list.

5. Those who adopt the list should spell and add pronunciation marks as preferred.

6. Geographical words in a name may be in noun or adjective form but must be consistent for that location (e.g., Canada, not Canadian).

7. Compound words conform to a series of rules that consistently address relationships between the two words and readability.

8. Use of hyphens is minimized.

9. For compound group names, hyphens are used only to connect two names that are birds or bird families (e.g., Eagle-Owl, Flycatcher-shrike) or when the name would be difficult to read (e.g., Silky-flycatcher, White-eye).

A detailed discussion of the thinking behind these rules follows.

1. **Capitalization.** An important rule adopted at the outset was that the words of an official bird's name begin with capital letters. While this is contrary to the general rules of spelling for mammals, birds, insects, fish, and other life forms (i.e., use lowercase letters), the committee believed the initial capital to be preferable for the name of a bird species in an ornithological context, first because it has been the customary spelling in bird books for some years, and also because it distinguishes a taxonomic species from a general description of a bird. Several species of sparrows could be described as "white-throated sparrows," but a "White-throated Sparrow" is a particular taxonomic species.

2. **Patronyms and accents.** It was agreed that if a name contained a patronym it would be stated in the possessive case (e.g., Smith's Longspur), and if the patronym ended with an *s* the apostrophe would be followed by an *s* (e.g., Ross's Turaco). There was general agreement to spell a patronym the way the person spelled it, even where the name was not English and the English spelling of the name differed (e.g., spelling a German name with an umlaut over the *u*, not the English *ue*). Initially the committee decided to use diacriticals on all words that in the language of origin were spelled with accents, even though accents are not used in English spelling, such as the French grave and acute accents, the Spanish cedilla and accents for Spanish place names, and the

German umlaut. A major point of contention was whether to adopt the glottal and other diacritical marks used in the Hawaiian language since, unlike other accent marks, they are almost totally unfamiliar to English-speakers. The committee decided against using such accents for that reason. This then led to a reconsideration of the use of accents generally. In the end the committee chairs decided to follow the precedent of the American Ornithologists' Union (AOU) Committee on Classification and Nomenclature and the *New York Times Atlas* among others and to use no accents, except umlauts for certain proper names of people.

Supporting this difficult decision is our view that the list of International English names is not a guide to correct pronunciation, the sole purpose of using accents in local languages of the world. That said, the committee is neutral as to the wishes of authors of regional works, who should feel free to add pronunciation marks that they consider to be appropriate for their intended audience.

3. **British versus American spellings.** The names reflect the committee's view that spelling should be consistent throughout the list. Easily stated and on its face obvious, this rule became very difficult to apply where the same words have for centuries been spelled differently in different English-speaking countries. The problem essentially involves British and American spellings, with some countries being on one side and some on the other. The gray/grey difference is the most pervasive and best known, but other variant words are color/colour, mustache/moustache, racket/racquet, ocher/ochre, somber/sombre, saber/sabre, miter/mitre, sulfur/sulphur, and perhaps others. The committee decided to encourage each author and publisher to select whatever spelling of these words is deemed appropriate (since that would undoubtedly happen anyway). But in publishing its master list the committee decided to select one spelling for each variant word, because to state these words in the alternative in every case would produce a cumbersome list. The spellings selected by the

committee represent a compromise. *Grey* is used because far more taxa have traditionally used that spelling than *gray*. The list likewise adopts the British spelling of sombre, sabre, sulphur, mitre, ochre, and moustache, and the American spelling of color and racket. This tilt to the British side is justified by the fact that both spellings of every one of these variant words is considered correct in typical American dictionaries, such as the unabridged *Merriam-Webster Dictionary*. We hope this solution will find favor with most users of the list.

The list of recommended names uses particular spellings merely as dictated by the decision to provide one name. Those who use the list should feel free to adopt the appropriate spelling.

4. Geographical nouns versus adjectives. An additional spelling question surfaced during the course of the project: whether to spell a geographical word in its noun or adjective form. An in-depth review of existing names revealed that, in general, places of large size have been spelled in the adjective form (e.g., African, Mexican, Japanese), while smaller places are spelled as nouns (e.g., Timor, Kentucky, Nepal). Continents and major regions have always been spelled in adjective form, while small islands and cities have always been spelled as nouns. Countries and large islands are treated inconsistently. Some countries are always found in adjective form (e.g., Egyptian, Chinese), while others are always in noun form (e.g., Canada, Gabon). The same is true of large islands (e.g., Javan and Bornean, on the one hand, and Madagascar and Sulawesi on the other). The committee decided that to achieve complete consistency among names would require the wholesale changing of familiar names. It would also pose too many difficult decisions on which way to go—noun or adjective—and where to draw the line between large and small. We decided to leave the names the way they were, and to make only such changes as were necessary to create consistency in the use of each individual name (e.g., to use Tahiti consistently and not have both Tahiti and Tahitian). This required remarkably few changes.

5. Compound names. The most difficult problem to resolve, because of widely disparate attitudes within the committee, was the spelling of compound words, particularly where found in group names. In general, a compound word is a combination of two words that in theory could be spelled as one word, as two words, or as two words hyphenated (e.g., Woodpigeon, Wood-Pigeon, or Wood Pigeon). In bird names a fourth alternative spelling is to follow the hyphen with a lowercase letter (e.g., Wood-pigeon). The problem is complicated by the use of variant spellings over many years. For example, Audubon used hyphens freely (as in Meadow-lark), in cases where now single words are used. The trend has been toward greater use of single words because it achieves a greater distinctiveness for the species. (Here the committee decided that usage was not as important in resolving spelling questions as it was in name selection, because it is hard to establish usage. Attitudes about hyphens have changed repeatedly over the decades.) The committee adopted the following principles:

A. *Single words*. Compound names are spelled as single words if the second word is *bird* (e.g., Bluebird, Tropicbird, Secretarybird) or its equivalent (e.g., Woodcock, Waterhen); or where the second word is a body part of a bird (e.g., Hookbill, Bufflehead, Yellowlegs); or if the name describes a bird's call or song (e.g., Chickadee, Dickcissel, Poorwill, Killdeer); or if it describes a bird's behavior or activity (e.g., Flycatcher, Roadrunner, Honeyeater). The only exception is to use a hyphen if otherwise the name would be hard to pronounce or would look odd (e.g., White-eye, Wattle-eye, Thick-knee, Huet-huet, Chuck-will's-widow). "Whip-poor-will" was deemed borderline and the committee decided to follow perceived general usage.

Another category of compound words eligible for use as single words includes those where the second word is a kind of bird (e.g., Nighthawk, Bushtit, Waterthrush, Meadowlark). The critical point here is that the spelling chosen should not suggest that the taxon is a member of the bird family named if it is not one. A Meadowlark is not a Lark; a Cuckooshrike is not a Shrike. Thus the name cannot be spelled as two words without a hyphen (e.g., Meadow Lark), or spelled with a hyphen followed by a capital letter (e.g., Cuckoo-Shrike). The committee adopted the rule that a single word will be used except where it would be hard to pronounce or look odd (e.g., Silky-flycatcher, Stone-curlew, Flycatcher-shrike).

A corollary of this rule is that if the second word is a type of bird and the taxon is in that bird family, the name would be spelled with two words, either without a hyphen or with a hyphen followed by a capital letter (e.g., Bush Lark, Eagle-Owl). Converting these to single words can suggest that the taxon is not in that family but is rather something different. Exceptions have been made in a few cases where long and widespread usage dictates a single word, such as Goldfinch, Skylark, Woodlark, and Sparrowhawk.

B. *Two words*. The most difficult problem is with compound words that are not to be spelled as single words. The choices for Storm Petrel, for example, are Storm Petrel, Storm-Petrel, or Storm-petrel. After much debate and in the absence of a clear majority in favor of any one of the alternative relevant rules we decided that the third of these—a hyphen followed by a lowercase letter—was appropriate only where the taxon is not a member of the family or taxon stated, such as Silky-flycatcher or Stone-curlew. That is the only correct spelling of such names if they are not spelled as a single word.

The choice, then, in most such cases was whether to hyphenate the two words or not, and this became the single most contentious point in the entire project because the committee members had very different attitudes toward the hyphen. At one extreme was the position that a hyphen should never be used except when absolutely necessary to clarify pronunciation or make a necessary word connection. Tied to this position were arguments that hyphens tend to violate otherwise ordinary rules of grammar; that common usage usually does not support hyphens; and that hyphens violate the principle that names should be simple. At the other extreme is the view that hyphens should be used liberally in bird nomenclature to indicate relationships among taxa, and that if two or more taxa have the same "last name" the words should be hyphenated.

Faced with these differing viewpoints, the committee decided that a middle ground was essential. It adopted the following rules for the use and spelling of two-word compound names:

1. Two words should be used to spell all names not falling within the rules for single-word names.

2. As a general rule a hyphen should not be used, and both words should begin with capital letters (e.g., Black Tyrant, Screech Owl, Green Pigeon, Storm Petrel, Wood Partridge).

3. Where both words are the names of birds or bird families a hyphen should be inserted to signify that the taxon belongs to the family of the second word, not the first (e.g., Eagle-Owl, Nightingale-Thrush).

4. If a name covered by #3 is of a taxon that is not a member of the stated bird family, the letter after the hyphen should be lowercase to clarify that status (e.g., Flycatcher-shrike). This is a companion to the rule, described above, applicable to single-word names that hyphenates them to avoid confusion, as in Silky-flycatcher or Stone-curlew.

5. If application of any of the above rules would produce a name that is contrary to long-established and widespread usage, the rule may be modified or not applied. For example, Goldfinch, Skylark, and Sparrowhawk—all taxa that are within the family name stated and thus do not come within the single-word rules described above—can nevertheless be spelled as single words, despite #1, because of long usage.

Because the foregoing rules allow for exceptions (see #4 and #5, above) the results produce a fair number of inconsistent names. A notable example is the use of "finch," where we have eleven single-word names and twenty-one two-word names. We concluded that perfect consistency is impossible without offending many people or turning usage on its ear. We strove to minimize these exceptions.

Throughout, the committee adopted conservative views on changing names. The temptation was great to standardize group names within genera, for example, to name all species of *Columba* "pigeons" or all species of *Turdus* "thrushes." But the recommended standardization of bird names will be useful only insofar as the birding public and ornithologists accept it. Various committee members from time to time suggested more radical changes in bird names. One interesting suggestion was to scrap most of the current names for taxa in the bird-of-paradise family in favor of new, more attractive, and more interesting names, like those of hummingbirds for example. The committee could not find substantial approval of changes like these. But many of the ideas so far expressed are good ones and are at least worthy of further consideration. These should commend themselves to bird-name committees of the future.

In the end most of the difficult decisions were the result of great teamwork and compromises by the subcommittees. We decided some by executive decision, playing Solomon and striving to balance wins and losses of preferred names. Radical name changes, however, are few.

One example of an executive recommendation is that of "Angel Tern" for *Gygis alba*. Resolution between its previous two names, "Fairy Tern" and "White Tern," was not possible without an executive decision. "Fairy Tern" was assigned years ago to *Sterna nereis* of Australia and New Zealand, leaving us with the truly bland generic name "White Tern" for one of the world's most endearing seabirds. "White Noddy" arose as a possible solution, but the evidence supporting its

relationship to the *Anous* noddies was deemed not yet conclusive. So we sought an improvement, and found comfort in "Angel Tern," a name that fits the bird and also invites interesting possibilities for naming potential new species of *Gygis*.

RANGES

A brief description of the geographical region occupied by each species is included to clarify the species to which the name refers and to allow for electronic sorting of the list. Geographical terminology and abbreviations used include the following:

General regions

- North America (NA)—includes the Caribbean
- Middle America (MA)—Mexico through Panama
- South America (SA)
- Latin America (LA)—Middle and South America
- Africa (AF)—entire continent rather than south of Sahara
- Eurasia (EU)—Europe, Asia from the Middle East through central Asia north of the Himalayas, Siberia and northern China to Japan
- Oriental Region (OR)—South Asia from Pakistan to Taiwan, plus Southeast Asia, the Philippines, and Greater Sundas
- Australasia (AU)—Wallacea (Indonesian islands east of Wallace's line), New Guinea and its islands, Australia, New Zealand and its subantarctic islands, the Solomons, New Caledonia, and Vanuatu
- Atlantic, Pacific, Indian, Tropical, Temperate, and Southern oceans (AO, PO, IO, TrO, TO, SO)
- Antarctica (AN)

The Excel files on the CD include more information on the range of each species. A second column provides a qualifier from the most general "widespread" to "e, se," referring the general region specified in the first column to the more specific countries or parts thereof, for example, "e, ne China" to "New Caledonia." A third column specifies a species' non-breeding range if it differs substantially from the breeding range.

INDEX

The index includes both English and scientific group names, primarily genera and families, of birds. We assume some familiarity with current classifications of the birds of the world, such that the reader will easily locate the family, genus, or group name of interest and then home in quickly on the target species of interest. We list the bird families and their starting page numbers in the preceding section of front matter. Full indices of scientific names are available in Dickinson (2003), a valued companion volume and guide to synonymies of avian taxonomy down to the subspecies level.

ELECTRONIC VERSIONS

We include with the book a CD that contains the three principal files that composed this work: (1) Nonpasserines; (2) Suboscine Passerines; (3) Oscine Passerines. These species files are formatted in Excel spreadsheets, which allows many options for sorting, finding, editing, and exporting to other widely used word processing and database programs. The files also include additional details on the range of each species.

PERMISSION TO USE IN OTHER WORKS

Wide dissemination, use, and improvement of the recommended International English names are our only goals. Gratis license to use this list in derivative works, if needed, can be obtained by writing Frank B. Gill, the registered holder of the copyright, at Box 428, Rushland, PA 18956.

THE INTERNATIONAL ORNITHO-LOGICAL CONGRESS (IOC)

The IOC is the preeminent international forum of ornithologists. It promotes worldwide collaboration and cooperation in ornithology and the other biological sciences through its meetings every four years and through its standing committees.

ACKNOWLEDGMENTS

This was a volunteer, community effort. All participants have given freely of their valuable time and institutional resources. We waived royalty rights to maximize the quality and affordability of the product. Most important were the contributions of the twenty-eight committee members who participated in the construction of the rules and their application. These were (region in parentheses): Per Alström (PAL); Mark Beaman (PAL); Aldo Berutti (AFR); Clive Barlow (AFR); David Bishop (AUS); Murray Bruce (AUS); Paul Coopmans (NEO); W. Richard J. Dean (AFR); Brian Gill (AUS); Simon Harrap (ORI); Steven L. Hilty (NEO); Steve N. G. Howell (NEO); Tim Inskipp (ORI); Michael Irwin (AFR); Kenn Kaufman (NEA); G. Stuart Keith (AFR); Ben King (ORI); David Parkin (PAL); Christopher Perrins (PAL); H. Douglas Pratt (AUS); Nigel Redman (ORI); Peter G. Ryan (AFR); Robert S. Ridgely (NEO); Phillip Round (ORI); Stephen M. Russell (NEA); Richard Schodde (AUS); Donald Turner (AFR); and Harrison B. Tordoff (NEA). Advising each of these committee members were a host of their personal friends and colleagues. We thank, in particular, Gary Wiles for his helpful perspective on the birds of Micronesia, and Guy Tudor for his extraordinary knowledge of the birds of the world.

Two other champions of this project merit special recognition and our heartfelt thanks.

David B. Donsker, MD, joined our team in the final years as taxonomic editor. He had at his disposal Phoebe Snetsinger's comprehensive database on taxonomic changes of world birds, which he keeps current in real time. He polished the taxonomic scholarship of the list not only with respect to current species splits and generic changes but also with respect to the agreements in gender between generic and species names.

Our special thanks go also to Sally Conyne, who contributed in three major ways. First, she led the compilation of one master list from the recommendations of the six subcommittees. That collation was a gargantuan and at times never-ending task, but she tackled it with steady and accurate determination. Second, she also led the solution to hyphenating group names, cutting the Gordian knot of disparate opinions with a clear understanding of the rules of English language outside the world of ornithology. Third, she added the abbreviated ranges to each species included on the CD. This required designing a system and then applying it, which consumed countless hours of diligent work.

We also thank Robert Kirk and Ellen Foos of Princeton University Press, who shared our view of the value of this work and made it a reality.

Lastly and with greatest possible appreciation, we thank all our IOC colleagues, who encouraged us in this project and who waited both patiently and optimistically for it to appear. It proved to be a much bigger challenge than we ever imagined it would be. In that spirit of realized humility, we dedicate this work to Burt L. Monroe Jr. We just finished the first phase of what he started.

We accept full responsibility for the errors of accuracy that surely still lurk in this first edition work.

Frank Gill and Minturn Wright
Co-chairs, IOC Standing Committee on English Names
December 2005

LITERATURE CITED

Bernis, F. *Diccionario de nombres vernaculos de aves.* Madrid: Editorial Gredos, 1995.

Devillers, P., and H. Ouellet. *Noms français des oiseaux du monde avec les équivalents latins et anglais. Commission internationale des noms français des oiseaux.* Sainte-Foy, Québec, and Chabaud, Bayonne, France: Multimondes, 1993.

Dickinson, E. C., ed. *The Howard & Moore Complete Checklist of the Birds of the World.* 3rd ed. Princeton, N.J.: Princeton University Press, 2003.

Sibley, C. G., and B. L. Monroe Jr. *Distribution and Taxonomy of the Birds of the World.* New Haven, Conn.: Yale University Press, 1990.

INTERNATIONAL ENGLISH NAME	SCIENTIFIC NAME	REGION(S)
	ORDER TINAMIFORMES	
TINAMOUS	**Family Tinamidae**	
—Grey Tinamou	*Tinamus tao*	SA
—Solitary Tinamou	*Tinamus solitarius*	SA
—Black Tinamou	*Tinamus osgoodi*	SA
—Great Tinamou	*Tinamus major*	LA
—White-throated Tinamou	*Tinamus guttatus*	SA
—Highland Tinamou	*Nothocercus bonapartei*	LA
—Tawny-breasted Tinamou	*Nothocercus julius*	SA
—Hooded Tinamou	*Nothocercus nigrocapillus*	SA
—Berlepsch's Tinamou	*Crypturellus berlepschi*	SA
—Cinereous Tinamou	*Crypturellus cinereus*	SA
—Little Tinamou	*Crypturellus soui*	LA
—Tepui Tinamou	*Crypturellus ptaritepui*	SA
—Brown Tinamou	*Crypturellus obsoletus*	SA
—Undulated Tinamou	*Crypturellus undulatus*	SA
—Pale-browed Tinamou	*Crypturellus transfasciatus*	SA
—Brazilian Tinamou	*Crypturellus strigulosus*	SA
—Grey-legged Tinamou	*Crypturellus duidae*	SA
—Red-legged Tinamou	*Crypturellus erythropus*	SA
—Magdalena Tinamou	*Crypturellus saltuarius*	SA
—Yellow-legged Tinamou	*Crypturellus noctivagus*	SA
—Black-capped Tinamou	*Crypturellus atrocapillus*	SA
—Thicket Tinamou	*Crypturellus cinnamomeus*	MA
—Slaty-breasted Tinamou	*Crypturellus boucardi*	MA
—Choco Tinamou	*Crypturellus kerriae*	LA
—Variegated Tinamou	*Crypturellus variegatus*	SA
—Rusty Tinamou	*Crypturellus brevirostris*	SA
—Bartlett's Tinamou	*Crypturellus bartletti*	SA
—Small-billed Tinamou	*Crypturellus parvirostris*	SA
—Barred Tinamou	*Crypturellus casiquiare*	SA
—Tataupa Tinamou	*Crypturellus tataupa*	SA
—Red-winged Tinamou	*Rhynchotus rufescens*	SA
—Huayco Tinamou	*Rhynchotus maculicollis*	SA
—Taczanowski's Tinamou	*Nothoprocta taczanowskii*	SA
—Kalinowski's Tinamou	*Nothoprocta kalinowskii*	SA
—Ornate Tinamou	*Nothoprocta ornata*	SA
—Chilean Tinamou	*Nothoprocta perdicaria*	SA
—Brushland Tinamou	*Nothoprocta cinerascens*	SA
—Andean Tinamou	*Nothoprocta pentlandii*	SA
—Curve-billed Tinamou	*Nothoprocta curvirostris*	SA
—White-bellied Nothura	*Nothura boraquira*	SA
—Lesser Nothura	*Nothura minor*	SA
—Darwin's Nothura	*Nothura darwinii*	SA
—Spotted Nothura	*Nothura maculosa*	SA
—Chaco Nothura	*Nothura chacoensis*	SA
—Dwarf Tinamou	*Taoniscus nanus*	SA
—Elegant Crested Tinamou	*Eudromia elegans*	SA
—Quebracho Crested Tinamou	*Eudromia formosa*	SA
—Puna Tinamou	*Tinamotis pentlandii*	SA
—Patagonian Tinamou	*Tinamotis ingoufi*	SA

INTERNATIONAL ENGLISH NAME	SCIENTIFIC NAME	REGION(S)
	ORDER STRUTHIONIFORMES	
OSTRICHES	**Family Struthionidae**	
—Common Ostrich	*Struthio camelus*	AF
—Somali Ostrich	*Struthio molybdophanes*	AF
	ORDER RHEIFORMES	
RHEAS	**Family Rheidae**	
—Greater Rhea	*Rhea americana*	SA
—Darwin's Rhea	*Pterocnemia pennata*	SA
	ORDER CASUARIIFORMES	
CASSOWARIES	**Family Casuariidae**	
—Southern Cassowary	*Casuarius casuarius*	AU
—Dwarf Cassowary	*Casuarius bennetti*	AU
—Northern Cassowary	*Casuarius unappendiculatus*	AU
EMUS	**Family Dromaiidae**	
—Emu	*Dromaius novaehollandiae*	
	ORDER DINORNITHIFORMES	
KIWIS	**Family Apterygidae**	
—Southern Brown Kiwi	*Apteryx australis*	AU
—North Island Brown Kiwi	*Apteryx mantelli*	AU
—Okarito Kiwi	*Apteryx rowi*	AU
—Little Spotted Kiwi	*Apteryx owenii*	AU
—Great Spotted Kiwi	*Apteryx haastii*	AU
	ORDER GALLIFORMES	
MEGAPODES	**Family Megapodiidae**	
—Australian Brushturkey	*Alectura lathami*	AU
—Wattled Brushturkey	*Aepypodius arfakianus*	AU
—Waigeo Brushturkey	*Aepypodius bruijnii*	AU
—Red-billed Brushturkey	*Talegalla cuvieri*	AU
—Black-billed Brushturkey	*Talegalla fuscirostris*	AU
—Collared Brushturkey	*Talegalla jobiensis*	AU
—Malleefowl	*Leipoa ocellata*	AU
—Maleo	*Macrocephalon maleo*	AU
—Moluccan Megapode	*Eulipoa wallacei*	AU
—Tongan Megapode	*Megapodius pritchardii*	PO
—Micronesian Megapode	*Megapodius laperouse*	PO
—Nicobar Megapode	*Megapodius nicobariensis*	OR
—Philippine Megapode	*Megapodius cumingii*	OR
—Sula Megapode	*Megapodius bernsteinii*	AU
—Tanimbar Megapode	*Megapodius tenimberensis*	AU
—Dusky Megapode	*Megapodius freycinet*	AU
—Forsten's Megapode	*Megapodius forstenii*	AU

INTERNATIONAL ENGLISH NAME	SCIENTIFIC NAME	REGION(S)
—Biak Megapode	*Megapodius geelvinkianus*	AU
—Melanesian Megapode	*Megapodius eremita*	AU
—Vanuatu Megapode	*Megapodius layardi*	AU
—New Guinea Megapode	*Megapodius decollatus*	AU
—Scrubfowl	*Megapodius reinwardt*	AU
CHACHALACAS, CURASSOWS, GUANS	**Family Cracidae**	
—Plain Chachalaca	*Ortalis vetula*	NA, MA
—Grey-headed Chachalaca	*Ortalis cinereiceps*	LA
—Chestnut-winged Chachalaca	*Ortalis garrula*	SA
—Rufous-vented Chachalaca	*Ortalis ruficauda*	SA
—Rufous-headed Chachalaca	*Ortalis erythroptera*	SA
—Rufous-bellied Chachalaca	*Ortalis wagleri*	MA
—West Mexican Chachalaca	*Ortalis poliocephala*	MA
—Chaco Chachalaca	*Ortalis canicollis*	SA
—White-bellied Chachalaca	*Ortalis leucogastra*	MA
—Speckled Chachalaca	*Ortalis guttata*	SA
—East Brazilian Chachalaca	*Ortalis araucuan*	SA
—Scaled Chachalaca	*Ortalis squamata*	SA
—Colombian Chachalaca	*Ortalis columbiana*	SA
—Little Chachalaca	*Ortalis motmot*	SA
—Chestnut-headed Chachalaca	*Ortalis ruficeps*	SA
—Buff-browed Chachalaca	*Ortalis superciliaris*	SA
—Band-tailed Guan	*Penelope argyrotis*	SA
—Bearded Guan	*Penelope barbata*	SA
—Baudo Guan	*Penelope ortoni*	SA
—Andean Guan	*Penelope montagnii*	SA
—Marail Guan	*Penelope marail*	SA
—Rusty-margined Guan	*Penelope superciliaris*	SA
—Red-faced Guan	*Penelope dabbenei*	SA
—Crested Guan	*Penelope purpurascens*	LA
—Cauca Guan	*Penelope perspicax*	SA
—White-winged Guan	*Penelope albipennis*	SA
—Spix's Guan	*Penelope jacquacu*	SA
—Dusky-legged Guan	*Penelope obscura*	SA
—White-crested Guan	*Penelope pileata*	SA
—Chestnut-bellied Guan	*Penelope ochrogaster*	SA
—White-browed Guan	*Penelope jacucaca*	SA
—Common Piping Guan	*Pipile pipile*	SA
—Black-fronted Piping Guan	*Pipile jacutinga*	SA
—Wattled Guan	*Aburria aburri*	SA
—Black Guan	*Chamaepetes unicolor*	MA
—Sickle-winged Guan	*Chamaepetes goudotii*	SA
—Highland Guan	*Penelopina nigra*	MA
—Horned Guan	*Oreophasis derbianus*	MA
—Nocturnal Curassow	*Nothocrax urumutum*	SA
—Crestless Curassow	*Mitu tomentosum*	SA
—Salvin's Curassow	*Mitu salvini*	SA
—Razor-billed Curassow	*Mitu tuberosum*	SA
—Alagoas Curassow	*Mitu mitu*	SA
—Northern Helmeted Curassow	*Pauxi pauxi*	SA
—Southern Helmeted Curassow	*Pauxi unicornis*	SA
—Great Curassow	*Crax rubra*	LA

INTERNATIONAL ENGLISH NAME	SCIENTIFIC NAME	REGION(S)
__Blue-knobbed Curassow	*Crax alberti*	SA
__Yellow-knobbed Curassow	*Crax daubentoni*	SA
__Black Curassow	*Crax alector*	SA
__Wattled Curassow	*Crax globulosa*	SA
__Bare-faced Curassow	*Crax fasciolata*	SA
__Red-knobbed Curassow	*Crax blumenbachii*	SA
GUINEAFOWL	**Family Numididae**	
__White-breasted Guineafowl	*Agelastes meleagrides*	AF
__Black Guineafowl	*Agelastes niger*	AF
__Helmeted Guineafowl	*Numida meleagris*	AF
__Plumed Guineafowl	*Guttera plumifera*	AF
__Crested Guineafowl	*Guttera pucherani*	AF
__Vulturine Guineafowl	*Acryllium vulturinum*	AF
NEW WORLD QUAIL	**Family Odontophoridae**	
__Bearded Wood Partridge	*Dendrortyx barbatus*	MA
__Long-tailed Wood Partridge	*Dendrortyx macroura*	MA
__Buffy-crowned Wood Partridge	*Dendrortyx leucophrys*	MA
__Mountain Quail	*Oreortyx pictus*	NA, MA
__Scaled Quail	*Callipepla squamata*	NA, MA
__Elegant Quail	*Callipepla douglasii*	MA
__California Quail	*Callipepla californica*	NA, MA
__Gambel's Quail	*Callipepla gambelii*	NA, MA
__Banded Quail	*Philortyx fasciatus*	MA
__Northern Bobwhite	*Colinus virginianus*	NA, MA
__Yucatan Bobwhite	*Colinus nigrogularis*	MA
__Spot-bellied Bobwhite	*Colinus leucopogon*	MA
__Crested Bobwhite	*Colinus cristatus*	LA
__Marbled Wood Quail	*Odontophorus gujanensis*	LA
__Spot-winged Wood Quail	*Odontophorus capueira*	SA
__Black-eared Wood Quail	*Odontophorus melanotis*	MA
__Rufous-fronted Wood Quail	*Odontophorus erythrops*	SA
__Black-fronted Wood Quail	*Odontophorus atrifrons*	SA
__Chestnut Wood Quail	*Odontophorus hyperythrus*	SA
__Dark-backed Wood Quail	*Odontophorus melanonotus*	SA
__Rufous-breasted Wood Quail	*Odontophorus speciosus*	SA
__Tacarcuna Wood Quail	*Odontophorus dialeucos*	LA
__Gorgeted Wood Quail	*Odontophorus strophium*	SA
__Venezuelan Wood Quail	*Odontophorus columbianus*	SA
__Black-breasted Wood Quail	*Odontophorus leucolaemus*	MA
__Stripe-faced Wood Quail	*Odontophorus balliviani*	SA
__Starred Wood Quail	*Odontophorus stellatus*	SA
__Spotted Wood Quail	*Odontophorus guttatus*	MA
__Singing Quail	*Dactylortyx thoracicus*	MA
__Montezuma Quail	*Cyrtonyx montezumae*	NA, MA
__Ocellated Quail	*Cyrtonyx ocellatus*	MA
__Tawny-faced Quail	*Rhynchortyx cinctus*	LA
PHEASANTS, FOWL & ALLIES	**Family Phasianidae**	
__Wild Turkey	*Meleagris gallopavo*	NA, MA
__Ocellated Turkey	*Meleagris ocellata*	MA
__Ruffed Grouse	*Bonasa umbellus*	NA

INTERNATIONAL ENGLISH NAME	SCIENTIFIC NAME	REGION(S)
—Hazel Grouse	*Tetrastes bonasia*	EU
—Severtzov's Grouse	*Tetrastes sewerzowi*	EU
—Siberian Grouse	*Falcipennis falcipennis*	EU
—Spruce Grouse	*Falcipennis canadensis*	NA
—Western Capercaillie	*Tetrao urogallus*	EU
—Black-billed Capercaillie	*Tetrao parvirostris*	EU
—Black Grouse	*Lyrurus tetrix*	EU
—Caucasian Grouse	*Lyrurus mlokosiewiczi*	EU
—Sage Grouse	*Centrocercus urophasianus*	NA
—Gunnison Grouse	*Centrocercus minimus*	NA
—Blue Grouse	*Dendragapus obscurus*	NA
—Sharp-tailed Grouse	*Tympanuchus phasianellus*	NA
—Lesser Prairie Chicken	*Tympanuchus pallidicinctus*	NA
—Greater Prairie Chicken	*Tympanuchus cupido*	NA
—White-tailed Ptarmigan	*Lagopus leucura*	NA
—Rock Ptarmigan	*Lagopus muta*	NA, EU
—Willow Ptarmigan	*Lagopus lagopus*	NA, EU
—Snow Partridge	*Lerwa lerwa*	EU
—Verreaux's Monal-Partridge	*Tetraophasis obscurus*	EU
—Szechenyi's Monal-Partridge	*Tetraophasis szechenyii*	EU
—Caucasian Snowcock	*Tetraogallus caucasicus*	EU
—Caspian Snowcock	*Tetraogallus caspius*	EU
—Himalayan Snowcock	*Tetraogallus himalayensis*	EU
—Tibetan Snowcock	*Tetraogallus tibetanus*	EU
—Altai Snowcock	*Tetraogallus altaicus*	EU
—Rock Partridge	*Alectoris graeca*	EU
—Chukar Partridge	*Alectoris chukar*	EU
—Przevalski's Partridge	*Alectoris magna*	EU
—Philby's Partridge	*Alectoris philbyi*	EU
—Barbary Partridge	*Alectoris barbara*	AF
—Red-legged Partridge	*Alectoris rufa*	EU
—Arabian Partridge	*Alectoris melanocephala*	EU
—See-see Partridge	*Ammoperdix griseogularis*	EU
—Sand Partridge	*Ammoperdix heyi*	EU, AF
—Stone Partridge	*Ptilopachus petrosus*	AF
—Nahan's Francolin	*Ptilopachus nahani*	AF
—Black Francolin	*Francolinus francolinus*	EU, OR
—Painted Francolin	*Francolinus pictus*	OR
—Chinese Francolin	*Francolinus pintadeanus*	OR
—Grey Francolin	*Francolinus pondicerianus*	EU, OR
—Swamp Francolin	*Francolinus gularis*	OR
—Forest Francolin	*Peliperdix lathami*	AF
—Coqui Francolin	*Peliperdix coqui*	AF
—White-throated Francolin	*Peliperdix albogularis*	AF
—Schlegel's Francolin	*Peliperdix schlegelii*	AF
—Ring-necked Francolin	*Scleroptila streptophorus*	AF
—Grey-winged Francolin	*Scleroptila africana*	AF
—Red-winged Francolin	*Scleroptila levaillantii*	AF
—Finsch's Francolin	*Scleroptila finschi*	AF
—Shelley's Francolin	*Scleroptila shelleyi*	AF
—Moorland Francolin	*Scleroptila psilolaemus*	AF
—Orange River Francolin	*Scleroptila levaillantoides*	AF
—Crested Francolin	*Dendroperdix sephaena*	AF

INTERNATIONAL ENGLISH NAME	SCIENTIFIC NAME	REGION(S)
__Scaly Francolin	*Pternistis squamatus*	AF
__Ahanta Francolin	*Pternistis ahantensis*	AF
__Grey-striped Francolin	*Pternistis griseostriatus*	AF
__Hildebrandt's Francolin	*Pternistis hildebrandti*	AF
__Double-spurred Francolin	*Pternistis bicalcaratus*	AF
__Heuglin's Francolin	*Pternistis icterorhynchus*	AF
__Clapperton's Francolin	*Pternistis clappertoni*	AF
__Harwood's Francolin	*Pternistis harwoodi*	AF
__Swierstra's Francolin	*Pternistis swierstrai*	AF
__Mount Cameroon Francolin	*Pternistis camerunensis*	AF
__Handsome Francolin	*Pternistis nobilis*	AF
__Jackson's Francolin	*Pternistis jacksoni*	AF
__Chestnut-naped Francolin	*Pternistis castaneicollis*	AF
__Djibouti Francolin	*Pternistis ochropectus*	AF
__Erckel's Francolin	*Pternistis erckelii*	AF
__Hartlaub's Spurfowl	*Pternistis hartlaubi*	AF
__Red-billed Spurfowl	*Pternistis adspersus*	AF
__Cape Spurfowl	*Pternistis capensis*	AF
__Natal Spurfowl	*Pternistis natalensis*	AF
__Yellow-necked Spurfowl	*Pternistis leucoscepus*	AF
__Grey-breasted Spurfowl	*Pternistis rufopictus*	AF
__Red-necked Spurfowl	*Pternistis afer*	AF
__Swainson's Spurfowl	*Pternistis swainsonii*	AF
__Grey Partridge	*Perdix perdix*	EU
__Daurian Partridge	*Perdix dauurica*	EU
__Tibetan Partridge	*Perdix hodgsoniae*	EU
__Long-billed Partridge	*Rhizothera longirostris*	OR
__Hose's Partridge	*Rhizothera dulitensis*	OR
__Madagascar Partridge	*Margaroperdix madagascariensis*	AF
__Black Partridge	*Melanoperdix niger*	OR
__Common Quail	*Coturnix coturnix*	AF, EU
__Japanese Quail	*Coturnix japonica*	EU
__Rain Quail	*Coturnix coromandelica*	OR
__Harlequin Quail	*Coturnix delegorguei*	AF
__Stubble Quail	*Coturnix pectoralis*	AU
__Brown Quail	*Coturnix ypsilophora*	AU
__King Quail	*Coturnix chinensis*	OR, AU
__Blue Quail	*Coturnix adansonii*	AF
__Snow Mountains Quail	*Anurophasis monorthonyx*	AU
__Jungle Bush Quail	*Perdicula asiatica*	OR
__Rock Bush Quail	*Perdicula argoondah*	OR
__Painted Bush Quail	*Perdicula erythrorhyncha*	OR
__Manipur Bush Quail	*Perdicula manipurensis*	OR
__Udzungwa Forest Partridge	*Xenoperdix udzungwensis*	AF
__Hill Partridge	*Arborophila torqueola*	OR
__Rufous-throated Partridge	*Arborophila rufogularis*	OR
__White-cheeked Partridge	*Arborophila atrogularis*	OR
__Taiwan Partridge	*Arborophila crudigularis*	OR
__Chestnut-breasted Partridge	*Arborophila mandellii*	OR
__Bar-backed Partridge	*Arborophila brunneopectus*	OR
__Sichuan Partridge	*Arborophila rufipectus*	OR
__White-necklaced Partridge	*Arborophila gingica*	OR
__Orange-necked Partridge	*Arborophila davidi*	OR

INTERNATIONAL ENGLISH NAME	SCIENTIFIC NAME	REGION(S)
—Chestnut-headed Partridge	*Arborophila cambodiana*	OR
—Siamese Partridge	*Arborophila diversa*	OR
—Malaysian Partridge	*Arborophila campbelli*	OR
—Roll's Partridge	*Arborophila rolli*	OR
—Sumatran Partridge	*Arborophila sumatrana*	OR
—Grey-breasted Partridge	*Arborophila orientalis*	OR
—Chestnut-bellied Partridge	*Arborophila javanica*	OR
—Red-billed Partridge	*Arborophila rubrirostris*	OR
—Red-breasted Partridge	*Arborophila hyperythra*	OR
—Hainan Partridge	*Arborophila ardens*	OR
—Scaly-breasted Partridge	*Arborophila charltonii*	OR
—Green-legged Partridge	*Arborophila chloropus*	OR
—Ferruginous Partridge	*Caloperdix oculeus*	OR
—Crimson-headed Partridge	*Haematortyx sanguiniceps*	OR
—Crested Partridge	*Rollulus rouloul*	OR
—Mountain Bamboo Partridge	*Bambusicola fytchii*	OR
—Chinese Bamboo Partridge	*Bambusicola thoracicus*	OR
—Red Spurfowl	*Galloperdix spadicea*	OR
—Painted Spurfowl	*Galloperdix lunulata*	OR
—Sri Lanka Spurfowl	*Galloperdix bicalcarata*	OR
—Blood Pheasant	*Ithaginis cruentus*	OR
—Western Tragopan	*Tragopan melanocephalus*	OR
—Satyr Tragopan	*Tragopan satyra*	OR
—Blyth's Tragopan	*Tragopan blythii*	OR
—Temminck's Tragopan	*Tragopan temminckii*	OR
—Cabot's Tragopan	*Tragopan caboti*	OR
—Koklass Pheasant	*Pucrasia macrolopha*	OR
—Himalayan Monal	*Lophophorus impejanus*	OR
—Sclater's Monal	*Lophophorus sclateri*	OR
—Chinese Monal	*Lophophorus lhuysii*	OR
—Red Junglefowl	*Gallus gallus*	OR
—Grey Junglefowl	*Gallus sonneratii*	OR
—Sri Lanka Junglefowl	*Gallus lafayetii*	OR
—Green Junglefowl	*Gallus varius*	OR
—Kalij Pheasant	*Lophura leucomelanos*	OR
—Silver Pheasant	*Lophura nycthemera*	OR
—Edwards's Pheasant	*Lophura edwardsi*	OR
—Vietnamese Pheasant	*Lophura hatinhensis*	OR
—Swinhoe's Pheasant	*Lophura swinhoii*	OR
—Hoogerwerf's Pheasant	*Lophura hoogerwerfi*	OR
—Salvadori's Pheasant	*Lophura inornata*	OR
—Crestless Fireback	*Lophura erythrophthalma*	OR
—Crested Fireback	*Lophura ignita*	OR
—Siamese Fireback	*Lophura diardi*	OR
—Bulwer's Pheasant	*Lophura bulweri*	OR
—White Eared Pheasant	*Crossoptilon crossoptilon*	OR
—Tibetan Eared Pheasant	*Crossoptilon harmani*	OR
—Brown Eared Pheasant	*Crossoptilon mantchuricum*	EU
—Blue Eared Pheasant	*Crossoptilon auritum*	EU
—Cheer Pheasant	*Catreus wallichi*	EU
—Elliot's Pheasant	*Syrmaticus ellioti*	OR
—Mrs. Hume's Pheasant	*Syrmaticus humiae*	OR
—Mikado Pheasant	*Syrmaticus mikado*	OR

INTERNATIONAL ENGLISH NAME	SCIENTIFIC NAME	REGION(S)
__Copper Pheasant	*Syrmaticus soemmerringii*	EU
__Reeves's Pheasant	*Syrmaticus reevesii*	EU
__Common Pheasant	*Phasianus colchicus*	EU
__Golden Pheasant	*Chrysolophus pictus*	OR
__Lady Amherst's Pheasant	*Chrysolophus amherstiae*	OR
__Bronze-tailed Peacock-Pheasant	*Polyplectron chalcurum*	OR
__Mountain Peacock-Pheasant	*Polyplectron inopinatum*	OR
__Germain's Peacock-Pheasant	*Polyplectron germaini*	OR
__Grey Peacock-Pheasant	*Polyplectron bicalcaratum*	OR
__Malayan Peacock-Pheasant	*Polyplectron malacense*	OR
__Bornean Peacock-Pheasant	*Polyplectron schleiermacheri*	OR
__Palawan Peacock-Pheasant	*Polyplectron napoleonis*	OR
__Crested Argus	*Rheinardia ocellata*	OR
__Great Argus	*Argusianus argus*	OR
__Indian Peafowl	*Pavo cristatus*	OR
__Green Peafowl	*Pavo muticus*	OR
__Congo Peacock	*Afropavo congensis*	AF

ORDER ANSERIFORMES

SCREAMERS	**Family Anhimidae**	
__Horned Screamer	*Anhima cornuta*	SA
__Northern Screamer	*Chauna chavaria*	SA
__Southern Screamer	*Chauna torquata*	SA
MAGPIE GOOSE	**Family Anseranatidae**	
__Magpie Goose	*Anseranas semipalmata*	AU
DUCKS, GEESE, SWANS	**Family Anatidae**	
__White-faced Whistling Duck	*Dendrocygna viduata*	AF, SA
__Black-bellied Whistling Duck	*Dendrocygna autumnalis*	NA, LA
__Spotted Whistling Duck	*Dendrocygna guttata*	OR, AU
__West Indian Whistling Duck	*Dendrocygna arborea*	NA
__Fulvous Whistling Duck	*Dendrocygna bicolor*	NA, LA, AF, OR
__Plumed Whistling Duck	*Dendrocygna eytoni*	AU
__Wandering Whistling Duck	*Dendrocygna arcuata*	OR, AU
__Lesser Whistling Duck	*Dendrocygna javanica*	OR
__White-backed Duck	*Thalassornis leuconotus*	AF
__Cape Barren Goose	*Cereopsis novaehollandiae*	AU
__Swan Goose	*Anser cygnoides*	EU
__Bean Goose	*Anser fabalis*	EU
__Pink-footed Goose	*Anser brachyrhynchus*	EU
__Greylag Goose	*Anser anser*	EU
__Greater White-fronted Goose	*Anser albifrons*	NA, MA, EU
__Lesser White-fronted Goose	*Anser erythropus*	EU
__Bar-headed Goose	*Anser indicus*	EU
__Snow Goose	*Chen caerulescens*	NA
__Ross's Goose	*Chen rossii*	NA
__Emperor Goose	*Chen canagica*	NA, EU
__Canada Goose	*Branta canadensis*	NA
__Cackling Goose	*Branta hutchinsii*	NA
__Nene	*Branta sandvicensis*	PO
__Brant Goose	*Branta bernicla*	NA, EU

INTERNATIONAL ENGLISH NAME	SCIENTIFIC NAME	REGION(S)
—Barnacle Goose	*Branta leucopsis*	EU
—Red-breasted Goose	*Branta ruficollis*	EU
—Coscoroba Swan	*Coscoroba coscoroba*	SA
—Black Swan	*Cygnus atratus*	AU
—Black-necked Swan	*Cygnus melanocoryphus*	SA
—Mute Swan	*Cygnus olor*	EU
—Trumpeter Swan	*Cygnus buccinator*	NA
—Tundra Swan	*Cygnus columbianus*	EU, NA
—Whooper Swan	*Cygnus cygnus*	EU
—Freckled Duck	*Stictonetta naevosa*	AU
—Blue Duck	*Hymenolaimus malacorhynchos*	AU
—Flying Steamer Duck	*Tachyeres patachonicus*	SA
—Fuegian Steamer Duck	*Tachyeres pteneres*	SA
—Falkland Steamer Duck	*Tachyeres brachypterus*	SA
—Chubut Steamer Duck	*Tachyeres leucocephalus*	SA
—Torrent Duck	*Merganetta armata*	SA
—Spur-winged Goose	*Plectropterus gambensis*	AF
—Comb Duck	*Sarkidiornis sylvicola*	SA
—Knob-billed Duck	*Sarkidiornis melanotos*	AF, OR
—Blue-winged Goose	*Cyanochen cyanoptera*	AF
—Egyptian Goose	*Alopochen aegyptiaca*	AF
—Orinoco Goose	*Neochen jubata*	SA
—Andean Goose	*Chloephaga melanoptera*	SA
—Upland Goose	*Chloephaga picta*	SA
—Kelp Goose	*Chloephaga hybrida*	SA
—Ashy-headed Goose	*Chloephaga poliocephala*	SA
—Ruddy-headed Goose	*Chloephaga rubidiceps*	SA
—Common Shelduck	*Tadorna tadorna*	EU, AF
—Raja Shelduck	*Tadorna radjah*	AU
—Ruddy Shelduck	*Tadorna ferruginea*	EU
—South African Shelduck	*Tadorna cana*	AF
—Australian Shelduck	*Tadorna tadornoides*	AU
—Paradise Shelduck	*Tadorna variegata*	AU
—Pink-eared Duck	*Malacorhynchus membranaceus*	AU
—Salvadori's Teal	*Salvadorina waigiuensis*	AU
—Muscovy Duck	*Cairina moschata*	NA, LA
—White-winged Duck	*Asacornis scutulata*	OR
—Hartlaub's Duck	*Pteronetta hartlaubii*	AF
—Wood Duck	*Aix sponsa*	NA
—Mandarin Duck	*Aix galericulata*	EU
—Maned Duck	*Chenonetta jubata*	AU
—African Pygmy Goose	*Nettapus auritus*	AF
—Cotton Pygmy Goose	*Nettapus coromandelianus*	OR
—Green Pygmy Goose	*Nettapus pulchellus*	AU
—Brazilian Teal	*Amazonetta brasiliensis*	SA
—Ringed Teal	*Callonetta leucophrys*	SA
—Crested Duck	*Lophonetta specularioides*	SA
—Bronze-winged Duck	*Speculanas specularis*	SA
—Cape Teal	*Anas capensis*	AF
—Gadwall	*Anas strepera*	NA, EU
—Falcated Duck	*Anas falcata*	EU
—Chiloe Wigeon	*Anas sibilatrix*	SA
—Eurasian Wigeon	*Anas penelope*	EU

INTERNATIONAL ENGLISH NAME	SCIENTIFIC NAME	REGION(S)
—American Wigeon	*Anas americana*	NA
—African Black Duck	*Anas sparsa*	AF
—American Black Duck	*Anas rubripes*	NA
—Mallard	*Anas platyrhynchos*	NA, EU
—Mexican Duck	*Anas diazi*	NA, MA
—Mottled Duck	*Anas fulvigula*	NA
—Hawaiian Duck	*Anas wyvilliana*	PO
—Laysan Duck	*Anas laysanensis*	PO
—Philippine Duck	*Anas luzonica*	OR
—Pacific Black Duck	*Anas superciliosa*	AU
—Indian Spot-billed Duck	*Anas poecilorhyncha*	OR
—Eastern Spot-billed Duck	*Anas zonorhyncha*	OR
—Yellow-billed Duck	*Anas undulata*	AF
—Meller's Duck	*Anas melleri*	AF
—Blue-winged Teal	*Anas discors*	NA
—Cinnamon Teal	*Anas cyanoptera*	NA, LA
—Cape Shoveler	*Anas smithii*	AF
—Red Shoveler	*Anas platalea*	SA
—Australasian Shoveler	*Anas rhynchotis*	AU
—Northern Shoveler	*Anas clypeata*	NA, EU
—Bernier's Teal	*Anas bernieri*	AF
—Sunda Teal	*Anas gibberifrons*	OR
—Grey Teal	*Anas gracilis*	AU
—Chestnut Teal	*Anas castanea*	AU
—Brown Teal	*Anas aucklandica*	AU
—White-cheeked Pintail	*Anas bahamensis*	SA
—Red-billed Teal	*Anas erythrorhyncha*	AF
—Speckled Teal	*Anas flavirostris*	SA
—Andean Teal	*Anas andium*	SA
—Yellow-billed Pintail	*Anas georgica*	SA
—Northern Pintail	*Anas acuta*	NA, EU
—Eaton's Pintail	*Anas eatoni*	IO
—Garganey	*Anas querquedula*	EU
—Baikal Teal	*Anas formosa*	EU
—Eurasian Teal	*Anas crecca*	EU
—Green-winged Teal	*Anas carolinensis*	NA
—Silver Teal	*Anas versicolor*	SA
—Puna Teal	*Anas puna*	SA
—Hottentot Teal	*Anas hottentota*	AF
—Marbled Duck	*Marmaronetta angustirostris*	EU
—Red-crested Pochard	*Netta rufina*	EU
—Rosy-billed Pochard	*Netta peposaca*	SA
—Southern Pochard	*Netta erythrophthalma*	AF, SA
—Canvasback	*Aythya valisineria*	NA
—Redhead	*Aythya americana*	NA
—Common Pochard	*Aythya ferina*	EU
—Hardhead	*Aythya australis*	AU
—Madagascar Pochard	*Aythya innotata*	AF
—Baer's Pochard	*Aythya baeri*	EU
—Ferruginous Duck	*Aythya nyroca*	EU
—New Zealand Scaup	*Aythya novaeseelandiae*	AU
—Ring-necked Duck	*Aythya collaris*	NA
—Tufted Duck	*Aythya fuligula*	EU

INTERNATIONAL ENGLISH NAME	SCIENTIFIC NAME	REGION(S)
—Greater Scaup	*Aythya marila*	NA, EU
—Lesser Scaup	*Aythya affinis*	NA
—Steller's Eider	*Polysticta stelleri*	NA, EU
—Spectacled Eider	*Somateria fischeri*	NA, EU
—King Eider	*Somateria spectabilis*	NA, EU
—Common Eider	*Somateria mollissima*	NA, EU
—Harlequin Duck	*Histrionicus histrionicus*	NA, EU
—Surf Scoter	*Melanitta perspicillata*	NA
—Velvet Scoter	*Melanitta fusca*	EU
—White-winged Scoter	*Melanitta deglandi*	NA
—Black Scoter	*Melanitta nigra*	EU
—American Scoter	*Melanitta americana*	NA
—Long-tailed Duck	*Clangula hyemalis*	NA, EU
—Bufflehead	*Bucephala albeola*	NA
—Common Goldeneye	*Bucephala clangula*	NA, EU
—Barrow's Goldeneye	*Bucephala islandica*	NA
—Smew	*Mergellus albellus*	EU
—Hooded Merganser	*Lophodytes cucullatus*	NA
—Brazilian Merganser	*Mergus octosetaceus*	SA
—Common Merganser	*Mergus merganser*	NA, EU
—Red-breasted Merganser	*Mergus serrator*	NA, EU
—Scaly-sided Merganser	*Mergus squamatus*	EU
—Black-headed Duck	*Heteronetta atricapilla*	SA
—Masked Duck	*Nomonyx dominicus*	LA
—Ruddy Duck	*Oxyura jamaicensis*	NA, MA
—Andean Duck	*Oxyura ferruginea*	SA
—Lake Duck	*Oxyura vittata*	SA
—Blue-billed Duck	*Oxyura australis*	AU
—Maccoa Duck	*Oxyura maccoa*	AF
—White-headed Duck	*Oxyura leucocephala*	EU
—Musk Duck	*Biziura lobata*	AU

ORDER SPHENISCIFORMES

PENGUINS	**Family Spheniscidae**	
—King Penguin	*Aptenodytes patagonicus*	SO
—Emperor Penguin	*Aptenodytes forsteri*	AN
—Gentoo Penguin	*Pygoscelis papua*	SO
—Adelie Penguin	*Pygoscelis adeliae*	SO, AN
—Chinstrap Penguin	*Pygoscelis antarcticus*	SO, AN
—Fiordland Penguin	*Eudyptes pachyrhynchus*	AU
—Snares Penguin	*Eudyptes robustus*	AU
—Erect-crested Penguin	*Eudyptes sclateri*	AU
—Rockhopper Penguin	*Eudyptes chrysocome*	SO
—Royal Penguin	*Eudyptes schlegeli*	AU
—Macaroni Penguin	*Eudyptes chrysolophus*	SO
—Yellow-eyed Penguin	*Megadyptes antipodes*	AU
—Fairy Penguin	*Eudyptula minor*	AU
—Jackass Penguin	*Spheniscus demersus*	AF
—Magellanic Penguin	*Spheniscus magellanicus*	SA
—Humboldt Penguin	*Spheniscus humboldti*	SA
—Galapagos Penguin	*Spheniscus mendiculus*	SA

INTERNATIONAL ENGLISH NAME	SCIENTIFIC NAME	REGION(S)
	ORDER GAVIIFORMES	
LOONS	**Family Gaviidae**	
—Red-throated Loon	*Gavia stellata*	NA, EU
—Black-throated Loon	*Gavia arctica*	EU
—Pacific Loon	*Gavia pacifica*	NA
—Great Northern Loon	*Gavia immer*	NA, EU
—Yellow-billed Loon	*Gavia adamsii*	NA, EU
	ORDER PROCELLARIIFORMES	
ALBATROSSES	**Family Diomedeidae**	
—Laysan Albatross	*Phoebastria immutabilis*	PO
—Black-footed Albatross	*Phoebastria nigripes*	PO
—Waved Albatross	*Phoebastria irrorata*	PO
—Short-tailed Albatross	*Phoebastria albatrus*	PO
—Royal Albatross	*Diomedea epomophora*	PO
—Wandering Albatross	*Diomedea exulans*	SO
—Sooty Albatross	*Phoebetria fusca*	IO, AO
—Light-mantled Albatross	*Phoebetria palpebrata*	SO
—Yellow-nosed Albatross	*Thalassarche chlororhynchos*	IO, AO
—Grey-headed Albatross	*Thalassarche chrysostoma*	SO
—Black-browed Albatross	*Thalassarche melanophrys*	SO
—Buller's Albatross	*Thalassarche bulleri*	PO
—Shy Albatross	*Thalassarche cauta*	IO, PO
PETRELS, SHEARWATERS	**Family Procellariidae**	
—Southern Giant Petrel	*Macronectes giganteus*	SO, AN
—Northern Giant Petrel	*Macronectes halli*	SO
—Northern Fulmar	*Fulmarus glacialis*	NO
—Southern Fulmar	*Fulmarus glacialoides*	SO, AN
—Antarctic Petrel	*Thalassoica antarctica*	SO, AN
—Cape Petrel	*Daption capense*	SO, AN
—Snow Petrel	*Pagodroma nivea*	SO, AN
—Blue Petrel	*Halobaena caerulea*	SO
—Broad-billed Prion	*Pachyptila vittata*	SO
—Salvin's Prion	*Pachyptila salvini*	IO
—Antarctic Prion	*Pachyptila desolata*	SO, AN
—Slender-billed Prion	*Pachyptila belcheri*	SO
—Fairy Prion	*Pachyptila turtur*	SO
—Fulmar Prion	*Pachyptila crassirostris*	SO
—Kerguelen Petrel	*Aphrodroma brevirostris*	SO
—Great-winged Petrel	*Pterodroma macroptera*	SO
—White-headed Petrel	*Pterodroma lessonii*	SO
—Atlantic Petrel	*Pterodroma incerta*	AO
—Providence Petrel	*Pterodroma solandri*	PO
—Magenta Petrel	*Pterodroma magentae*	PO
—Murphy's Petrel	*Pterodroma ultima*	PO
—Soft-plumaged Petrel	*Pterodroma mollis*	SO
—Zino's Petrel	*Pterodroma madeira*	AO
—Fea's Petrel	*Pterodroma feae*	AO
—Cahow	*Pterodroma cahow*	AO
—Black-capped Petrel	*Pterodroma hasitata*	AO

INTERNATIONAL ENGLISH NAME	SCIENTIFIC NAME	REGION(S)
—Juan Fernandez Petrel	*Pterodroma externa*	PO
—Vanuatu Petrel	*Pterodroma occulta*	PO
—Kermadec Petrel	*Pterodroma neglecta*	PO
—Herald Petrel	*Pterodroma heraldica*	PO
—Trindade Petrel	*Pterodroma arminjoniana*	AO
—Henderson Petrel	*Pterodroma atrata*	PO
—Phoenix Petrel	*Pterodroma alba*	PO
—Barau's Petrel	*Pterodroma baraui*	IO
—Hawaiian Petrel	*Pterodroma sandwichensis*	PO
—Galapagos Petrel	*Pterodroma phaeopygia*	PO
—Mottled Petrel	*Pterodroma inexpectata*	PO, IO
—White-necked Petrel	*Pterodroma cervicalis*	PO
—Black-winged Petrel	*Pterodroma nigripennis*	PO
—Chatham Petrel	*Pterodroma axillaris*	PO
—Bonin Petrel	*Pterodroma hypoleuca*	PO
—Gould's Petrel	*Pterodroma leucoptera*	PO
—Collared Petrel	*Pterodroma brevipes*	PO
—Cook's Petrel	*Pterodroma cookii*	PO
—De Filippi's Petrel	*Pterodroma defilippiana*	PO
—Stejneger's Petrel	*Pterodroma longirostris*	PO
—Pycroft's Petrel	*Pterodroma pycrofti*	PO
—Mascarene Petrel	*Pseudobulweria aterrima*	IO
—Tahiti Petrel	*Pseudobulweria rostrata*	PO
—Fiji Petrel	*Pseudobulweria macgillivrayi*	PO
—Pediunker	*Procellaria cinerea*	SO
—White-chinned Petrel	*Procellaria aequinoctialis*	SO
—Spectacled Petrel	*Procellaria conspicillata*	SO
—Black Petrel	*Procellaria parkinsoni*	PO
—Westland Petrel	*Procellaria westlandica*	PO
—Streaked Shearwater	*Calonectris leucomelas*	PO
—Cory's Shearwater	*Calonectris diomedea*	AO
—Cape Verde Shearwater	*Calonectris edwardsii*	AO
—Christmas Shearwater	*Puffinus nativitatis*	PO
—Wedge-tailed Shearwater	*Puffinus pacificus*	PO, IO
—Buller's Shearwater	*Puffinus bulleri*	PO
—Manx Shearwater	*Puffinus puffinus*	AO
—Yelkouan Shearwater	*Puffinus yelkouan*	AO
—Balearic Shearwater	*Puffinus mauretanicus*	AO
—Black-vented Shearwater	*Puffinus opisthomelas*	PO
—Townsend's Shearwater	*Puffinus auricularis*	PO
—Fluttering Shearwater	*Puffinus gavia*	PO
—Hutton's Shearwater	*Puffinus huttoni*	PO
—Audubon's Shearwater	*Puffinus lherminieri*	TrO
—Bannerman's Shearwater	*Puffinus bannermani*	PO
—Heinroth's Shearwater	*Puffinus heinrothi*	PO
—Little Shearwater	*Puffinus assimilis*	AO, SO
—Sooty Shearwater	*Puffinus griseus*	Worldwide
—Short-tailed Shearwater	*Puffinus tenuirostris*	PO
—Pink-footed Shearwater	*Puffinus creatopus*	PO
—Flesh-footed Shearwater	*Puffinus carneipes*	PO, IO
—Great Shearwater	*Puffinus gravis*	AO
—Bulwer's Petrel	*Bulweria bulwerii*	TrO,TO
—Jouanin's Petrel	*Bulweria fallax*	IO

INTERNATIONAL ENGLISH NAME	SCIENTIFIC NAME	REGION(S)
STORM PETRELS	**Family Hydrobatidae**	
—Wilson's Storm Petrel	*Oceanites oceanicus*	TO, SO
—New Zealand Storm Petrel	*Oceanites maorianus*	PO
—White-vented Storm Petrel	*Oceanites gracilis*	PO
—Grey-backed Storm Petrel	*Garrodia nereis*	SO
—White-faced Storm Petrel	*Pelagodroma marina*	TrO, TO
—White-bellied Storm Petrel	*Fregetta grallaria*	SO
—Black-bellied Storm Petrel	*Fregetta tropica*	SO
—Polynesian Storm Petrel	*Nesofregetta fuliginosa*	PO
—European Storm Petrel	*Hydrobates pelagicus*	AO
—Least Storm Petrel	*Oceanodroma microsoma*	PO
—Wedge-rumped Storm Petrel	*Oceanodroma tethys*	PO
—Band-rumped Storm Petrel	*Oceanodroma castro*	PO, AO
—Swinhoe's Storm Petrel	*Oceanodroma monorhis*	IO, PO
—Leach's Storm Petrel	*Oceanodroma leucorhoa*	PO, AO
—Markham's Storm Petrel	*Oceanodroma markhami*	PO
—Tristram's Storm Petrel	*Oceanodroma tristrami*	PO
—Black Storm Petrel	*Oceanodroma melania*	PO
—Matsudaira's Storm Petrel	*Oceanodroma matsudairae*	IO, PO
—Ashy Storm Petrel	*Oceanodroma homochroa*	PO
—Hornby's Storm Petrel	*Oceanodroma hornbyi*	PO
—Fork-tailed Storm Petrel	*Oceanodroma furcata*	PO
DIVING PETRELS	**Family Pelecanoididae**	
—Peruvian Diving Petrel	*Pelecanoides garnotii*	SA
—Magellanic Diving Petrel	*Pelecanoides magellani*	SA
—South Georgia Diving Petrel	*Pelecanoides georgicus*	SO
—Common Diving Petrel	*Pelecanoides urinatrix*	SO

ORDER PODICIPEDIFORMES

GREBES	**Family Podicipedidae**	
—Alaotra Grebe	*Tachybaptus rufolavatus*	AF
—Little Grebe	*Tachybaptus ruficollis*	EU, AF, OR
—Australasian Grebe	*Tachybaptus novaehollandiae*	AU
—Madagascar Grebe	*Tachybaptus pelzelnii*	AF
—Least Grebe	*Tachybaptus dominicus*	NA, LA
—Pied-billed Grebe	*Podilymbus podiceps*	NA, LA
—Atitlan Grebe	*Podilymbus gigas*	MA
—White-tufted Grebe	*Rollandia rolland*	SA
—Titicaca Grebe	*Rollandia microptera*	SA
—Hoary-headed Grebe	*Poliocephalus poliocephalus*	AU
—New Zealand Grebe	*Poliocephalus rufopectus*	AU
—Great Grebe	*Podiceps major*	SA
—Red-necked Grebe	*Podiceps grisegena*	NA, EU
—Great Crested Grebe	*Podiceps cristatus*	EU
—Horned Grebe	*Podiceps auritus*	NA, EU
—Black-necked Grebe	*Podiceps nigricollis*	EU, AF, NA, MA
—Silvery Grebe	*Podiceps occipitalis*	SA
—Junin Grebe	*Podiceps taczanowskii*	SA
—Hooded Grebe	*Podiceps gallardoi*	SA
—Western Grebe	*Aechmophorus occidentalis*	NA, MA
—Clark's Grebe	*Aechmophorus clarkii*	NA, MA

INTERNATIONAL ENGLISH NAME	SCIENTIFIC NAME	REGION(S)
	ORDER PHOENICOPTERIFORMES	
FLAMINGOS	**Family Phoenicopteridae**	
—Greater Flamingo	*Phoenicopterus roseus*	EU, AF
—American Flamingo	*Phoenicopterus ruber*	LA
—Chilean Flamingo	*Phoenicopterus chilensis*	SA
—Lesser Flamingo	*Phoeniconaias minor*	AF
—Andean Flamingo	*Phoenicoparrus andinus*	SA
—James's Flamingo	*Phoenicoparrus jamesi*	SA
	ORDER CICONIIFORMES	
STORKS	**Family Ciconiidae**	
—Wood Stork	*Mycteria americana*	NA, LA
—Milky Stork	*Mycteria cinerea*	OR
—Yellow-billed Stork	*Mycteria ibis*	AF
—Painted Stork	*Mycteria leucocephala*	OR
—Asian Openbill	*Anastomus oscitans*	OR
—African Openbill	*Anastomus lamelligerus*	AF
—Black Stork	*Ciconia nigra*	AF, EU
—Abdim's Stork	*Ciconia abdimii*	AF
—Woolly-necked Stork	*Ciconia episcopus*	AF, OR
—Storm's Stork	*Ciconia stormi*	OR
—Maguari Stork	*Ciconia maguari*	SA
—White Stork	*Ciconia ciconia*	EU
—Oriental Stork	*Ciconia boyciana*	EU
—Black-necked Stork	*Ephippiorhynchus asiaticus*	OR, AU
—Saddle-billed Stork	*Ephippiorhynchus senegalensis*	AF
—Jabiru	*Jabiru mycteria*	LA
—Lesser Adjutant	*Leptoptilos javanicus*	OR
—Greater Adjutant	*Leptoptilos dubius*	OR
—Marabou Stork	*Leptoptilos crumeniferus*	AF
IBISES, SPOONBILLS	**Family Threskiornithidae**	
—Sacred Ibis	*Threskiornis aethiopicus*	AF
—Black-headed Ibis	*Threskiornis melanocephalus*	OR
—Australian White Ibis	*Threskiornis molucca*	AU
—Straw-necked Ibis	*Threskiornis spinicollis*	AU
—Red-naped Ibis	*Pseudibis papillosa*	OR
—White-shouldered Ibis	*Pseudibis davisoni*	OR
—Giant Ibis	*Pseudibis gigantea*	OR
—Northern Bald Ibis	*Geronticus eremita*	AF
—Southern Bald Ibis	*Geronticus calvus*	AF
—Crested Ibis	*Nipponia nippon*	EU
—Olive Ibis	*Bostrychia olivacea*	AF
—Sao Tome Ibis	*Bostrychia bocagei*	AF
—Spot-breasted Ibis	*Bostrychia rara*	AF
—Hadada Ibis	*Bostrychia hagedash*	AF
—Wattled Ibis	*Bostrychia carunculata*	AF
—Plumbeous Ibis	*Theristicus caerulescens*	SA
—Buff-necked Ibis	*Theristicus caudatus*	SA
—Black-faced Ibis	*Theristicus melanopis*	SA
—Sharp-tailed Ibis	*Cercibis oxycerca*	SA

INTERNATIONAL ENGLISH NAME	SCIENTIFIC NAME	REGION(S)
__Green Ibis	*Mesembrinibis cayennensis*	SA
__Bare-faced Ibis	*Phimosus infuscatus*	SA
__American White Ibis	*Eudocimus albus*	NA, LA
__Scarlet Ibis	*Eudocimus ruber*	SA
__Glossy Ibis	*Plegadis falcinellus*	Worldwide
__White-faced Ibis	*Plegadis chihi*	NA, LA
__Puna Ibis	*Plegadis ridgwayi*	SA
__Madagascar Ibis	*Lophotibis cristata*	AF
__Eurasian Spoonbill	*Platalea leucorodia*	AF, EU, OR
__Black-faced Spoonbill	*Platalea minor*	EU
__African Spoonbill	*Platalea alba*	AF
__Royal Spoonbill	*Platalea regia*	AU
__Yellow-billed Spoonbill	*Platalea flavipes*	AU
__Roseate Spoonbill	*Platalea ajaja*	NA, LA

HERONS, BITTERNS	**Family Ardeidae**	
__Forest Bittern	*Zonerodius heliosylus*	AU
__White-crested Tiger Heron	*Tigriornis leucolopha*	AF
__Rufescent Tiger Heron	*Tigrisoma lineatum*	LA
__Fasciated Tiger Heron	*Tigrisoma fasciatum*	LA
__Bare-throated Tiger Heron	*Tigrisoma mexicanum*	LA
__Agami Heron	*Agamia agami*	LA
__Boat-billed Heron	*Cochlearius cochlearius*	LA
__Zigzag Heron	*Zebrilus undulatus*	SA
__Eurasian Bittern	*Botaurus stellaris*	EU
__Australasian Bittern	*Botaurus poiciloptilus*	AU
__American Bittern	*Botaurus lentiginosus*	NA
__Pinnated Bittern	*Botaurus pinnatus*	LA
__Stripe-backed Bittern	*Ixobrychus involucris*	SA
__Least Bittern	*Ixobrychus exilis*	NA, LA
__Little Bittern	*Ixobrychus minutus*	EU, AF, AU, OR
__New Zealand Bittern	*Ixobrychus novaezelandiae*	AU
__Yellow Bittern	*Ixobrychus sinensis*	OR
__Von Schrenck's Bittern	*Ixobrychus eurhythmus*	EU
__Cinnamon Bittern	*Ixobrychus cinnamomeus*	OR
__Dwarf Bittern	*Ixobrychus sturmii*	AF
__Black Bittern	*Dupetor flavicollis*	OR, AU
__White-eared Night Heron	*Gorsachius magnificus*	OR
__Japanese Night Heron	*Gorsachius goisagi*	EU
__Malayan Night Heron	*Gorsachius melanolophus*	OR
__White-backed Night Heron	*Gorsachius leuconotus*	AF
__Black-crowned Night Heron	*Nycticorax nycticorax*	Worldwide
__Rufous Night Heron	*Nycticorax caledonicus*	AU
__Yellow-crowned Night Heron	*Nyctanassa violacea*	NA, LA
__Green Heron	*Butorides virescens*	NA, MA
__Lava Heron	*Butorides sundevalli*	SA
__Striated Heron	*Butorides striata*	SA, EU, AF, AU
__Squacco Heron	*Ardeola ralloides*	EU, AF
__Indian Pond Heron	*Ardeola grayii*	EU, OR
__Chinese Pond Heron	*Ardeola bacchus*	OR
__Javan Pond Heron	*Ardeola speciosa*	OR
__Malagasy Pond Heron	*Ardeola idae*	AF

INTERNATIONAL ENGLISH NAME	SCIENTIFIC NAME	REGION(S)
__Rufous-bellied Heron	*Ardeola rufiventris*	AF
__Cattle Egret	*Bubulcus ibis*	Worldwide
__Grey Heron	*Ardea cinerea*	EU, AF, OR
__Great Blue Heron	*Ardea herodias*	NA, MA
__Cocoi Heron	*Ardea cocoi*	SA
__White-necked Heron	*Ardea pacifica*	AU
__Black-headed Heron	*Ardea melanocephala*	AF
__Humblot's Heron	*Ardea humbloti*	AF
__White-bellied Heron	*Ardea insignis*	OR
__Great-billed Heron	*Ardea sumatrana*	OR, AU
__Goliath Heron	*Ardea goliath*	AF
__Purple Heron	*Ardea purpurea*	EU, OR, AF
__Great Egret	*Ardea alba*	Worldwide
__Capped Heron	*Pilherodius pileatus*	LA
__Whistling Heron	*Syrigma sibilatrix*	SA
__Yellow-billed Egret	*Egretta intermedia*	OR, AF, AU
__Pied Heron	*Egretta picata*	AU
__White-faced Heron	*Egretta novaehollandiae*	AU
__Reddish Egret	*Egretta rufescens*	NA, MA
__Black Heron	*Egretta ardesiaca*	AF
__Slaty Egret	*Egretta vinaceigula*	AF
__Tricolored Heron	*Egretta tricolor*	NA, LA
__Little Blue Heron	*Egretta caerulea*	NA, LA
__Snowy Egret	*Egretta thula*	NA, LA
__Little Egret	*Egretta garzetta*	EU, AF, OR, AU
__Western Reef Heron	*Egretta gularis*	AF, EU, OR
__Dimorphic Egret	*Egretta dimorpha*	AF
__Pacific Reef Heron	*Egretta sacra*	OR, AU
__Chinese Egret	*Egretta eulophotes*	EU

ORDER PELECANIFORMES

TROPICBIRDS	**Family Phaethontidae**	
__Red-billed Tropicbird	*Phaethon aethereus*	TrO
__Red-tailed Tropicbird	*Phaethon rubricauda*	TrO
__White-tailed Tropicbird	*Phaethon lepturus*	TrO
FRIGATEBIRDS	**Family Fregatidae**	
__Ascension Frigatebird	*Fregata aquila*	AO
__Christmas Frigatebird	*Fregata andrewsi*	IO
__Magnificent Frigatebird	*Fregata magnificens*	AO, PO
__Great Frigatebird	*Fregata minor*	TrO
__Lesser Frigatebird	*Fregata ariel*	TrO
HAMERKOP	**Family Scopidae**	
__Hamerkop	*Scopus umbretta*	AF
SHOEBILL	**Family Balaenicipitidae**	
__Shoebill	*Balaeniceps rex*	AF

INTERNATIONAL ENGLISH NAME	SCIENTIFIC NAME	REGION(S)
PELICANS	**Family Pelecanidae**	
—Great White Pelican	*Pelecanus onocrotalus*	EU
—Pink-backed Pelican	*Pelecanus rufescens*	AF
—Spot-billed Pelican	*Pelecanus philippensis*	OR
—Dalmatian Pelican	*Pelecanus crispus*	EU
—Australian Pelican	*Pelecanus conspicillatus*	AU
—American White Pelican	*Pelecanus erythrorhynchos*	NA
—Brown Pelican	*Pelecanus occidentalis*	NA, LA
—Peruvian Pelican	*Pelecanus thagus*	SA
GANNETS, BOOBIES	**Family Sulidae**	
—Northern Gannet	*Morus bassanus*	AO
—Cape Gannet	*Morus capensis*	AF
—Australasian Gannet	*Morus serrator*	AU
—Abbott's Booby	*Papasula abbotti*	IO
—Blue-footed Booby	*Sula nebouxii*	PO
—Peruvian Booby	*Sula variegata*	SA
—Masked Booby	*Sula dactylatra*	TrO
—Nazca Booby	*Sula granti*	PO
—Red-footed Booby	*Sula sula*	TrO
—Brown Booby	*Sula leucogaster*	TrO
CORMORANTS	**Family Phalacrocoracidae**	
—Little Pied Cormorant	*Phalacrocorax melanoleucos*	AU
—Reed Cormorant	*Phalacrocorax africanus*	AF
—Crowned Cormorant	*Phalacrocorax coronatus*	AF
—Little Cormorant	*Phalacrocorax niger*	OR
—Pygmy Cormorant	*Phalacrocorax pygmeus*	EU
—Brandt's Cormorant	*Phalacrocorax penicillatus*	NA
—Flightless Cormorant	*Phalacrocorax harrisi*	SA
—Bank Cormorant	*Phalacrocorax neglectus*	AF
—Black-faced Cormorant	*Phalacrocorax fuscescens*	AU
—Neotropic Cormorant	*Phalacrocorax brasilianus*	LA
—Double-crested Cormorant	*Phalacrocorax auritus*	NA, MA
—Indian Cormorant	*Phalacrocorax fuscicollis*	OR
—Little Black Cormorant	*Phalacrocorax sulcirostris*	AU
—Australian Pied Cormorant	*Phalacrocorax varius*	AU
—Great Cormorant	*Phalacrocorax carbo*	EU, AU, OR
—White-breasted Cormorant	*Phalacrocorax lucidus*	AF
—Japanese Cormorant	*Phalacrocorax capillatus*	EU
—Socotra Cormorant	*Leucocarbo nigrogularis*	EU
—Cape Cormorant	*Leucocarbo capensis*	AF
—Guanay Cormorant	*Leucocarbo bougainvillii*	SA
—Rock Shag	*Leucocarbo magellanicus*	SA
—Pelagic Shag	*Leucocarbo pelagicus*	PO
—Red-faced Shag	*Leucocarbo urile*	PO
—European Shag	*Leucocarbo aristotelis*	EU
—Red-legged Shag	*Leucocarbo gaimardi*	SA
—Spotted Shag	*Leucocarbo punctatus*	AU
—Pitt Shag	*Leucocarbo featherstoni*	AU
—Imperial Shag	*Leucocarbo atriceps*	SA
—South Georgia Shag	*Leucocarbo georgianus*	SO
—King Shag	*Leucocarbo albiventer*	SA

INTERNATIONAL ENGLISH NAME	SCIENTIFIC NAME	REGION(S)
—Antarctic Shag	*Leucocarbo bransfieldensis*	AN
—Kerguelen Shag	*Leucocarbo verrucosus*	IO
—Rough-faced Shag	*Leucocarbo carunculatus*	AU
—Bronze Shag	*Leucocarbo chalconotus*	AU
—Chatham Shag	*Leucocarbo onslowi*	AU
—Campbell Shag	*Leucocarbo campbelli*	AU
—Auckland Shag	*Leucocarbo colensoi*	AU
—Bounty Shag	*Leucocarbo ranfurlyi*	AU
ANHINGAS	**Family Anhingidae**	
—Darter	*Anhinga melanogaster*	AF, OR, AU
—Anhinga	*Anhinga anhinga*	NA, LA
	ORDER FALCONIFORMES	
NEW WORLD VULTURES	**Family Cathartidae**	
—Turkey Vulture	*Cathartes aura*	NA, LA
—Lesser Yellow-headed Vulture	*Cathartes burrovianus*	LA
—Greater Yellow-headed Vulture	*Cathartes melambrotus*	SA
—Black Vulture	*Coragyps atratus*	NA, LA
—King Vulture	*Sarcoramphus papa*	LA
—California Condor	*Gymnogyps californianus*	NA
—Andean Condor	*Vultur gryphus*	SA
CARACARAS, FALCONS	**Family Falconidae**	
—Black Caracara	*Daptrius ater*	SA
—Red-throated Caracara	*Ibycter americanus*	LA
—Carunculated Caracara	*Phalcoboenus carunculatus*	SA
—Mountain Caracara	*Phalcoboenus megalopterus*	SA
—White-throated Caracara	*Phalcoboenus albogularis*	SA
—Striated Caracara	*Phalcoboenus australis*	SA
—Northern Crested Caracara	*Caracara cheriway*	NA, LA
—Southern Crested Caracara	*Caracara plancus*	SA
—Yellow-headed Caracara	*Milvago chimachima*	LA
—Chimango Caracara	*Milvago chimango*	SA
—Laughing Falcon	*Herpetotheres cachinnans*	LA
—Barred Forest Falcon	*Micrastur ruficollis*	LA
—Plumbeous Forest Falcon	*Micrastur plumbeus*	SA
—Lined Forest Falcon	*Micrastur gilvicollis*	SA
—Cryptic Forest Falcon	*Micrastur mintoni*	SA
—Slaty-backed Forest Falcon	*Micrastur mirandollei*	LA
—Collared Forest Falcon	*Micrastur semitorquatus*	LA
—Buckley's Forest Falcon	*Micrastur buckleyi*	SA
—Spot-winged Falconet	*Spiziapteryx circumcincta*	SA
—Pygmy Falcon	*Polihierax semitorquatus*	AF
—White-rumped Falcon	*Polihierax insignis*	OR
—Collared Falconet	*Microhierax caerulescens*	OR
—Black-thighed Falconet	*Microhierax fringillarius*	OR
—White-fronted Falconet	*Microhierax latifrons*	OR
—Philippine Falconet	*Microhierax erythrogenys*	OR
—Pied Falconet	*Microhierax melanoleucos*	OR
—Lesser Kestrel	*Falco naumanni*	EU

INTERNATIONAL ENGLISH NAME	SCIENTIFIC NAME	REGION(S)
__Common Kestrel	*Falco tinnunculus*	EU, AF
__Malagasy Kestrel	*Falco newtoni*	AF
__Mauritius Kestrel	*Falco punctatus*	AF
__Seychelles Kestrel	*Falco araeus*	AF
__Spotted Kestrel	*Falco moluccensis*	AU
__Nankeen Kestrel	*Falco cenchroides*	AU
__American Kestrel	*Falco sparverius*	NA, LA
__Greater Kestrel	*Falco rupicoloides*	AF
__Fox Kestrel	*Falco alopex*	AF
__Grey Kestrel	*Falco ardosiaceus*	AF
__Dickinson's Kestrel	*Falco dickinsoni*	AF
__Banded Kestrel	*Falco zoniventris*	AF
__Red-necked Falcon	*Falco chicquera*	AF, OR
__Red-footed Falcon	*Falco vespertinus*	EU
__Amur Falcon	*Falco amurensis*	EU
__Eleonora's Falcon	*Falco eleonorae*	EU
__Sooty Falcon	*Falco concolor*	AF, EU
__Aplomado Falcon	*Falco femoralis*	LA
__Merlin	*Falco columbarius*	NA, EU
__Bat Falcon	*Falco rufigularis*	LA
__Orange-breasted Falcon	*Falco deiroleucus*	LA
__Eurasian Hobby	*Falco subbuteo*	EU
__African Hobby	*Falco cuvierii*	AF
__Oriental Hobby	*Falco severus*	OR, AU
__Australian Hobby	*Falco longipennis*	AU
__New Zealand Falcon	*Falco novaeseelandiae*	AU
__Brown Falcon	*Falco berigora*	AU
__Grey Falcon	*Falco hypoleucos*	AU
__Black Falcon	*Falco subniger*	AU
__Lanner Falcon	*Falco biarmicus*	EU, AF
__Laggar Falcon	*Falco jugger*	OR
__Saker Falcon	*Falco cherrug*	EU
__Gyrfalcon	*Falco rusticolus*	NA, EU
__Prairie Falcon	*Falco mexicanus*	NA, MA
__Peregrine Falcon	*Falco peregrinus*	Worldwide
__Barbary Falcon	*Falco pelegrinoides*	EU
__Taita Falcon	*Falco fasciinucha*	AF
KITES, HAWKS, EAGLES	**Family Accipitridae**	
__Secretarybird	*Sagittarius serpentarius*	AF
__Osprey	*Pandion haliaetus*	Worldwide
__African Cuckoo-Hawk	*Aviceda cuculoides*	AF
__Madagascar Cuckoo-Hawk	*Aviceda madagascariensis*	AF
__Jerdon's Baza	*Aviceda jerdoni*	OR
__Pacific Baza	*Aviceda subcristata*	AU
__Black Baza	*Aviceda leuphotes*	OR
__Grey-headed Kite	*Leptodon cayanensis*	LA
__White-collared Kite	*Leptodon forbesi*	SA
__Hook-billed Kite	*Chondrohierax uncinatus*	NA, LA
__Cuban Kite	*Chondrohierax wilsoni*	NA
__Long-tailed Honey Buzzard	*Henicopernis longicauda*	AU
__Black Honey Buzzard	*Henicopernis infuscatus*	AU
__European Honey Buzzard	*Pernis apivorus*	EU

INTERNATIONAL ENGLISH NAME	SCIENTIFIC NAME	REGION(S)
—Crested Honey Buzzard	*Pernis ptilorhynchus*	EU, OR
—Barred Honey Buzzard	*Pernis celebensis*	OR, AU
—Square-tailed Kite	*Lophoictinia isura*	AU
—Black-breasted Buzzard	*Hamirostra melanosternon*	AU
—Swallow-tailed Kite	*Elanoides forficatus*	NA, LA
—Bat Hawk	*Macheiramphus alcinus*	AF, OR
—Pearl Kite	*Gampsonyx swainsonii*	SA
—Black-winged Kite	*Elanus caeruleus*	AF, OR
—Black-shouldered Kite	*Elanus axillaris*	AU
—White-tailed Kite	*Elanus leucurus*	NA, LA
—Letter-winged Kite	*Elanus scriptus*	AU
—Scissor-tailed Kite	*Chelictinia riocourii*	AF
—Snail Kite	*Rostrhamus sociabilis*	NA, LA
—Slender-billed Kite	*Rostrhamus hamatus*	LA
—Double-toothed Kite	*Harpagus bidentatus*	LA
—Rufous-thighed Kite	*Harpagus diodon*	SA
—Mississippi Kite	*Ictinia mississippiensis*	NA
—Plumbeous Kite	*Ictinia plumbea*	LA
—Red Kite	*Milvus milvus*	EU
—Black Kite	*Milvus migrans*	EU, AF, OR, AU
—Whistling Kite	*Haliastur sphenurus*	AU
—Brahminy Kite	*Haliastur indus*	OR, AU
—White-bellied Sea Eagle	*Haliaeetus leucogaster*	OR, AU
—Forest Fish Eagle	*Haliaeetus sanfordi*	AU
—African Fish Eagle	*Haliaeetus vocifer*	AF
—Madagascar Fish Eagle	*Haliaeetus vociferoides*	AF
—Pallas's Fish Eagle	*Haliaeetus leucoryphus*	EU
—White-tailed Eagle	*Haliaeetus albicilla*	EU
—Bald Eagle	*Haliaeetus leucocephalus*	NA
—Steller's Sea Eagle	*Haliaeetus pelagicus*	EU
—Lesser Fish Eagle	*Ichthyophaga humilis*	OR
—Grey-headed Fish Eagle	*Ichthyophaga ichthyaetus*	OR
—Palm-nut Vulture	*Gypòhierax angolensis*	AF
—Bearded Vulture	*Gypaetus barbatus*	AF, EU
—Egyptian Vulture	*Neophron percnopterus*	AF, EU, OR
—Hooded Vulture	*Necrosyrtes monachus*	AF
—White-backed Vulture	*Gyps africanus*	AF
—White-rumped Vulture	*Gyps bengalensis*	OR
—Indian Vulture	*Gyps indicus*	OR
—Slender-billed Vulture	*Gyps tenuirostris*	OR
—Rüppell's Vulture	*Gyps rueppellii*	AF
—Himalayan Vulture	*Gyps himalayensis*	OR
—Griffon Vulture	*Gyps fulvus*	AF, EU
—Cape Vulture	*Gyps coprotheres*	AF
—Red-headed Vulture	*Sarcogyps calvus*	OR
—White-headed Vulture	*Aegypius occipitalis*	AF
—Cinereous Vulture	*Aegypius monachus*	EU
—Lappet-faced Vulture	*Aegypius tracheliotus*	AF
—Short-toed Snake Eagle	*Circaetus gallicus*	EU, OR
—Beaudouin's Snake Eagle	*Circaetus beaudouini*	AF
—Black-chested Snake Eagle	*Circaetus pectoralis*	AF
—Brown Snake Eagle	*Circaetus cinereus*	AF
—Southern Banded Snake Eagle	*Circaetus fasciolatus*	AF

INTERNATIONAL ENGLISH NAME	SCIENTIFIC NAME	REGION(S)
__Western Banded Snake Eagle	*Circaetus cinerascens*	AF
__Bateleur	*Terathopius ecaudatus*	AF
__Crested Serpent Eagle	*Spilornis cheela*	OR
__Nicobar Serpent Eagle	*Spilornis minimus*	OR
__Mountain Serpent Eagle	*Spilornis kinabaluensis*	OR
__Sulawesi Serpent Eagle	*Spilornis rufipectus*	OR
__Philippine Serpent Eagle	*Spilornis holospilus*	OR
__Andaman Serpent Eagle	*Spilornis elgini*	OR
__Congo Serpent Eagle	*Dryotriorchis spectabilis*	AF
__Madagascar Serpent Eagle	*Eutriorchis astur*	AF
__Western Marsh Harrier	*Circus aeruginosus*	EU
__Eastern Marsh Harrier	*Circus spilonotus*	EU
__Swamp Harrier	*Circus approximans*	AU
__African Marsh Harrier	*Circus ranivorus*	AF
__Malagasy Marsh Harrier	*Circus maillardi*	AF
__Long-winged Harrier	*Circus buffoni*	SA
__Spotted Harrier	*Circus assimilis*	AU
__Black Harrier	*Circus maurus*	AF
__Northern Harrier	*Circus cyaneus*	NA, EU
__Cinereous Harrier	*Circus cinereus*	SA
__Pallid Harrier	*Circus macrourus*	EU
__Pied Harrier	*Circus melanoleucos*	EU
__Montagu's Harrier	*Circus pygargus*	EU
__African Harrier-Hawk	*Polyboroides typus*	AF
__Madagascar Harrier-Hawk	*Polyboroides radiatus*	AF
__Dark Chanting Goshawk	*Melierax metabates*	AF
__Eastern Chanting Goshawk	*Melierax poliopterus*	AF
__Pale Chanting Goshawk	*Melierax canorus*	AF
__Gabar Goshawk	*Micronisus gabar*	AF
__Grey-bellied Hawk	*Accipiter poliogaster*	SA
__Crested Goshawk	*Accipiter trivirgatus*	OR
__Sulawesi Goshawk	*Accipiter griseiceps*	AU
__Red-chested Goshawk	*Accipiter toussenelii*	AF
__African Goshawk	*Accipiter tachiro*	AF
__Chestnut-flanked Sparrowhawk	*Accipiter castanilius*	AF
__Shikra	*Accipiter badius*	AF, OR
__Nicobar Sparrowhawk	*Accipiter butleri*	OR
__Levant Sparrowhawk	*Accipiter brevipes*	EU
__Chinese Sparrowhawk	*Accipiter soloensis*	EU
__Frances's Sparrowhawk	*Accipiter francesii*	AF
__Spot-tailed Sparrowhawk	*Accipiter trinotatus*	AU
__Grey Goshawk	*Accipiter novaehollandiae*	AU
__Brown Goshawk	*Accipiter fasciatus*	AU
__Black-mantled Goshawk	*Accipiter melanochlamys*	AU
__Pied Goshawk	*Accipiter albogularis*	AU
__White-bellied Goshawk	*Accipiter haplochrous*	AU
__Fiji Goshawk	*Accipiter rufitorques*	AU
__Moluccan Goshawk	*Accipiter henicogrammus*	AU
__Slaty-mantled Goshawk	*Accipiter luteoschistaceus*	AU
__Imitator Goshawk	*Accipiter imitator*	AU
__Grey-headed Goshawk	*Accipiter poliocephalus*	AU
__New Britain Goshawk	*Accipiter princeps*	AU
__Tiny Hawk	*Accipiter superciliosus*	LA

INTERNATIONAL ENGLISH NAME	SCIENTIFIC NAME	REGION(S)
—Semicollared Hawk	*Accipiter collaris*	SA
—Red-thighed Sparrowhawk	*Accipiter erythropus*	AF
—Little Sparrowhawk	*Accipiter minullus*	AF
—Japanese Sparrowhawk	*Accipiter gularis*	EU
—Besra	*Accipiter virgatus*	OR
—Dwarf Sparrowhawk	*Accipiter nanus*	AU
—Rufous-necked Sparrowhawk	*Accipiter erythrauchen*	AU
—Collared Sparrowhawk	*Accipiter cirrocephalus*	AU
—Grey Sparrowhawk	*Accipiter brachyurus*	AU
—Vinous-breasted Sparrowhawk	*Accipiter rhodogaster*	AU
—Madagascar Sparrowhawk	*Accipiter madagascariensis*	AF
—Ovambo Sparrowhawk	*Accipiter ovampensis*	AF
—Eurasian Sparrowhawk	*Accipiter nisus*	EU
—Rufous-breasted Sparrowhawk	*Accipiter rufiventris*	AF
—Sharp-shinned Hawk	*Accipiter striatus*	NA, MA
—White-breasted Hawk	*Accipiter chionogaster*	MA
—Plain-breasted Hawk	*Accipiter ventralis*	SA
—Rufous-thighed Hawk	*Accipiter erythronemius*	SA
—Cooper's Hawk	*Accipiter cooperii*	NA, MA
—Gundlach's Hawk	*Accipiter gundlachi*	NA
—Bicolored Hawk	*Accipiter bicolor*	LA
—Chilean Hawk	*Accipiter chilensis*	SA
—Black Sparrowhawk	*Accipiter melanoleucus*	AF
—Henst's Goshawk	*Accipiter henstii*	AF
—Northern Goshawk	*Accipiter gentilis*	NA, MA, EU
—Meyer's Goshawk	*Accipiter meyerianus*	AU
—Chestnut-shouldered Goshawk	*Erythrotriorchis buergersi*	AU
—Red Goshawk	*Erythrotriorchis radiatus*	AU
—Doria's Goshawk	*Megatriorchis doriae*	AU
—Long-tailed Hawk	*Urotriorchis macrourus*	AF
—Lizard Buzzard	*Kaupifalco monogrammicus*	AF
—Grasshopper Buzzard	*Butastur rufipennis*	AF
—White-eyed Buzzard	*Butastur teesa*	OR
—Rufous-winged Buzzard	*Butastur liventer*	OR
—Grey-faced Buzzard	*Butastur indicus*	EU
—Crane Hawk	*Geranospiza caerulescens*	LA
—Plumbeous Hawk	*Leucopternis plumbeus*	SA
—Slate-colored Hawk	*Leucopternis schistaceus*	SA
—Barred Hawk	*Leucopternis princeps*	LA
—Black-faced Hawk	*Leucopternis melanops*	SA
—White-browed Hawk	*Leucopternis kuhli*	SA
—White-necked Hawk	*Leucopternis lacernulatus*	SA
—Semiplumbeous Hawk	*Leucopternis semiplumbeus*	LA
—White Hawk	*Leucopternis albicollis*	LA
—Grey-backed Hawk	*Leucopternis occidentalis*	SA
—Mantled Hawk	*Leucopternis polionotus*	SA
—Rufous Crab Hawk	*Buteogallus aequinoctialis*	SA
—Common Black Hawk	*Buteogallus anthracinus*	NA, LA
—Great Black Hawk	*Buteogallus urubitinga*	LA
—Savanna Hawk	*Buteogallus meridionalis*	LA
—Harris's Hawk	*Parabuteo unicinctus*	NA, LA
—Black-collared Hawk	*Busarellus nigricollis*	LA
—Black-chested Buzzard-Eagle	*Geranoaetus melanoleucus*	SA

INTERNATIONAL ENGLISH NAME	SCIENTIFIC NAME	REGION(S)
—Montane Solitary Eagle	*Harpyhaliaetus solitarius*	LA
—Crowned Solitary Eagle	*Harpyhaliaetus coronatus*	SA
—Grey-lined Hawk	*Buteo nitida*	NA, LA
—Roadside Hawk	*Buteo magnirostris*	LA
—Red-shouldered Hawk	*Buteo lineatus*	NA
—Ridgway's Hawk	*Buteo ridgwayi*	NA
—Broad-winged Hawk	*Buteo platypterus*	NA
—White-rumped Hawk	*Buteo leucorrhous*	SA
—Short-tailed Hawk	*Buteo brachyurus*	LA
—White-throated Hawk	*Buteo albigula*	SA
—Swainson's Hawk	*Buteo swainsoni*	NA, MA
—White-tailed Hawk	*Buteo albicaudatus*	NA, LA
—Galapagos Hawk	*Buteo galapagoensis*	SA
—Variable Hawk	*Buteo polyosoma*	SA
—Zone-tailed Hawk	*Buteo albonotatus*	NA, LA
—Hawaiian Hawk	*Buteo solitarius*	PO
—Red-tailed Hawk	*Buteo jamaicensis*	NA, MA
—Rufous-tailed Hawk	*Buteo ventralis*	SA
—Common Buzzard	*Buteo buteo*	EU
—Mountain Buzzard	*Buteo oreophilus*	AF
—Forest Buzzard	*Buteo trizonatus*	AF
—Madagascar Buzzard	*Buteo brachypterus*	AF
—Long-legged Buzzard	*Buteo rufinus*	EU, AF
—Upland Buzzard	*Buteo hemilasius*	EU
—Ferruginous Hawk	*Buteo regalis*	NA
—Roughleg	*Buteo lagopus*	NA, EU
—Red-necked Buzzard	*Buteo auguralis*	AF
—Augur Buzzard	*Buteo augur*	AF
—Jackal Buzzard	*Buteo rufofuscus*	AF
—Crested Eagle	*Morphnus guianensis*	LA
—Harpy Eagle	*Harpia harpyja*	LA
—Papuan Eagle	*Harpyopsis novaeguineae*	AU
—Philippine Eagle	*Pithecophaga jefferyi*	OR
—Black Eagle	*Ictinaetus malayensis*	OR
—Lesser Spotted Eagle	*Aquila pomarina*	EU
—Indian Spotted Eagle	*Aquila hastata*	OR
—Greater Spotted Eagle	*Aquila clanga*	EU
—Tawny Eagle	*Aquila rapax*	AF
—Steppe Eagle	*Aquila nipalensis*	EU
—Spanish Imperial Eagle	*Aquila adalberti*	EU
—Asian Imperial Eagle	*Aquila heliaca*	EU
—Gurney's Eagle	*Aquila gurneyi*	AU
—Golden Eagle	*Aquila chrysaetos*	NA, MA, EU
—Wedge-tailed Eagle	*Aquila audax*	AU
—Verreaux's Eagle	*Aquila verreauxii*	AF
—Wahlberg's Eagle	*Aquila wahlbergi*	AF
—Bonelli's Eagle	*Hieraaetus fasciatus*	EU, OR
—African Hawk-Eagle	*Hieraaetus spilogaster*	AF
—Booted Eagle	*Hieraaetus pennatus*	EU
—Little Eagle	*Hieraaetus morphnoides*	AU
—Ayres's Hawk-Eagle	*Hieraaetus ayresii*	AF
—Rufous-bellied Eagle	*Hieraaetus kienerii*	OR
—Martial Eagle	*Polemaetus bellicosus*	AF

INTERNATIONAL ENGLISH NAME	SCIENTIFIC NAME	REGION(S)
—Black-and-white Hawk-Eagle	*Spizastur melanoleucus*	LA
—Long-crested Eagle	*Lophaetus occipitalis*	AF
—Cassin's Hawk-Eagle	*Spizaetus africanus*	AF
—Crested Hawk-Eagle	*Spizaetus cirrhatus*	OR
—Changeable Hawk-Eagle	*Spizaetus limnaeetus*	OR
—Flores Hawk-Eagle	*Spizaetus floris*	AU
—Mountain Hawk-Eagle	*Spizaetus nipalensis*	OR
—Blyth's Hawk-Eagle	*Spizaetus alboniger*	OR
—Javan Hawk-Eagle	*Spizaetus bartelsi*	OR
—Sulawesi Hawk-Eagle	*Spizaetus lanceolatus*	AU
—Philippine Hawk-Eagle	*Spizaetus philippensis*	OR
—Wallace's Hawk-Eagle	*Spizaetus nanus*	OR
—Black Hawk-Eagle	*Spizaetus tyrannus*	LA
—Ornate Hawk-Eagle	*Spizaetus ornatus*	LA
—Crowned Eagle	*Stephanoaetus coronatus*	AF
—Black-and-chestnut Eagle	*Oroaetus isidori*	SA

ORDER GRUIFORMES

BUSTARDS	**Family Otidae**	
—Great Bustard	*Otis tarda*	EU
—Arabian Bustard	*Ardeotis arabs*	AF
—Kori Bustard	*Ardeotis kori*	AF
—Great Indian Bustard	*Ardeotis nigriceps*	OR
—Australian Bustard	*Ardeotis australis*	AU
—Houbara Bustard	*Chlamydotis undulata*	AF
—Macqueen's Bustard	*Chlamydotis macqueenii*	EU
—Ludwig's Bustard	*Neotis ludwigii*	AF
—Denham's Bustard	*Neotis denhami*	AF
—Heuglin's Bustard	*Neotis heuglinii*	AF
—Nubian Bustard	*Neotis nuba*	AF
—White-bellied Bustard	*Eupodotis senegalensis*	AF
—Barrow's Korhaan	*Eupodotis barrowii*	AF
—Blue Korhaan	*Eupodotis caerulescens*	AF
—Karoo Korhaan	*Eupodotis vigorsii*	AF
—Rüppell's Korhaan	*Eupodotis rueppellii*	AF
—Little Brown Bustard	*Eupodotis humilis*	AF
—Savile's Bustard	*Lophotis savilei*	AF
—Buff-crested Bustard	*Lophotis gindiana*	AF
—Red-crested Korhaan	*Lophotis ruficrista*	AF
—Southern Black Korhaan	*Afrotis afra*	AF
—Northern Black Korhaan	*Afrotis afraoides*	AF
—Black-bellied Bustard	*Lissotis melanogaster*	AF
—Hartlaub's Bustard	*Lissotis hartlaubii*	AF
—Bengal Florican	*Houbaropsis bengalensis*	OR
—Lesser Florican	*Sypheotides indica*	OR
—Little Bustard	*Tetrax tetrax*	EU

MESITES	**Family Mesitornithidae**	
—White-breasted Mesite	*Mesitornis variegatus*	AF
—Brown Mesite	*Mesitornis unicolor*	AF
—Subdesert Mesite	*Monias benschi*	AF

INTERNATIONAL ENGLISH NAME	SCIENTIFIC NAME	REGION(S)
SERIEMAS	**Family Cariamidae**	
—Red-legged Seriema	*Cariama cristata*	SA
—Black-legged Seriema	*Chunga burmeisteri*	SA
KAGU	**Family Rhynochetidae**	
—Kagu	*Rhynochetos jubatus*	AU
SUNBITTERN	**Family Eurypygidae**	
—Sunbittern	*Eurypyga helias*	LA
FLUFFTAILS	**Family Sarothruridae**	
—White-spottéd Flufftail	*Sarothrura pulchra*	AF
—Buff-spotted Flufftail	*Sarothrura elegans*	AF
—Red-chested Flufftail	*Sarothrura rufa*	AF
—Chestnut-headed Flufftail	*Sarothrura lugens*	AF
—Streaky-breasted Flufftail	*Sarothrura boehmi*	AF
—Striped Flufftail	*Sarothrura affinis*	AF
—Madagascar Flufftail	*Sarothrura insularis*	AF
—White-winged Flufftail	*Sarothrura ayresi*	AF
—Slender-billed Flufftail	*Sarothrura watersi*	AF
RAILS, CRAKES, COOTS	**Family Rallidae**	
—Nkulengu Rail	*Himantornis haematopus*	AF
—Grey-throated Rail	*Canirallus oculeus*	AF
—Madagascar Wood Rail	*Canirallus kioloides*	AF
—Swinhoe's Rail	*Coturnicops exquisitus*	EU
—Yellow Rail	*Coturnicops noveboracensis*	NA
—Speckled Crake	*Coturnicops notatus*	SA
—Ocellated Crake	*Micropygia schomburgkii*	SA
—Chestnut Forest Crake	*Rallina rubra*	AU
—White-striped Forest Crake	*Rallina leucospila*	AU
—Forbes's Forest Crake	*Rallina forbesi*	AU
—Mayr's Forest Crake	*Rallina mayri*	AU
—Red-necked Crake	*Rallina tricolor*	AU
—Andaman Crake	*Rallina canningi*	OR
—Red-legged Crake	*Rallina fasciata*	OR
—Slaty-legged Crake	*Rallina eurizonoides*	OR
—Chestnut-headed Crake	*Anurolimnas castaneiceps*	SA
—Russet-crowned Crake	*Laterallus viridis*	SA
—Black-banded Crake	*Laterallus fasciatus*	SA
—Rufous-sided Crake	*Laterallus melanophaius*	SA
—Rusty-flanked Crake	*Laterallus levraudi*	SA
—Ruddy Crake	*Laterallus ruber*	MA
—White-throated Crake	*Laterallus albigularis*	LA
—Grey-breasted Crake	*Laterallus exilis*	LA
—Black Rail	*Laterallus jamaicensis*	NA, LA
—Junin Crake	*Laterallus tuerosi*	SA
—Galapagos Crake	*Laterallus spilonotus*	SA
—Red-and-white Crake	*Laterallus leucopyrrhus*	SA
—Rufous-faced Crake	*Laterallus xenopterus*	SA
—Bar-winged Rail	*Nesoclopeus poecilopterus*	AU
—Woodford's Rail	*Nesoclopeus woodfordi*	AU

INTERNATIONAL ENGLISH NAME	SCIENTIFIC NAME	REGION(S)
__Weka	*Gallirallus australis*	AU
__Calayan Rail	*Gallirallus calayanensis*	OR
__New Caledonian Rail	*Gallirallus lafresnayanus*	AU
__Lord Howe Woodhen	*Gallirallus sylvestris*	AU
__Okinawa Rail	*Gallirallus okinawae*	EU
__Barred Rail	*Gallirallus torquatus*	AU
__Pink-legged Rail	*Gallirallus insignis*	AU
__Buff-banded Rail	*Gallirallus philippensis*	AU
__Guam Rail	*Gallirallus owstoni*	AU
__Roviana Rail	*Gallirallus rovianae*	AU
__Slaty-breasted Rail	*Gallirallus striatus*	OR
__Clapper Rail	*Rallus longirostris*	NA, LA
__King Rail	*Rallus elegans*	NA, MA
__Plain-flanked Rail	*Rallus wetmorei*	SA
__Virginia Rail	*Rallus limicola*	NA
__Ecuadorian Rail	*Rallus aequatorialis*	SA
__Bogota Rail	*Rallus semiplumbeus*	SA
__Austral Rail	*Rallus antarcticus*	SA
__Water Rail	*Rallus aquaticus*	EU
__African Rail	*Rallus caerulescens*	AF
__Madagascar Rail	*Rallus madagascariensis*	AF
__Brown-banded Rail	*Lewinia mirifica*	OR
__Lewin's Rail	*Lewinia pectoralis*	AU
__Auckland Rail	*Lewinia muelleri*	AU
__White-throated Rail	*Dryolimnas cuvieri*	AF
__African Crake	*Crex egregia*	AF
__Corn Crake	*Crex crex*	EU
__Rouget's Rail	*Rougetius rougetii*	AF
__Snoring Rail	*Aramidopsis plateni*	AU
__Inaccessible Island Rail	*Atlantisia rogersi*	AO
__Little Wood Rail	*Aramides mangle*	SA
__Rufous-necked Wood Rail	*Aramides axillaris*	LA
__Grey-necked Wood Rail	*Aramides cajanea*	LA
__Brown Wood Rail	*Aramides wolfi*	SA
__Giant Wood Rail	*Aramides ypecaha*	SA
__Slaty-breasted Wood Rail	*Aramides saracura*	SA
__Red-winged Wood Rail	*Aramides calopterus*	SA
__Uniform Crake	*Amaurolimnas concolor*	LA
__Blue-faced Rail	*Gymnocrex rosenbergii*	AU
__Talaud Rail	*Gymnocrex talaudensis*	AU
__Bare-eyed Rail	*Gymnocrex plumbeiventris*	AU
__Brown Bush-hen	*Amaurornis akool*	OR
__Isabelline Bush-hen	*Amaurornis isabellina*	AU
__Plain Bush-hen	*Amaurornis olivacea*	OR, AU
__Talaud Bush-hen	*Amaurornis magnirostris*	AU
__White-breasted Waterhen	*Amaurornis phoenicurus*	OR
__Black Crake	*Amaurornis flavirostra*	AF
__Sakalava Rail	*Amaurornis olivieri*	AF
__Black-tailed Crake	*Porzana bicolor*	OR
__Little Crake	*Porzana parva*	EU
__Baillon's Crake	*Porzana pusilla*	EU, AF
__Spotted Crake	*Porzana porzana*	EU

INTERNATIONAL ENGLISH NAME	SCIENTIFIC NAME	REGION(S)
__Australian Crake	*Porzana fluminea*	AU
__Sora	*Porzana carolina*	NA
__Dot-winged Crake	*Porzana spiloptera*	SA
__Ash-throated Crake	*Porzana albicollis*	SA
__Ruddy-breasted Crake	*Porzana fusca*	OR
__Band-bellied Crake	*Porzana paykullii*	EU
__Spotless Crake	*Porzana tabuensis*	AU
__Red-eyed Crake	*Porzana atra*	PO
__Yellow-breasted Crake	*Porzana flaviventer*	NA, LA
__White-browed Crake	*Porzana cinerea*	OR, AU
__Striped Crake	*Aenigmatolimnas marginalis*	AF
__Zapata Rail	*Cyanolimnas cerverai*	NA
__Colombian Crake	*Neocrex colombiana*	LA
__Paint-billed Crake	*Neocrex erythrops*	SA
__Spotted Rail	*Pardirallus maculatus*	LA
__Blackish Rail	*Pardirallus nigricans*	SA
__Plumbeous Rail	*Pardirallus sanguinolentus*	SA
__Chestnut Rail	*Eulabeornis castaneoventris*	AU
__Invisible Rail	*Habroptila wallacii*	AU
__Papuan Flightless Rail	*Megacrex inepta*	AU
__Watercock	*Gallicrex cinerea*	OR
__Purple Swamphen	*Porphyrio porphyrio*	AF, EU, OR, AU
__African Swamphen	*Porphyrio madagascariensis*	AF
__Takahe	*Porphyrio hochstetteri*	AU
__Allen's Gallinule	*Porphyrio alleni*	AF
__Purple Gallinule	*Porphyrio martinicus*	NA, LA
__Azure Gallinule	*Porphyrio flavirostris*	SA
__Makira Woodhen	*Gallinula silvestris*	AU
__Tristan Gallinule	*Gallinula nesiotis*	AO
__Common Moorhen	*Gallinula chloropus*	Worldwide
__Dusky Moorhen	*Gallinula tenebrosa*	AU
__Lesser Moorhen	*Gallinula angulata*	AF
__Spot-flanked Gallinule	*Gallinula melanops*	SA
__Black-tailed Nativehen	*Gallinula ventralis*	AU
__Tasmanian Nativehen	*Gallinula mortierii*	AU
__Red-knobbed Coot	*Fulica cristata*	AF
__Eurasian Coot	*Fulica atra*	EU, OR, AU
__Hawaiian Coot	*Fulica alai*	PO
__American Coot	*Fulica americana*	NA, MA
__Caribbean Coot	*Fulica caribaea*	NA
__White-winged Coot	*Fulica leucoptera*	SA
__Andean Coot	*Fulica ardesiaca*	SA
__Red-gartered Coot	*Fulica armillata*	SA
__Red-fronted Coot	*Fulica rufifrons*	SA
__Giant Coot	*Fulica gigantea*	SA
__Horned Coot	*Fulica cornuta*	SA

FINFOOTS	**Family Heliornithidae**	
__African Finfoot	*Podica senegalensis*	AF
__Masked Finfoot	*Heliopais personatus*	OR
__Sungrebe	*Heliornis fulica*	LA

INTERNATIONAL ENGLISH NAME	SCIENTIFIC NAME	REGION(S)
TRUMPETERS	**Family Psophiidae**	
—Grey-winged Trumpeter	*Psophia crepitans*	SA
—Pale-winged Trumpeter	*Psophia leucoptera*	SA
—Dark-winged Trumpeter	*Psophia viridis*	SA
CRANES	**Family Gruidae**	
—Grey Crowned Crane	*Balearica regulorum*	AF
—Black Crowned Crane	*Balearica pavonina*	AF
—Demoiselle Crane	*Anthropoides virgo*	EU
—Blue Crane	*Anthropoides paradiseus*	AF
—Wattled Crane	*Grus carunculatus*	AF
—Siberian Crane	*Grus leucogeranus*	EU
—Sandhill Crane	*Grus canadensis*	NA
—Sarus Crane	*Grus antigone*	OR, AU
—Brolga	*Grus rubicunda*	AU
—White-naped Crane	*Grus vipio*	EU
—Common Crane	*Grus grus*	EU
—Hooded Crane	*Grus monacha*	EU
—Whooping Crane	*Grus americana*	NA
—Black-necked Crane	*Grus nigricollis*	EU
—Red-crowned Crane	*Grus japonensis*	EU
LIMPKIN	**Family Aramidae**	
—Limpkin	*Aramus guarauna*	NA, LA
BUTTONQUAIL	**Family Turnicidae**	
—Kurrichane Buttonquail	*Turnix sylvaticus*	AF, OR
—Red-backed Buttonquail	*Turnix maculosus*	AU
—Black-rumped Buttonquail	*Turnix hottentottus*	AF
—Yellow-legged Buttonquail	*Turnix tanki*	OR
—Spotted Buttonquail	*Turnix ocellatus*	OR
—Barred Buttonquail	*Turnix suscitator*	OR
—Madagascar Buttonquail	*Turnix nigricollis*	AF
—Black-breasted Buttonquail	*Turnix melanogaster*	AU
—Chestnut-backed Buttonquail	*Turnix castanotus*	AU
—Buff-breasted Buttonquail	*Turnix olivii*	AU
—Painted Buttonquail	*Turnix varius*	AU
—Worcester's Buttonquail	*Turnix worcesteri*	OR
—Sumba Buttonquail	*Turnix everetti*	AU
—Red-chested Buttonquail	*Turnix pyrrhothorax*	AU
—Little Buttonquail	*Turnix velox*	AU
—Quail-plover	*Ortyxelos meiffrenii*	AF
	ORDER CHARADRIIFORMES	
STONE-CURLEWS, THICK-KNEES	**Family Burhinidae**	
—Eurasian Stone-curlew	*Burhinus oedicnemus*	EU
—Senegal Thick-knee	*Burhinus senegalensis*	AF
—Water Thick-knee	*Burhinus vermiculatus*	AF
—Spotted Thick-knee	*Burhinus capensis*	AF
—Double-striped Thick-knee	*Burhinus bistriatus*	LA
—Peruvian Thick-knee	*Burhinus superciliaris*	SA

INTERNATIONAL ENGLISH NAME	SCIENTIFIC NAME	REGION(S)
—Bush Stone-curlew	*Burhinus grallarius*	AU
—Great Stone-curlew	*Esacus recurvirostris*	OR
—Beach Stone-curlew	*Esacus neglectus*	OR, AU
SHEATHBILLS & ALLIES	**Family Chionidae**	
—Snowy Sheathbill	*Chionis albus*	AN
—Black-faced Sheathbill	*Chionis minor*	IO Is.
—Magellanic Plover	*Pluvianellus socialis*	SA
OYSTERCATCHERS	**Family Haematopodidae**	
—Magellanic Oystercatcher	*Haematopus leucopodus*	SA
—Blackish Oystercatcher	*Haematopus ater*	SA
—Black Oystercatcher	*Haematopus bachmani*	NA
—American Oystercatcher	*Haematopus palliatus*	NA, LA
—African Oystercatcher	*Haematopus moquini*	AF
—Eurasian Oystercatcher	*Haematopus ostralegus*	EU
—South Island Oystercatcher	*Haematopus finschi*	AU
—Pied Oystercatcher	*Haematopus longirostris*	AU
—Variable Oystercatcher	*Haematopus unicolor*	AU
—Sooty Oystercatcher	*Haematopus fuliginosus*	AU
CRAB-PLOVER	**Family Dromadidae**	
—Crab-plover	*Dromas ardeola*	AF, IO
IBISBILL	**Family Ibidorhynchidae**	
—Ibisbill	*Ibidorhyncha struthersii*	EU
STILTS, AVOCETS	**Family Recurvirostridae**	
—Black-winged Stilt	*Himantopus himantopus*	EU, AF, OR
—White-headed Stilt	*Himantopus leucocephalus*	AU
—Black-necked Stilt	*Himantopus mexicanus*	NA, LA
—White-backed Stilt	*Himantopus melanurus*	SA
—Black Stilt	*Himantopus novaezelandiae*	AU
—Banded Stilt	*Cladorhynchus leucocephalus*	AU
—Pied Avocet	*Recurvirostra avosetta*	AF, EU
—American Avocet	*Recurvirostra americana*	NA
—Red-necked Avocet	*Recurvirostra novaehollandiae*	AU
—Andean Avocet	*Recurvirostra andina*	SA
PLOVERS	**Family Charadriidae**	
—Northern Lapwing	*Vanellus vanellus*	EU
—Long-toed Lapwing	*Vanellus crassirostris*	AF
—Blacksmith Lapwing	*Vanellus armatus*	AF
—Spur-winged Lapwing	*Vanellus spinosus*	AF
—River Lapwing	*Vanellus duvaucelii*	OR
—Black-headed Lapwing	*Vanellus tectus*	AF
—Yellow-wattled Lapwing	*Vanellus malabaricus*	OR
—White-crowned Lapwing	*Vanellus albiceps*	AF
—Senegal Lapwing	*Vanellus lugubris*	AF
—Black-winged Lapwing	*Vanellus melanopterus*	AF
—Crowned Lapwing	*Vanellus coronatus*	AF
—African Wattled Lapwing	*Vanellus senegallus*	AF
—Spot-breasted Lapwing	*Vanellus melanocephalus*	AF
—Brown-chested Lapwing	*Vanellus superciliosus*	AF

INTERNATIONAL ENGLISH NAME	SCIENTIFIC NAME	REGION(S)
__Grey-headed Lapwing	*Vanellus cinereus*	EU
__Red-wattled Lapwing	*Vanellus indicus*	OR
__Javan Lapwing	*Vanellus macropterus*	OR
__Banded Lapwing	*Vanellus tricolor*	AU
__Masked Lapwing	*Vanellus miles*	AU
__Sociable Lapwing	*Vanellus gregarius*	EU
__White-tailed Lapwing	*Vanellus leucurus*	EU
__Southern Lapwing	*Vanellus chilensis*	SA
__Andean Lapwing	*Vanellus resplendens*	SA
__Red-kneed Dotterel	*Erythrogonys cinctus*	AU
__European Golden Plover	*Pluvialis apricaria*	EU
__Pacific Golden Plover	*Pluvialis fulva*	EU
__American Golden Plover	*Pluvialis dominica*	NA
__Grey Plover	*Pluvialis squatarola*	NA, EU
__New Zealand Plover	*Charadrius obscurus*	AU
__Common Ringed Plover	*Charadrius hiaticula*	EU
__Semipalmated Plover	*Charadrius semipalmatus*	NA
__Long-billed Plover	*Charadrius placidus*	EU
__Little Ringed Plover	*Charadrius dubius*	EU, OR
__Wilson's Plover	*Charadrius wilsonia*	NA, LA
__Killdeer	*Charadrius vociferus*	NA, LA
__Piping Plover	*Charadrius melodus*	NA
__Madagascar Plover	*Charadrius thoracicus*	AF
__Kittlitz's Plover	*Charadrius pecuarius*	AF
__St. Helena Plover	*Charadrius sanctaehelenae*	AO
__Three-banded Plover	*Charadrius tricollaris*	AF
__Forbes's Plover	*Charadrius forbesi*	AF
__White-fronted Plover	*Charadrius marginatus*	AF
__Kentish Plover	*Charadrius alexandrinus*	EU, AF, OR
__Snowy Plover	*Charadrius nivosus*	NA, LA
__Javan Plover	*Charadrius javanicus*	OR
__Red-capped Plover	*Charadrius ruficapillus*	AU
__Malaysian Plover	*Charadrius peronii*	OR
__Chestnut-banded Plover	*Charadrius pallidus*	AF
__Collared Plover	*Charadrius collaris*	LA
__Puna Plover	*Charadrius alticola*	SA
__Two-banded Plover	*Charadrius falklandicus*	SA
__Double-banded Plover	*Charadrius bicinctus*	AU
__Lesser Sand Plover	*Charadrius mongolus*	EU
__Greater Sand Plover	*Charadrius leschenaultii*	EU
__Caspian Plover	*Charadrius asiaticus*	EU
__Oriental Plover	*Charadrius veredus*	EU
__Eurasian Dotterel	*Charadrius morinellus*	EU
__Rufous-chested Plover	*Charadrius modestus*	SA
__Mountain Plover	*Charadrius montanus*	NA
__Inland Plover	*Charadrius australis*	AU
__Hooded Dotterel	*Thinornis rubricollis*	AU
__Shore Dotterel	*Thinornis novaeseelandiae*	AU
__Black-fronted Dotterel	*Elseyornis melanops*	AU
__Tawny-throated Dotterel	*Oreopholus ruficollis*	SA
__Wrybill	*Anarhynchus frontalis*	AU
__Diademed Plover	*Phegornis mitchellii*	SA
__Pied Plover	*Hoploxypterus cayanus*	SA

INTERNATIONAL ENGLISH NAME	SCIENTIFIC NAME	REGION(S)
PAINTED SNIPES	**Family Rostratulidae**	
—Greater Painted Snipe	*Rostratula benghalensis*	AF, OR, AU
—South American Painted Snipe	*Nycticryphes semicollaris*	SA
JACANAS	**Family Jacanidae**	
—Lesser Jacana	*Microparra capensis*	AF
—African Jacana	*Actophilornis africanus*	AF
—Madagascar Jacana	*Actophilornis albinucha*	AF
—Comb-crested Jacana	*Irediparra gallinacea*	AU
—Pheasant-tailed Jacana	*Hydrophasianus chirurgus*	OR
—Bronze-winged Jacana	*Metopidius indicus*	OR
—Northern Jacana	*Jacana spinosa*	MA
—Wattled Jacana	*Jacana jacana*	SA
PLAINS-WANDERER	**Family Pedionomidae**	
—Plains-wanderer	*Pedionomus torquatus*	AU
SEEDSNIPES	**Family Thinocoridae**	
—Rufous-bellied Seedsnipe	*Attagis gayi*	SA
—White-bellied Seedsnipe	*Attagis malouinus*	SA
—Grey-breasted Seedsnipe	*Thinocorus orbignyianus*	SA
—Least Seedsnipe	*Thinocorus rumicivorus*	SA
SANDPIPERS, SNIPES	**Family Scolopacidae**	
—Eurasian Woodcock	*Scolopax rusticola*	EU
—Amami Woodcock	*Scolopax mira*	EU
—Javan Woodcock	*Scolopax saturata*	OR
—New Guinea Woodcock	*Scolopax rosenbergi*	AU
—Bukidnon Woodcock	*Scolopax bukidnonensis*	OR
—Sulawesi Woodcock	*Scolopax celebensis*	AU
—Moluccan Woodcock	*Scolopax rochussenii*	AU
—American Woodcock	*Scolopax minor*	NA
—Chatham Snipe	*Coenocorypha pusilla*	AU
—New Zealand Snipe	*Coenocorypha aucklandica*	AU
—Jack Snipe	*Lymnocryptes minimus*	EU
—Solitary Snipe	*Gallinago solitaria*	EU
—Latham's Snipe	*Gallinago hardwickii*	EU
—Wood Snipe	*Gallinago nemoricola*	OR
—Pin-tailed Snipe	*Gallinago stenura*	EU
—Swinhoe's Snipe	*Gallinago megala*	EU
—African Snipe	*Gallinago nigripennis*	AF
—Madagascar Snipe	*Gallinago macrodactyla*	AF
—Great Snipe	*Gallinago media*	EU
—Common Snipe	*Gallinago gallinago*	EU
—Wilson's Snipe	*Gallinago delicata*	NA, LA
—South American Snipe	*Gallinago paraguaiae*	SA
—Puna Snipe	*Gallinago andina*	SA
—Noble Snipe	*Gallinago nobilis*	SA
—Giant Snipe	*Gallinago undulata*	SA
—Fuegian Snipe	*Gallinago stricklandii*	SA
—Andean Snipe	*Gallinago jamesoni*	SA
—Imperial Snipe	*Gallinago imperialis*	SA
—Short-billed Dowitcher	*Limnodromus griseus*	NA

INTERNATIONAL ENGLISH NAME	SCIENTIFIC NAME	REGION(S)
—Long-billed Dowitcher	*Limnodromus scolopaceus*	EU
—Asian Dowitcher	*Limnodromus semipalmatus*	EU
—Black-tailed Godwit	*Limosa limosa*	EU
—Hudsonian Godwit	*Limosa haemastica*	NA
—Bar-tailed Godwit	*Limosa lapponica*	EU
—Marbled Godwit	*Limosa fedoa*	NA
—Little Curlew	*Numenius minutus*	EU
—Eskimo Curlew	*Numenius borealis*	NA
—Whimbrel	*Numenius phaeopus*	NA, EU
—Bristle-thighed Curlew	*Numenius tahitiensis*	NA
—Slender-billed Curlew	*Numenius tenuirostris*	EU
—Eurasian Curlew	*Numenius arquata*	EU
—Eastern Curlew	*Numenius madagascariensis*	EU
—Long-billed Curlew	*Numenius americanus*	NA
—Upland Sandpiper	*Bartramia longicauda*	NA
—Spotted Redshank	*Tringa erythropus*	EU
—Common Redshank	*Tringa totanus*	EU
—Marsh Sandpiper	*Tringa stagnatilis*	EU
—Common Greenshank	*Tringa nebularia*	EU
—Nordmann's Greenshank	*Tringa guttifer*	EU
—Greater Yellowlegs	*Tringa melanoleuca*	NA
—Lesser Yellowlegs	*Tringa flavipes*	NA
—Green Sandpiper	*Tringa ochropus*	EU
—Solitary Sandpiper	*Tringa solitaria*	NA
—Wood Sandpiper	*Tringa glareola*	EU
—Terek Sandpiper	*Xenus cinerea*	EU
—Common Sandpiper	*Actitis hypoleucos*	EU
—Spotted Sandpiper	*Actitis macularius*	NA
—Grey-tailed Tattler	*Heteroscelus brevipes*	EU
—Wandering Tattler	*Heteroscelus incanus*	NA
—Willet	*Catoptrophorus semipalmatus*	NA
—Tuamotu Sandpiper	*Aechmorhynchus parvirostris*	PO
—Tahiti Sandpiper	*Prosobonia leucoptera*	PO
—Ruddy Turnstone	*Arenaria interpres*	NA, EU
—Black Turnstone	*Arenaria melanocephala*	NA
—Surfbird	*Aphriza virgata*	NA
—Great Knot	*Calidris tenuirostris*	EU
—Red Knot	*Calidris canutus*	NA, EU
—Sanderling	*Calidris alba*	NA, EU
—Semipalmated Sandpiper	*Calidris pusilla*	NA
—Western Sandpiper	*Calidris mauri*	NA
—Red-necked Stint	*Calidris ruficollis*	EU
—Little Stint	*Calidris minuta*	EU
—Temminck's Stint	*Calidris temminckii*	EU
—Long-toed Stint	*Calidris subminuta*	EU
—Least Sandpiper	*Calidris minutilla*	NA
—White-rumped Sandpiper	*Calidris fuscicollis*	NA
—Baird's Sandpiper	*Calidris bairdii*	NA
—Pectoral Sandpiper	*Calidris melanotos*	NA, EU
—Sharp-tailed Sandpiper	*Calidris acuminata*	EU
—Curlew Sandpiper	*Calidris ferruginea*	EU
—Purple Sandpiper	*Calidris maritima*	NA, EU
—Rock Sandpiper	*Calidris ptilocnemis*	EU, NA

INTERNATIONAL ENGLISH NAME	SCIENTIFIC NAME	REGION(S)
—Dunlin	*Calidris alpina*	NA, EU
—Stilt Sandpiper	*Calidris himantopus*	NA
—Spoon-billed Sandpiper	*Eurynorhynchus pygmeus*	EU
—Broad-billed Sandpiper	*Limicola falcinellus*	EU
—Buff-breasted Sandpiper	*Tryngites subruficollis*	NA
—Ruff	*Philomachus pugnax*	EU
—Wilson's Phalarope	*Phalaropus tricolor*	NA
—Red-necked Phalarope	*Phalaropus lobatus*	NA, EU
—Red Phalarope	*Phalaropus fulicarius*	NA, EU

COURSERS, PRATINCOLES	**Family Glareolidae**	
—Egyptian Plover	*Pluvianus aegyptius*	AF
—Cream-colored Courser	*Cursorius cursor*	AF
—Somali Courser	*Cursorius somalensis*	AF
—Burchell's Courser	*Cursorius rufus*	AF
—Temminck's Courser	*Cursorius temminckii*	AF
—Indian Courser	*Cursorius coromandelicus*	OR
—Double-banded Courser	*Rhinoptilus africanus*	AF
—Three-banded Courser	*Rhinoptilus cinctus*	AF
—Bronze-winged Courser	*Rhinoptilus chalcopterus*	AF
—Jerdon's Courser	*Rhinoptilus bitorquatus*	OR
—Australian Pratincole	*Stiltia isabella*	AU
—Collared Pratincole	*Glareola pratincola*	AF, EU
—Oriental Pratincole	*Glareola maldivarum*	EU, OR
—Black-winged Pratincole	*Glareola nordmanni*	EU
—Madagascar Pratincole	*Glareola ocularis*	AF
—Rock Pratincole	*Glareola nuchalis*	AF
—Grey Pratincole	*Glareola cinerea*	AF
—Small Pratincole	*Glareola lactea*	OR

GULLS, TERNS, SKIMMERS	**Family Laridae**	
—Dolphin Gull	*Leucophaeus scoresbii*	
—Pacific Gull	*Larus pacificus*	AU
—Band-tailed Gull	*Larus belcheri*	SA
—Olrog's Gull	*Larus atlanticus*	SA
—Black-tailed Gull	*Larus crassirostris*	EU
—Grey Gull	*Larus modestus*	SA
—Heermann's Gull	*Larus heermanni*	NA, MA
—White-eyed Gull	*Larus leucophthalmus*	AF
—Sooty Gull	*Larus hemprichii*	AF, EU
—Mew Gull	*Larus canus*	NA, EU
—Audouin's Gull	*Larus audouinii*	EU, AF
—Ring-billed Gull	*Larus delawarensis*	NA, MA
—California Gull	*Larus californicus*	NA, MA
—Great Black-backed Gull	*Larus marinus*	NA, EU
—Kelp Gull	*Larus dominicanus*	SA, AU, AF
—Glaucous-winged Gull	*Larus glaucescens*	EU, NA
—Western Gull	*Larus occidentalis*	NA
—Yellow-footed Gull	*Larus livens*	NA, MA
—Glaucous Gull	*Larus hyperboreus*	EU, NA
—Iceland Gull	*Larus glaucoides*	NA, EU
—Thayer's Gull	*Larus thayeri*	NA

INTERNATIONAL ENGLISH NAME	SCIENTIFIC NAME	REGION(S)
—Herring Gull	*Larus argentatus*	NA, MA, EU
—Vega Gull	*Larus vegae*	EU
—Yellow-legged Gull	*Larus cachinnans*	EU
—Armenian Gull	*Larus armenicus*	EU
—Slaty-backed Gull	*Larus schistisagus*	EU
—Lesser Black-backed Gull	*Larus fuscus*	EU
—Great Black-headed Gull	*Larus ichthyaetus*	EU
—Brown-headed Gull	*Larus brunnicephalus*	EU
—Grey-hooded Gull	*Larus cirrocephalus*	SA, AF
—Hartlaub's Gull	*Larus hartlaubii*	AF
—Silver Gull	*Larus novaehollandiae*	AU
—Red-billed Gull	*Larus scopulinus*	AU
—Black-billed Gull	*Larus bulleri*	AU
—Brown-hooded Gull	*Larus maculipennis*	SA
—Common Black-headed Gull	*Larus ridibundus*	EU
—Slender-billed Gull	*Larus genei*	EU
—Bonaparte's Gull	*Larus philadelphia*	NA
—Saunders's Gull	*Larus saundersi*	EU
—Andean Gull	*Larus serranus*	SA
—Mediterranean Gull	*Larus melanocephalus*	EU
—Relict Gull	*Larus relictus*	EU
—Lava Gull	*Larus fuliginosus*	SA
—Laughing Gull	*Larus atricilla*	NA, LA
—Franklin's Gull	*Larus pipixcan*	NA
—Little Gull	*Larus minutus*	EU, NA
—Ivory Gull	*Pagophila eburnea*	EU, NA
—Ross's Gull	*Rhodostethia rosea*	EU, NA
—Sabine's Gull	*Xema sabini*	EU, NA
—Swallow-tailed Gull	*Creagrus furcatus*	SA
—Black-legged Kittiwake	*Rissa tridactyla*	EU, NA
—Red-legged Kittiwake	*Rissa brevirostris*	NA
—Gull-billed Tern	*Sterna nilotica*	Worldwide
—Caspian Tern	*Sterna caspia*	Worldwide
—Elegant Tern	*Sterna elegans*	NA, LA
—Lesser Crested Tern	*Sterna bengalensis*	AF, OR, AU
—Sandwich Tern	*Sterna sandvicensis*	NA, LA, AF, EU
—Cayenne Tern	*Sterna eurygnatha*	SA
—Chinese Crested Tern	*Sterna bernsteini*	EU
—Royal Tern	*Sterna maxima*	NA, LA, AF
—Swift Tern	*Sterna bergii*	AU, OR, AF
—River Tern	*Sterna aurantia*	OR
—Roseate Tern	*Sterna dougallii*	Worldwide
—White-fronted Tern	*Sterna striata*	AU
—Black-naped Tern	*Sterna sumatrana*	AF, OR, AU
—South American Tern	*Sterna hirundinacea*	SA
—Common Tern	*Sterna hirundo*	EU, NA
—White-cheeked Tern	*Sterna repressa*	AF, EU
—Arctic Tern	*Sterna paradisaea*	EU, NA
—Antarctic Tern	*Sterna vittata*	SO
—Kerguelen Tern	*Sterna virgata*	IO
—Forster's Tern	*Sterna forsteri*	NA, MA
—Snowy-crowned Tern	*Sterna trudeaui*	SA
—Little Tern	*Sterna albifrons*	AF, EU, OR, AU

INTERNATIONAL ENGLISH NAME	SCIENTIFIC NAME	REGION(S)
__Saunders's Tern	*Sterna saundersi*	AF, EU
__Least Tern	*Sterna antillarum*	NA, MA
__Yellow-billed Tern	*Sterna superciliaris*	SA
__Peruvian Tern	*Sterna lorata*	SA
__Fairy Tern	*Sterna nereis*	AU
__Damara Tern	*Sterna balaenarum*	AF
__Black-bellied Tern	*Sterna acuticauda*	OR
__Aleutian Tern	*Sterna aleutica*	EU, NA
__Spectacled Tern	*Sterna lunata*	PO
__Bridled Tern	*Sterna anaethetus*	TrO
__Sooty Tern	*Sterna fuscata*	TrO
__Black-fronted Tern	*Sterna albostriata*	AU
__Whiskered Tern	*Chlidonias hybrida*	AF, EU, OR, AU
__White-winged Tern	*Chlidonias leucopterus*	EU
__Black Tern	*Chlidonias niger*	NA, EU
__Large-billed Tern	*Phaetusa simplex*	SA
__Brown Noddy	*Anous stolidus*	TrO
__Sooty Noddy	*Anous tenuirostris*	IO
__Black Noddy	*Anous minutus*	PO, AO
__Blue Noddy	*Procelsterna cerulea*	PO
__Grey Noddy	*Procelsterna albivitta*	PO
__Angel Tern	*Gygis alba*	TrO
__Inca Tern	*Larosterna inca*	SA
__Black Skimmer	*Rynchops niger*	NA, LA
__African Skimmer	*Rynchops flavirostris*	AF
__Indian Skimmer	*Rynchops albicollis*	OR
SKUAS	**Family Stercorariidae**	
__Chilean Skua	*Stercorarius chilensis*	SA
__South Polar Skua	*Stercorarius maccormicki*	AN
__Subantarctic Skua	*Stercorarius antarcticus*	SO
__Great Skua	*Stercorarius skua*	EU
__Pomarine Skua	*Stercorarius pomarinus*	NA, EU
__Parasitic Jaeger	*Stercorarius parasiticus*	NA, EU
__Long-tailed Jaeger	*Stercorarius longicaudus*	NA, EU
AUKS	**Family Alcidae**	
__Little Auk	*Alle alle*	NA, EU
__Thick-billed Murre	*Uria lomvia*	NA, EU
__Common Murre	*Uria aalge*	NA, EU
__Razorbill	*Alca torda*	NA, EU
__Black Guillemot	*Cepphus grylle*	NA, EU
__Pigeon Guillemot	*Cepphus columba*	EU, NA
__Spectacled Guillemot	*Cepphus carbo*	EU
__Marbled Murrelet	*Brachyramphus marmoratus*	NA
__Long-billed Murrelet	*Brachyramphus perdix*	EU
__Kittlitz's Murrelet	*Brachyramphus brevirostris*	EU, NA
__Xantus's Murrelet	*Synthliboramphus hypoleucus*	NA, MA
__Craveri's Murrelet	*Synthliboramphus craveri*	NA, MA
__Ancient Murrelet	*Synthliboramphus antiquus*	EU, NA
__Japanese Murrelet	*Synthliboramphus wumizusume*	EU
__Cassin's Auklet	*Ptychoramphus aleuticus*	NA
__Parakeet Auklet	*Aethia psittacula*	EU, NA

INTERNATIONAL ENGLISH NAME	SCIENTIFIC NAME	REGION(S)
—Least Auklet	*Aethia pusilla*	EU, NA
—Whiskered Auklet	*Aethia pygmaea*	EU, NA
—Crested Auklet	*Aethia cristatella*	EU, NA
—Rhinoceros Auklet	*Cerorhinca monocerata*	EU, NA
—Atlantic Puffin	*Fratercula arctica*	EU, NA
—Horned Puffin	*Fratercula corniculata*	EU, NA
—Tufted Puffin	*Fratercula cirrhata*	EU, NA
SANDGROUSE	**Family Pteroclididae**	
—Tibetan Sandgrouse	*Syrrhaptes tibetanus*	EU
—Pallas's Sandgrouse	*Syrrhaptes paradoxus*	EU
—Pin-tailed Sandgrouse	*Pterocles alchata*	EU
—Namaqua Sandgrouse	*Pterocles namaqua*	AF
—Chestnut-bellied Sandgrouse	*Pterocles exustus*	AF, EU, OR
—Spotted Sandgrouse	*Pterocles senegallus*	AF, EU
—Black-bellied Sandgrouse	*Pterocles orientalis*	EU
—Yellow-throated Sandgrouse	*Pterocles gutturalis*	AF
—Crowned Sandgrouse	*Pterocles coronatus*	AF, EU
—Black-faced Sandgrouse	*Pterocles decoratus*	AF
—Madagascar Sandgrouse	*Pterocles personatus*	AF
—Lichtenstein's Sandgrouse	*Pterocles lichtensteinii*	AF, EU
—Painted Sandgrouse	*Pterocles indicus*	OR
—Four-banded Sandgrouse	*Pterocles quadricinctus*	AF
—Double-banded Sandgrouse	*Pterocles bicinctus*	AF
—Burchell's Sandgrouse	*Pterocles burchelli*	AF

ORDER COLUMBIFORMES

PIGEONS, DOVES	Family Columbidae	
PIGEONS, DOVES	**Family Columbidae**	
—Common Pigeon	*Columba livia*	Worldwide
—Hill Pigeon	*Columba rupestris*	EU
—Snow Pigeon	*Columba leuconota*	EU
—Speckled Pigeon	*Columba guinea*	AF
—White-collared Pigeon	*Columba albitorques*	AF
—Stock Dove	*Columba oenas*	EU
—Yellow-eyed Pigeon	*Columba eversmanni*	EU
—Somali Pigeon	*Columba oliviae*	AF
—Common Wood Pigeon	*Columba palumbus*	EU
—Trocaz Pigeon	*Columba trocaz*	AF
—Bolle's Pigeon	*Columba bollii*	AF
—Laurel Pigeon	*Columba junoniae*	AF
—Afep Pigeon	*Columba unicincta*	AF
—African Olive Pigeon	*Columba arquatrix*	AF
—Cameroon Olive Pigeon	*Columba sjostedti*	AF
—Sao Tome Olive Pigeon	*Columba thomensis*	AF
—Comoros Olive Pigeon	*Columba pollenii*	AF
—Speckled Wood Pigeon	*Columba hodgsonii*	OR
—White-naped Pigeon	*Columba albinucha*	AF
—Ashy Wood Pigeon	*Columba pulchricollis*	OR
—Nilgiri Wood Pigeon	*Columba elphinstonii*	OR
—Sri Lanka Wood Pigeon	*Columba torringtoni*	OR
—Pale-capped Pigeon	*Columba punicea*	OR
—Silvery Pigeon	*Columba argentina*	OR

INTERNATIONAL ENGLISH NAME	SCIENTIFIC NAME	REGION(S)
__Andaman Wood Pigeon	*Columba palumboides*	OR
__Japanese Wood Pigeon	*Columba janthina*	EU
__Metallic Pigeon	*Columba vitiensis*	OR, AU
__White-headed Pigeon	*Columba leucomela*	AU
__Yellow-legged Pigeon	*Columba pallidiceps*	AU
__Eastern Bronze-naped Pigeon	*Columba delegorguei*	AF
__Western Bronze-naped Pigeon	*Columba iriditorques*	AF
__Island Bronze-naped Pigeon	*Columba malherbii*	AF
__Lemon Dove	*Columba larvata*	AF
__White-crowned Pigeon	*Patagioenas leucocephala*	NA, MA
__Scaly-naped Pigeon	*Patagioenas squamosa*	NA
__Scaled Pigeon	*Patagioenas speciosa*	LA
__Picazuro Pigeon	*Patagioenas picazuro*	SA
__Bare-eyed Pigeon	*Patagioenas corensis*	SA
__Spot-winged Pigeon	*Patagioenas maculosa*	SA
__Band-tailed Pigeon	*Patagioenas fasciata*	NA, LA
__Chilean Pigeon	*Patagioenas araucana*	SA
__Ring-tailed Pigeon	*Patagioenas caribaea*	NA
__Pale-vented Pigeon	*Patagioenas cayennensis*	LA
__Red-billed Pigeon	*Patagioenas flavirostris*	MA
__Maranon Pigeon	*Patagioenas oenops*	SA
__Plain Pigeon	*Patagioenas inornata*	NA
__Plumbeous Pigeon	*Patagioenas plumbea*	SA
__Ruddy Pigeon	*Patagioenas subvinacea*	LA
__Short-billed Pigeon	*Patagioenas nigrirostris*	LA
__Dusky Pigeon	*Patagioenas goodsoni*	SA
__Pink Pigeon	*Nesoenas mayeri*	AF
__European Turtle Dove	*Streptopelia turtur*	EU
__Dusky Turtle Dove	*Streptopelia lugens*	AF
__Adamawa Turtle Dove	*Streptopelia hypopyrrha*	AF
__Oriental Turtle Dove	*Streptopelia orientalis*	EU, OR
__Island Collared Dove	*Streptopelia bitorquata*	OR
__Eurasian Collared Dove	*Streptopelia decaocto*	EU, OR
__African Collared Dove	*Streptopelia roseogrisea*	AF
__White-winged Collared Dove	*Streptopelia reichenowi*	AF
__Mourning Collared Dove	*Streptopelia decipiens*	AF
__Red-eyed Dove	*Streptopelia semitorquata*	AF
__Ring-necked Dove	*Streptopelia capicola*	AF
__Vinaceous Dove	*Streptopelia vinacea*	AF
__Red Turtle Dove	*Streptopelia tranquebarica*	OR
__Malagasy Turtle Dove	*Streptopelia picturata*	AF
__Spotted Dove	*Streptopelia chinensis*	OR
__Laughing Dove	*Streptopelia senegalensis*	AF, EU, OR
__Barred Cuckoo-Dove	*Macropygia unchall*	OR
__Brown Cuckoo-Dove	*Macropygia amboinensis*	AU
__Bar-necked Cuckoo-Dove	*Macropygia magna*	AU
__Andaman Cuckoo-Dove	*Macropygia rufipennis*	OR
__Black-billed Cuckoo-Dove	*Macropygia nigrirostris*	OR
__Spot-breasted Cuckoo-Dove	*Macropygia mackinlayi*	AU
__Little Cuckoo-Dove	*Macropygia ruficeps*	OR
__Great Cuckoo-Dove	*Reinwardtoena reinwardtii*	AU
__Pied Cuckoo-Dove	*Reinwardtoena browni*	AU
__Crested Cuckoo-Dove	*Reinwardtoena crassirostris*	AU

INTERNATIONAL ENGLISH NAME	SCIENTIFIC NAME	REGION(S)
—White-faced Dove	*Turacoena manadensis*	AU
—Black Dove	*Turacoena modesta*	AU
—Emerald-spotted Wood Dove	*Turtur chalcospilos*	AF
—Black-billed Wood Dove	*Turtur abyssinicus*	AF
—Blue-spotted Wood Dove	*Turtur afer*	AF
—Tambourine Dove	*Turtur tympanistria*	AF
—Blue-headed Wood Dove	*Turtur brehmeri*	AF
—Namaqua Dove	*Oena capensis*	AF
—Common Emerald Dove	*Chalcophaps indica*	OR, AU
—Stephan's Emerald Dove	*Chalcophaps stephani*	AU
—New Guinea Bronzewing	*Henicophaps albifrons*	AU
—New Britain Bronzewing	*Henicophaps foersteri*	AU
—Common Bronzewing	*Phaps chalcoptera*	AU
—Brush Bronzewing	*Phaps elegans*	AU
—Flock Bronzewing	*Phaps histrionica*	AU
—Crested Pigeon	*Ocyphaps lophotes*	AU
—Spinifex Pigeon	*Geophaps plumifera*	AU
—Squatter Pigeon	*Geophaps scripta*	AU
—Partridge Pigeon	*Geophaps smithii*	AU
—Thick-billed Ground Pigeon	*Trugon terrestris*	AU
—Wonga Pigeon	*Leucosarcia melanoleuca*	AU
—Chestnut-quilled Rock Pigeon	*Petrophassa rufipennis*	AU
—White-quilled Rock Pigeon	*Petrophassa albipennis*	AU
—Diamond Dove	*Geopelia cuneata*	AU
—Zebra Dove	*Geopelia striata*	OR
—Peaceful Dove	*Geopelia placida*	AU
—Barred Dove	*Geopelia maugei*	AU
—Bar-shouldered Dove	*Geopelia humeralis*	AU
—Mourning Dove	*Zenaida macroura*	NA, MA
—Socorro Dove	*Zenaida graysoni*	MA
—Eared Dove	*Zenaida auriculata*	SA
—Zenaida Dove	*Zenaida aurita*	NA
—Galapagos Dove	*Zenaida galapagoensis*	SA
—White-winged Dove	*Zenaida asiatica*	NA, MA
—West Peruvian Dove	*Zenaida meloda*	SA
—Inca Dove	*Scardafella inca*	NA, MA
—Scaled Dove	*Scardafella squammata*	SA
—Common Ground Dove	*Columbina passerina*	NA, LA
—Plain-breasted Ground Dove	*Columbina minuta*	LA
—Ecuadorian Ground Dove	*Columbina buckleyi*	SA
—Ruddy Ground Dove	*Columbina talpacoti*	LA
—Picui Ground Dove	*Columbina picui*	SA
—Croaking Ground Dove	*Columbina cruziana*	SA
—Blue-eyed Ground Dove	*Columbina cyanopis*	SA
—Blue Ground Dove	*Claravis pretiosa*	LA
—Purple-winged Ground Dove	*Claravis godefrida*	SA
—Maroon-chested Ground Dove	*Claravis mondetoura*	LA
—Bare-faced Ground Dove	*Metriopelia ceciliae*	SA
—Moreno's Ground Dove	*Metriopelia morenoi*	SA
—Black-winged Ground Dove	*Metriopelia melanoptera*	SA
—Golden-spotted Ground Dove	*Metriopelia aymara*	SA
—Long-tailed Ground Dove	*Uropelia campestris*	SA
—White-tipped Dove	*Leptotila verreauxi*	LA

INTERNATIONAL ENGLISH NAME	SCIENTIFIC NAME	REGION(S)
__Yungas Dove	*Leptotila megalura*	SA
__Grey-fronted Dove	*Leptotila rufaxilla*	SA
__Grey-headed Dove	*Leptotila plumbeiceps*	LA
__Pallid Dove	*Leptotila pallida*	SA
__Azuero Dove	*Leptotila battyi*	MA
__Grenada Dove	*Leptotila wellsi*	NA
__Caribbean Dove	*Leptotila jamaicensis*	NA, MA
__Grey-chested Dove	*Leptotila cassini*	LA
__Ochre-bellied Dove	*Leptotila ochraceiventris*	SA
__Tolima Dove	*Leptotila conoveri*	SA
__Purplish-backed Quail-Dove	*Geotrygon lawrencii*	MA
__Tuxtla Quail-Dove	*Geotrygon carrikeri*	MA
__Buff-fronted Quail-Dove	*Geotrygon costaricensis*	MA
__Russet-crowned Quail-Dove	*Geotrygon goldmani*	LA
__Sapphire Quail-Dove	*Geotrygon saphirina*	SA
__Olive-backed Quail-Dove	*Geotrygon veraguensis*	LA
__Indigo-crowned Quail-Dove	*Geotrygon purpurata*	SA
__Grey-fronted Quail-Dove	*Geotrygon caniceps*	NA
__White-fronted Quail-Dove	*Geotrygon leucometopia*	NA
__Crested Quail-Dove	*Geotrygon versicolor*	NA
__White-faced Quail-Dove	*Geotrygon albifacies*	MA
__Chiriqui Quail-Dove	*Geotrygon chiriquensis*	MA
__Lined Quail-Dove	*Geotrygon linearis*	SA
__White-throated Quail-Dove	*Geotrygon frenata*	SA
__Key West Quail-Dove	*Geotrygon chrysia*	NA
__Bridled Quail-Dove	*Geotrygon mystacea*	NA
__Violaceous Quail-Dove	*Geotrygon violacea*	LA
__Ruddy Quail-Dove	*Geotrygon montana*	LA
__Blue-headed Quail-Dove	*Starnoenas cyanocephala*	NA
__Nicobar Pigeon	*Caloenas nicobarica*	OR, AU
__Luzon Bleeding-heart	*Gallicolumba luzonica*	OR
__Mindanao Bleeding-heart	*Gallicolumba crinigera*	OR
__Mindoro Bleeding-heart	*Gallicolumba platenae*	OR
__Negros Bleeding-heart	*Gallicolumba keayi*	OR
__Sulu Bleeding-heart	*Gallicolumba menagei*	OR
__Cinnamon Ground Dove	*Gallicolumba rufigula*	AU
__Sulawesi Ground Dove	*Gallicolumba tristigmata*	AU
__Wetar Ground Dove	*Gallicolumba hoedtii*	AU
__Purple Ground Dove	*Gallicolumba jobiensis*	AU
__White-fronted Ground Dove	*Gallicolumba kubaryi*	PO
__Polynesian Ground Dove	*Gallicolumba erythroptera*	PO
__White-throated Ground Dove	*Gallicolumba xanthonura*	PO
__Tongan Ground Dove	*Gallicolumba stairi*	PO
__Santa Cruz Ground Dove	*Gallicolumba sanctaecrucis*	AU
__Thick-billed Ground Dove	*Gallicolumba salamonis*	AU
__Marquesan Ground Dove	*Gallicolumba rubescens*	PO
__Bronze Ground Dove	*Gallicolumba beccarii*	AU
__Palau Ground Dove	*Gallicolumba canifrons*	AU
__Pheasant Pigeon	*Otidiphaps nobilis*	AU
__Western Crowned Pigeon	*Goura cristata*	AU
__Southern Crowned Pigeon	*Goura scheepmakeri*	AU
__Victoria Crowned Pigeon	*Goura victoria*	AU
__Tooth-billed Pigeon	*Didunculus strigirostris*	PO

INTERNATIONAL ENGLISH NAME	SCIENTIFIC NAME	REGION(S)
—White-eared Brown Dove	*Phapitreron leucotis*	OR
—Amethyst Brown Dove	*Phapitreron amethystinus*	OR
—Dark-eared Brown Dove	*Phapitreron cinereiceps*	OR
—Cinnamon-headed Green Pigeon	*Treron fulvicollis*	OR
—Little Green Pigeon	*Treron olax*	OR
—Pink-necked Green Pigeon	*Treron vernans*	OR
—Orange-breasted Green Pigeon	*Treron bicinctus*	OR
—Pompadour Green Pigeon	*Treron pompadora*	OR
—Thick-billed Green Pigeon	*Treron curvirostra*	OR
—Grey-cheeked Green Pigeon	*Treron griseicauda*	OR, AU
—Sumba Green Pigeon	*Treron teysmannii*	AU
—Flores Green Pigeon	*Treron floris*	AU
—Timor Green Pigeon	*Treron psittaceus*	AU
—Large Green Pigeon	*Treron capellei*	OR
—Yellow-footed Green Pigeon	*Treron phoenicopterus*	OR
—Bruce's Green Pigeon	*Treron waalia*	AF
—Madagascar Green Pigeon	*Treron australis*	AF
—Comoros Green Pigeon	*Treron griveaudi*	AF
—African Green Pigeon	*Treron calvus*	AF
—Pemba Green Pigeon	*Treron pembaensis*	AF
—Sao Tome Green Pigeon	*Treron sanctithomae*	AF
—Pin-tailed Green Pigeon	*Treron apicauda*	OR
—Sumatran Green Pigeon	*Treron oxyurus*	OR
—Yellow-vented Green Pigeon	*Treron seimundi*	OR
—Wedge-tailed Green Pigeon	*Treron sphenurus*	OR
—White-bellied Green Pigeon	*Treron sieboldii*	EU, OR
—Whistling Green Pigeon	*Treron formosae*	EU, OR
—Banded Fruit Dove	*Ptilinopus cinctus*	AU
—Red-naped Fruit Dove	*Ptilinopus dohertyi*	AU
—Pink-headed Fruit Dove	*Ptilinopus porphyreus*	OR
—Flame-breasted Fruit Dove	*Ptilinopus marchei*	OR
—Cream-breasted Fruit Dove	*Ptilinopus merrilli*	OR
—Yellow-breasted Fruit Dove	*Ptilinopus occipitalis*	OR
—Red-eared Fruit Dove	*Ptilinopus fischeri*	AU
—Jambu Fruit Dove	*Ptilinopus jambu*	OR
—Maroon-chinned Fruit Dove	*Ptilinopus subgularis*	AU
—Black-chinned Fruit Dove	*Ptilinopus leclancheri*	OR
—Scarlet-breasted Fruit Dove	*Ptilinopus bernsteinii*	AU
—Wompoo Fruit Dove	*Ptilinopus magnificus*	AU
—Pink-spotted Fruit Dove	*Ptilinopus perlatus*	AU
—Ornate Fruit Dove	*Ptilinopus ornatus*	AU
—Tanna Fruit Dove	*Ptilinopus tannensis*	AU
—Orange-fronted Fruit Dove	*Ptilinopus aurantiifrons*	AU
—Wallace's Fruit Dove	*Ptilinopus wallacii*	AU
—Superb Fruit Dove	*Ptilinopus superbus*	AU
—Many-colored Fruit Dove	*Ptilinopus perousii*	PO
—Crimson-crowned Fruit Dove	*Ptilinopus porphyraceus*	PO
—Palau Fruit Dove	*Ptilinopus pelewensis*	AU
—Lilac-crowned Fruit Dove	*Ptilinopus rarotongensis*	PO
—Mariana Fruit Dove	*Ptilinopus roseicapilla*	PO
—Rose-crowned Fruit Dove	*Ptilinopus regina*	AU
—Silver-capped Fruit Dove	*Ptilinopus richardsii*	AU
—Grey-green Fruit Dove	*Ptilinopus purpuratus*	PO

INTERNATIONAL ENGLISH NAME	SCIENTIFIC NAME	REGION(S)
__Makatea Fruit Dove	*Ptilinopus chalcurus*	PO
__Atoll Fruit Dove	*Ptilinopus coralensis*	PO
__Red-bellied Fruit Dove	*Ptilinopus greyii*	AU
__Rapa Fruit Dove	*Ptilinopus huttoni*	PO
__White-capped Fruit Dove	*Ptilinopus dupetithouarsii*	PO
__Moustached Fruit Dove	*Ptilinopus mercierii*	PO
__Scarlet-capped Fruit Dove	*Ptilinopus insularis*	PO
__Coroneted Fruit Dove	*Ptilinopus coronulatus*	AU
__Beautiful Fruit Dove	*Ptilinopus pulchellus*	AU
__Blue-capped Fruit Dove	*Ptilinopus monacha*	AU
__White-bibbed Fruit Dove	*Ptilinopus rivoli*	AU
__Yellow-bibbed Fruit Dove	*Ptilinopus solomonensis*	AU
__Claret-breasted Fruit Dove	*Ptilinopus viridis*	AU
__White-headed Fruit Dove	*Ptilinopus eugeniae*	AU
__Orange-bellied Fruit Dove	*Ptilinopus iozonus*	AU
__Knob-billed Fruit Dove	*Ptilinopus insolitus*	AU
__Grey-headed Fruit Dove	*Ptilinopus hyogastrus*	AU
__Carunculated Fruit Dove	*Ptilinopus granulifrons*	AU
__Black-naped Fruit Dove	*Ptilinopus melanospilus*	OR, AU
__Dwarf Fruit Dove	*Ptilinopus nainus*	AU
__Negros Fruit Dove	*Ptilinopus arcanus*	OR
__Orange Fruit Dove	*Ptilinopus victor*	PO
__Golden Fruit Dove	*Ptilinopus luteovirens*	PO
__Whistling Fruit Dove	*Ptilinopus layardi*	PO
__Cloven-feathered Dove	*Drepanoptila holosericea*	AU
__Madagascar Blue Pigeon	*Alectroenas madagascariensis*	AF
__Comoros Blue Pigeon	*Alectroenas sganzini*	AF
__Seychelles Blue Pigeon	*Alectroenas pulcherrima*	AF
__Pink-bellied Imperial Pigeon	*Ducula poliocephala*	OR
__White-bellied Imperial Pigeon	*Ducula forsteni*	AU
__Mindoro Imperial Pigeon	*Ducula mindorensis*	OR
__Grey-headed Imperial Pigeon	*Ducula radiata*	AU
__Spotted Imperial Pigeon	*Ducula carola*	OR
__Green Imperial Pigeon	*Ducula aenea*	OR
__Spectacled Imperial Pigeon	*Ducula perspicillata*	AU
__Elegant Imperial Pigeon	*Ducula concinna*	AU
__Pacific Imperial Pigeon	*Ducula pacifica*	PO
__Micronesian Imperial Pigeon	*Ducula oceanica*	PO
__Polynesian Imperial Pigeon	*Ducula aurorae*	PO
__Marquesan Imperial Pigeon	*Ducula galeata*	PO
__Red-knobbed Imperial Pigeon	*Ducula rubricera*	AU
__Spice Imperial Pigeon	*Ducula myristicivora*	AU
__Purple-tailed Imperial Pigeon	*Ducula rufigaster*	AU
__Cinnamon Imperial Pigeon	*Ducula basilica*	AU
__Growling Imperial Pigeon	*Ducula finschii*	AU
__Shining Imperial Pigeon	*Ducula chalconota*	AU
__Floury Imperial Pigeon	*Ducula pistrinaria*	AU
__Pink-headed Imperial Pigeon	*Ducula rosacea*	AU
__Christmas Imperial Pigeon	*Ducula whartoni*	OR
__Grey Imperial Pigeon	*Ducula pickeringii*	OR
__Barking Imperial Pigeon	*Ducula latrans*	PO
__Chestnut-bellied Imperial Pigeon	*Ducula brenchleyi*	AU
__Vanuatu Imperial Pigeon	*Ducula bakeri*	AU

INTERNATIONAL ENGLISH NAME	SCIENTIFIC NAME	REGION(S)
—Goliath Imperial Pigeon	*Ducula goliath*	AU
—Pinon Imperial Pigeon	*Ducula pinon*	AU
—Black Imperial Pigeon	*Ducula melanochroa*	AU
—Collared Imperial Pigeon	*Ducula mullerii*	AU
—Zoe Imperial Pigeon	*Ducula zoeae*	AU
—Mountain Imperial Pigeon	*Ducula badia*	OR
—Dark-backed Imperial Pigeon	*Ducula lacernulata*	OR, AU
—Timor Imperial Pigeon	*Ducula cineracea*	AU
—Pied Imperial Pigeon	*Ducula bicolor*	OR
—Torresian Imperial Pigeon	*Ducula spilorrhoa*	AU
—Bismarck Imperial Pigeon	*Ducula subflavescens*	AU
—Topknot Pigeon	*Lopholaimus antarcticus*	AU
—New Zealand Pigeon	*Hemiphaga novaeseelandiae*	AU
—Sombre Pigeon	*Cryptophaps poecilorrhoa*	AU
—Papuan Mountain Pigeon	*Gymnophaps albertisii*	AU
—Long-tailed Mountain Pigeon	*Gymnophaps mada*	AU
—Pale Mountain Pigeon	*Gymnophaps solomonensis*	AU

ORDER PSITTACIFORMES

COCKATOOS, PARROTS	**Family Psittacidae**	
—Kea	*Nestor notabilis*	AU
—New Zealand Kaka	*Nestor meridionalis*	AU
—Kakapo	*Strigops habroptila*	AU
—Pesquet's Parrot	*Psittrichas fulgidus*	AU
—Vernal Hanging Parrot	*Loriculus vernalis*	OR
—Sri Lanka Hanging Parrot	*Loriculus beryllinus*	OR
—Philippine Hanging Parrot	*Loriculus philippensis*	OR
—Blue-crowned Hanging Parrot	*Loriculus galgulus*	OR
—Great Hanging Parrot	*Loriculus stigmatus*	AU
—Moluccan Hanging Parrot	*Loriculus amabilis*	AU
—Sangihe Hanging Parrot	*Loriculus catamene*	AU
—Orange-fronted Hanging Parrot	*Loriculus aurantiifrons*	AU
—Green-fronted Hanging Parrot	*Loriculus tener*	AU
—Pygmy Hanging Parrot	*Loriculus exilis*	AU
—Yellow-throated Hanging Parrot	*Loriculus pusillus*	OR
—Wallace's Hanging Parrot	*Loriculus flosculus*	AU
—Yellow-capped Pygmy Parrot	*Micropsitta keiensis*	AU
—Geelvink Pygmy Parrot	*Micropsitta geelvinkiana*	AU
—Buff-faced Pygmy Parrot	*Micropsitta pusio*	AU
—Citrine Pygmy Parrot	*Micropsitta meeki*	AU
—Emerald Pygmy Parrot	*Micropsitta finschii*	AU
—Rose-breasted Pygmy Parrot	*Micropsitta bruijnii*	AU
—Palm Cockatoo	*Probosciger aterrimus*	AU
—Red-tailed Black Cockatoo	*Calyptorhynchus banksii*	AU
—Glossy Black Cockatoo	*Calyptorhynchus lathami*	AU
—Yellow-tailed Black Cockatoo	*Calyptorhynchus funereus*	AU
—Short-billed Black Cockatoo	*Calyptorhynchus latirostris*	AU
—Long-billed Black Cockatoo	*Calyptorhynchus baudinii*	AU
—Gang-gang Cockatoo	*Callocephalon fimbriatum*	AU
—Galah	*Eolophus roseicapilla*	AU
—Long-billed Corella	*Cacatua tenuirostris*	AU
—Western Corella	*Cacatua pastinator*	AU

INTERNATIONAL ENGLISH NAME	SCIENTIFIC NAME	REGION(S)
__Little Corella	*Cacatua sanguinea*	AU
__Tanimbar Corella	*Cacatua goffiniana*	AU
__Broad-crested Corella	*Cacatua ducorpsii*	AU
__Red-vented Cockatoo	*Cacatua haematuropygia*	OR
__Major Mitchell's Cockatoo	*Cacatua leadbeateri*	AU
__Yellow-crested Cockatoo	*Cacatua sulphurea*	AU
__Sulphur-crested Cockatoo	*Cacatua galerita*	AU
__Blue-eyed Cockatoo	*Cacatua ophthalmica*	AU
__White Cockatoo	*Cacatua alba*	AU
Salmon-crested Cockatoo	*Cacatua moluccensis*	AU
__Cockatiel	*Nymphicus hollandicus*	AU
__Black Lory	*Chalcopsitta atra*	AU
__Brown Lory	*Chalcopsitta duivenbodei*	AU
__Streaked Lory	*Chalcopsitta sintillata*	AU
__Cardinal Lory	*Chalcopsitta cardinalis*	AU
__Red-and-blue Lory	*Eos histrio*	AU
__Violet-necked Lory	*Eos squamata*	AU
__Red Lory	*Eos rubra*	AU
__Blue-streaked Lory	*Eos reticulata*	AU
__Black-winged Lory	*Eos cyanogenia*	AU
__Blue-eared Lory	*Eos semilarvata*	AU
__Dusky Lory	*Pseudeos fuscata*	AU
__Ornate Lorikeet	*Trichoglossus ornatus*	AU
__Sunset Lorikeet	*Trichoglossus forsteni*	AU
__Leaf Lorikeet	*Trichoglossus weberi*	AU
__Marigold Lorikeet	*Trichoglossus capistratus*	AU
__Coconut Lorikeet	*Trichoglossus haematodus*	AU
__Shawl-collared Lorikeet	*Trichoglossus rosenbergii*	AU
__Rainbow Lorikeet	*Trichoglossus moluccanus*	AU
__Red-collared Lorikeet	*Trichoglossus rubritorquis*	AU
__Olive-headed Lorikeet	*Trichoglossus euteles*	AU
__Citrine Lorikeet	*Trichoglossus flavoviridis*	AU
__Mindanao Lorikeet	*Trichoglossus johnstoniae*	OR
__Pohnpei Lorikeet	*Trichoglossus rubiginosus*	PO
__Scaly-breasted Lorikeet	*Trichoglossus chlorolepidotus*	AU
__Varied Lorikeet	*Psitteuteles versicolor*	AU
__Iris Lorikeet	*Psitteuteles iris*	AU
__Goldie's Lorikeet	*Psitteuteles goldiei*	AU
__Chattering Lory	*Lorius garrulus*	AU
__Purple-naped Lory	*Lorius domicella*	AU
__Black-capped Lory	*Lorius lory*	AU
__Purple-bellied Lory	*Lorius hypoinochrous*	AU
__White-naped Lory	*Lorius albidinucha*	AU
__Yellow-bibbed Lory	*Lorius chlorocercus*	AU
__Collared Lory	*Phigys solitarius*	PO
__Blue-crowned Lorikeet	*Vini australis*	PO
__Kuhl's Lorikeet	*Vini kuhlii*	PO
__Stephen's Lorikeet	*Vini stepheni*	PO
__Violet Lorikeet	*Vini peruviana*	PO
__Ultramarine Lorikeet	*Vini ultramarina*	PO
__Musk Lorikeet	*Glossopsitta concinna*	AU
__Little Lorikeet	*Glossopsitta pusilla*	AU
__Purple-crowned Lorikeet	*Glossopsitta porphyrocephala*	AU

INTERNATIONAL ENGLISH NAME	SCIENTIFIC NAME	REGION(S)
—Palm Lorikeet	*Charmosyna palmarum*	AU
—Red-chinned Lorikeet	*Charmosyna rubrigularis*	AU
—Meek's Lorikeet	*Charmosyna meeki*	AU
—Blue-fronted Lorikeet	*Charmosyna toxopei*	AU
—Striated Lorikeet	*Charmosyna multistriata*	AU
—Pygmy Lorikeet	*Charmosyna wilhelminae*	AU
—Red-fronted Lorikeet	*Charmosyna rubronotata*	AU
—Red-flanked Lorikeet	*Charmosyna placentis*	AU
—Red-throated Lorikeet	*Charmosyna amabilis*	PO
—Duchess Lorikeet	*Charmosyna margarethae*	AU
—Fairy Lorikeet	*Charmosyna pulchella*	AU
—Josephine's Lorikeet	*Charmosyna josefinae*	AU
—Papuan Lorikeet	*Charmosyna papou*	AU
—Plum-faced Lorikeet	*Oreopsittacus arfaki*	AU
—Yellow-billed Lorikeet	*Neopsittacus musschenbroekii*	AU
—Orange-billed Lorikeet	*Neopsittacus pullicauda*	AU
—Crimson Shining Parrot	*Prosopeia splendens*	PO
—Masked Shining Parrot	*Prosopeia personata*	PO
—Maroon Shining Parrot	*Prosopeia tabuensis*	PO
—Horned Parakeet	*Eunymphicus cornutus*	AU
—Red-crowned Parakeet	*Cyanoramphus saisseti*	AU
—Norfolk Parakeet	*Cyanoramphus cookii*	AU
—Antipodes Parakeet	*Cyanoramphus unicolor*	AU
—Yellow-crowned Parakeet	*Cyanoramphus auriceps*	AU
—Red-fronted Parakeet	*Cyanoramphus novaezelandiae*	AU
—Red-capped Parrot	*Purpureicephalus spurius*	AU
—Australian Ringneck	*Barnardius zonarius*	AU
—Green Rosella	*Platycercus caledonicus*	AU
—Crimson Rosella	*Platycercus elegans*	AU
—White-cheeked Rosella	*Platycercus adscitus*	AU
—Western Rosella	*Platycercus icterotis*	AU
—Bluebonnet	*Northiella haematogaster*	AU
—Red-rumped Parrot	*Psephotus haematonotus*	AU
—Mulga Parrot	*Psephotus varius*	AU
—Hooded Parrot	*Psephotus dissimilis*	AU
—Golden-shouldered Parrot	*Psephotus chrysopterygius*	AU
—Bourke's Parrot	*Neopsephotus bourkii*	AU
—Blue-winged Parrot	*Neophema chrysostoma*	AU
—Elegant Parrot	*Neophema elegans*	AU
—Rock Parrot	*Neophema petrophila*	AU
—Orange-bellied Parrot	*Neophema chrysogaster*	AU
—Turquoise Parrot	*Neophema pulchella*	AU
—Scarlet-chested Parrot	*Neophema splendida*	AU
—Swift Parrot	*Lathamus discolor*	AU
—Budgerigar	*Melopsittacus undulatus*	AU
—Ground Parrot	*Pezoporus wallicus*	AU
—Night Parrot	*Pezoporus occidentalis*	AU
—Brehm's Tiger Parrot	*Psittacella brehmii*	AU
—Painted Tiger Parrot	*Psittacella picta*	AU
—Modest Tiger Parrot	*Psittacella modesta*	AU
—Madarasz's Tiger Parrot	*Psittacella madaraszi*	AU
—Blue-rumped Parrot	*Psittinus cyanurus*	OR
—Red-cheeked Parrot	*Geoffroyus geoffroyi*	AU

INTERNATIONAL ENGLISH NAME	SCIENTIFIC NAME	REGION(S)
—Blue-collared Parrot	*Geoffroyus simplex*	AU
—Singing Parrot	*Geoffroyus heteroclitus*	AU
—Montane Racket-tail	*Prioniturus montanus*	OR
—Blue-headed Racket-tail	*Prioniturus platenae*	OR
—Green Racket-tail	*Prioniturus luconensis*	OR
—Blue-crowned Racket-tail	*Prioniturus discurus*	OR
—Blue-winged Racket-tail	*Prioniturus verticalis*	OR
—Yellow-breasted Racket-tail	*Prioniturus flavicans*	AU
—Golden-mantled Racket-tail	*Prioniturus platurus*	AU
—Buru Racket-tail	*Prioniturus mada*	AU
—Great-billed Parrot	*Tanygnathus megalorynchos*	AU
—Blue-naped Parrot	*Tanygnathus lucionensis*	OR
—Blue-backed Parrot	*Tanygnathus sumatranus*	OR, AU
—Black-lored Parrot	*Tanygnathus gramineus*	AU
—Eclectus Parrot	*Eclectus roratus*	AU
—Moluccan King Parrot	*Alisterus amboinensis*	AU
—Papuan King Parrot	*Alisterus chloropterus*	AU
—Australian King Parrot	*Alisterus scapularis*	AU
—Jonquil Parrot	*Aprosmictus jonquillaceus*	AU
—Red-winged Parrot	*Aprosmictus erythropterus*	AU
—Superb Parrot	*Polytelis swainsonii*	AU
—Regent Parrot	*Polytelis anthopeplus*	AU
—Princess Parrot	*Polytelis alexandrae*	AU
—Alexandrine Parakeet	*Psittacula eupatria*	OR
—Rose-ringed Parakeet	*Psittacula krameri*	AF, OR
—Mauritius Parakeet	*Psittacula echo*	AF
—Slaty-headed Parakeet	*Psittacula himalayana*	OR
—Grey-headed Parakeet	*Psittacula finschii*	OR
—Plum-headed Parakeet	*Psittacula cyanocephala*	OR
—Blossom-headed Parakeet	*Psittacula roseata*	OR
—Blue-winged Parakeet	*Psittacula columboides*	OR
—Layard's Parakeet	*Psittacula calthropae*	OR
—Lord Derby's Parakeet	*Psittacula derbiana*	OR
—Red-breasted Parakeet	*Psittacula alexandri*	OR
—Nicobar Parakeet	*Psittacula caniceps*	OR
—Long-tailed Parakeet	*Psittacula longicauda*	OR
—Grey-headed Lovebird	*Agapornis canus*	AF
—Red-headed Lovebird	*Agapornis pullarius*	AF
—Black-winged Lovebird	*Agapornis taranta*	AF
—Black-collared Lovebird	*Agapornis swindernianus*	AF
—Rosy-faced Lovebird	*Agapornis roseicollis*	AF
—Fischer's Lovebird	*Agapornis fischeri*	AF
—Yellow-collared Lovebird	*Agapornis personatus*	AF
—Lilian's Lovebird	*Agapornis lilianae*	AF
—Black-cheeked Lovebird	*Agapornis nigrigenis*	AF
—Greater Vasa Parrot	*Coracopsis vasa*	AF
—Lesser Vasa Parrot	*Coracopsis nigra*	AF
—Grey Parrot	*Psittacus erithacus*	AF
—Brown-necked Parrot	*Poicephalus fuscicollis*	AF
—Cape Parrot	*Poicephalus robustus*	AF
—Red-fronted Parrot	*Poicephalus gulielmi*	AF
—Meyer's Parrot	*Poicephalus meyeri*	AF
—Rüppell's Parrot	*Poicephalus rueppellii*	AF

INTERNATIONAL ENGLISH NAME	SCIENTIFIC NAME	REGION(S)
—Brown-headed Parrot	*Poicephalus cryptoxanthus*	AF
—Niam-niam Parrot	*Poicephalus crassus*	AF
—Red-bellied Parrot	*Poicephalus rufiventris*	AF
—Senegal Parrot	*Poicephalus senegalus*	AF
—Yellow-fronted Parrot	*Poicephalus flavifrons*	AF
—Hyacinth Macaw	*Anodorhynchus hyacinthinus*	SA
—Lear's Macaw	*Anodorhynchus leari*	SA
—Spix's Macaw	*Cyanopsitta spixii*	SA
—Blue-and-yellow Macaw	*Ara ararauna*	SA
—Blue-throated Macaw	*Ara glaucogularis*	SA
—Military Macaw	*Ara militaris*	LA
—Great Green Macaw	*Ara ambiguus*	LA
—Scarlet Macaw	*Ara macao*	LA
—Red-and-green Macaw	*Ara chloropterus*	SA
—Red-fronted Macaw	*Ara rubrogenys*	SA
—Chestnut-fronted Macaw	*Ara severus*	LA
—Red-bellied Macaw	*Orthopsittaca manilata*	SA
—Blue-headed Macaw	*Primolius couloni*	SA
—Blue-winged Macaw	*Primolius maracana*	SA
—Golden-collared Macaw	*Primolius auricollis*	SA
—Red-shouldered Macaw	*Diopsittaca nobilis*	SA
—Thick-billed Parrot	*Rhynchopsitta pachyrhyncha*	MA
—Maroon-fronted Parrot	*Rhynchopsitta terrisi*	MA
—Yellow-eared Parrot	*Ognorhynchus icterotis*	SA
—Golden Parakeet	*Guaruba guarouba*	SA
—Blue-crowned Parakeet	*Aratinga acuticaudata*	SA
—Green Parakeet	*Aratinga holochlora*	MA
—Socorro Parakeet	*Aratinga brevipes*	MA
—Red-throated Parakeet	*Aratinga rubritorquis*	MA
—Pacific Parakeet	*Aratinga strenua*	MA
—Scarlet-fronted Parakeet	*Aratinga wagleri*	SA
—Mitred Parakeet	*Aratinga mitrata*	SA
—Red-masked Parakeet	*Aratinga erythrogenys*	SA
—Finsch's Parakeet	*Aratinga finschi*	MA
—White-eyed Parakeet	*Aratinga leucophthalma*	SA
—Cuban Parakeet	*Aratinga euops*	NA
—Hispaniolan Parakeet	*Aratinga chloroptera*	NA
—Sun Parakeet	*Aratinga solstitialis*	SA
—Jandaya Parakeet	*Aratinga jandaya*	SA
—Golden-capped Parakeet	*Aratinga auricapillus*	SA
—Dusky-headed Parakeet	*Aratinga weddellii*	SA
—Jamaican Parakeet	*Aratinga nana*	NA
—Aztec Parakeet	*Aratinga astec*	MA
—Orange-fronted Parakeet	*Aratinga canicularis*	MA
—Peach-fronted Parakeet	*Aratinga aurea*	SA
—Brown-throated Parakeet	*Aratinga pertinax*	LA
—Caatinga Parakeet	*Aratinga cactorum*	SA
—Nanday Parakeet	*Nandayus nenday*	SA
—Golden-plumed Parakeet	*Leptosittaca branickii*	SA
—Burrowing Parrot	*Cyanoliseus patagonus*	SA
—Ochre-marked Parakeet	*Pyrrhura cruentata*	SA
—Blaze-winged Parakeet	*Pyrrhura devillei*	SA
—Reddish-bellied Parakeet	*Pyrrhura frontalis*	SA

INTERNATIONAL ENGLISH NAME	SCIENTIFIC NAME	REGION(S)
—Pearly Parakeet	*Pyrrhura lepida*	SA
—Crimson-bellied Parakeet	*Pyrrhura perlata*	SA
—Green-cheeked Parakeet	*Pyrrhura molinae*	SA
—Painted Parakeet	*Pyrrhura picta*	SA
—White-eared Parakeet	*Pyrrhura leucotis*	SA
—Pfrimer's Parakeet	*Pyrrhura pfrimeri*	SA
—Grey-breasted Parakeet	*Pyrrhura anaca*	SA
—Venezuelan Parakeet	*Pyrrhura emma*	SA
—Santa Marta Parakeet	*Pyrrhura viridicata*	SA
—Fiery-shouldered Parakeet	*Pyrrhura egregia*	SA
—Maroon-tailed Parakeet	*Pyrrhura melanura*	SA
—El Oro Parakeet	*Pyrrhura orcesi*	SA
—Black-capped Parakeet	*Pyrrhura rupicola*	SA
—White-breasted Parakeet	*Pyrrhura albipectus*	SA
—Flame-winged Parakeet	*Pyrrhura calliptera*	SA
—Blood-eared Parakeet	*Pyrrhura hoematotis*	SA
—Rose-crowned Parakeet	*Pyrrhura rhodocephala*	SA
—Sulphur-winged Parakeet	*Pyrrhura hoffmanni*	MA
—Austral Parakeet	*Enicognathus ferrugineus*	SA
—Slender-billed Parakeet	*Enicognathus leptorhynchus*	SA
—Monk Parakeet	*Myiopsitta monachus*	SA
—Cliff Parakeet	*Myiopsitta luchsi*	SA
—Grey-hooded Parakeet	*Psilopsiagon aymara*	SA
—Mountain Parakeet	*Psilopsiagon aurifrons*	SA
—Barred Parakeet	*Bolborhynchus lineola*	LA
—Andean Parakeet	*Bolborhynchus orbygnesius*	SA
—Rufous-fronted Parakeet	*Bolborhynchus ferrugineifrons*	SA
—Mexican Parrotlet	*Forpus cyanopygius*	MA
—Green-rumped Parrotlet	*Forpus passerinus*	SA
—Blue-winged Parrotlet	*Forpus xanthopterygius*	SA
—Spectacled Parrotlet	*Forpus conspicillatus*	LA
—Dusky-billed Parrotlet	*Forpus sclateri*	SA
—Pacific Parrotlet	*Forpus coelestis*	SA
—Yellow-faced Parrotlet	*Forpus xanthops*	SA
—Plain Parakeet	*Brotogeris tirica*	SA
—White-winged Parakeet	*Brotogeris versicolurus*	SA
—Yellow-chevroned Parakeet	*Brotogeris chiriri*	SA
—Grey-cheeked Parakeet	*Brotogeris pyrrhoptera*	SA
—Orange-chinned Parakeet	*Brotogeris jugularis*	LA
—Cobalt-winged Parakeet	*Brotogeris cyanoptera*	SA
—Golden-winged Parakeet	*Brotogeris chrysoptera*	SA
—Tui Parakeet	*Brotogeris sanctithomae*	SA
—Tepui Parrotlet	*Nannopsittaca panychlora*	SA
—Manu Parrotlet	*Nannopsittaca dachilleae*	SA
—Lilac-tailed Parrotlet	*Touit batavicus*	SA
—Scarlet-shouldered Parrotlet	*Touit huetii*	SA
—Red-fronted Parrotlet	*Touit costaricensis*	MA
—Blue-fronted Parrotlet	*Touit dilectissimus*	LA
—Sapphire-rumped Parrotlet	*Touit purpuratus*	SA
—Brown-backed Parrotlet	*Touit melanonotus*	SA
—Golden-tailed Parrotlet	*Touit surdus*	SA
—Spot-winged Parrotlet	*Touit stictopterus*	SA
—Black-headed Parrot	*Pionites melanocephalus*	SA

INTERNATIONAL ENGLISH NAME	SCIENTIFIC NAME	REGION(S)
—White-bellied Parrot	*Pionites leucogaster*	SA
—Vulturine Parrot	*Pionopsitta vulturina*	SA
—Bald Parrot	*Pionopsitta aurantiocephala*	SA
—Brown-hooded Parrot	*Pionopsitta haematotis*	LA
—Rose-faced Parrot	*Pionopsitta pulchra*	SA
—Orange-cheeked Parrot	*Pionopsitta barrabandi*	SA
—Saffron-headed Parrot	*Pionopsitta pyrilia*	LA
—Caica Parrot	*Pionopsitta caica*	SA
—Pileated Parrot	*Pionopsitta pileata*	SA
—Black-winged Parrot	*Hapalopsittaca melanotis*	SA
—Rusty-faced Parrot	*Hapalopsittaca amazonina*	SA
—Fuertes's Parrot	*Hapalopsittaca fuertesi*	SA
—Red-faced Parrot	*Hapalopsittaca pyrrhops*	SA
—Short-tailed Parrot	*Graydidascalus brachyurus*	SA
—Blue-headed Parrot	*Pionus menstruus*	LA
—Red-billed Parrot	*Pionus sordidus*	SA
—Scaly-headed Parrot	*Pionus maximiliani*	SA
—Plum-crowned Parrot	*Pionus tumultuosus*	SA
—White-capped Parrot	*Pionus seniloides*	SA
—White-crowned Parrot	*Pionus senilis*	MA
—Bronze-winged Parrot	*Pionus chalcopterus*	SA
—Dusky Parrot	*Pionus fuscus*	SA
—Cuban Amazon	*Amazona leucocephala*	NA
—Yellow-billed Amazon	*Amazona collaria*	NA
—Hispaniolan Amazon	*Amazona ventralis*	NA
—White-fronted Amazon	*Amazona albifrons*	MA
—Yucatan Amazon	*Amazona xantholora*	MA
—Black-billed Amazon	*Amazona agilis*	NA
—Puerto Rican Amazon	*Amazona vittata*	NA
—Tucuman Amazon	*Amazona tucumana*	SA
—Red-spectacled Amazon	*Amazona pretrei*	SA
—Red-crowned Amazon	*Amazona viridigenalis*	MA
—Lilac-crowned Amazon	*Amazona finschi*	MA
—Red-lored Amazon	*Amazona autumnalis*	LA
—Diademed Amazon	*Amazona diadema*	SA
—Blue-cheeked Amazon	*Amazona dufresniana*	SA
—Red-browed Amazon	*Amazona rhodocorytha*	SA
—Red-tailed Amazon	*Amazona brasiliensis*	SA
—Festive Amazon	*Amazona festiva*	SA
—Yellow-faced Amazon	*Amazona xanthops*	SA
—Yellow-shouldered Amazon	*Amazona barbadensis*	SA
—Turquoise-fronted Amazon	*Amazona aestiva*	SA
—Yellow-headed Amazon	*Amazona oratrix*	MA
—Yellow-naped Amazon	*Amazona auropalliata*	MA
—Yellow-crowned Amazon	*Amazona ochrocephala*	LA
—Orange-winged Amazon	*Amazona amazonica*	SA
—Scaly-naped Amazon	*Amazona mercenaria*	SA
—White-cheeked Amazon	*Amazona kawalli*	SA
—Mealy Amazon	*Amazona farinosa*	LA
—Vinaceous-breasted Amazon	*Amazona vinacea*	SA
—St. Lucia Amazon	*Amazona versicolor*	NA
—Red-necked Amazon	*Amazona arausiaca*	NA

INTERNATIONAL ENGLISH NAME	SCIENTIFIC NAME	REGION(S)
—St. Vincent Amazon	*Amazona guildingii*	NA
—Imperial Amazon	*Amazona imperialis*	NA
—Red-fan Parrot	*Deroptyus accipitrinus*	SA
—Blue-bellied Parrot	*Triclaria malachitacea*	SA
—Orange-breasted Fig Parrot	*Cyclopsitta gulielmitertii*	AU
—Double-eyed Fig Parrot	*Cyclopsitta diophthalma*	AU
—Flame-headed Fig Parrot	*Psittaculirostris desmarestii*	AU
—Scarlet-cheeked Fig Parrot	*Psittaculirostris edwardsii*	AU
—Yellow-cheeked Fig Parrot	*Psittaculirostris salvadorii*	AU
—Guaiabero	*Bolbopsittacus lunulatus*	OR

ORDER OPISTHOCOMIFORMES

HOATZIN

Family Opisthocomidae

—Hoatzin	*Opisthocomus hoazin*	SA

ORDER MUSOPHAGIFORMES

TURACOS

Family Musophagidae

—Great Blue Turaco	*Corythaeola cristata*	AF
—Guinea Turaco	*Tauraco persa*	AF
—Livingstone's Turaco	*Tauraco livingstonii*	AF
—Schalow's Turaco	*Tauraco schalowi*	AF
—Knysna Turaco	*Tauraco corythaix*	AF
—Black-billed Turaco	*Tauraco schuettii*	AF
—Fischer's Turaco	*Tauraco fischeri*	AF
—Yellow-billed Turaco	*Tauraco macrorhynchus*	AF
—White-crested Turaco	*Tauraco leucolophus*	AF
—Bannerman's Turaco	*Tauraco bannermani*	AF
—Red-crested Turaco	*Tauraco erythrolophus*	AF
—Hartlaub's Turaco	*Tauraco hartlaubi*	AF
—White-cheeked Turaco	*Tauraco leucotis*	AF
—Ruspoli's Turaco	*Tauraco ruspolii*	AF
—Purple-crested Turaco	*Tauraco porphyreolophus*	AF
—Ruwenzori Turaco	*Ruwenzorornis johnstoni*	AF
—Violet Turaco	*Musophaga violacea*	AF
—Ross's Turaco	*Musophaga rossae*	AF
—Grey Go-away-bird	*Corythaixoides concolor*	AF
—Bare-faced Go-away-bird	*Corythaixoides personatus*	AF
—White-bellied Go-away-bird	*Corythaixoides leucogaster*	AF
—Western Plantain-eater	*Crinifer piscator*	AF
—Eastern Plantain-eater	*Crinifer zonurus*	AF

ORDER CUCULIFORMES

CUCKOOS

Family Cuculidae

—Guira Cuckoo	*Guira guira*	SA
—Greater Ani	*Crotophaga major*	LA
—Smooth-billed Ani	*Crotophaga ani*	NA, LA
—Groove-billed Ani	*Crotophaga sulcirostris*	LA
—Striped Cuckoo	*Tapera naevia*	LA
—Pheasant Cuckoo	*Dromococcyx phasianellus*	LA

INTERNATIONAL ENGLISH NAME	SCIENTIFIC NAME	REGION(S)
—Pavonine Cuckoo	*Dromococcyx pavoninus*	SA
—Lesser Ground Cuckoo	*Morococcyx erythropygus*	MA
—Greater Roadrunner	*Geococcyx californianus*	NA, MA
—Lesser Roadrunner	*Geococcyx velox*	MA
—Rufous-vented Ground Cuckoo	*Neomorphus geoffroyi*	LA
—Banded Ground Cuckoo	*Neomorphus radiolosus*	SA
—Rufous-winged Ground Cuckoo	*Neomorphus rufipennis*	SA
—Red-billed Ground Cuckoo	*Neomorphus pucheranii*	SA
—Buff-headed Coucal	*Centropus milo*	AU
—Pied Coucal	*Centropus ateralbus*	AU
—Ivory-billed Coucal	*Centropus menbeki*	AU
—Biak Coucal	*Centropus chalybeus*	AU
—Rufous Coucal	*Centropus unirufus*	OR
—Green-billed Coucal	*Centropus chlororhynchos*	OR
—Black-faced Coucal	*Centropus melanops*	OR
—Black-hooded Coucal	*Centropus steerii*	OR
—Short-toed Coucal	*Centropus rectunguis*	OR
—Bay Coucal	*Centropus celebensis*	AU
—Gabon Coucal	*Centropus anselli*	AF
—Black-throated Coucal	*Centropus leucogaster*	AF
—Senegal Coucal	*Centropus senegalensis*	AF
—Blue-headed Coucal	*Centropus monachus*	AF
—Coppery-tailed Coucal	*Centropus cupreicaudus*	AF
—White-browed Coucal	*Centropus superciliosus*	AF
—Neumann's Coucal	*Centropus neumanni*	AF
—Burchell's Coucal	*Centropus burchelli*	AF
—Sunda Coucal	*Centropus nigrorufus*	OR
—Greater Coucal	*Centropus sinensis*	OR
—Malagasy Coucal	*Centropus toulou*	AF
—Goliath Coucal	*Centropus goliath*	AU
—Black Coucal	*Centropus grillii*	AF
—Philippine Coucal	*Centropus viridis*	OR
—Lesser Coucal	*Centropus bengalensis*	OR
—Violet Coucal	*Centropus violaceus*	AU
—Black-billed Coucal	*Centropus bernsteini*	AU
—Pheasant Coucal	*Centropus phasianinus*	AU
—Andaman Coucal	*Centropus andamanensis*	OR
—Kai Coucal	*Centropus spilopterus*	AU
—Bornean Ground Cuckoo	*Carpococcyx radiceus*	OR
—Sumatran Ground Cuckoo	*Carpococcyx viridis*	OR
—Coral-billed Ground Cuckoo	*Carpococcyx renauldi*	OR
—Crested Coua	*Coua cristata*	AF
—Verreaux's Coua	*Coua verreauxi*	AF
—Blue Coua	*Coua caerulea*	AF
—Red-capped Coua	*Coua ruficeps*	AF
—Red-fronted Coua	*Coua reynaudii*	AF
—Coquerel's Coua	*Coua coquereli*	AF
—Running Coua	*Coua cursor*	AF
—Giant Coua	*Coua gigas*	AF
—Red-breasted Coua	*Coua serriana*	AF
—Raffles's Malkoha	*Rhinortha chlorophaea*	OR
—Green Malkoha	*Ceuthmochares aereus*	AF
—Sirkeer Malkoha	*Taccocua leschenaultii*	OR

INTERNATIONAL ENGLISH NAME	SCIENTIFIC NAME	REGION(S)
__Red-billed Malkoha	*Zanclostomus javanicus*	OR
__Yellow-billed Malkoha	*Rhamphococcyx calyorhynchus*	AU
__Chestnut-breasted Malkoha	*Phaenicophaeus curvirostris*	OR
__Red-faced Malkoha	*Phaenicophaeus pyrrhocephalus*	OR
__Chestnut-bellied Malkoha	*Phaenicophaeus sumatranus*	OR
__Blue-faced Malkoha	*Phaenicophaeus viridirostris*	OR
__Black-bellied Malkoha	*Phaenicophaeus diardi*	OR
__Green-billed Malkoha	*Phaenicophaeus tristis*	OR
__Rough-crested Malkoha	*Dasylophus superciliosus*	OR
__Scale-feathered Malkoha	*Dasylophus cumingi*	OR
__Chestnut-winged Cuckoo	*Clamator coromandus*	OR
__Great Spotted Cuckoo	*Clamator glandarius*	AF, EU
__Levaillant's Cuckoo	*Clamator levaillantii*	AF
__Jacobin Cuckoo	*Clamator jacobinus*	AF, OR
__Little Cuckoo	*Coccycua minuta*	LA
__Dwarf Cuckoo	*Coccycua pumila*	SA
__Ash-colored Cuckoo	*Coccycua cinerea*	SA
__Squirrel Cuckoo	*Piaya cayana*	LA
__Black-bellied Cuckoo	*Piaya melanogaster*	SA
__Dark-billed Cuckoo	*Coccyzus melacoryphus*	SA
__Yellow-billed Cuckoo	*Coccyzus americanus*	NA, MA
__Pearly-breasted Cuckoo	*Coccyzus euleri*	SA
__Mangrove Cuckoo	*Coccyzus minor*	NA, LA
__Cocos Cuckoo	*Coccyzus ferrugineus*	MA
__Black-billed Cuckoo	*Coccyzus erythropthalmus*	NA
__Grey-capped Cuckoo	*Coccyzus lansbergi*	SA
__Chestnut-bellied Cuckoo	*Coccyzus pluvialis*	NA
__Bay-breasted Cuckoo	*Coccyzus rufigularis*	NA
__Jamaican Lizard Cuckoo	*Coccyzus vetula*	NA
__Great Lizard Cuckoo	*Coccyzus merlini*	NA
__Puerto Rican Lizard Cuckoo	*Coccyzus vieilloti*	NA
__Hispaniolan Lizard Cuckoo	*Coccyzus longirostris*	NA
__Thick-billed Cuckoo	*Pachycoccyx audeberti*	AF
__Dwarf Koel	*Microdynamis parva*	AU
__Asian Koel	*Eudynamys scolopaceus*	OR
__Black-billed Koel	*Eudynamys melanorhynchus*	AU
__Pacific Koel	*Eudynamys orientalis*	AU
__Pacific Long-tailed Cuckoo	*Urodynamis taitensis*	AU
__Channel-billed Cuckoo	*Scythrops novaehollandiae*	AU
__Asian Emerald Cuckoo	*Chrysococcyx maculatus*	OR
__Violet Cuckoo	*Chrysococcyx xanthorhynchus*	OR
__Dideric Cuckoo	*Chrysococcyx caprius*	AF
__Klaas's Cuckoo	*Chrysococcyx klaas*	AF
__Yellow-throated Cuckoo	*Chrysococcyx flavigularis*	AF
__African Emerald Cuckoo	*Chrysococcyx cupreus*	AF
__Long-billed Cuckoo	*Chrysococcyx megarhynchus*	AU
__Horsfield's Bronze Cuckoo	*Chrysococcyx basalis*	AU
__Black-eared Cuckoo	*Chrysococcyx osculans*	AU
__Rufous-throated Bronze Cuckoo	*Chrysococcyx ruficollis*	AU
__Shining Bronze Cuckoo	*Chrysococcyx lucidus*	AU
__White-eared Bronze Cuckoo	*Chrysococcyx meyeri*	AU
__Little Bronze Cuckoo	*Chrysococcyx minutillus*	OR, AU
__Pied Bronze Cuckoo	*Chrysococcyx crassirostris*	AU

INTERNATIONAL ENGLISH NAME	SCIENTIFIC NAME	REGION(S)
__Pallid Cuckoo	*Cacomantis pallidus*	AU
__White-crowned Cuckoo	*Cacomantis leucolophus*	AU
__Chestnut-breasted Cuckoo	*Cacomantis castaneiventris*	AU
__Fan-tailed Cuckoo	*Cacomantis flabelliformis*	AU
__Banded Bay Cuckoo	*Cacomantis sonneratii*	OR
__Plaintive Cuckoo	*Cacomantis merulinus*	OR
__Grey-bellied Cuckoo	*Cacomantis passerinus*	OR
__Brush Cuckoo	*Cacomantis variolosus*	AU
__Rusty-breasted Cuckoo	*Cacomantis sepulcralis*	OR
__Moluccan Cuckoo	*Cacomantis heinrichi*	AU
__Dusky Long-tailed Cuckoo	*Cercococcyx mechowi*	AF
__Olive Long-tailed Cuckoo	*Cercococcyx olivinus*	AF
__Barred Long-tailed Cuckoo	*Cercococcyx montanus*	AF
__Philippine Drongo-Cuckoo	*Surniculus velutinus*	OR
__Asian Drongo-Cuckoo	*Surniculus lugubris*	OR
__Moustached Hawk-Cuckoo	*Hierococcyx vagans*	OR
__Large Hawk-Cuckoo	*Hierococcyx sparverioides*	OR
__Common Hawk-Cuckoo	*Hierococcyx varius*	OR
__Rufous Hawk-Cuckoo	*Hierococcyx hyperythrus*	EU
__Sulawesi Hawk-Cuckoo	*Hierococcyx crassirostris*	AU
__Philippine Hawk-Cuckoo	*Hierococcyx pectoralis*	OR
__Malaysian Hawk-Cuckoo	*Hierococcyx fugax*	OR
__Hodgson's Hawk-Cuckoo	*Hierococcyx nisicolor*	OR
__Black Cuckoo	*Cuculus clamosus*	AF
__Red-chested Cuckoo	*Cuculus solitarius*	AF
__Lesser Cuckoo	*Cuculus poliocephalus*	EU
__Sulawesi Cuckoo	*Cuculus crassirostris*	AU
__Indian Cuckoo	*Cuculus micropterus*	OR
__Madagascar Cuckoo	*Cuculus rochii*	AF
__African Cuckoo	*Cuculus gularis*	AF
__Oriental Cuckoo	*Cuculus saturatus*	OR
__Common Cuckoo	*Cuculus canorus*	EU

ORDER STRIGIFORMES

BARN OWLS	**Family Tytonidae**	
__Greater Sooty Owl	*Tyto tenebricosa*	AU
__Lesser Sooty Owl	*Tyto multipunctata*	AU
__Minahassa Masked Owl	*Tyto inexspectata*	AU
__Taliabu Masked Owl	*Tyto nigrobrunnea*	AU
__Moluccan Masked Owl	*Tyto sororcula*	AU
__Manus Masked Owl	*Tyto manusi*	AU
__Golden Masked Owl	*Tyto aurantia*	AU
__Australian Masked Owl	*Tyto novaehollandiae*	AU
__Sulawesi Masked Owl	*Tyto rosenbergii*	AU
__Red Owl	*Tyto soumagnei*	AF
__Barn Owl	*Tyto alba*	Worldwide
__Ashy-faced Owl	*Tyto glaucops*	NA
__Grass Owl	*Tyto capensis*	AF, OR, AU
__Congo Bay Owl	*Phodilus prigoginei*	AF
__Oriental Bay Owl	*Phodilus badius*	OR

INTERNATIONAL ENGLISH NAME	SCIENTIFIC NAME	REGION(S)
OWLS	**Family Strigidae**	
__White-fronted Scops Owl	*Otus sagittatus*	OR
__Reddish Scops Owl	*Otus rufescens*	OR
__Serendib Scops Owl	*Otus thilohoffmanni*	OR
__Sandy Scops Owl	*Otus icterorhynchus*	AF
__Sokoke Scops Owl	*Otus ireneae*	AF
__Andaman Scops Owl	*Otus balli*	OR
__Flores Scops Owl	*Otus alfredi*	AU
__Mountain Scops Owl	*Otus spilocephalus*	OR
__Rajah Scops Owl	*Otus brookii*	OR
__Javan Scops Owl	*Otus angelinae*	OR
__Mentawai Scops Owl	*Otus mentawi*	OR
__Collared Scops Owl	*Otus bakkamoena*	OR
__Palawan Scops Owl	*Otus fuliginosus*	OR
__Philippine Scops Owl	*Otus megalotis*	OR
__Wallace's Scops Owl	*Otus silvicola*	AU
__Mindanao Scops Owl	*Otus mirus*	OR
__Luzon Scops Owl	*Otus longicornis*	OR
__Mindoro Scops Owl	*Otus mindorensis*	OR
__Pallid Scops Owl	*Otus brucei*	EU
__African Scops Owl	*Otus senegalensis*	AF
__Eurasian Scops Owl	*Otus scops*	EU
__Oriental Scops Owl	*Otus sunia*	OR
__Moluccan Scops Owl	*Otus magicus*	AU
__Sula Scops Owl	*Otus sulaensis*	AU
__Siau Scops Owl	*Otus siaoensis*	AU
__Mantanani Scops Owl	*Otus mantananensis*	OR
__Ryukyu Scops Owl	*Otus elegans*	OR
__Sulawesi Scops Owl	*Otus manadensis*	AU
__Sangihe Scops Owl	*Otus collari*	AU
__Biak Scops Owl	*Otus beccarii*	AU
__Seychelles Scops Owl	*Otus insularis*	IO
__Simeulue Scops Owl	*Otus umbra*	OR
__Nicobar Scops Owl	*Otus alius*	OR
__Pemba Scops Owl	*Otus pembaensis*	AF
__Karthala Scops Owl	*Otus pauliani*	AF
__Moheli Scops Owl	*Otus moheliensis*	AF
__Mayotte Scops Owl	*Otus mayottensis*	AF
__Torotoroka Scops Owl	*Otus madagascariensis*	AF
__Rainforest Scops Owl	*Otus rutilus*	AF
__Sao Tome Scops Owl	*Otus hartlaubi*	AF
__Flammulated Owl	*Megascops flammeolus*	NA, MA
__Eastern Screech Owl	*Megascops asio*	NA, MA
__Western Screech Owl	*Megascops kennicottii*	NA, MA
__Balsas Screech Owl	*Megascops seductus*	MA
__Pacific Screech Owl	*Megascops cooperi*	MA
__Whiskered Screech Owl	*Megascops trichopsis*	NA, MA
__Tropical Screech Owl	*Megascops choliba*	LA
__West Peruvian Screech Owl	*Megascops roboratus*	SA
__Koepcke's Screech Owl	*Megascops koepckeae*	SA
__Bare-shanked Screech Owl	*Megascops clarkii*	LA
__Bearded Screech Owl	*Megascops barbarus*	MA
__Rufescent Screech Owl	*Megascops ingens*	SA

INTERNATIONAL ENGLISH NAME	SCIENTIFIC NAME	REGION(S)
__Cinnamon Screech Owl	*Megascops petersoni*	SA
__Cloud-forest Screech Owl	*Megascops marshalli*	SA
__Tawny-bellied Screech Owl	*Megascops watsonii*	SA
__Vermiculated Screech Owl	*Megascops guatemalae*	LA
__Choco Screech Owl	*Megascops centralis*	SA
__Yungas Screech Owl	*Megascops hoyi*	SA
__Black-capped Screech Owl	*Megascops atricapilla*	SA
__Long-tufted Screech Owl	*Megascops sanctaecatarinae*	SA
__Foothill Screech Owl	*Megascops roraimae*	SA
__Puerto Rican Screech Owl	*Megascops nudipes*	NA
__White-throated Screech Owl	*Megascops albogularis*	SA
__Palau Owl	*Pyrroglaux podarginus*	AU
__Bare-legged Owl	*Gymnoglaux lawrencii*	NA
__Northern White-faced Owl	*Ptilopsis leucotis*	AF
__Southern White-faced Owl	*Ptilopsis granti*	AF
__Giant Scops Owl	*Mimizuku gurneyi*	OR
__Snowy Owl	*Bubo scandiaca*	NA, EU
__Great Horned Owl	*Bubo virginianus*	NA, LA
__Lesser Horned Owl	*Bubo magellanicus*	SA
__Eurasian Eagle-Owl	*Bubo bubo*	EU
__Pharaoh Eagle-Owl	*Bubo ascalaphus*	AF
__Cape Eagle-Owl	*Bubo capensis*	AF
__Spotted Eagle-Owl	*Bubo africanus*	AF
__Greyish Eagle-Owl	*Bubo cinerascens*	AF
__Fraser's Eagle-Owl	*Bubo poensis*	AF
__Usambara Eagle-Owl	*Bubo vosseleri*	AF
__Spot-bellied Eagle-Owl	*Bubo nipalensis*	OR
__Barred Eagle-Owl	*Bubo sumatranus*	OR
__Shelley's Eagle-Owl	*Bubo shelleyi*	AF
__Verreaux's Eagle-Owl	*Bubo lacteus*	AF
__Dusky Eagle-Owl	*Bubo coromandus*	OR
__Akun Eagle-Owl	*Bubo leucostictus*	AF
__Philippine Eagle-Owl	*Bubo philippensis*	OR
__Blakiston's Fish Owl	*Bubo blakistoni*	EU
__Brown Fish Owl	*Ketupa zeylonensis*	OR, EU
__Tawny Fish Owl	*Ketupa flavipes*	OR
__Buffy Fish Owl	*Ketupa ketupu*	OR
__Pel's Fishing Owl	*Scotopelia peli*	AF
__Rufous Fishing Owl	*Scotopelia ussheri*	AF
__Vermiculated Fishing Owl	*Scotopelia bouvieri*	AF
__Spotted Wood Owl	*Strix seloputo*	OR
__Mottled Wood Owl	*Strix ocellata*	OR
__Brown Wood Owl	*Strix leptogrammica*	OR
__Tawny Owl	*Strix aluco*	EU
__Hume's Owl	*Strix butleri*	EU
__Spotted Owl	*Strix occidentalis*	NA, MA
__Barred Owl	*Strix varia*	NA, MA
__Fulvous Owl	*Strix fulvescens*	MA
__Rusty-barred Owl	*Strix hylophila*	SA
__Chaco Owl	*Strix chacoensis*	SA
__Rufous-legged Owl	*Strix rufipes*	SA
__Ural Owl	*Strix uralensis*	EU
__Pere David's Owl	*Strix davidi*	EU

INTERNATIONAL ENGLISH NAME	SCIENTIFIC NAME	REGION(S)
__Great Grey Owl	*Strix nebulosa*	NA, EU
__African Wood Owl	*Strix woodfordii*	AF
__Mottled Owl	*Strix virgata*	LA
__Rufous-banded Owl	*Strix albitarsis*	SA
__Black-and-white Owl	*Strix nigrolineata*	LA
__Black-banded Owl	*Strix huhula*	SA
__Maned Owl	*Jubula lettii*	AF
__Crested Owl	*Lophostrix cristata*	LA
__Spectacled Owl	*Pulsatrix perspicillata*	LA
__Tawny-browed Owl	*Pulsatrix koeniswaldiana*	SA
__Band-bellied Owl	*Pulsatrix melanota*	SA
__Northern Hawk-Owl	*Surnia ulula*	NA, EU
__Eurasian Pygmy Owl	*Glaucidium passerinum*	EU
__Collared Owlet	*Glaucidium brodiei*	OR
__Pearl-spotted Owlet	*Glaucidium perlatum*	AF
__Northern Pygmy Owl	*Glaucidium californicum*	NA
__Mountain Pygmy Owl	*Glaucidium gnoma*	NA, MA
__Cape Pygmy Owl	*Glaucidium hoskinsii*	MA
__Costa Rican Pygmy Owl	*Glaucidium costaricanum*	MA
__Andean Pygmy Owl	*Glaucidium jardinii*	SA
__Cloud-forest Pygmy Owl	*Glaucidium nubicola*	SA
__Yungas Pygmy Owl	*Glaucidium bolivianum*	SA
__Colima Pygmy Owl	*Glaucidium palmarum*	MA
__Tamaulipas Pygmy Owl	*Glaucidium sanchezi*	MA
__Pernambuco Pygmy Owl	*Glaucidium mooreorum*	SA
__Central American Pygmy Owl	*Glaucidium griseiceps*	MA
__Subtropical Pygmy Owl	*Glaucidium parkeri*	SA
__Amazonian Pygmy Owl	*Glaucidium hardyi*	SA
__East Brazilian Pygmy Owl	*Glaucidium minutissimum*	SA
__Ferruginous Pygmy Owl	*Glaucidium brasilianum*	LA
__Pacific Pygmy Owl	*Glaucidium peruanum*	SA
__Austral Pygmy Owl	*Glaucidium nana*	SA
__Cuban Pygmy Owl	*Glaucidium siju*	NA
__Red-chested Owlet	*Glaucidium tephronotum*	AF
__Sjostedt's Barred Owlet	*Glaucidium sjostedti*	AF
__Asian Barred Owlet	*Glaucidium cuculoides*	OR
__Javan Owlet	*Glaucidium castanopterum*	OR
__Jungle Owlet	*Glaucidium radiatum*	OR
__Chestnut-backed Owlet	*Glaucidium castanonotum*	OR
__African Barred Owlet	*Glaucidium capense*	AF
__Long-whiskered Owlet	*Xenoglaux loweryi*	SA
__Elf Owl	*Micrathene whitneyi*	NA, MA
__Little Owl	*Athene noctua*	EU, AF
__Spotted Owlet	*Athene brama*	OR, EU
__Burrowing Owl	*Athene cunicularia*	NA, LA
__Forest Owlet	*Heteroglaux blewitti*	OR
__Boreal Owl	*Aegolius funereus*	NA, EU
__Northern Saw-whet Owl	*Aegolius acadicus*	NA
__Unspotted Saw-whet Owl	*Aegolius ridgwayi*	MA
__Buff-fronted Owl	*Aegolius harrisii*	SA
__Rufous Boobook	*Ninox rufa*	AU
__Togian Boobook	*Ninox burhani*	AU
__Powerful Boobook	*Ninox strenua*	AU

INTERNATIONAL ENGLISH NAME	SCIENTIFIC NAME	REGION(S)
—Barking Boobook	*Ninox connivens*	AU
—Sumba Boobook	*Ninox rudolfi*	AU
—Southern Boobook	*Ninox boobook*	AU
—Morepork	*Ninox novaeseelandiae*	AU
—Brown Hawk-Owl	*Ninox scutulata*	OR, EU
—Andaman Hawk-Owl	*Ninox affinis*	OR
—White-browed Hawk-Owl	*Ninox superciliaris*	AF
—Philippine Hawk-Owl	*Ninox philippensis*	OR
—Ochre-bellied Boobook	*Ninox ochracea*	AU
—Cinnabar Boobook	*Ninox ios*	AU
—Moluccan Boobook	*Ninox squamipila*	AU
—Christmas Boobook	*Ninox natalis*	IO
—Jungle Boobook	*Ninox theomacha*	AU
—Manus Boobook	*Ninox meeki*	AU
—Speckled Boobook	*Ninox punctulata*	AU
—Barred Boobook	*Ninox variegata*	AU
—Spangled Boobook	*Ninox odiosa*	AU
—Solomons Boobook	*Ninox jacquinoti*	AU
—Little Sumba Hawk-Owl	*Ninox sumbensis*	AU
—Papuan Hawk-Owl	*Uroglaux dimorpha*	AU
—Jamaican Owl	*Pseudoscops grammicus*	NA
—Striped Owl	*Pseudoscops clamator*	LA
—Fearful Owl	*Nesasio solomonensis*	AU
—Stygian Owl	*Asio stygius*	LA
—Long-eared Owl	*Asio otus*	NA, MA, EU
—Abyssinian Owl	*Asio abyssinicus*	AF
—Madagascar Owl	*Asio madagascariensis*	AF
—Short-eared Owl	*Asio flammeus*	Worldwide
—Marsh Owl	*Asio capensis*	AF

ORDER CAPRIMULGIFORMES

FROGMOUTHS	**Family Podargidae**	
—Marbled Frogmouth	*Podargus ocellatus*	AU
—Papuan Frogmouth	*Podargus papuensis*	AU
—Tawny Frogmouth	*Podargus strigoides`*	AU
—Cinnamon Frogmouth.	*Podargus inexpectatus*	AU
—Large Frogmouth	*Batrachostomus auritus*	OR
—Dulit Frogmouth	*Batrachostomus harterti*	OR
—Philippine Frogmouth	*Batrachostomus septimus*	OR
—Gould's Frogmouth	*Batrachostomus stellatus*	OR
—Sri Lanka Frogmouth	*Batrachostomus moniliger*	OR
—Hodgson's Frogmouth	*Batrachostomus hodgsoni*	OR
—Short-tailed Frogmouth	*Batrachostomus poliolophus*	OR
—Javan Frogmouth	*Batrachostomus javensis*	OR
—Sunda Frogmouth	*Batrachostomus cornutus*	OR
OILBIRD	**Family Steatornithidae**	
—Oilbird	*Steatornis caripensis*	SA
POTOOS	**Family Nyctibiidae**	
—Great Potoo	*Nyctibius grandis*	LA
—Long-tailed Potoo	*Nyctibius aethereus*	SA

INTERNATIONAL ENGLISH NAME	SCIENTIFIC NAME	REGION(S)
—Northern Potoo	*Nyctibius jamaicensis*	MA
—Common Potoo	*Nyctibius griseus*	LA
—Andean Potoo	*Nyctibius maculosus*	SA
—White-winged Potoo	*Nyctibius leucopterus*	SA
—Rufous Potoo	*Nyctibius bracteatus*	SA
NIGHTJARS	**Family Caprimulgidae**	
—Short-tailed Nighthawk	*Lurocalis semitorquatus*	LA
—Rufous-bellied Nighthawk	*Lurocalis rufiventris*	SA
—Least Nighthawk	*Chordeiles pusillus*	SA
—Sand-colored Nighthawk	*Chordeiles rupestris*	SA
—Lesser Nighthawk	*Chordeiles acutipennis*	NA, LA
—Common Nighthawk	*Chordeiles minor*	NA, MA
—Antillean Nighthawk	*Chordeiles gundlachii*	NA
—Band-tailed Nighthawk	*Nyctiprogne leucopyga*	SA
—Plain-tailed Nighthawk	*Nyctiprogne vielliardi*	SA
—Nacunda Nighthawk	*Podager nacunda*	SA
—Spotted Nightjar	*Eurostopodus argus*	AU
—White-throated Nightjar	*Eurostopodus mystacalis*	AU
—Satanic Nightjar	*Eurostopodus diabolicus*	AU
—Papuan Nightjar	*Eurostopodus papuensis*	AU
—Cloud-forest Nightjar	*Eurostopodus archboldi*	AU
—Malaysian Eared Nightjar	*Eurostopodus temminckii*	OR
—Great Eared Nightjar	*Eurostopodus macrotis*	OR
—Brown Nightjar	*Veles binotatus*	AF
—Pauraque	*Nyctidromus albicollis*	LA
—Common Poorwill	*Phalaenoptilus nuttallii*	NA, MA
—Least Poorwill	*Siphonorhis brewsteri*	NA
—Eared Poorwill	*Nyctiphrynus mcleodii*	MA
—Yucatan Poorwill	*Nyctiphrynus yucatanicus*	MA
—Ocellated Poorwill	*Nyctiphrynus ocellatus*	LA
—Choco Poorwill	*Nyctiphrynus rosenbergi*	SA
—Chuck-will's-widow	*Caprimulgus carolinensis*	NA
—Rufous Nightjar	*Caprimulgus rufus*	LA
—Greater Antillean Nightjar	*Caprimulgus cubanensis*	NA
—Tawny-collared Nightjar	*Caprimulgus salvini*	MA
—Yucatan Nightjar	*Caprimulgus badius*	MA
—Silky-tailed Nightjar	*Caprimulgus sericocaudatus*	SA
—Buff-collared Nightjar	*Caprimulgus ridgwayi*	MA
—Whip-poor-will	*Caprimulgus vociferus*	NA
—Puerto Rican Nightjar	*Caprimulgus noctitherus*	NA
—Dusky Nightjar	*Caprimulgus saturatus*	MA
—Band-winged Nightjar	*Caprimulgus longirostris*	SA
—White-tailed Nightjar	*Caprimulgus cayennensis*	LA
—White-winged Nightjar	*Caprimulgus candicans*	SA
—Spot-tailed Nightjar	*Caprimulgus maculicaudus*	LA
—Little Nightjar	*Caprimulgus parvulus*	SA
—Anthony's Nightjar	*Caprimulgus anthonyi*	SA
—Cayenne Nightjar	*Caprimulgus maculosus*	SA
—Blackish Nightjar	*Caprimulgus nigrescens*	SA
—Roraiman Nightjar	*Caprimulgus whitelyi*	SA
—Pygmy Nightjar	*Caprimulgus hirundinaceus*	SA
—Red-necked Nightjar	*Caprimulgus ruficollis*	EU, AF

INTERNATIONAL ENGLISH NAME	SCIENTIFIC NAME	REGION(S)
—Grey Nightjar	*Caprimulgus indicus*	OR
—European Nightjar	*Caprimulgus europaeus*	EU
—Sombre Nightjar	*Caprimulgus fraenatus*	AF
—Rufous-cheeked Nightjar	*Caprimulgus rufigena*	AF
—Egyptian Nightjar	*Caprimulgus aegyptius*	EU, AF
—Sykes's Nightjar	*Caprimulgus mahrattensis*	EU
—Vaurie's Nightjar	*Caprimulgus centralasicus*	EU
—Nubian Nightjar	*Caprimulgus nubicus*	AF
—Golden Nightjar	*Caprimulgus eximius*	AF
—Jerdon's Nightjar	*Caprimulgus atripennis*	OR
—Large-tailed Nightjar	*Caprimulgus macrurus*	OR, AU
—Philippine Nightjar	*Caprimulgus manillensis*	OR
—Sulawesi Nightjar	*Caprimulgus celebensis*	AU
—Donaldson-Smith's Nightjar	*Caprimulgus donaldsoni*	AF
—Black-shouldered Nightjar	*Caprimulgus nigriscapularis*	AF
—Fiery-necked Nightjar	*Caprimulgus pectoralis*	AF
—Montane Nightjar	*Caprimulgus poliocephalus*	AF
—Ruwenzori Nightjar	*Caprimulgus ruwenzorii*	AF
—Indian Nightjar	*Caprimulgus asiaticus*	OR
—Madagascar Nightjar	*Caprimulgus madagascariensis*	AF
—Swamp Nightjar	*Caprimulgus natalensis*	AF
—Nechisar Nightjar	*Caprimulgus solala*	AF
—Plain Nightjar	*Caprimulgus inornatus*	AF
—Star-spotted Nightjar	*Caprimulgus stellatus*	AF
—Savanna Nightjar	*Caprimulgus affinis*	OR
—Freckled Nightjar	*Caprimulgus tristigma*	AF
—Bonaparte's Nightjar	*Caprimulgus concretus*	OR
—Salvadori's Nightjar	*Caprimulgus pulchellus*	OR
—Prigogine's Nightjar	*Caprimulgus prigoginei*	AF
—Collared Nightjar	*Caprimulgus enarratus*	AF
—Bates's Nightjar	*Caprimulgus batesi*	AF
—Long-tailed Nightjar	*Caprimulgus climacurus*	AF
—Slender-tailed Nightjar	*Caprimulgus clarus*	AF
—Square-tailed Nightjar	*Caprimulgus fossii*	AF
—Standard-winged Nightjar	*Macrodipteryx longipennis*	AF
—Pennant-winged Nightjar	*Macrodipteryx vexillarius*	AF
—Ladder-tailed Nightjar	*Hydropsalis climacocerca*	SA
—Scissor-tailed Nightjar	*Hydropsalis torquata*	SA
—Swallow-tailed Nightjar	*Uropsalis segmentata*	SA
—Lyre-tailed Nightjar	*Uropsalis lyra*	SA
—Long-trained Nightjar	*Macropsalis forcipata*	SA
—Sickle-winged Nightjar	*Eleothreptus anomalus*	SA
OWLET-NIGHTJARS	**Family Aegothelidae**	
—Feline Owlet-Nightjar	*Euaegotheles insignis*	AU
—Spangled Owlet-Nightjar	*Euaegotheles tatei*	AU
—Moluccan Owlet-Nightjar	*Euaegotheles crinifrons*	AU
—Wallace's Owlet-Nightjar	*Aegotheles wallacii*	AU
—Archbold's Owlet-Nightjar	*Aegotheles archboldi*	AU
—Mountain Owlet-Nightjar	*Aegotheles albertisi*	AU
—Enigmatic Owlet-Nightjar	*Aegotheles savesi*	AU
—Barred Owlet-Nightjar	*Aegotheles bennettii*	AU
—Australian Owlet-Nightjar	*Aegotheles cristatus*	AU

INTERNATIONAL ENGLISH NAME	SCIENTIFIC NAME	REGION(S)
	ORDER APODIFORMES	
TREESWIFTS	**Family Hemiprocnidae**	
—Crested Treeswift	*Hemiprocne coronata*	OR
—Grey-rumped Treeswift	*Hemiprocne longipennis*	OR, AU
—Whiskered Treeswift	*Hemiprocne comata*	OR
—Moustached Treeswift	*Hemiprocne mystacea*	OR
SWIFTS	**Family Apodidae**	
—Spot-fronted Swift	*Cypseloides cherriei*	LA
—White-chinned Swift	*Cypseloides cryptus*	LA
—White-fronted Swift	*Cypseloides storeri*	MA
—Sooty Swift	*Cypseloides fumigatus*	SA
—Rothschild's Swift	*Cypseloides rothschildi*	SA
—American Black Swift	*Cypseloides niger*	NA, MA
—White-chested Swift	*Cypseloides lemosi*	SA
—Great Dusky Swift	*Cypseloides senex*	SA
—Tepui Swift	*Cypseloides phelpsi*	SA
—Chestnut-collared Swift	*Cypseloides rutilus*	LA
—White-collared Swift	*Streptoprocne zonaris*	LA
—Biscutate Swift	*Streptoprocne biscutata*	SA
—White-naped Swift	*Streptoprocne semicollaris*	MA
—Giant Swiftlet	*Hydrochous gigas*	OR
—Glossy Swiftlet	*Collocalia esculenta*	OR, AU
—Cave Swiftlet	*Collocalia linchi*	OR
—Pygmy Swiftlet	*Collocalia troglodytes*	OR
—Seychelles Swiftlet	*Aerodramus elaphrus*	IO
—Mascarene Swiftlet	*Aerodramus francicus*	IO
—Indian Swiftlet	*Aerodramus unicolor*	OR
—Philippine Swiftlet	*Aerodramus mearnsi`*	OR
—Moluccan Swiftlet	*Aerodramus infuscatus*	AU
—Mountain Swiftlet	*Aerodramus hirundinaceus*	AU
—White-rumped Swiftlet	*Aerodramus spodiopygius*	AU
—Australian Swiftlet	*Aerodramus terraereginae*	AU
—Himalayan Swiftlet	*Aerodramus brevirostris*	OR
—Volcano Swiftlet	*Aerodramus vulcanorum*	OR
—Whitehead's Swiftlet	*Aerodramus whiteheadi*	OR
—Bare-legged Swiftlet	*Aerodramus nuditarsus*	AU
—Mayr's Swiftlet	*Aerodramus orientalis*	AU
—Mossy-nest Swiftlet	*Aerodramus salangana*	OR
—Uniform Swiftlet	*Aerodramus vanikorensis*	AU
—Palau Swiftlet	*Aerodramus pelewensis*	AU
—Mariana Swiftlet	*Aerodramus bartschi*	PO
—Island Swiftlet	*Aerodramus inquieta*	PO
—Tahiti Swiftlet	*Aerodramus leucophaeus*	PO
—Atiu Swiftlet	*Aerodramus sawtelli*	PO
—Marquesan Swiftlet	*Aerodramus ocistus*	PO
—Black-nest Swiftlet	*Aerodramus maximus*	OR
—Edible-nest Swiftlet	*Aerodramus fuciphagus*	OR, AU
—Germain's Swiftlet	*Aerodramus germani*	OR
—Three-toed Swiftlet	*Aerodramus papuensis*	AU
—Scarce Swift	*Schoutedenapus myoptilus*	AF
—Schouteden's Swift	*Schoutedenapus schoutedeni*	AF

INTERNATIONAL ENGLISH NAME	SCIENTIFIC NAME	REGION(S)
—Philippine Spine-tailed Swift	*Mearnsia picina*	OR
—Papuan Spine-tailed Swift	*Mearnsia novaeguineae*	AU
—Madagascar Spinetail	*Zoonavena grandidieri*	AF
—Sao Tome Spinetail	*Zoonavena thomensis*	AF
—White-rumped Spinetail	*Zoonavena sylvatica*	OR
—Mottled Spinetail	*Telacanthura ussheri*	AF
—Black Spinetail	*Telacanthura melanopygia*	AF
—Silver-rumped Spinetail	*Rhaphidura leucopygialis*	OR
—Sabine's Spinetail	*Rhaphidura sabini*	AF
—Cassin's Spinetail	*Neafrapus cassini*	AF
—Böhm's Spinetail	*Neafrapus boehmi*	AF
—White-throated Needletail	*Hirundapus caudacutus*	EU
—Silver-backed Needletail	*Hirundapus cochinchinensis*	OR
—Brown-backed Needletail	*Hirundapus giganteus*	OR
—Purple Needletail	*Hirundapus celebensis*	OR, AU
—Lesser Antillean Swift	*Chaetura martinica*	NA
—Band-rumped Swift	*Chaetura spinicaudus*	LA
—Costa Rican Swift	*Chaetura fumosa*	MA
—Pale-rumped Swift	*Chaetura egregia*	SA
—Grey-rumped Swift	*Chaetura cinereiventris*	LA
—Vaux's Swift	*Chaetura vauxi*	NA, LA
—Ashy-tailed Swift	*Chaetura meridionalis*	SA
—Chimney Swift	*Chaetura pelagica*	NA
—Chapman's Swift	*Chaetura chapmani*	LA
—Mato Grosso Swift	*Chaetura viridipennis*	SA
—Short-tailed Swift	*Chaetura brachyura*	LA
—Tumbes Swift	*Chaetura ocypetes*	SA
—White-throated Swift	*Aeronautes saxatalis*	NA, MA
—White-tipped Swift	*Aeronautes montivagus*	SA
—Andean Swift	*Aeronautes andecolus*	SA
—Antillean Palm Swift	*Tachornis phoenicobia*	NA
—Pygmy Palm Swift	*Tachornis furcata*	SA
—Neotropical Palm Swift	*Tachornis squamata*	SA
—Great Swallow-tailed Swift	*Panyptila sanctihieronymi*	MA
—Lesser Swallow-tailed Swift	*Panyptila cayennensis*	LA
—African Palm Swift	*Cypsiurus parvus*	AF
—Asian Palm Swift	*Cypsiurus balasiensis*	OR
—Alpine Swift	*Tachymarptis melba*	EU, AF
—Mottled Swift	*Tachymarptis aequatorialis*	AF
—Cape Verde Swift	*Apus alexandri*	AF
—Common Swift	*Apus apus*	EU
—Plain Swift	*Apus unicolor*	AF
—Nyanza Swift	*Apus niansae*	AF
—Pallid Swift	*Apus pallidus*	EU, AF
—African Black Swift	*Apus barbatus*	AF
—Malagasy Black Swift	*Apus balstoni*	AF
—Fernando Po Swift	*Apus sladeniae*	AF
—Forbes-Watson's Swift	*Apus berliozi*	AF
—Bradfield's Swift	*Apus bradfieldi*	AF
—Fork-tailed Swift	*Apus pacificus*	EU
—Dark-rumped Swift	*Apus acuticauda*	OR
—Little Swift	*Apus affinis*	AF
—House Swift	*Apus nipalensis*	OR

INTERNATIONAL ENGLISH NAME	SCIENTIFIC NAME	REGION(S)
—Horus Swift	*Apus horus*	AF
—White-rumped Swift	*Apus caffer*	AF
—Bates's Swift	*Apus batesi*	AF
HUMMINGBIRDS	**Family Trochilidae**	
—Saw-billed Hermit	*Ramphodon naevius*	SA
—White-tipped Sicklebill	*Eutoxeres aquila*	LA
—Buff-tailed Sicklebill	*Eutoxeres condamini*	SA
—Hook-billed Hermit	*Glaucis dohrnii*	SA
—Rufous-breasted Hermit	*Glaucis hirsutus*	LA
—Bronzy Hermit	*Glaucis aeneus*	LA
—Band-tailed Barbthroat	*Threnetes ruckeri*	LA
—Pale-tailed Barbthroat	*Threnetes niger*	SA
—Broad-tipped Hermit	*Anopetia gounellei*	SA
—White-whiskered Hermit	*Phaethornis yaruqui*	SA
—Green Hermit	*Phaethornis guy*	LA
—White-bearded Hermit	*Phaethornis hispidus*	SA
—Long-billed Hermit	*Phaethornis longirostris*	LA
—Mexican Hermit	*Phaethornis mexicanus*	MA
—Baron's Hermit	*Phaethornis baroni*	SA
—Long-tailed Hermit	*Phaethornis superciliosus*	SA
—Great-billed Hermit	*Phaethornis malaris*	SA
—Tawny-bellied Hermit	*Phaethornis syrmatophorus*	SA
—Koepcke's Hermit	*Phaethornis koepckeae*	SA
—Needle-billed Hermit	*Phaethornis philippii*	SA
—Straight-billed Hermit	*Phaethornis bourcieri*	SA
—Pale-bellied Hermit	*Phaethornis anthophilus*	LA
—Scale-throated Hermit	*Phaethornis eurynome*	SA
—Planalto Hermit	*Phaethornis pretrei*	SA
—Sooty-capped Hermit	*Phaethornis augusti*	SA
—Buff-bellied Hermit	*Phaethornis subochraceus*	SA
—Dusky-throated Hermit	*Phaethornis squalidus*	SA
—Streak-throated Hermit	*Phaethornis rupurumii*	SA
—Little Hermit	*Phaethornis longuemareus*	SA
—Minute Hermit	*Phaethornis idaliae*	SA
—Cinnamon-throated Hermit	*Phaethornis nattereri*	SA
—Reddish Hermit	*Phaethornis ruber*	SA
—White-browed Hermit	*Phaethornis stuarti*	SA
—Black-throated Hermit	*Phaethornis atrimentalis*	SA
—Stripe-throated Hermit	*Phaethornis striigularis*	LA
—Grey-chinned Hermit	*Phaethornis griseogularis*	SA
—Tooth-billed Hummingbird	*Androdon aequatorialis*	LA
—Green-fronted Lancebill	*Doryfera ludovicae*	LA
—Blue-fronted Lancebill	*Doryfera johannae*	SA
—Scaly-breasted Hummingbird	*Campylopterus cuvierii*	LA
—Wedge-tailed Sabrewing	*Campylopterus curvipennis*	MA
—Long-tailed Sabrewing	*Campylopterus excellens*	MA
—Grey-breasted Sabrewing	*Campylopterus largipennis*	SA
—Rufous Sabrewing	*Campylopterus rufus*	MA
—Rufous-breasted Sabrewing	*Campylopterus hyperythrus*	SA
—Violet Sabrewing	*Campylopterus hemileucurus*	MA
—White-tailed Sabrewing	*Campylopterus ensipennis*	SA
—Lazuline Sabrewing	*Campylopterus falcatus*	SA

INTERNATIONAL ENGLISH NAME	SCIENTIFIC NAME	REGION(S)
—Santa Marta Sabrewing	*Campylopterus phainopeplus*	SA
—Napo Sabrewing	*Campylopterus villaviscensio*	SA
—Buff-breasted Sabrewing	*Campylopterus duidae*	SA
—Sombre Hummingbird	*Aphantochroa cirrochloris*	SA
—Swallow-tailed Hummingbird	*Eupetomena macroura*	SA
—White-necked Jacobin	*Florisuga mellivora*	LA
—Black Jacobin	*Florisuga fusca*	SA
—Brown Violetear	*Colibri delphinae*	LA
—Green Violetear	*Colibri thalassinus*	LA
—Sparkling Violetear	*Colibri coruscans*	SA
—White-vented Violetear	*Colibri serrirostris*	SA
—Green-throated Mango	*Anthracothorax viridigula*	SA
—Green-breasted Mango	*Anthracothorax prevostii*	LA
—Black-throated Mango	*Anthracothorax nigricollis*	LA
—Veraguan Mango	*Anthracothorax veraguensis*	MA
—Antillean Mango	*Anthracothorax dominicus*	NA
—Green Mango	*Anthracothorax viridis*	NA
—Jamaican Mango	*Anthracothorax mango*	NA
—Fiery-tailed Awlbill	*Avocettula recurvirostris*	SA
—Crimson Topaz	*Topaza pella*	SA
—Fiery Topaz	*Topaza pyra*	SA
—Purple-throated Carib	*Eulampis jugularis*	NA
—Green-throated Carib	*Eulampis holosericeus*	NA
—Ruby Topaz	*Chrysolampis mosquitus*	LA
—Antillean Crested Hummingbird	*Orthorhyncus cristatus*	NA
—Violet-headed Hummingbird	*Klais guimeti*	LA
—Black-breasted Plovercrest	*Stephanoxis lalandi*	SA
—Emerald-chinned Hummingbird	*Abeillia abeillei*	MA
—Tufted Coquette	*Lophornis ornatus*	SA
—Dot-eared Coquette	*Lophornis gouldii*	SA
—Frilled Coquette	*Lophornis magnificus*	SA
—Short-crested Coquette	*Lophornis brachylophus*	MA
—Rufous-crested Coquette	*Lophornis delattrei*	LA
—Spangled Coquette	*Lophornis stictolophus*	SA
—Festive Coquette	*Lophornis chalybeus*	SA
—Peacock Coquette	*Lophornis pavoninus*	SA
—Black-crested Coquette	*Lophornis helenae*	MA
—White-crested Coquette	*Lophornis adorabilis*	MA
—Wire-crested Thorntail	*Popelairia popelairii*	SA
—Black-bellied Thorntail	*Popelairia langsdorffi*	SA
—Letitia's Thorntail	*Popelairia letitiae*	SA
—Green Thorntail	*Popelairia conversii*	LA
—Racket-tailed Coquette	*Discosura longicaudus*	SA
—Red-billed Streamertail	*Trochilus polytmus*	NA
—Black-billed Streamertail	*Trochilus scitulus*	NA
—Blue-chinned Sapphire	*Chlorestes notatus*	SA
—Golden-crowned Emerald	*Chlorostilbon auriceps*	MA
—Cozumel Emerald	*Chlorostilbon forficatus*	MA
—Canivet's Emerald	*Chlorostilbon canivetii*	MA
—Salvin's Emerald	*Chlorostilbon salvini*	MA
—Garden Emerald	*Chlorostilbon assimilis*	MA
—Blue-tailed Emerald	*Chlorostilbon mellisugus*	SA
—Western Emerald	*Chlorostilbon melanorhynchus*	SA

INTERNATIONAL ENGLISH NAME	SCIENTIFIC NAME	REGION(S)
__Red-billed Emerald	*Chlorostilbon gibsoni*	SA
__Chiribiquete Emerald	*Chlorostilbon olivaresi*	SA
__Glittering-bellied Emerald	*Chlorostilbon aureoventris*	SA
__Cuban Emerald	*Chlorostilbon ricordii*	NA
__Hispaniolan Emerald	*Chlorostilbon swainsonii*	NA
__Puerto Rican Emerald	*Chlorostilbon maugaeus*	NA
__Coppery Emerald	*Chlorostilbon russatus*	SA
__Narrow-tailed Emerald	*Chlorostilbon stenurus*	SA
__Green-tailed Emerald	*Chlorostilbon alice*	SA
__Short-tailed Emerald	*Chlorostilbon poortmani*	SA
__Fiery-throated Hummingbird	*Panterpe insignis*	MA
__White-tailed Emerald	*Elvira chionura*	MA
__Coppery-headed Emerald	*Elvira cupreiceps*	MA
__Oaxaca Hummingbird	*Eupherusa cyanophrys*	MA
__White-tailed Hummingbird	*Eupherusa poliocerca*	MA
__Stripe-tailed Hummingbird	*Eupherusa eximia*	MA
__Black-bellied Hummingbird	*Eupherusa nigriventris*	MA
__Pirre Hummingbird	*Goethalsia bella*	LA
__Violet-capped Hummingbird	*Goldmania violiceps*	LA
__Dusky Hummingbird	*Cynanthus sordidus*	MA
__Broad-billed Hummingbird	*Cynanthus latirostris*	NA, MA
__Doubleday's Hummingbird	*Cynanthus doubledayi*	MA
__Blue-headed Hummingbird	*Cyanophaia bicolor*	NA
__Mexican Woodnymph	*Thalurania ridgwayi*	MA
__Violet-crowned Woodnymph	*Thalurania colombica*	LA
__Green-crowned Woodnymph	*Thalurania fannyi*	LA
__Emerald-bellied Woodnymph	*Thalurania hypochlora*	SA
__Fork-tailed Woodnymph	*Thalurania furcata*	SA
__Long-tailed Woodnymph	*Thalurania watertonii*	SA
__Violet-capped Woodnymph	*Thalurania glaucopis*	SA
__Violet-bellied Hummingbird	*Damophila julie*	LA
__Sapphire-throated Hummingbird	*Lepidopyga coeruleogularis*	LA
__Sapphire-bellied Hummingbird	*Lepidopyga lilliae*	SA
__Shining-green Hummingbird	*Lepidopyga goudoti*	SA
__Blue-throated Sapphire	*Hylocharis eliciae*	LA
__Rufous-throated Sapphire	*Hylocharis sapphirina*	SA
__White-chinned Sapphire	*Hylocharis cyanus*	SA
__Gilded Sapphire	*Hylocharis chrysura*	SA
__Blue-headed Sapphire	*Hylocharis grayi*	SA
__Humboldt's Sapphire	*Hylocharis humboldtii*	LA
__Golden-tailed Sapphire	*Chrysuronia oenone*	SA
__White-throated Hummingbird	*Leucochloris albicollis*	SA
__White-tailed Goldenthroat	*Polytmus guainumbi*	SA
__Tepui Goldenthroat	*Polytmus milleri*	SA
__Green-tailed Goldenthroat	*Polytmus theresiae*	SA
__Buffy Hummingbird	*Leucippus fallax*	SA
__Tumbes Hummingbird	*Leucippus baeri*	SA
__Spot-throated Hummingbird	*Leucippus taczanowskii*	SA
__Olive-spotted Hummingbird	*Leucippus chlorocercus*	SA
__White-bellied Hummingbird	*Leucippus chionogaster*	SA
__Green-and-white Hummingbird	*Leucippus viridicauda*	SA
__Many-spotted Hummingbird	*Taphrospilus hypostictus*	SA
__Cinnamon Hummingbird	*Amazilia rutila*	MA

INTERNATIONAL ENGLISH NAME	SCIENTIFIC NAME	REGION(S)
—Buff-bellied Hummingbird	*Amazilia yucatanensis*	MA
—Rufous-tailed Hummingbird	*Amazilia tzacatl*	LA
—Escudo Hummingbird	*Amazilia handleyi*	MA
—Chestnut-bellied Hummingbird	*Amazilia castaneiventris*	LA
—Amazilia Hummingbird	*Amazilia amazilia*	LA
—Loja Hummingbird	*Amazilia alticola*	LA
—Plain-bellied Emerald	*Amazilia leucogaster*	SA
—Versicolored Emerald	*Amazilia versicolor*	SA
—Rondonia Emerald	*Amazilia rondoniae*	SA
—White-chested Emerald	*Amazilia brevirostris*	SA
—Andean Emerald	*Amazilia franciae*	SA
—White-bellied Emerald	*Amazilia candida*	MA
—Azure-crowned Hummingbird	*Amazilia cyanocephala*	MA
—Violet-crowned Hummingbird	*Amazilia violiceps*	NA, MA
—Green-fronted Hummingbird	*Amazilia viridifrons*	MA
—Cinnamon-sided Hummingbird	*Amazilia wagneri*	MA
—Glittering-throated Emerald	*Amazilia fimbriata*	SA
—Sapphire-spangled Emerald	*Amazilia lactea*	SA
—Blue-chested Hummingbird	*Amazilia amabilis*	LA
—Charming Hummingbird	*Amazilia decora*	MA
—Purple-chested Hummingbird	*Amazilia rosenbergi*	SA
—Mangrove Hummingbird	*Amazilia boucardi*	MA
—Honduran Emerald	*Amazilia luciae*	MA
—Steely-vented Hummingbird	*Amazilia saucerrottei*	LA
—Indigo-capped Hummingbird	*Amazilia cyanifrons*	SA
—Snowy-bellied Hummingbird	*Amazilia edward*	MA
—Blue-tailed Hummingbird	*Amazilia cyanura*	MA
—Berylline Hummingbird	*Amazilia beryllina*	MA
—Green-bellied Hummingbird	*Amazilia viridigaster*	SA
—Tepui Hummingbird	*Amazilia cupreicauda*	SA
—Copper-rumped Hummingbird	*Amazilia tobaci*	SA
—Snowcap	*Microchera albocoronata*	MA
—Blossomcrown	*Anthocephala floriceps*	SA
—White-vented Plumeleteer	*Chalybura buffonii*	LA
—Bronze-tailed Plumeleteer	*Chalybura urochrysia*	LA
—Blue-throated Mountaingem	*Lampornis clemenciae*	NA, MA
—Amethyst-throated Mountaingem	*Lampornis amethystinus*	MA
—Green-throated Mountaingem	*Lampornis viridipallens*	MA
—Green-breasted Mountaingem	*Lampornis sybillae*	MA
—White-bellied Mountaingem	*Lampornis hemileucus*	MA
—Purple-throated Mountaingem	*Lampornis calolaemus*	MA
—White-throated Mountaingem	*Lampornis castaneoventris*	MA
—Grey-tailed Mountaingem	*Lampornis cinereicauda*	MA
—Xantus's Hummingbird	*Basilinna xantusii*	MA
—White-eared Hummingbird	*Basilinna leucotis*	MA
—Garnet-throated Hummingbird	*Lamprolaima rhami*	MA
—Speckled Hummingbird	*Adelomyia melanogenys*	SA
—Ecuadorian Piedtail	*Phlogophilus hemileucurus*	SA
—Peruvian Piedtail	*Phlogophilus harterti*	SA
—Brazilian Ruby	*Clytolaema rubricauda*	SA
—Velvet-browed Brilliant	*Heliodoxa xanthogonys*	SA
—Pink-throated Brilliant	*Heliodoxa gularis*	SA
—Rufous-webbed Brilliant	*Heliodoxa branickii*	SA

INTERNATIONAL ENGLISH NAME	SCIENTIFIC NAME	REGION(S)
—Black-throated Brilliant	*Heliodoxa schreibersii*	SA
—Gould's Jewelfront	*Heliodoxa aurescens*	SA
—Fawn-breasted Brilliant	*Heliodoxa rubinoides*	SA
—Green-crowned Brilliant	*Heliodoxa jacula*	LA
—Empress Brilliant	*Heliodoxa imperatrix*	SA
—Violet-fronted Brilliant	*Heliodoxa leadbeateri*	SA
—Magnificent Hummingbird	*Eugenes fulgens*	NA, MA
—Scissor-tailed Hummingbird	*Hylonympha macrocerca*	SA
—Violet-chested Hummingbird	*Sternoclyta cyanopectus*	SA
—White-tailed Hillstar	*Urochroa bougueri*	SA
—Buff-tailed Coronet	*Boissonneaua flavescens*	SA
—Chestnut-breasted Coronet	*Boissonneaua matthewsii*	SA
—Velvet-purple Coronet	*Boissonneaua jardini*	SA
—Shining Sunbeam	*Aglaeactis cupripennis*	SA
—Purple-backed Sunbeam	*Aglaeactis aliciae*	SA
—White-tufted Sunbeam	*Aglaeactis castelnaudii*	SA
—Black-hooded Sunbeam	*Aglaeactis pamela*	SA
—Ecuadorian Hillstar	*Oreotrochilus chimborazo*	SA
—Andean Hillstar	*Oreotrochilus estella*	SA
—White-sided Hillstar	*Oreotrochilus leucopleurus*	SA
—Black-breasted Hillstar	*Oreotrochilus melanogaster*	SA
—Wedge-tailed Hillstar	*Oreotrochilus adela*	SA
—Mountain Velvetbreast	*Lafresnaya lafresnayi*	SA
—Bronzy Inca	*Coeligena coeligena*	SA
—Brown Inca	*Coeligena wilsoni*	SA
—Black Inca	*Coeligena prunellei*	SA
—Collared Inca	*Coeligena torquata*	SA
—Gould's Inca	*Coeligena inca*	SA
—White-tailed Starfrontlet	*Coeligena phalerata*	SA
—Golden-bellied Starfrontlet	*Coeligena bonapartei*	SA
—Golden-tailed Starfrontlet	*Coeligena eos*	SA
—Blue-throated Starfrontlet	*Coeligena helianthea*	SA
—Buff-winged Starfrontlet	*Coeligena lutetiae*	SA
—Violet-throated Starfrontlet	*Coeligena violifer*	SA
—Rainbow Starfrontlet	*Coeligena iris*	SA
—Sword-billed Hummingbird	*Ensifera ensifera*	SA
—Great Sapphirewing	*Pterophanes cyanopterus*	SA
—Giant Hummingbird	*Patagona gigas*	SA
—Green-backed Firecrown	*Sephanoides sephaniodes*	SA
—Juan Fernandez Firecrown	*Sephanoides fernandensis*	SA
—Orange-throated Sunangel	*Heliangelus mavors*	SA
—Amethyst-throated Sunangel	*Heliangelus amethysticollis*	SA
—Longuemare's Sunangel	*Heliangelus clarisse*	SA
—Gorgeted Sunangel	*Heliangelus strophianus*	SA
—Tourmaline Sunangel	*Heliangelus exortis*	SA
—Flame-throated Sunangel	*Heliangelus micraster*	SA
—Purple-throated Sunangel	*Heliangelus viola*	SA
—Bogota Sunangel	*Heliangelus zusii*	SA
—Royal Sunangel	*Heliangelus regalis*	SA
—Black-breasted Puffleg	*Eriocnemis nigrivestis*	SA
—Glowing Puffleg	*Eriocnemis vestita*	SA
—Black-thighed Puffleg	*Eriocnemis derbyi*	SA
—Turquoise-throated Puffleg	*Eriocnemis godini*	SA

INTERNATIONAL ENGLISH NAME	SCIENTIFIC NAME	REGION(S)
—Coppery-bellied Puffleg	*Eriocnemis cupreoventris*	SA
—Sapphire-vented Puffleg	*Eriocnemis luciani*	SA
—Coppery-naped Puffleg	*Eriocnemis sapphiropygia*	SA
—Golden-breasted Puffleg	*Eriocnemis mosquera*	SA
—Blue-capped Puffleg	*Eriocnemis glaucopoides*	SA
—Colorful Puffleg	*Eriocnemis mirabilis*	SA
—Emerald-bellied Puffleg	*Eriocnemis alinae*	SA
—Greenish Puffleg	*Haplophaedia aureliae*	LA
—Buff-thighed Puffleg	*Haplophaedia assimilis*	SA
—Hoary Puffleg	*Haplophaedia lugens*	SA
—Purple-bibbed Whitetip	*Urosticte benjamini*	SA
—Rufous-vented Whitetip	*Urosticte ruficrissa*	SA
—Booted Racket-tail	*Ocreatus underwoodii*	SA
—Black-tailed Trainbearer	*Lesbia victoriae*	SA
—Green-tailed Trainbearer	*Lesbia nuna*	SA
—Red-tailed Comet	*Sappho sparganura*	SA
—Bronze-tailed Comet	*Polyonymus caroli*	SA
—Black-backed Thornbill	*Ramphomicron dorsale*	SA
—Purple-backed Thornbill	*Ramphomicron microrhynchum*	SA
—Bearded Mountaineer	*Oreonympha nobilis*	SA
—Bearded Helmetcrest	*Oxypogon guerinii*	SA
—Tyrian Metaltail	*Metallura tyrianthina*	SA
—Perija Metaltail	*Metallura iracunda*	SA
—Viridian Metaltail	*Metallura williami*	SA
—Violet-throated Metaltail	*Metallura baroni*	SA
—Neblina Metaltail	*Metallura odomae*	SA
—Coppery Metaltail	*Metallura theresiae*	SA
—Fiery-throated Metaltail	*Metallura eupogon*	SA
—Scaled Metaltail	*Metallura aeneocauda*	SA
—Black Metaltail	*Metallura phoebe*	SA
—Rufous-capped Thornbill	*Chalcostigma ruficeps*	SA
—Olivaceous Thornbill	*Chalcostigma olivaceum*	SA
—Blue-mantled Thornbill	*Chalcostigma stanleyi*	SA
—Bronze-tailed Thornbill	*Chalcostigma heteropogon*	SA
—Rainbow-bearded Thornbill	*Chalcostigma herrani*	SA
—Mountain Avocetbill	*Opisthoprora euryptera*	SA
—Grey-bellied Comet	*Taphrolesbia griseiventris*	SA
—Long-tailed Sylph	*Aglaiocercus kingi*	SA
—Venezuelan Sylph	*Aglaiocercus berlepschi*	SA
—Violet-tailed Sylph	*Aglaiocercus coelestis*	SA
—Hyacinth Visorbearer	*Augastes scutatus*	SA
—Hooded Visorbearer	*Augastes lumachella*	SA
—Wedge-billed Hummingbird	*Schistes geoffroyi*	SA
—Purple-crowned Fairy	*Heliothryx barroti*	LA
—Black-eared Fairy	*Heliothryx auritus*	SA
—Horned Sungem	*Heliactin bilopha*	SA
—Marvelous Spatuletail	*Loddigesia mirabilis*	SA
—Plain-capped Starthroat	*Heliomaster constantii*	MA
—Long-billed Starthroat	*Heliomaster longirostris*	LA
—Stripe-breasted Starthroat	*Heliomaster squamosus*	SA
—Blue-tufted Starthroat	*Heliomaster furcifer*	SA
—Oasis Hummingbird	*Rhodopis vesper*	SA
—Peruvian Sheartail	*Thaumastura cora*	SA

INTERNATIONAL ENGLISH NAME	SCIENTIFIC NAME	REGION(S)
—Sparkling-tailed Woodstar	*Tilmatura dupontii*	MA
—Slender Sheartail	*Doricha enicura*	MA
—Mexican Sheartail	*Doricha eliza*	MA
—Amethyst Woodstar	*Calliphlox amethystina*	SA
—Bahama Woodstar	*Calliphlox evelynae*	NA
—Magenta-throated Woodstar	*Calliphlox bryantae*	MA
—Purple-throated Woodstar	*Calliphlox mitchellii*	LA
—Slender-tailed Woodstar	*Microstilbon burmeisteri*	SA
—Lucifer Sheartail	*Calothorax lucifer*	NA
—Beautiful Sheartail	*Calothorax pulcher*	MA
—Vervain Hummingbird	*Mellisuga minima*	NA
—Bee Hummingbird	*Mellisuga helenae*	NA
—Ruby-throated Hummingbird	*Archilochus colubris*	NA
—Black-chinned Hummingbird	*Archilochus alexandri*	NA
—Anna's Hummingbird	*Calypte anna*	NA
—Costa's Hummingbird	*Calypte costae*	NA
—Bumblebee Hummingbird	*Atthis heloisa*	MA
—Wine-throated Hummingbird	*Atthis ellioti*	MA
—Purple-collared Woodstar	*Myrtis fanny*	SA
—Chilean Woodstar	*Eulidia yarrellii*	SA
—Short-tailed Woodstar	*Myrmia micrura*	SA
—White-bellied Woodstar	*Chaetocercus mulsant*	SA
—Little Woodstar	*Chaetocercus bombus*	SA
—Gorgeted Woodstar	*Chaetocercus heliodor*	SA
—Santa Marta Woodstar	*Chaetocercus astreans*	SA
—Esmeraldas Woodstar	*Chaetocercus berlepschi*	SA
—Rufous-shafted Woodstar	*Chaetocercus jourdanii*	SA
—Broad-tailed Hummingbird	*Selasphorus platycercus*	NA
—Rufous Hummingbird	*Selasphorus rufus*	NA
—Allen's Hummingbird	*Selasphorus sasin*	NA
—Volcano Hummingbird	*Selasphorus flammula*	MA
—Glow-throated Hummingbird	*Selasphorus ardens*	MA
—Scintillant Hummingbird	*Selasphorus scintilla*	MA
—Calliope Hummingbird	*Stellula calliope*	NA

ORDER COLIIFORMES

MOUSEBIRDS	**Family Coliidae**	
—Speckled Mousebird	*Colius striatus*	AF
—White-headed Mousebird	*Colius leucocephalus*	AF
—Red-backed Mousebird	*Colius castanotus*	AF
—White-backed Mousebird	*Colius colius*	AF
—Blue-naped Mousebird	*Urocolius macrourus*	AF
—Red-faced Mousebird	*Urocolius indicus*	AF

ORDER TROGONIFORMES

TROGONS	**Family Trogonidae**	
—Narina Trogon	*Apaloderma narina*	AF
—Bare-cheeked Trogon	*Apaloderma aequatoriale*	AF
—Bar-tailed Trogon	*Apaloderma vittatum*	AF
—Blue-tailed Trogon	*Apalharpactes reinwardtii*	OR
—Sumatran Trogon	*Apalharpactes mackloti*	OR
—Malabar Trogon	*Harpactes fasciatus*	OR

INTERNATIONAL ENGLISH NAME	SCIENTIFIC NAME	REGION(S)
—Red-naped Trogon	*Harpactes kasumba*	OR
—Diard's Trogon	*Harpactes diardii*	OR
—Philippine Trogon	*Harpactes ardens*	OR
—Whitehead's Trogon	*Harpactes whiteheadi*	OR
—Cinnamon-rumped Trogon	*Harpactes orrhophaeus*	OR
—Scarlet-rumped Trogon	*Harpactes duvaucelii*	OR
—Orange-breasted Trogon	*Harpactes oreskios*	OR
—Red-headed Trogon	*Harpactes erythrocephalus*	OR
—Ward's Trogon	*Harpactes wardi*	OR
—Cuban Trogon	*Priotelus temnurus*	NA
—Hispaniolan Trogon	*Priotelus roseigaster*	NA
—Black-headed Trogon	*Trogon melanocephalus*	MA
—Citreoline Trogon	*Trogon citreolus*	MA
—Amazonian White-tailed Trogon	*Trogon viridis*	SA
—Western White-tailed Trogon	*Trogon chionurus*	LA
—Baird's Trogon	*Trogon bairdii*	MA
—Surucua Trogon	*Trogon surrucura*	SA
—Blue-crowned Trogon	*Trogon curucui*	SA
—Violaceous Trogon	*Trogon violaceus*	SA
—Gartered Trogon	*Trogon caligatus*	LA
—Mountain Trogon	*Trogon mexicanus*	MA
—Elegant Trogon	*Trogon elegans*	NA, MA
—Collared Trogon	*Trogon collaris*	LA
—Masked Trogon	*Trogon personatus*	SA
—Black-throated Trogon	*Trogon rufus*	LA
—Slaty-tailed Trogon	*Trogon massena*	LA
—Lattice-tailed Trogon	*Trogon clathratus*	MA
—Black-tailed Trogon	*Trogon melanurus*	LA
—Ecuadorian Trogon	*Trogon mesurus*	SA
—Choco Trogon	*Trogon comptus*	SA
—Eared Quetzal	*Euptilotis neoxenus*	MA
—Pavonine Quetzal	*Pharomachrus pavoninus*	SA
—Golden-headed Quetzal	*Pharomachrus auriceps*	SA
—White-tipped Quetzal	*Pharomachrus fulgidus*	SA
—Resplendent Quetzal	*Pharomachrus mocinno*	MA
—Crested Quetzal	*Pharomachrus antisianus*	SA

ORDER CORACIIFORMES

ROLLERS	**Family Coraciidae**	
—Purple Roller	*Coracias naevius*	AF
—Indian Roller	*Coracias benghalensis*	EU, OR
—Purple-winged Roller	*Coracias temminckii*	AU
—Racket-tailed Roller	*Coracias spatulatus*	AF
—Lilac-breasted Roller	*Coracias caudatus*	AF
—Abyssinian Roller	*Coracias abyssinicus*	AU
—European Roller	*Coracias garrulus*	EU
—Blue-bellied Roller	*Coracias cyanogaster*	AF
—Blue-throated Roller	*Eurystomus gularis*	AF
—Broad-billed Roller	*Eurystomus glaucurus*	AF
—Oriental Dollarbird	*Eurystomus orientalis*	EU, OR, AU
—Azure Dollarbird	*Eurystomus azureus*	AU

INTERNATIONAL ENGLISH NAME	SCIENTIFIC NAME	REGION(S)
GROUND ROLLERS	**Family Brachypteraciidae**	
—Short-legged Ground Roller	*Brachypteracias leptosomus*	AF
—Scaly Ground Roller	*Geobiastes squamiger*	AF
—Pitta-like Ground Roller	*Atelornis pittoides*	AF
—Rufous-headed Ground Roller	*Atelornis crossleyi*	AF
—Long-tailed Ground Roller	*Uratelornis chimaera*	AF
CUCKOO ROLLER	**Family Leptosomatidae**	
—Cuckoo Roller	*Leptosomus discolor*	AF
KINGFISHERS	**Family Alcedinidae**	
—Green-backed Kingfisher	*Actenoides monachus*	AU
—Scaly-breasted Kingfisher	*Actenoides princeps*	AU
—Moustached Kingfisher	*Actenoides bougainvillei*	AU
—Spotted Wood Kingfisher	*Actenoides lindsayi*	OR
—Hombron's Kingfisher	*Actenoides hombroni*	OR
—Rufous-collared Kingfisher	*Actenoides concretus*	OR
—Hook-billed Kingfisher	*Melidora macrorrhina*	AU
—Banded Kingfisher	*Lacedo pulchella*	OR
—Galatea Paradise Kingfisher	*Tanysiptera galatea*	AU
—Kofiau Paradise Kingfisher	*Tanysiptera ellioti*	AU
—Biak Paradise Kingfisher	*Tanysiptera riedelii*	AU
—Cobalt Paradise Kingfisher	*Tanysiptera carolinae*	AU
—Little Paradise Kingfisher	*Tanysiptera hydrocharis*	AU
—Buff-breasted Paradise Kingfisher	*Tanysiptera sylvia*	AU
—Black-capped Paradise Kingfisher	*Tanysiptera nigriceps*	AU
—Fairy Paradise Kingfisher	*Tanysiptera nympha*	AU
—Russet Paradise Kingfisher	*Tanysiptera danae*	AU
—Lilac Kingfisher	*Cittura cyanotis*	AU
—Shovel-billed Kookaburra	*Clytoceyx rex*	AU
—Laughing Kookaburra	*Dacelo novaeguineae*	AU
—Blue-winged Kookaburra	*Dacelo leachii*	AU
—Spangled Kookaburra	*Dacelo tyro*	AU
—Rufous-bellied Kookaburra	*Dacelo gaudichaud*	AU
—Glittering Kingfisher	*Caridonax fulgidus*	AU
—Stork-billed Kingfisher	*Pelargopsis capensis*	OR
—Great-billed Kingfisher	*Pelargopsis melanorhyncha*	AU
—Brown-winged Kingfisher	*Pelargopsis amauroptera*	OR
—Ruddy Kingfisher	*Halcyon coromanda*	OR
—White-throated Kingfisher	*Halcyon smyrnensis*	OR
—Javan Kingfisher	*Halcyon cyanoventris*	OR
—Chocolate-backed Kingfisher	*Halcyon badia*	AF
—Black-capped Kingfisher	*Halcyon pileata*	OR
—Grey-headed Kingfisher	*Halcyon leucocephala*	AF
—Brown-hooded Kingfisher	*Halcyon albiventris*	AF
—Striped Kingfisher	*Halcyon chelicuti*	AF
—Blue-breasted Kingfisher	*Halcyon malimbica*	AF
—Woodland Kingfisher	*Halcyon senegalensis*	AF
—Mangrove Kingfisher	*Halcyon senegaloides*	AF
—Blue-black Kingfisher	*Todiramphus nigrocyaneus*	AU
—Winchell's Kingfisher	*Todiramphus winchelli*	OR
—Blue-and-white Kingfisher	*Todiramphus diops*	AU

INTERNATIONAL ENGLISH NAME	SCIENTIFIC NAME	REGION(S)
__Lazuli Kingfisher	*Todiramphus lazuli*	AU
__Forest Kingfisher	*Todiramphus macleayii*	AU
__White-mantled Kingfisher	*Todiramphus albonotatus*	AU
__Ultramarine Kingfisher	*Todiramphus leucopygius*	AU
__Vanuatu Kingfisher	*Todiramphus farquhari*	AU
__Sombre Kingfisher	*Todiramphus funebris*	AU
__Collared Kingfisher	*Todiramphus chloris*	OR, AU
__Talaud Kingfisher	*Todiramphus enigma*	AU
__Micronesian Kingfisher	*Todiramphus cinnamominus*	PO
__Beach Kingfisher	*Todiramphus saurophagus*	AU
__Sacred Kingfisher	*Todiramphus sanctus*	OR, AU
__Flat-billed Kingfisher	*Todiramphus recurvirostris*	PO
__Cinnamon-banded Kingfisher	*Todiramphus australasia*	AU
__Chattering Kingfisher	*Todiramphus tutus*	PO
__Mewing Kingfisher	*Todiramphus ruficollaris*	PO
__Society Kingfisher	*Todiramphus veneratus*	PO
__Tuamotu Kingfisher	*Todiramphus gambieri*	PO
__Marquesan Kingfisher	*Todiramphus godeffroyi*	PO
__Red-backed Kingfisher	*Todiramphus pyrrhopygius*	AU
__Yellow-billed Kingfisher	*Syma torotoro*	AU
__Mountain Kingfisher	*Syma megarhyncha*	AU
__African Dwarf Kingfisher	*Ispidina lecontei*	AF
__African Pygmy Kingfisher	*Ispidina picta*	AF
__Madagascar Pygmy Kingfisher	*Ispidina madagascariensis*	AF
__Oriental Dwarf Kingfisher	*Ceyx erithaca*	OR
__Philippine Dwarf Kingfisher	*Ceyx melanurus*	OR
__Sulawesi Dwarf Kingfisher	*Ceyx fallax*	AU
__Chameleon Dwarf Kingfisher	*Ceyx lepidus*	AU
__White-bellied Kingfisher	*Alcedo leucogaster*	AF
__Principe Kingfisher	*Alcedo nais*	AF
__Malachite Kingfisher	*Alcedo cristata*	AF
__Sao Tome Kingfisher	*Alcedo thomensis*	AF
__Malagasy Kingfisher	*Alcedo vintsioides*	AF
__Indigo-banded Kingfisher	*Alcedo cyanopectus*	OR
__Silvery Kingfisher	*Alcedo argentata*	OR
__Cerulean Kingfisher	*Alcedo coerulescens*	OR, AU
__Blue-banded Kingfisher	*Alcedo euryzona*	OR
__Shining-blue Kingfisher	*Alcedo quadribrachys*	AF
__Azure Kingfisher	*Alcedo azurea*	AU
__Bismarck Kingfisher	*Alcedo websteri*	AU
__Little Kingfisher	*Alcedo pusilla*	AU
__Blue-eared Kingfisher	*Alcedo meninting*	OR
__Common Kingfisher	*Alcedo atthis*	EU, OR
__Half-collared Kingfisher	*Alcedo semitorquata*	AF
__Blyth's Kingfisher	*Alcedo hercules*	OR
__American Pygmy Kingfisher	*Chloroceryle aenea*	LA
__Green-and-rufous Kingfisher	*Chloroceryle inda*	LA
__Green Kingfisher	*Chloroceryle americana*	NA, LA
__Amazon Kingfisher	*Chloroceryle amazona*	LA
__Crested Kingfisher	*Megaceryle lugubris*	OR, EU
__Giant Kingfisher	*Megaceryle maxima*	AF
__Ringed Kingfisher	*Megaceryle torquata*	NA, LA

INTERNATIONAL ENGLISH NAME	SCIENTIFIC NAME	REGION(S)
—Belted Kingfisher	*Megaceryle alcyon*	NA
—Pied Kingfisher	*Ceryle rudis*	AF, OR
TODIES	**Family Todidae**	
—Cuban Tody	*Todus multicolor*	NA
—Broad-billed Tody	*Todus subulatus*	NA
—Narrow-billed Tody	*Todus angustirostris*	NA
—Jamaican Tody	*Todus todus*	NA
—Puerto Rican Tody	*Todus mexicanus*	NA
MOTMOTS	**Family Momotidae**	
—Tody Motmot	*Hylomanes momotula*	LA
—Blue-throated Motmot	*Aspatha gularis*	MA
—Russet-crowned Motmot	*Momotus mexicanus*	MA
—Blue-crowned Motmot	*Momotus momota*	LA
—Highland Motmot	*Momotus aequatorialis*	SA
—Rufous Motmot	*Baryphthengus martii*	LA
—Rufous-capped Motmot	*Baryphthengus ruficapillus*	SA
—Keel-billed Motmot	*Electron carinatum*	MA
—Broad-billed Motmot	*Electron platyrhynchum*	LA
—Turquoise-browed Motmot	*Eumomota superciliosa*	MA
BEE-EATERS	**Family Meropidae**	
—Red-bearded Bee-eater	*Nyctyornis amictus*	OR
—Blue-bearded Bee-eater	*Nyctyornis athertoni*	OR
—Purple-bearded Bee-eater	*Meropogon forsteni*	AU
—Black-headed Bee-eater	*Merops breweri*	AF
—Blue-headed Bee-eater	*Merops muelleri*	AF
—Black Bee-eater	*Merops gularis*	AF
—Swallow-tailed Bee-eater	*Merops hirundineus*	AF
—Little Bee-eater	*Merops pusillus*	AF
—Blue-breasted Bee-eater	*Merops variegatus*	AF
—Cinnamon-chested Bee-eater	*Merops oreobates*	AF
—Red-throated Bee-eater	*Merops bullocki*	AF
—White-fronted Bee-eater	*Merops bullockoides*	AF
—Somali Bee-eater	*Merops revoilii*	AF
—White-throated Bee-eater	*Merops albicollis*	AF
—Böhm's Bee-eater	*Merops boehmi*	AF
—Green Bee-eater	*Merops orientalis*	AF, EU, OR
—Blue-cheeked Bee-eater	*Merops persicus*	EU
—Olive Bee-eater	*Merops superciliosus*	AF
—Blue-tailed Bee-eater	*Merops philippinus*	OR
—Rainbow Bee-eater	*Merops ornatus*	AU
—Blue-throated Bee-eater	*Merops viridis*	OR
—Chestnut-headed Bee-eater	*Merops leschenaulti*	OR
—European Bee-eater	*Merops apiaster*	EU
—Rosy Bee-eater	*Merops malimbicus*	AF
—Northern Carmine Bee-eater	*Merops nubicus*	AF
—Southern Carmine Bee-eater	*Merops nubicoides*	AF
HOOPOES	**Family Upupidae**	
—Eurasian Hoopoe	*Upupa epops*	EU, OR
—African Hoopoe	*Upupa africana*	AF
—Madagascar Hoopoe	*Upupa marginata*	AF

INTERNATIONAL ENGLISH NAME	SCIENTIFIC NAME	REGION(S)
WOOD HOOPOES	**Family Phoeniculidae**	
—Forest Wood Hoopoe	*Phoeniculus castaneiceps*	AF
—White-headed Wood Hoopoe	*Phoeniculus bollei*	AF
—Green Wood Hoopoe	*Phoeniculus purpureus*	AF
—Black-billed Wood Hoopoe	*Phoeniculus somaliensis*	AF
—Violet Wood Hoopoe	*Phoeniculus damarensis*	AF
—Grant's Wood Hoopoe	*Phoeniculus granti*	AF
—Black Scimitarbill	*Rhinopomastus aterrimus*	AF
—Common Scimitarbill	*Rhinopomastus cyanomelas*	AF
—Abyssinian Scimitarbill	*Rhinopomastus minor*	AF
HORNBILLS	**Family Bucerotidae**	
—Brown Hornbill	*Anorrhinus tickelli*	OR
—Bushy-crested Hornbill	*Anorrhinus galeritus*	OR
—Crowned Hornbill	*Tockus alboterminatus*	AF
—Bradfield's Hornbill	*Tockus bradfieldi*	AF
—African Pied Hornbill	*Tockus fasciatus*	AF
—Hemprich's Hornbill	*Tockus hemprichii*	AF
—Pale-billed Hornbill	*Tockus pallidirostris*	AF
—African Grey Hornbill	*Tockus nasutus*	AF
—Monteiro's Hornbill	*Tockus monteiri*	AF
—Red-billed Hornbill	*Tockus erythrorhynchus*	AF
—Southern Yellow-billed Hornbill	*Tockus leucomelas*	AF
—Northern Yellow-billed Hornbill	*Tockus flavirostris*	AF
—Von der Decken's Hornbill	*Tockus deckeni*	AF
—Jackson's Hornbill	*Tockus jacksoni*	AF
—Black Dwarf Hornbill	*Tockus hartlaubi*	AF
—Red-billed Dwarf Hornbill	*Tockus camurus*	AF
—White-crested Hornbill	*Tropicranus albocristatus*	AF
—Malabar Grey Hornbill	*Ocyceros griseus*	OR
—Sri Lanka Grey Hornbill	*Ocyceros gingalensis*	OR
—Indian Grey Hornbill	*Ocyceros birostris*	OR
—Malabar Pied Hornbill	*Anthracoceros coronatus*	OR
—Oriental Pied Hornbill	*Anthracoceros albirostris*	OR
—Palawan Hornbill	*Anthracoceros marchei*	OR
—Black Hornbill	*Anthracoceros malayanus*	OR
—Sulu Hornbill	*Anthracoceros montani*	OR
—Great Hornbill	*Buceros bicornis*	OR
—Rhinoceros Hornbill	*Buceros rhinoceros*	OR
—Rufous Hornbill	*Buceros hydrocorax*	OR
—Helmeted Hornbill	*Rhinoplax vigil*	OR
—Sulawesi Hornbill	*Penelopides exarhatus*	AU
—Tarictic Hornbill	*Penelopides panini*	OR
—White-crowned Hornbill	*Berenicornis comatus*	OR
—Rufous-necked Hornbill	*Aceros nipalensis*	OR
—Knobbed Hornbill	*Aceros cassidix*	AU
—Wrinkled Hornbill	*Aceros corrugatus*	OR
—Walden's Hornbill	*Aceros waldeni*	OR
—Writhed Hornbill	*Aceros leucocephalus*	OR
—Blyth's Hornbill	*Rhyticeros plicatus*	AU
—Narcondam Hornbill	*Rhyticeros narcondami*	OR
—Plain-pouched Hornbill	*Rhyticeros subruficollis*	OR
—Wreathed Hornbill	*Rhyticeros undulatus*	OR

INTERNATIONAL ENGLISH NAME	SCIENTIFIC NAME	REGION(S)
—Sumba Hornbill	*Rhyticeros everetti*	AU
—Piping Hornbill	*Bycanistes fistulator*	AF
—Trumpeter Hornbill	*Bycanistes bucinator*	AF
—Brown-cheeked Hornbill	*Bycanistes cylindricus*	AF
—White-thighed Hornbill	*Bycanistes albotibialis*	AF
—Black-and-white-casqued Hornbill	*Bycanistes subcylindricus*	AF
—Silvery-cheeked Hornbill	*Bycanistes brevis*	AF
—Black-casqued Wattled Hornbill	*Ceratogymna atrata*	AF
—Yellow-casqued Wattled Hornbill	*Ceratogymna elata*	AF
GROUND HORNBILLS	**Family Bucorvidae**	
—Abyssinian Ground Hornbill	*Bucorvus abyssinicus*	AF
—Southern Ground Hornbill	*Bucorvus leadbeateri*	AF

ORDER PICIFORMES

TOUCANS, BARBETS	**Family Ramphastidae**	
—Emerald Toucanet	*Aulacorhynchus prasinus*	LA
—Groove-billed Toucanet	*Aulacorhynchus sulcatus*	SA
—Yellow-billed Toucanet	*Aulacorhynchus calorhynchus*	SA
—Chestnut-tipped Toucanet	*Aulacorhynchus derbianus*	SA
—Crimson-rumped Toucanet	*Aulacorhynchus haematopygus*	SA
—Yellow-browed Toucanet	*Aulacorhynchus huallagae*	SA
—Blue-banded Toucanet	*Aulacorhynchus coeruleicinctis*	SA
—Green Aracari	*Pteroglossus viridis*	SA
—Lettered Aracari	*Pteroglossus inscriptus*	SA
—Red-necked Aracari	*Pteroglossus bitorquatus*	SA
—Ivory-billed Aracari	*Pteroglossus azara*	SA
—Brown-mandibled Aracari	*Pteroglossus mariae*	SA
—Black-necked Aracari	*Pteroglossus aracari*	SA
—Chestnut-eared Aracari	*Pteroglossus castanotis*	SA
—Many-banded Aracari	*Pteroglossus pluricinctus*	SA
—Collared Aracari	*Pteroglossus torquatus*	LA
—Stripe-billed Aracari	*Pteroglossus sanguineus*	SA
—Pale-mandibled Aracari	*Pteroglossus erythropygius*	SA
—Fiery-billed Aracari	*Pteroglossus frantzii*	MA
—Curl-crested Aracari	*Pteroglossus beauharnaesii*	SA
—Saffron Toucanet	*Pteroglossus bailloni*	SA
—Yellow-eared Toucanet	*Selenidera spectabilis*	LA
—Guianan Toucanet	*Selenidera culik*	SA
—Golden-collared Toucanet	*Selenidera reinwardtii*	SA
—Tawny-tufted Toucanet	*Selenidera nattereri*	SA
—Gould's Toucanet	*Selenidera gouldii*	SA
—Spot-billed Toucanet	*Selenidera maculirostris*	SA
—Grey-breasted Mountain Toucan	*Andigena hypoglauca*	SA
—Plate-billed Mountain Toucan	*Andigena laminirostris*	SA
—Hooded Mountain Toucan	*Andigena cucullata*	SA
—Black-billed Mountain Toucan	*Andigena nigrirostris*	SA
—Green-billed Toucan	*Ramphastos dicolorus*	SA
—Channel-billed Toucan	*Ramphastos vitellinus*	SA
—Citron-throated Toucan	*Ramphastos citreolaemus*	SA
—Choco Toucan	*Ramphastos brevis*	SA
Keel-billed Toucan	*Ramphastos sulfuratus*	LA

INTERNATIONAL ENGLISH NAME	SCIENTIFIC NAME	REGION(S)
__Toco Toucan	*Ramphastos toco*	SA
__White-throated Toucan	*Ramphastos tucanus*	SA
__Chestnut-mandibled Toucan	*Ramphastos swainsonii*	LA
__Black-mandibled Toucan	*Ramphastos ambiguus*	SA
__Scarlet-crowned Barbet	*Capito aurovirens*	SA
__Scarlet-banded Barbet	*Capito wallacei*	SA
__Spot-crowned Barbet	*Capito maculicoronatus*	LA
__Orange-fronted Barbet	*Capito squamatus*	SA
__White-mantled Barbet	*Capito hypoleucus*	SA
__Black-girdled Barbet	*Capito dayi*	SA
__Brown-chested Barbet	*Capito brunneipectus*	SA
__Black-spotted Barbet	*Capito niger*	SA
__Gilded Barbet	*Capito auratus*	SA
__Five-colored Barbet	*Capito quinticolor*	SA
__Lemon-throated Barbet	*Eubucco richardsoni*	SA
__Red-headed Barbet	*Eubucco bourcierii*	LA
__Scarlet-hooded Barbet	*Eubucco tucinkae*	SA
__Versicolored Barbet	*Eubucco versicolor*	SA
__Prong-billed Barbet	*Semnornis frantzii*	MA
__Toucan Barbet	*Semnornis ramphastinus*	SA
__Fire-tufted Barbet	*Psilopogon pyrolophus*	OR
__Great Barbet	*Megalaima virens*	OR
__Red-vented Barbet	*Megalaima lagrandieri*	OR
__Brown-headed Barbet	*Megalaima zeylanica*	OR
__Lineated Barbet	*Megalaima lineata*	OR
__White-cheeked Barbet	*Megalaima viridis*	OR
__Green-eared Barbet	*Megalaima faiostricta*	OR
__Brown-throated Barbet	*Megalaima corvina*	OR
__Golden-whiskered Barbet	*Megalaima chrysopogon*	OR
__Red-crowned Barbet	*Megalaima rafflesii*	OR
__Red-throated Barbet	*Megalaima mystacophanos*	OR
__Black-banded Barbet	*Megalaima javensis*	OR
__Yellow-fronted Barbet	*Megalaima flavifrons*	OR
__Golden-throated Barbet	*Megalaima franklinii*	OR
__Black-browed Barbet	*Megalaima oorti*	OR
__Blue-throated Barbet	*Megalaima asiatica*	OR
__Mountain Barbet	*Megalaima monticola*	OR
__Moustached Barbet	*Megalaima incognita*	OR
__Yellow-crowned Barbet	*Megalaima henricii*	OR
__Flame-fronted Barbet	*Megalaima armillaris*	OR
__Golden-naped Barbet	*Megalaima pulcherrima*	OR
__Blue-eared Barbet	*Megalaima australis*	OR
__Bornean Barbet	*Megalaima eximia*	OR
__Crimson-fronted Barbet	*Megalaima rubricapillus*	OR
__Coppersmith Barbet	*Megalaima haemacephala*	OR
__Brown Barbet	*Calorhamphus fuliginosus*	OR
__Sladen's Barbet	*Gymnobucco sladeni*	AF
__Bristle-nosed Barbet	*Gymnobucco peli*	AF
__Naked-faced Barbet	*Gymnobucco calvus*	AF
__White-eared Barbet	*Stactolaema leucotis*	AF
__Whyte's Barbet	*Stactolaema whytii*	AF
__Anchieta's Barbet	*Stactolaema anchietae*	AF
__Green Barbet	*Stactolaema olivacea*	AF

INTERNATIONAL ENGLISH NAME	SCIENTIFIC NAME	REGION(S)
—Speckled Tinkerbird	*Pogoniulus scolopaceus*	AF
—Green Tinkerbird	*Pogoniulus simplex*	AF
—Moustached Tinkerbird	*Pogoniulus leucomystax*	AF
—Western Tinkerbird	*Pogoniulus coryphaeus*	AF
—Red-rumped Tinkerbird	*Pogoniulus atroflavus*	AF
—Yellow-throated Tinkerbird	*Pogoniulus subsulphureus*	AF
—Yellow-rumped Tinkerbird	*Pogoniulus bilineatus*	AF
—Red-fronted Tinkerbird	*Pogoniulus pusillus*	AF
—Yellow-fronted Tinkerbird	*Pogoniulus chrysoconus*	AF
—Yellow-spotted Barbet	*Buccanodon duchaillui*	AF
—Hairy breasted Barbet	*Tricholaema hirsuta*	AF
—Red-fronted Barbet	*Tricholaema diademata*	AF
—Miombo Pied Barbet	*Tricholaema frontata*	AF
—Acacia Pied Barbet	*Tricholaema leucomelas*	AF
—Spot-flanked Barbet	*Tricholaema lacrymosa*	AF
—Black-throated Barbet	*Tricholaema melanocephala*	AF
—Banded Barbet	*Lybius undatus*	AF
—Vieillot's Barbet	*Lybius vieilloti*	AF
—White-headed Barbet	*Lybius leucocephalus*	AF
—Chaplin's Barbet	*Lybius chaplini*	AF
—Red-faced Barbet	*Lybius rubrifacies*	AF
—Black-billed Barbet	*Lybius guifsobalito*	AF
—Black-collared Barbet	*Lybius torquatus*	AF
—Brown-breasted Barbet	*Lybius melanopterus*	AF
—Black-backed Barbet	*Lybius minor*	AF
—Double-toothed Barbet	*Lybius bidentatus*	AF
—Bearded Barbet	*Lybius dubius*	AF
—Black-breasted Barbet	*Lybius rolleti*	AF
—Yellow-billed Barbet	*Trachyphonus purpuratus*	AF
—Crested Barbet	*Trachyphonus vaillantii*	AF
—Red-and-yellow Barbet	*Trachyphonus erythrocephalus*	AF
—Yellow-breasted Barbet	*Trachyphonus margaritatus*	AF
—D'Arnaud's Barbet	*Trachyphonus darnaudii*	AF

HONEYGUIDES	Family Indicatoridae	
—Cassin's Honeybird	*Prodotiscus insignis*	AF
—Green-backed Honeybird	*Prodotiscus zambesiae*	AF
—Brown-backed Honeybird	*Prodotiscus regulus*	AF
—Zenker's Honeyguide	*Melignomon zenkeri*	AF
—Yellow-footed Honeyguide	*Melignomon eisentrauti*	AF
—Dwarf Honeyguide	*Indicator pumilio*	AF
—Willcocks's Honeyguide	*Indicator willcocksi*	AF
—Pallid Honeyguide	*Indicator meliphilus*	AF
—Least Honeyguide	*Indicator exilis*	AF
—Thick-billed Honeyguide	*Indicator conirostris*	AF
—Lesser Honeyguide	*Indicator minor*	AF
—Spotted Honeyguide	*Indicator maculatus*	AF
—Scaly-throated Honeyguide	*Indicator variegatus*	AF
—Yellow-rumped Honeyguide	*Indicator xanthonotus*	OR
—Malaysian Honeyguide	*Indicator archipelagicus*	OR
—Greater Honeyguide	*Indicator indicator*	AF
—Lyre-tailed Honeyguide	*Melichneutes robustus*	AF

INTERNATIONAL ENGLISH NAME	SCIENTIFIC NAME	REGION(S)
WOODPECKERS	**Family Picidae**	
—Eurasian Wryneck	*Jynx torquilla*	EU
—Red-throated Wryneck	*Jynx ruficollis*	AF
—Speckled Piculet	*Picumnus innominatus*	OR
—Bar-breasted Piculet	*Picumnus aurifrons*	SA
—Lafresnaye's Piculet	*Picumnus lafresnayi*	SA
—Orinoco Piculet	*Picumnus pumilus*	SA
—Golden-spangled Piculet	*Picumnus exilis*	SA
—Black-dotted Piculet	*Picumnus nigropunctatus*	SA
—Ecuadorian Piculet	*Picumnus sclateri*	SA
—Scaled Piculet	*Picumnus squamulatus*	SA
—White-bellied Piculet	*Picumnus spilogaster*	SA
—Arrowhead Piculet	*Picumnus minutissimus*	SA
—Spotted Piculet	*Picumnus pygmaeus*	SA
—Speckle-chested Piculet	*Picumnus steindachneri*	SA
—Varzea Piculet	*Picumnus varzeae*	SA
—White-barred Piculet	*Picumnus cirratus*	SA
—Ocellated Piculet	*Picumnus dorbygnianus*	SA
—Ochre-collared Piculet	*Picumnus temminckii*	SA
—White-wedged Piculet	*Picumnus albosquamatus*	SA
—Rusty-necked Piculet	*Picumnus fuscus*	SA
—Rufous-breasted Piculet	*Picumnus rufiventris*	SA
—Ochraceous Piculet	*Picumnus limae*	SA
—Tawny Piculet	*Picumnus fulvescens*	SA
—Mottled Piculet	*Picumnus nebulosus*	SA
—Plain-breasted Piculet	*Picumnus castelnau*	SA
—Fine-barred Piculet	*Picumnus subtilis*	SA
—Olivaceous Piculet	*Picumnus olivaceus*	LA
—Greyish Piculet	*Picumnus granadensis*	SA
—Chestnut Piculet	*Picumnus cinnamomeus*	SA
—African Piculet	*Sasia africana*	AF
—Rufous Piculet	*Sasia abnormis*	OR
—White-browed Piculet	*Sasia ochracea*	OR
—Antillean Piculet	*Nesoctites micromegas*	NA
—White Woodpecker	*Leuconerpes candidus*	SA
—Lewis's Woodpecker	*Melanerpes lewis*	NA
—Guadeloupe Woodpecker	*Melanerpes herminieri*	NA
—Puerto Rican Woodpecker	*Melanerpes portoricensis*	NA
—Red-headed Woodpecker	*Melanerpes erythrocephalus*	NA
—Acorn Woodpecker	*Melanerpes formicivorus*	NA, LA
—Yellow-tufted Woodpecker	*Melanerpes cruentatus*	SA
—Yellow-fronted Woodpecker	*Melanerpes flavifrons*	SA
—Golden-naped Woodpecker	*Melanerpes chrysauchen*	MA
—Beautiful Woodpecker	*Melanerpes pulcher*	SA
—Black-cheeked Woodpecker	*Melanerpes pucherani*	LA
—White-fronted Woodpecker	*Melanerpes cactorum*	SA
—Hispaniolan Woodpecker	*Melanerpes striatus*	NA
—Jamaican Woodpecker	*Melanerpes radiolatus*	NA
—Golden-cheeked Woodpecker	*Melanerpes chrysogenys*	MA
—Grey-breasted Woodpecker	*Melanerpes hypopolius*	MA
—Yucatan Woodpecker	*Melanerpes pygmaeus*	MA
—Red-crowned Woodpecker	*Melanerpes rubricapillus*	LA
—Gila Woodpecker	*Melanerpes uropygialis*	NA, MA

INTERNATIONAL ENGLISH NAME	SCIENTIFIC NAME	REGION(S)
__Hoffmann's Woodpecker	*Melanerpes hoffmannii*	MA
__Golden-fronted Woodpecker	*Melanerpes aurifrons*	NA, MA
__Red-bellied Woodpecker	*Melanerpes carolinus*	NA
__West Indian Woodpecker	*Melanerpes superciliaris*	NA
__Williamson's Sapsucker	*Sphyrapicus thyroideus*	NA
__Yellow-bellied Sapsucker	*Sphyrapicus varius*	NA
__Red-naped Sapsucker	*Sphyrapicus nuchalis*	NA
__Red-breasted Sapsucker	*Sphyrapicus ruber*	NA
__Cuban Green Woodpecker	*Xiphidiopicus percussus*	NA
__Fine-spotted Woodpecker	*Campethera punctuligera*	AF
__Bennett's Woodpecker	*Campethera bennettii*	AF
__Speckle-throated Woodpecker	*Campethera scriptoricauda*	AF
__Nubian Woodpecker	*Campethera nubica*	AF
__Golden-tailed Woodpecker	*Campethera abingoni*	AF
__Mombasa Woodpecker	*Campethera mombassica*	AF
__Knysna Woodpecker	*Campethera notata*	AF
__Green-backed Woodpecker	*Campethera cailliautii*	AF
__Little Green Woodpecker	*Campethera maculosa*	AF
__Tullberg's Woodpecker	*Campethera tullbergi*	AF
__Buff-spotted Woodpecker	*Campethera nivosa*	AF
__Brown-eared Woodpecker	*Campethera caroli*	AF
__Ground Woodpecker	*Geocolaptes olivaceus*	AF
__Little Grey Woodpecker	*Dendropicos elachus*	AF
__Speckle-breasted Woodpecker	*Dendropicos poecilolaemus*	AF
__Abyssinian Woodpecker	*Dendropicos abyssinicus*	AF
__Cardinal Woodpecker	*Dendropicos fuscescens*	AF
__Gabon Woodpecker	*Dendropicos gabonensis*	AF
__Stierling's Woodpecker	*Dendropicos stierlingi*	AF
__Bearded Woodpecker	*Dendropicos namaquus*	AF
__Yellow-crested Woodpecker	*Dendropicos xantholophus*	AF
__Fire-bellied Woodpecker	*Dendropicos pyrrhogaster*	AF
__Elliot's Woodpecker	*Dendropicos elliotii*	AF
__African Grey Woodpecker	*Dendropicos goertae*	AF
__Olive Woodpecker	*Dendropicos griseocephalus*	AF
__Rufous-bellied Woodpecker	*Dendrocopos hyperythrus*	OR
__Sulawesi Pygmy Woodpecker	*Dendrocopos temminckii*	AU
__Philippine Pygmy Woodpecker	*Dendrocopos maculatus*	OR
__Sunda Pygmy Woodpecker	*Dendrocopos moluccensis*	OR
__Brown-capped Pygmy Woodpecker	*Dendrocopos nanus*	OR
__Japanese Pygmy Woodpecker	*Dendrocopos kizuki*	EU
__Grey-capped Pygmy Woodpecker	*Dendrocopos canicapillus*	OR, EU
__Lesser Spotted Woodpecker	*Dendrocopos minor*	EU
__Fulvous-breasted Woodpecker	*Dendrocopos macei*	OR
__Stripe-breasted Woodpecker	*Dendrocopos atratus*	OR
__Brown-fronted Woodpecker	*Dendrocopos auriceps*	OR
__Yellow-crowned Woodpecker	*Dendrocopos mahrattensis*	OR
__Arabian Woodpecker	*Dendrocopos dorae*	EU
__Crimson-breasted Woodpecker	*Dendrocopos cathpharius*	OR, EU
__Darjeeling Woodpecker	*Dendrocopos darjellensis*	OR
__Middle Spotted Woodpecker	*Dendrocopos medius*	EU
__White-backed Woodpecker	*Dendrocopos leucotos*	EU
__Himalayan Woodpecker	*Dendrocopos himalayensis*	EU
__Sind Woodpecker	*Dendrocopos assimilis*	EU

INTERNATIONAL ENGLISH NAME	SCIENTIFIC NAME	REGION(S)
__Syrian Woodpecker	*Dendrocopos syriacus*	EU
__White-winged Woodpecker	*Dendrocopos leucopterus*	EU
__Great Spotted Woodpecker	*Dendrocopos major*	EU
__Brown-backed Woodpecker	*Picoides obsoletus*	AF
__Checkered Woodpecker	*Picoides mixtus*	SA
__Striped Woodpecker	*Picoides lignarius*	SA
__Ladder-backed Woodpecker	*Picoides scalaris*	NA, MA
__Nuttall's Woodpecker	*Picoides nuttallii*	NA
__Downy Woodpecker	*Picoides pubescens*	NA
__Hairy Woodpecker	*Picoides villosus*	NA, MA
__Arizona Woodpecker	*Picoides arizonae*	NA, MA
__Strickland's Woodpecker	*Picoides stricklandi*	MA
__Red-cockaded Woodpecker	*Picoides borealis*	NA
__White-headed Woodpecker	*Picoides albolarvatus*	NA
__Eurasian Three-toed Woodpecker	*Picoides tridactylus*	EU
__American Three-toed Woodpecker	*Picoides dorsalis*	NA
__Black-backed Woodpecker	*Picoides arcticus*	NA
__Scarlet-backed Woodpecker	*Veniliornis callonotus*	SA
__Yellow-vented Woodpecker	*Veniliornis dignus*	SA
__Bar-bellied Woodpecker	*Veniliornis nigriceps*	SA
__Smoky-brown Woodpecker	*Veniliornis fumigatus*	LA
__Little Woodpecker	*Veniliornis passerinus*	SA
__Dot-fronted Woodpecker	*Veniliornis frontalis*	SA
__White-spotted Woodpecker	*Veniliornis spilogaster*	SA
__Blood-colored Woodpecker	*Veniliornis sanguineus*	SA
__Red-rumped Woodpecker	*Veniliornis kirkii*	LA
__Red-stained Woodpecker	*Veniliornis affinis*	SA
__Choco Woodpecker	*Veniliornis chocoensis*	SA
__Golden-collared Woodpecker	*Veniliornis cassini*	SA
__Yellow-eared Woodpecker	*Veniliornis maculifrons*	SA
__Rufous-winged Woodpecker	*Piculus simplex*	MA
__Stripe-cheeked Woodpecker	*Piculus callopterus*	MA
__White-throated Woodpecker	*Piculus leucolaemus*	SA
__Lita Woodpecker	*Piculus litae*	SA
__Yellow-throated Woodpecker	*Piculus flavigula*	SA
__Golden-green Woodpecker	*Piculus chrysochloros*	LA
__Yellow-browed Woodpecker	*Piculus aurulentus*	SA
__Golden-olive Woodpecker	*Piculus rubiginosus*	MA
__Bronze-winged Woodpecker	*Piculus aeruginosus*	LA
__Grey-crowned Woodpecker	*Piculus auricularis*	MA
__Crimson-mantled Woodpecker	*Piculus rivolii*	SA
__Black-necked Woodpecker	*Chrysoptilus atricollis*	SA
__Spot-breasted Woodpecker	*Chrysoptilus punctigula*	LA
__Green-barred Woodpecker	*Chrysoptilus melanochloros*	SA
__Northern Flicker	*Colaptes auratus*	NA, MA
__Gilded Flicker	*Colaptes chrysoides*	NA, MA
__Fernandina's Flicker	*Colaptes fernandinae*	NA
__Chilean Flicker	*Colaptes pitius*	SA
__Andean Flicker	*Colaptes rupicola*	SA
__Campo Flicker	*Colaptes campestris*	SA
__Rufous Woodpecker	*Celeus brachyurus*	OR
__Cinnamon Woodpecker	*Celeus loricatus*	LA
__Waved Woodpecker	*Celeus undatus*	SA

INTERNATIONAL ENGLISH NAME	SCIENTIFIC NAME	REGION(S)
—Scaly-breasted Woodpecker	*Celeus grammicus*	SA
—Chestnut-colored Woodpecker	*Celeus castaneus*	MA
—Chestnut Woodpecker	*Celeus elegans*	SA
—Pale-crested Woodpecker	*Celeus lugubris*	SA
—Blond-crested Woodpecker	*Celeus flavescens*	SA
—Cream-colored Woodpecker	*Celeus flavus*	SA
—Rufous-headed Woodpecker	*Celeus spectabilis*	SA
—Piaui Woodpecker	*Celeus obrieni*	SA
—Ringed Woodpecker	*Celeus torquatus*	SA
—Helmeted Woodpecker	*Dryocopus galeatus*	SA
—Black-bodied Woodpecker	*Dryocopus schulzi*	SA
—Lineated Woodpecker	*Dryocopus lineatus*	LA
—Pileated Woodpecker	*Dryocopus pileatus*	NA
—White-bellied Woodpecker	*Dryocopus javensis*	OR
—Andaman Woodpecker	*Dryocopus hodgei*	OR
—Black Woodpecker	*Dryocopus martius*	EU
—Powerful Woodpecker	*Campephilus pollens*	SA
—Crimson-bellied Woodpecker	*Campephilus haematogaster*	LA
—Red-necked Woodpecker	*Campephilus rubricollis*	SA
—Robust Woodpecker	*Campephilus robustus*	SA
—Crimson-crested Woodpecker	*Campephilus melanoleucos*	SA
—Pale-billed Woodpecker	*Campephilus guatemalensis*	MA
—Guayaquil Woodpecker	*Campephilus gayaquilensis*	SA
—Cream-backed Woodpecker	*Campephilus leucopogon*	SA
—Magellanic Woodpecker	*Campephilus magellanicus*	SA
—Ivory-billed Woodpecker	*Campephilus principalis*	NA
—Imperial Woodpecker	*Campephilus imperialis*	MA
—Banded Woodpecker	*Picus mineaceus*	OR
—Crimson-winged Woodpecker	*Picus puniceus*	OR
—Lesser Yellownape	*Picus chlorolophus*	OR
—Checker-throated Woodpecker	*Picus mentalis*	OR
—Greater Yellownape	*Picus flavinucha*	OR
—Streak-breasted Woodpecker	*Picus viridanus*	OR
—Laced Woodpecker	*Picus vittatus*	OR
—Streak-throated Woodpecker	*Picus xanthopygaeus*	OR
—Scaly-bellied Woodpecker	*Picus squamatus*	EU
—Japanese Green Woodpecker	*Picus awokera*	EU
—European Green Woodpecker	*Picus viridis*	EU
—Levaillant's Woodpecker	*Picus vaillantii*	AF
—Red-collared Woodpecker	*Picus rabieri*	OR
—Black-headed Woodpecker	*Picus erythropygius*	OR
—Grey-headed Woodpecker	*Picus canus*	EU, OR
—Olive-backed Woodpecker	*Dinopium rafflesii*	OR
—Himalayan Goldenback	*Dinopium shorii*	OR
—Common Goldenback	*Dinopium javanense*	OR
—Lesser Goldenback	*Dinopium benghalense*	OR
—Greater Goldenback	*Chrysocolaptes lucidus*	OR
—White-naped Woodpecker	*Chrysocolaptes festivus*	OR
—Pale-headed Woodpecker	*Gecinulus grantia*	OR
—Bamboo Woodpecker	*Gecinulus viridis*	OR
—Okinawa Woodpecker	*Sapheopipo noguchii*	EU
—Maroon Woodpecker	*Blythipicus rubiginosus*	OR
—Bay Woodpecker	*Blythipicus pyrrhotis*	OR

INTERNATIONAL ENGLISH NAME	SCIENTIFIC NAME	REGION(S)
—Orange-backed Woodpecker	*Reinwardtipicus validus*	OR
—Buff-rumped Woodpecker	*Meiglyptes tristis*	OR
—Black-and-buff Woodpecker	*Meiglyptes jugularis*	OR
—Buff-necked Woodpecker	*Meiglyptes tukki*	OR
—Grey-and-buff Woodpecker	*Hemicircus concretus*	OR
—Heart-spotted Woodpecker	*Hemicircus canente*	OR
—Ashy Woodpecker	*Mulleripicus fulvus*	AU
—Sooty Woodpecker	*Mulleripicus funebris*	OR
—Great Slaty Woodpecker	*Mulleripicus pulverulentus*	OR

JACAMARS — Family Galbulidae

—White-eared Jacamar	*Galbalcyrhynchus leucotis*	SA
—Purus Jacamar	*Galbalcyrhynchus purusianus*	SA
—Dusky-backed Jacamar	*Brachygalba salmoni*	LA
—Pale-headed Jacamar	*Brachygalba goeringi*	SA
—Brown Jacamar	*Brachygalba lugubris*	SA
—White-throated Jacamar	*Brachygalba albogularis*	SA
—Three-toed Jacamar	*Jacamaralcyon tridactyla*	SA
—Yellow-billed Jacamar	*Galbula albirostris*	SA
—Blue-necked Jacamar	*Galbula cyanicollis*	SA
—Rufous-tailed Jacamar	*Galbula ruficauda*	LA
—Green-tailed Jacamar	*Galbula galbula*	SA
—Coppery-chested Jacamar	*Galbula pastazae*	SA
—White-chinned Jacamar	*Galbula tombacea*	SA
—Bluish-fronted Jacamar	*Galbula cyanescens*	SA
—Purplish Jacamar	*Galbula chalcothorax*	SA
—Bronzy Jacamar	*Galbula leucogastra*	SA
—Paradise Jacamar	*Galbula dea*	SA
—Great Jacamar	*Jacamerops aureus*	LA

PUFFBIRDS — Family Bucconidae

—White-necked Puffbird	*Notharchus macrorhynchos*	LA
—Buff-bellied Puffbird	*Notharchus swainsoni*	SA
—Black-breasted Puffbird	*Notharchus pectoralis*	LA
—Brown-banded Puffbird	*Notharchus ordii*	SA
—Pied Puffbird	*Notharchus tectus*	LA
—Chestnut-capped Puffbird	*Bucco macrodactylus*	SA
—Spotted Puffbird	*Bucco tamatia*	SA
—Sooty-capped Puffbird	*Bucco noanamae*	SA
—Collared Puffbird	*Bucco capensis*	SA
—Barred Puffbird	*Nystalus radiatus*	LA
—White-eared Puffbird	*Nystalus chacuru*	SA
—Striolated Puffbird	*Nystalus striolatus*	SA
—Caatinga Puffbird	*Nystalus maculatus*	SA
—Chaco Puffbird	*Nystalus striatipectus*	SA
—Russet-throated Puffbird	*Hypnelus ruficollis*	SA
—Crescent-chested Puffbird	*Malacoptila striata*	SA
—White-chested Puffbird	*Malacoptila fusca*	SA
—Semicollared Puffbird	*Malacoptila semicincta*	SA
—Black-streaked Puffbird	*Malacoptila fulvogularis*	SA
—Rufous-necked Puffbird	*Malacoptila rufa*	SA
—White-whiskered Puffbird	*Malacoptila panamensis*	LA
—Moustached Puffbird	*Malacoptila mystacalis*	SA

INTERNATIONAL ENGLISH NAME	SCIENTIFIC NAME	REGION(S)
—Lanceolated Monklet	*Micromonacha lanceolata*	LA
—Rusty-breasted Nunlet	*Nonnula rubecula*	SA
—Fulvous-chinned Nunlet	*Nonnula sclateri*	SA
—Brown Nunlet	*Nonnula brunnea*	SA
—Grey-cheeked Nunlet	*Nonnula frontalis*	LA
—Rufous-capped Nunlet	*Nonnula ruficapilla*	SA
—Chestnut-headed Nunlet	*Nonnula amaurocephala*	SA
—White-faced Nunbird	*Hapaloptila castanea*	SA
—Black Nunbird	*Monasa atra*	SA
—Black-fronted Nunbird	*Monasa nigrifrons*	SA
—White-fronted Nunbird	*Monasa morphoeus*	LA
—Yellow-billed Nunbird	*Monasa flavirostris*	SA
—Swallow-winged Puffbird	*Chelidoptera tenebrosa*	SA

INTERNATIONAL ENGLISH NAME	SCIENTIFIC NAME	REGION(S)
	ORDER PASSERIFORMES	
NEW ZEALAND WRENS	**Family Acanthisittidae**	
—Rifleman	*Acanthisitta chloris*	AU
—Bushwren	*Xenicus longipes*	AU
—New Zealand Rockwren	*Xenicus gilviventris*	AU
BROADBILLS	**Family Eurylaimidae**	
—African Broadbill	*Smithornis capensis*	AF
—Grey-headed Broadbill	*Smithornis sharpei*	AF
—Rufous-sided Broadbill	*Smithornis rufolateralis*	AF
—Green Broadbill	*Calyptomena viridis*	OR
—Hose's Broadbill	*Calyptomena hosii*	OR
—Whitehead's Broadbill	*Calyptomena whiteheadi*	OR
—Black-and-red Broadbill	*Cymbirhynchus macrorhynchos*	OR
—Long-tailed Broadbill	*Psarisomus dalhousiae*	OR
—Silver-breasted Broadbill	*Serilophus lunatus*	OR
—Banded Broadbill	*Eurylaimus javanicus*	OR
—Black-and-yellow Broadbill	*Eurylaimus ochromalus*	OR
—Wattled Broadbill	*Eurylaimus steerii*	OR
—Visayan Broadbill	*Eurylaimus samarensis*	OR
—Dusky Broadbill	*Corydon sumatranus*	OR
—Grauer's Broadbill	*Pseudocalyptomena graueri*	AF
ASITIES	**Family Philepittidae**	
—Velvet Asity	*Philepitta castanea*	AF
—Schlegel's Asity	*Philepitta schlegeli*	AF
—Common Sunbird-Asity	*Neodrepanis coruscans*	AF
—Yellow-bellied Sunbird-Asity	*Neodrepanis hypoxantha*	AF
SAPAYOA	**Family Sapayaoidae**	
—Broad-billed Sapayoa	*Sapayoa aenigma*	LA
PITTAS	**Family Pittidae**	
—Eared Pitta	*Pitta phayrei*	OR
—Blue-naped Pitta	*Pitta nipalensis*	OR
—Blue-rumped Pitta	*Pitta soror*	OR
—Rusty-naped Pitta	*Pitta oatesi*	OR
—Schneider's Pitta	*Pitta schneideri*	OR
—Giant Pitta	*Pitta caerulea*	OR
—Blue Pitta	*Pitta cyanea*	OR
—Bar-bellied Pitta	*Pitta elliotii*	OR
—Banded Pitta	*Pitta guajana*	OR
—Gurney's Pitta	*Pitta gurneyi*	OR
—Whiskered Pitta	*Pitta kochi*	OR
—Red-bellied Pitta	*Pitta erythrogaster*	AU
—Sula Pitta	*Pitta dohertyi*	AU
—Blue-banded Pitta	*Pitta arquata*	OR
—Garnet Pitta	*Pitta granatina*	OR
—Graceful Pitta	*Pitta venusta*	OR
—Black-crowned Pitta	*Pitta ussheri*	OR
—Blue-headed Pitta	*Pitta baudii*	OR

INTERNATIONAL ENGLISH NAME	SCIENTIFIC NAME	REGION(S)
—Hooded Pitta	*Pitta sordida*	OR, AU
—Ivory-breasted Pitta	*Pitta maxima*	AU
—Azure-breasted Pitta	*Pitta steerii*	OR
—Superb Pitta	*Pitta superba*	AU
—African Pitta	*Pitta angolensis*	AF
—Green-breasted Pitta	*Pitta reichenowi*	AF
—Indian Pitta	*Pitta brachyura*	OR
—Fairy Pitta	*Pitta nympha*	OR, EU
—Blue-winged Pitta	*Pitta moluccensis*	OR
—Mangrove Pitta	*Pitta megarhyncha*	OR
Elegant Pitta	*Pitta elegans*	AU
—Double-striped Pitta	*Pitta vigorsii*	AU
—Rainbow Pitta	*Pitta iris*	AU
—Noisy Pitta	*Pitta versicolor*	AU
—Black-faced Pitta	*Pitta anerythra*	AU

MANAKINS	**Family Pipridae**	
—Pin-tailed Manakin	*Ilicura militaris*	SA
—Golden-winged Manakin	*Masius chrysopterus*	SA
—White-throated Manakin	*Corapipo gutturalis*	SA
—White-ruffed Manakin	*Corapipo leucorrhoa*	LA
—Club-winged Manakin	*Machaeropterus deliciosus*	SA
—Eastern Striped Manakin	*Machaeropterus regulus*	SA
—Western Striped Manakin	*Machaeropterus striolatus*	SA
—Fiery-capped Manakin	*Machaeropterus pyrocephalus*	SA
—Blue-crowned Manakin	*Lepidothrix coronata*	LA
—Blue-rumped Manakin	*Lepidothrix isidorei*	SA
—Cerulean-capped Manakin	*Lepidothrix coeruleocapilla*	SA
—Snow-capped Manakin	*Lepidothrix nattereri*	SA
—Golden-crowned Manakin	*Lepidothrix vilasboasi*	SA
—Opal-crowned Manakin	*Lepidothrix iris*	SA
—White-fronted Manakin	*Lepidothrix serena*	SA
—Orange-bellied Manakin	*Lepidothrix suavissima*	SA
—White-bearded Manakin	*Manacus manacus*	SA
—White-collared Manakin	*Manacus candei*	MA
—Golden-collared Manakin	*Manacus vitellinus*	LA
—Orange-collared Manakin	*Manacus aurantiacus*	MA
—Araripe Manakin	*Antilophia bokermanni*	SA
—Helmeted Manakin	*Antilophia galeata*	SA
—Long-tailed Manakin	*Chiroxiphia linearis*	MA
—Lance-tailed Manakin	*Chiroxiphia lanceolata*	LA
—Blue-backed Manakin	*Chiroxiphia pareola*	SA
—Yungas Manakin	*Chiroxiphia boliviana*	SA
—Blue Manakin	*Chiroxiphia caudata*	SA
—Green Manakin	*Chloropipo holochlora*	LA
—Yellow-headed Manakin	*Chloropipo flavicapilla*	SA
—Jet Manakin	*Chloropipo unicolor*	SA
—Olive Manakin	*Chloropipo uniformis*	SA
—Black Manakin	*Xenopipo atronitens*	SA
—Orange-crested Manakin	*Heterocercus aurantiivertex*	SA
—Yellow-crested Manakin	*Heterocercus flavivertex*	SA
—Flame-crested Manakin	*Heterocercus linteatus*	SA

INTERNATIONAL ENGLISH NAME	SCIENTIFIC NAME	REGION(S)
—White-crowned Manakin	*Pipra pipra*	LA
—Crimson-hooded Manakin	*Pipra aureola*	SA
—Wire-tailed Manakin	*Pipra filicauda*	SA
—Band-tailed Manakin	*Pipra fasciicauda*	SA
—Scarlet-horned Manakin	*Pipra cornuta*	SA
—Red-capped Manakin	*Pipra mentalis*	LA
—Round-tailed Manakin	*Pipra chloromeros*	SA
—Golden-headed Manakin	*Pipra erythrocephala*	SA
—Red-headed Manakin	*Pipra rubrocapilla*	SA
COTINGAS	**Family Cotingidae**	
—Black-crowned Tityra	*Tityra inquisitor*	LA
—Black-tailed Tityra	*Tityra cayana*	SA
—Masked Tityra	*Tityra semifasciata*	LA
—Varzea Schiffornis	*Schiffornis major*	SA
—Thrush-like Schiffornis	*Schiffornis turdina*	LA
—Greenish Schiffornis	*Schiffornis virescens*	SA
—Speckled Mourner	*Laniocera rufescens*	LA
—Cinereous Mourner	*Laniocera hypopyrra*	SA
—Buff-throated Purpletuft	*Iodopleura pipra*	SA
—Dusky Purpletuft	*Iodopleura fusca*	SA
—White-browed Purpletuft	*Iodopleura isabellae*	SA
—Brazilian Laniisoma	*Laniisoma elegans*	SA
—Andean Laniisoma	*Laniisoma buckleyi*	SA
—White-naped Xenopsaris	*Xenopsaris albinucha*	SA
—Green-backed Becard	*Pachyramphus viridis*	SA
—Yellow-cheeked Becard	*Pachyramphus xanthogenys*	SA
—Barred Becard	*Pachyramphus versicolor*	LA
—Slaty Becard	*Pachyramphus spodiurus*	SA
—Cinereous Becard	*Pachyramphus rufus*	LA
—Chestnut-crowned Becard	*Pachyramphus castaneus*	SA
—Cinnamon Becard	*Pachyramphus cinnamomeus*	LA
—White-winged Becard	*Pachyramphus polychopterus*	LA
—Black-capped Becard	*Pachyramphus marginatus*	SA
—Black-and-white Becard	*Pachyramphus albogriseus*	LA
—Grey-collared Becard	*Pachyramphus major*	MA
—Glossy-backed Becard	*Pachyramphus surinamus*	SA
—Rose-throated Becard	*Platypsaris aglaiae*	MA
—One-colored Becard	*Platypsaris homochrous*	LA
—Pink-throated Becard	*Platypsaris minor*	SA
—Crested Becard	*Platypsaris validus*	SA
—Jamaican Becard	*Platypsaris niger*	NA
—Swallow-tailed Cotinga	*Phibalura flavirostris*	SA
—Palkachupa Cotinga	*Phibalura boliviana*	SA
—Red-crested Cotinga	*Ampelion rubrocristatus*	SA
—Chestnut-crested Cotinga	*Ampelion rufaxilla*	SA
—White-cheeked Cotinga	*Zaratornis stresemanni*	SA
—Chestnut-bellied Cotinga	*Doliornis remseni*	SA
—Bay-vented Cotinga	*Doliornis sclateri*	SA
—Peruvian Plantcutter	*Phytotoma raimondii*	SA
—White-tipped Plantcutter	*Phytotoma rutila*	SA
—Rufous-tailed Plantcutter	*Phytotoma rara*	SA
—Hooded Berryeater	*Carpornis cucullata*	SA

INTERNATIONAL ENGLISH NAME	SCIENTIFIC NAME	REGION(S)
__Black-headed Berryeater	*Carpornis melanocephala*	SA
__Green-and-black Fruiteater	*Pipreola riefferii*	SA
__Band-tailed Fruiteater	*Pipreola intermedia*	SA
__Barred Fruiteater	*Pipreola arcuata*	SA
__Golden-breasted Fruiteater	*Pipreola aureopectus*	SA
__Orange-breasted Fruiteater	*Pipreola jucunda*	SA
__Black-chested Fruiteater	*Pipreola lubomirskii*	SA
__Masked Fruiteater	*Pipreola pulchra*	SA
__Scarlet-breasted Fruiteater	*Pipreola frontalis*	SA
__Fiery-throated Fruiteater	*Pipreola chlorolepidota*	SA
Handsome Fruiteater	*Pipreola formosa*	SA
__Red-banded Fruiteater	*Pipreola whitelyi*	SA
__Sharpbill	*Oxyruncus cristatus*	SA
__Scaled Fruiteater	*Ampelioides tschudii*	SA
__Guianan Cock-of-the-rock	*Rupicola rupicola*	SA
__Andean Cock-of-the-rock	*Rupicola peruvianus*	SA
__Guianan Red Cotinga	*Phoenicircus carnifex*	SA
__Black-necked Red Cotinga	*Phoenicircus nigricollis*	SA
__Lovely Cotinga	*Cotinga amabilis*	MA
__Turquoise Cotinga	*Cotinga ridgwayi*	MA
__Blue Cotinga	*Cotinga nattererii*	LA
__Plum-throated Cotinga	*Cotinga maynana*	SA
__Purple-breasted Cotinga	*Cotinga cotinga*	SA
__Banded Cotinga	*Cotinga maculata*	SA
__Spangled Cotinga	*Cotinga cayana*	SA
__Three-wattled Bellbird	*Procnias tricarunculatus*	MA
__White Bellbird	*Procnias albus*	SA
__Bearded Bellbird	*Procnias averano*	SA
__Bare-throated Bellbird	*Procnias nudicollis*	SA
__Black-and-gold Cotinga	*Tijuca atra*	SA
__Grey-winged Cotinga	*Tijuca condita*	SA
__Chestnut-capped Piha	*Lipaugus weberi*	SA
__Dusky Piha	*Lipaugus fuscocinereus*	SA
__Scimitar-winged Piha	*Lipaugus uropygialis*	SA
__Rufous Piha	*Lipaugus unirufus*	LA
__Screaming Piha	*Lipaugus vociferans*	SA
__Cinnamon-vented Piha	*Lipaugus lanioides*	SA
__Rose-collared Piha	*Lipaugus streptophorus*	SA
__Black-faced Cotinga	*Conioptilon mcilhennyi*	SA
__Grey-tailed Piha	*Snowornis subalaris*	SA
__Olivaceous Piha	*Snowornis cryptolophus*	SA
__Purple-throated Cotinga	*Porphyrolaema porphyrolaema*	SA
__Pompadour Cotinga	*Xipholena punicea*	SA
__White-tailed Cotinga	*Xipholena lamellipennis*	SA
__White-winged Cotinga	*Xipholena atropurpurea*	SA
__Black-tipped Cotinga	*Carpodectes hopkei*	LA
__Snowy Cotinga	*Carpodectes nitidus*	MA
__Yellow-billed Cotinga	*Carpodectes antoniae*	MA
__Bare-necked Fruitcrow	*Gymnoderus foetidus*	SA
__Purple-throated Fruitcrow	*Querula purpurata*	LA
__Crimson Fruitcrow	*Haematoderus militaris*	SA
__Red-ruffed Fruitcrow	*Pyroderus scutatus*	SA
__ Capuchinbird	*Perissocephalus tricolor*	SA

INTERNATIONAL ENGLISH NAME	SCIENTIFIC NAME	REGION(S)
—Bare-necked Umbrellabird	*Cephalopterus glabricollis*	MA
—Amazonian Umbrellabird	*Cephalopterus ornatus*	SA
—Long-wattled Umbrellabird	*Cephalopterus penduliger*	SA
FAMILY UNCERTAIN	**Incertae Sedis**	
—Grey-headed Piprites	*Piprites griseiceps*	MA
—Wing-barred Piprites	*Piprites chloris*	SA
—Black-capped Piprites	*Piprites pileata*	SA
—Kinglet Calyptura	*Calyptura cristata*	SA
TYRANT FLYCATCHERS	**Family Tyrannidae**	
—Planalto Tyrannulet	*Phyllomyias fasciatus*	SA
—Rough-legged Tyrannulet	*Phyllomyias burmeisteri*	SA
—White-fronted Tyrannulet	*Phyllomyias zeledoni*	LA
—Greenish Tyrannulet	*Phyllomyias virescens*	SA
—Reiser's Tyrannulet	*Phyllomyias reiseri*	SA
—Urich's Tyrannulet	*Phyllomyias urichi*	SA
—Sclater's Tyrannulet	*Phyllomyias sclateri*	SA
—Grey-capped Tyrannulet	*Phyllomyias griseocapilla*	SA
—Sooty-headed Tyrannulet	*Phyllomyias griseiceps*	SA
—Plumbeous-crowned Tyrannulet	*Phyllomyias plumbeiceps*	SA
—Black-capped Tyrannulet	*Phyllomyias nigrocapillus*	SA
—Ashy-headed Tyrannulet	*Phyllomyias cinereiceps*	SA
—Tawny-rumped Tyrannulet	*Phyllomyias uropygialis*	SA
—Yellow-crowned Tyrannulet	*Tyrannulus elatus*	LA
—Forest Elaenia	*Myiopagis gaimardii*	LA
—Grey Elaenia	*Myiopagis caniceps*	SA
—Foothill Elaenia	*Myiopagis olallai*	SA
—Pacific Elaenia	*Myiopagis subplacens*	SA
—Yellow-crowned Elaenia	*Myiopagis flavivertex*	SA
—Greenish Elaenia	*Myiopagis viridicata*	LA
—Jamaican Elaenia	*Myiopagis cotta*	NA
—Yellow-bellied Elaenia	*Elaenia flavogaster*	LA
—Caribbean Elaenia	*Elaenia martinica*	NA
—Large Elaenia	*Elaenia spectabilis*	SA
—Noronha Elaenia	*Elaenia ridleyana*	SA
—White-crested Elaenia	*Elaenia albiceps*	SA
—Small-billed Elaenia	*Elaenia parvirostris*	SA
—Olivaceous Elaenia	*Elaenia mesoleuca*	SA
—Slaty Elaenia	*Elaenia strepera*	SA
—Mottle-backed Elaenia	*Elaenia gigas*	SA
—Brownish Elaenia	*Elaenia pelzelni*	SA
—Plain-crested Elaenia	*Elaenia cristata*	SA
—Lesser Elaenia	*Elaenia chiriquensis*	LA
—Rufous-crowned Elaenia	*Elaenia ruficeps*	SA
—Mountain Elaenia	*Elaenia frantzii*	LA
—Highland Elaenia	*Elaenia obscura*	SA
—Great Elaenia	*Elaenia dayi*	SA
—Sierran Elaenia	*Elaenia pallatangae*	SA
—Greater Antillean Elaenia	*Elaenia fallax*	NA
—Yellow-bellied Tyrannulet	*Ornithion semiflavum*	MA
—Brown-capped Tyrannulet	*Ornithion brunneicapillus*	LA

INTERNATIONAL ENGLISH NAME	SCIENTIFIC NAME	REGION(S)
__White-lored Tyrannulet	*Ornithion inerme*	SA
__Northern Beardless Tyrannulet	*Camptostoma imberbe*	MA
__Southern Beardless Tyrannulet	*Camptostoma obsoletum*	LA
__Chaco Suiriri	*Suiriri suiriri*	SA
__Campo Suiriri	*Suiriri affinis*	SA
__Chapada Suiriri	*Suiriri islerorum*	SA
__White-throated Tyrannulet	*Mecocerculus leucophrys*	SA
__White-tailed Tyrannulet	*Mecocerculus poecilocercus*	SA
__Buff-banded Tyrannulet	*Mecocerculus hellmayri*	SA
__Rufous-winged Tyrannulet	*Mecocerculus calopterus*	SA
Sulphur-bellied Tyrannulet	*Mecocerculus minor*	SA
__White-banded Tyrannulet	*Mecocerculus stictopterus*	SA
__Black-crested Tit-Tyrant	*Anairetes nigrocristatus*	SA
__Pied-crested Tit-Tyrant	*Anairetes reguloides*	SA
__Ash-breasted Tit-Tyrant	*Anairetes alpinus*	SA
__Yellow-billed Tit-Tyrant	*Anairetes flavirostris*	SA
__Tufted Tit-Tyrant	*Anairetes parulus*	SA
__Juan Fernandez Tit-Tyrant	*Anairetes fernandezianus*	SA
__Agile Tit-Tyrant	*Uromyias agilis*	SA
__Unstreaked Tit-Tyrant	*Uromyias agraphia*	SA
__Torrent Tyrannulet	*Serpophaga cinerea*	LA
__River Tyrannulet	*Serpophaga hypoleuca*	SA
__Sooty Tyrannulet	*Serpophaga nigricans*	SA
__White-crested Tyrannulet	*Serpophaga subcristata*	SA
__White-bellied Tyrannulet	*Serpophaga munda*	SA
__Mouse-colored Tyrannulet	*Phaeomyias murina*	LA
__Tumbesian Tyrannulet	*Phaeomyias tumbezana*	SA
__Yellow Tyrannulet	*Capsiempis flaveola*	LA
__Bearded Tachuri	*Polystictus pectoralis*	SA
__Grey-backed Tachuri	*Polystictus superciliaris*	SA
__Cocos Flycatcher	*Nesotriccus ridgwayi*	MA
__Dinelli's Doradito	*Pseudocolopteryx dinelliana*	SA
__Crested Doradito	*Pseudocolopteryx sclateri*	SA
__Subtropical Doradito	*Pseudocolopteryx acutipennis*	SA
__Warbling Doradito	*Pseudocolopteryx flaviventris*	SA
__Bronze-olive Pygmy Tyrant	*Pseudotriccus pelzelni*	SA
__Hazel-fronted Pygmy Tyrant	*Pseudotriccus simplex*	SA
__Rufous-headed Pygmy Tyrant	*Pseudotriccus ruficeps*	SA
__Ringed Antpipit	*Corythopis torquatus*	SA
__Southern Antpipit	*Corythopis delalandi*	SA
__Tawny-crowned Pygmy Tyrant	*Euscarthmus meloryphus*	SA
__Rufous-sided Pygmy Tyrant	*Euscarthmus rufomarginatus*	SA
__Grey-and-white Tyrannulet	*Pseudelaenia leucospodia*	SA
__Lesser Wagtail-Tyrant	*Stigmatura napensis*	SA
__Bahia Wagtail-Tyrant	*Stigmatura bahiae*	SA
__Greater Wagtail-Tyrant	*Stigmatura budytoides*	SA
__Caatinga Wagtail-Tyrant	*Stigmatura gracilis*	SA
__Paltry Tyrannulet	*Zimmerius vilissimus*	LA
__Venezuelan Tyrannulet	*Zimmerius improbus*	SA
__Bolivian Tyrannulet	*Zimmerius bolivianus*	SA
__Red-billed Tyrannulet	*Zimmerius cinereicapilla*	SA
__Mishana Tyrannulet	*Zimmerius villarejoi*	SA
__Slender-footed Tyrannulet	*Zimmerius gracilipes*	SA

INTERNATIONAL ENGLISH NAME	SCIENTIFIC NAME	REGION(S)
—Golden-faced Tyrannulet	*Zimmerius chrysops*	SA
—Loja Tyrannulet	*Zimmerius flavidifrons*	SA
—Peruvian Tyrannulet	*Zimmerius viridiflavus*	SA
—Variegated Bristle Tyrant	*Pogonotriccus poecilotis*	SA
—Chapman's Bristle Tyrant	*Pogonotriccus chapmani*	SA
—Marble-faced Bristle Tyrant	*Pogonotriccus ophthalmicus*	SA
—Spectacled Bristle Tyrant	*Pogonotriccus orbitalis*	SA
—Venezuelan Bristle Tyrant	*Pogonotriccus venezuelanus*	SA
—Antioquia Bristle Tyrant	*Pogonotriccus lanyoni*	SA
—Southern Bristle Tyrant	*Pogonotriccus eximius*	SA
—Mottle-cheeked Tyrannulet	*Phylloscartes ventralis*	SA
—Alagoas Tyrannulet	*Phylloscartes ceciliae*	SA
—Restinga Tyrannulet	*Phylloscartes kronei*	SA
—Bahia Tyrannulet	*Phylloscartes beckeri*	SA
—Panamanian Tyrannulet	*Phylloscartes flavovirens*	MA
—Guianan Tyrannulet	*Phylloscartes virescens*	SA
—Ecuadorian Tyrannulet	*Phylloscartes gualaquizae*	SA
—Black-fronted Tyrannulet	*Phylloscartes nigrifrons*	SA
—Rufous-browed Tyrannulet	*Phylloscartes superciliaris*	LA
—Rufous-lored Tyrannulet	*Phylloscartes flaviventris*	SA
—Cinnamon-faced Tyrannulet	*Phylloscartes parkeri*	SA
—Minas Gerais Tyrannulet	*Phylloscartes roquettei*	SA
—Sao Paulo Tyrannulet	*Phylloscartes paulista*	SA
—Oustalet's Tyrannulet	*Phylloscartes oustaleti*	SA
—Serra do Mar Tyrannulet	*Phylloscartes difficilis*	SA
—Bay-ringed Tyrannulet	*Phylloscartes sylviolus*	SA
—Streak-necked Flycatcher	*Mionectes striaticollis*	SA
—Olive-striped Flycatcher	*Mionectes olivaceus*	LA
—Ochre-bellied Flycatcher	*Mionectes oleagineus*	LA
—McConnell's Flycatcher	*Mionectes macconnelli*	SA
—Grey-hooded Flycatcher	*Mionectes rufiventris*	SA
—Sepia-capped Flycatcher	*Leptopogon amaurocephalus*	LA
—Slaty-capped Flycatcher	*Leptopogon superciliaris*	LA
—Rufous-breasted Flycatcher	*Leptopogon rufipectus*	SA
—Inca Flycatcher	*Leptopogon taczanowskii*	SA
—Northern Scrub Flycatcher	*Sublegatus arenarum*	LA
—Amazonian Scrub Flycatcher	*Sublegatus obscurior*	SA
—Southern Scrub Flycatcher	*Sublegatus modestus*	SA
—Slender-billed Inezia	*Inezia tenuirostris*	SA
—Plain Inezia	*Inezia inornata*	SA
—Amazonian Inezia	*Inezia subflava*	SA
—Pale-tipped Inezia	*Inezia caudata*	SA
—Flavescent Flycatcher	*Myiophobus flavicans*	SA
—Orange-crested Flycatcher	*Myiophobus phoenicomitra*	SA
—Unadorned Flycatcher	*Myiophobus inornatus*	SA
—Roraiman Flycatcher	*Myiophobus roraimae*	SA
—Handsome Flycatcher	*Myiophobus pulcher*	SA
—Orange-banded Flycatcher	*Myiophobus lintoni*	SA
—Ochraceous-breasted Flycatcher	*Myiophobus ochraceiventris*	SA
—Olive-chested Flycatcher	*Myiophobus cryptoxanthus*	SA
—Bran-colored Flycatcher	*Myiophobus fasciatus*	LA
—Ornate Flycatcher	*Myiotriccus ornatus*	SA
—Many-colored Rush Tyrant	*Tachuris rubrigastra*	SA

INTERNATIONAL ENGLISH NAME	SCIENTIFIC NAME	REGION(S)
__Sharp-tailed Grass Tyrant	*Culicivora caudacuta*	SA
__Drab-breasted Bamboo Tyrant	*Hemitriccus diops*	SA
__Brown-breasted Bamboo Tyrant	*Hemitriccus obsoletus*	SA
__Flammulated Bamboo Tyrant	*Hemitriccus flammulatus*	SA
__Snethlage's Tody-Tyrant	*Hemitriccus minor*	SA
__Yungas Tody-Tyrant	*Hemitriccus spodiops*	SA
__Boat-billed Tody-Tyrant	*Hemitriccus josephinae*	SA
__White-eyed Tody-Tyrant	*Hemitriccus zosterops*	SA
__White-bellied Tody-Tyrant	*Hemitriccus griseipectus*	SA
__Zimmer's Tody-Tyrant	*Hemitriccus minimus*	SA
__Eye-ringed Tody-Tyrant	*Hemitriccus orbitatus*	SA
__Johannes's Tody-Tyrant	*Hemitriccus iohannis*	SA
__Stripe-necked Tody-Tyrant	*Hemitriccus striaticollis*	SA
__Hangnest Tody-Tyrant	*Hemitriccus nidipendulus*	SA
__Pearly-vented Tody-Tyrant	*Hemitriccus margaritaceiventer*	SA
__Pelzeln's Tody-Tyrant	*Hemitriccus inornatus*	SA
__Black-throated Tody-Tyrant	*Hemitriccus granadensis*	SA
__Buff-breasted Tody-Tyrant	*Hemitriccus mirandae*	SA
__Cinnamon-breasted Tody-Tyrant	*Hemitriccus cinnamomeipectus*	SA
__Kaempfer's Tody-Tyrant	*Hemitriccus kaempferi*	SA
__Buff-throated Tody-Tyrant	*Hemitriccus rufigularis*	SA
__Fork-tailed Tody-Tyrant	*Hemitriccus furcatus*	SA
__Eared Pygmy Tyrant	*Myiornis auricularis*	SA
__White-bellied Pygmy Tyrant	*Myiornis albiventris*	SA
__Black-capped Pygmy Tyrant	*Myiornis atricapillus*	LA
__Short-tailed Pygmy Tyrant	*Myiornis ecaudatus*	SA
__Northern Bentbill	*Oncostoma cinereigulare*	MA
__Southern Bentbill	*Oncostoma olivaceum*	LA
__Scale-crested Pygmy Tyrant	*Lophotriccus pileatus*	LA
__Long-crested Pygmy Tyrant	*Lophotriccus eulophotes*	SA
__Double-banded Pygmy Tyrant	*Lophotriccus vitiosus*	SA
__Helmeted Pygmy Tyrant	*Lophotriccus galeatus*	SA
__Pale-eyed Pygmy Tyrant	*Lophotriccus pilaris*	LA
__Rufous-crowned Tody-Flycatcher	*Poecilotriccus ruficeps*	SA
__Lulu's Tody-Flycatcher	*Poecilotriccus luluae*	SA
__White-cheeked Tody-Flycatcher	*Poecilotriccus albifacies*	SA
__Black-and-white Tody-Flycatcher	*Poecilotriccus capitalis*	SA
__Buff-cheeked Tody-Flycatcher	*Poecilotriccus senex*	SA
__Ruddy Tody-Flycatcher	*Poecilotriccus russatum*	SA
__Ochre-faced Tody-Flycatcher	*Poecilotriccus plumbeiceps*	SA
__Smoky-fronted Tody-Flycatcher	*Poecilotriccus fumifrons*	SA
__Rusty-fronted Tody-Flycatcher	*Poecilotriccus latirostris*	SA
__Slaty-headed Tody-Flycatcher	*Poecilotriccus sylvia*	LA
__Golden-winged Tody-Flycatcher	*Poecilotriccus calopterum*	SA
__Black-backed Tody-Flycatcher	*Poecilotriccus pulchellum*	SA
__Black-chested Tyrant	*Taeniotriccus andrei*	SA
__Spotted Tody-Flycatcher	*Todirostrum maculatum*	SA
__Yellow-lored Tody-Flycatcher	*Todirostrum poliocephalum*	SA
__Common Tody-Flycatcher	*Todirostrum cinereum*	LA
__Maracaibo Tody-Flycatcher	*Todirostrum viridanum*	SA
__Painted Tody-Flycatcher	*Todirostrum pictum*	SA
__Yellow-browed Tody-Flycatcher	*Todirostrum chrysocrotaphum*	SA
__Black-headed Tody-Flycatcher	*Todirostrum nigriceps*	LA

INTERNATIONAL ENGLISH NAME	SCIENTIFIC NAME	REGION(S)
—Brownish Twistwing	*Cnipodectes subbrunneus*	LA
—Eye-ringed Flatbill	*Rhynchocyclus brevirostris*	MA
—Olivaceous Flatbill	*Rhynchocyclus olivaceus*	LA
—Pacific Flatbill	*Rhynchocyclus pacificus*	SA
—Fulvous-breasted Flatbill	*Rhynchocyclus fulvipectus*	SA
—Yellow-olive Flatbill	*Tolmomyias sulphurescens*	LA
—Orange-eyed Flatbill	*Tolmomyias traylori*	SA
—Zimmer's Flatbill	*Tolmomyias assimilis*	SA
—Yellow-margined Flatbill	*Tolmomyias flavotectus*	LA
—Grey-crowned Flatbill	*Tolmomyias poliocephalus*	SA
—Ochre-lored Flatbill	*Tolmomyias flaviventris*	SA
—Olive-faced Flatbill	*Tolmomyias viridiceps*	SA
—Cinnamon-crested Spadebill	*Platyrinchus saturatus*	SA
—Stub-tailed Spadebill	*Platyrinchus cancrominus*	MA
—White-throated Spadebill	*Platyrinchus mystaceus*	LA
—Golden-crowned Spadebill	*Platyrinchus coronatus*	LA
—Yellow-throated Spadebill	*Platyrinchus flavigularis*	SA
—White-crested Spadebill	*Platyrinchus platyrhynchos*	SA
—Russet-winged Spadebill	*Platyrinchus leucoryphus*	SA
—Amazonian Royal Flycatcher	*Onychorhynchus coronatus*	SA
—Northern Royal Flycatcher	*Onychorhynchus mexicanus*	LA
—Pacific Royal Flycatcher	*Onychorhynchus occidentalis*	SA
—Atlantic Royal Flycatcher	*Onychorhynchus swainsoni*	SA
—Tawny-breasted Myiobius	*Myiobius villosus*	SA
—Sulphur-rumped Myiobius	*Myiobius sulphureipygius*	LA
—Whiskered Myiobius	*Myiobius barbatus*	SA
—Yellow-rumped Myiobius	*Myiobius mastacalis*	SA
—Black-tailed Myiobius	*Myiobius atricaudus*	LA
—Ruddy-tailed Flycatcher	*Terenotriccus erythrurus*	LA
—Cinnamon Neopipo	*Neopipo cinnamomea*	SA
—Saffron-crested Neopelma	*Neopelma chrysocephalum*	SA
—Sulphur-bellied Neopelma	*Neopelma sulphureiventer*	SA
—Pale-bellied Neopelma	*Neopelma pallescens*	SA
—Wied's Neopelma	*Neopelma aurifrons*	SA
—Serra do Mar Neopelma	*Neopelma chrysolophum*	SA
—Dwarf Tyranneutes	*Tyranneutes stolzmanni*	SA
—Tiny Tyranneutes	*Tyranneutes virescens*	SA
—Cinnamon Flycatcher	*Pyrrhomyias cinnamomeus*	SA
—Cliff Flycatcher	*Hirundinea ferruginea*	SA
—Euler's Flycatcher	*Lathrotriccus euleri*	SA
—Grey-breasted Flycatcher	*Lathrotriccus griseipectus*	SA
—Tawny-chested Flycatcher	*Aphanotriccus capitalis*	MA
—Black-billed Flycatcher	*Aphanotriccus audax*	LA
—Fuscous Flycatcher	*Cnemotriccus fuscatus*	SA
—Belted Flycatcher	*Xenotriccus callizonus*	MA
—Pileated Flycatcher	*Xenotriccus mexicanus*	MA
—Eastern Phoebe	*Sayornis phoebe*	NA
—Black Phoebe	*Sayornis nigricans*	NA, LA
—Say's Phoebe	*Sayornis saya*	NA, MA
—Northern Tufted Flycatcher	*Mitrephanes phaeocercus*	LA
—Olive Tufted Flycatcher	*Mitrephanes olivaceus*	SA
—Olive-sided Flycatcher	*Contopus cooperi*	NA
—Greater Pewee	*Contopus pertinax*	NA, MA

INTERNATIONAL ENGLISH NAME	SCIENTIFIC NAME	REGION(S)
__Dark Pewee	*Contopus lugubris*	MA
__Smoke-colored Pewee	*Contopus fumigatus*	SA
__Ochraceous Pewee	*Contopus ochraceus*	MA
__Western Wood Pewee	*Contopus sordidulus*	NA, MA
__Eastern Wood Pewee	*Contopus virens*	NA
__Tropical Pewee	*Contopus cinereus*	LA
__Tumbes Pewee	*Contopus punensis*	SA
__White-throated Pewee	*Contopus albogularis*	SA
__Blackish Pewee	*Contopus nigrescens*	SA
__Cuban Pewee	*Contopus caribaeus*	NA
__Hispaniolan Pewee	*Contopus hispaniolensis*	NA
__Jamaican Pewee	*Contopus pallidus*	NA
__Lesser Antillean Pewee	*Contopus latirostris*	NA
__Yellow-bellied Flycatcher	*Empidonax flaviventris*	NA
__Acadian Flycatcher	*Empidonax virescens*	NA
__Willow Flycatcher	*Empidonax traillii*	NA
__Alder Flycatcher	*Empidonax alnorum*	NA
__White-throated Flycatcher	*Empidonax albigularis*	MA
__Least Flycatcher	*Empidonax minimus*	NA
__Hammond's Flycatcher	*Empidonax hammondii*	NA
__Dusky Flycatcher	*Empidonax oberholseri*	NA
__Grey Flycatcher	*Empidonax wrightii*	NA
__Pine Flycatcher	*Empidonax affinis*	MA
__Pacific-slope Flycatcher	*Empidonax difficilis*	NA
__Cordilleran Flycatcher	*Empidonax occidentalis*	NA
__Yellowish Flycatcher	*Empidonax flavescens*	MA
__Buff-breasted Flycatcher	*Empidonax fulvifrons*	NA, MA
__Black-capped Flycatcher	*Empidonax atriceps*	MA
__Vermilion Flycatcher	*Pyrocephalus rubinus*	NA, LA
__Darwin's Flycatcher	*Pyrocephalus nanus*	SA
__Patagonian Negrito	*Lessonia rufa*	SA
__Andean Negrito	*Lessonia oreas*	SA
__Cinereous Tyrant	*Knipolegus striaticeps*	SA
__Hudson's Black Tyrant	*Knipolegus hudsoni*	SA
__Amazonian Black Tyrant	*Knipolegus poecilocercus*	SA
__Andean Tyrant	*Knipolegus signatus*	SA
__Blue-billed Black Tyrant	*Knipolegus cyanirostris*	SA
__Rufous-tailed Tyrant	*Knipolegus poecilurus*	SA
__Riverside Tyrant	*Knipolegus orenocensis*	SA
__White-winged Black Tyrant	*Knipolegus aterrimus*	SA
__Caatinga Black Tyrant	*Knipolegus franciscanus*	SA
__Crested Black Tyrant	*Knipolegus lophotes*	SA
__Velvety Black Tyrant	*Knipolegus nigerrimus*	SA
__Spectacled Tyrant	*Hymenops perspicillatus*	SA
__Drab Water Tyrant	*Ochthornis littoralis*	SA
__Yellow-browed Tyrant	*Satrapa icterophrys*	SA
__Little Ground Tyrant	*Muscisaxicola fluviatilis*	SA
__Spot-billed Ground Tyrant	*Muscisaxicola maculirostris*	SA
__Plain-capped Ground Tyrant	*Muscisaxicola griseus*	SA
__Puna Ground Tyrant	*Muscisaxicola juninensis*	SA
__Cinereous Ground Tyrant	*Muscisaxicola cinereus*	SA
__White-fronted Ground Tyrant	*Muscisaxicola albifrons*	SA
__Ochre-naped Ground Tyrant	*Muscisaxicola flavinucha*	SA

INTERNATIONAL ENGLISH NAME	SCIENTIFIC NAME	REGION(S)
—Rufous-naped Ground Tyrant	*Muscisaxicola rufivertex*	SA
—Dark-faced Ground Tyrant	*Muscisaxicola maclovianus*	SA
—White-browed Ground Tyrant	*Muscisaxicola albilora*	SA
—Paramo Ground Tyrant	*Muscisaxicola alpinus*	SA
—Cinnamon-bellied Ground Tyrant	*Muscisaxicola capistratus*	SA
—Black-fronted Ground Tyrant	*Muscisaxicola frontalis*	SA
—Black-billed Shrike-Tyrant	*Agriornis montanus*	SA
—White-tailed Shrike-Tyrant	*Agriornis albicauda*	SA
—Great Shrike-Tyrant	*Agriornis lividus*	SA
—Grey-bellied Shrike-Tyrant	*Agriornis micropterus*	SA
—Lesser Shrike-Tyrant	*Agriornis murinus*	SA
—Fire-eyed Diucon	*Xolmis pyrope*	SA
—Grey Monjita	*Xolmis cinereus*	SA
—Black-crowned Monjita	*Xolmis coronatus*	SA
—White-rumped Monjita	*Xolmis velatus*	SA
—White Monjita	*Xolmis irupero*	SA
—Rusty-backed Monjita	*Xolmis rubetra*	SA
—Salinas Monjita	*Xolmis salinarum*	SA
—Black-and-white Monjita	*Heteroxolmis dominicanus*	SA
—Streak-throated Bush Tyrant	*Myiotheretes striaticollis*	SA
—Santa Marta Bush Tyrant	*Myiotheretes pernix*	SA
—Smoky Bush Tyrant	*Myiotheretes fumigatus*	SA
—Rufous-bellied Bush Tyrant	*Myiotheretes fuscorufus*	SA
—Red-rumped Bush Tyrant	*Cnemarchus erythropygius*	SA
—Rufous-webbed Bush Tyrant	*Polioxolmis rufipennis*	SA
—Chocolate-vented Tyrant	*Neoxolmis rufiventris*	SA
—Streamer-tailed Tyrant	*Gubernetes yetapa*	SA
—Shear-tailed Grey Tyrant	*Muscipipra vetula*	SA
—Pied Water Tyrant	*Fluvicola pica*	LA
—Black-backed Water Tyrant	*Fluvicola albiventer*	SA
—Masked Water Tyrant	*Fluvicola nengeta*	SA
—White-headed Marsh Tyrant	*Arundinicola leucocephala*	SA
—Cock-tailed Tyrant	*Alectrurus tricolor*	SA
—Strange-tailed Tyrant	*Alectrurus risora*	SA
—Tumbes Tyrant	*Tumbezia salvini*	SA
—Crowned Chat-Tyrant	*Ochthoeca frontalis*	SA
—Kalinowski's Chat-Tyrant	*Ochthoeca spodionota*	SA
—Golden-browed Chat-Tyrant	*Ochthoeca pulchella*	SA
—Yellow-bellied Chat-Tyrant	*Ochthoeca diadema*	SA
—Jelski's Chat-Tyrant	*Ochthoeca jelskii*	SA
—Slaty-backed Chat-Tyrant	*Ochthoeca cinnamomeiventris*	SA
—Blackish Chat-Tyrant	*Ochthoeca nigrita*	SA
—Maroon-belted Chat-Tyrant	*Ochthoeca thoracica*	SA
—Rufous-breasted Chat-Tyrant	*Ochthoeca rufipectoralis*	SA
—Brown-backed Chat-Tyrant	*Ochthoeca fumicolor*	SA
—d'Orbigny's Chat-Tyrant	*Ochthoeca oenanthoides*	SA
—White-browed Chat-Tyrant	*Ochthoeca leucophrys*	SA
—Piura Chat-Tyrant	*Ochthoeca piurae*	SA
—Patagonian Tyrant	*Colorhamphus parvirostris*	SA
—Long-tailed Tyrant	*Colonia colonus*	LA
—Short-tailed Field Tyrant	*Muscigralla brevicauda*	SA
—Cattle Tyrant	*Machetornis rixosa*	LA
—Piratic Flycatcher	*Legatus leucophaius*	LA

INTERNATIONAL ENGLISH NAME	SCIENTIFIC NAME	REGION(S)
—White-bearded Flycatcher	*Phelpsia inornata*	SA
—Rusty-margined Flycatcher	*Myiozetetes cayanensis*	LA
—Social Flycatcher	*Myiozetetes similis*	LA
—Grey-capped Flycatcher	*Myiozetetes granadensis*	LA
—Dusky-chested Flycatcher	*Myiozetetes luteiventris*	SA
—Great Kiskadee	*Pitangus sulphuratus*	NA, LA
—Lesser Kiskadee	*Philohydor lictor*	LA
—White-ringed Flycatcher	*Conopias albovittatus*	LA
—Yellow-throated Flycatcher	*Conopias parvus*	SA
—Three-striped Flycatcher	*Conopias trivirgatus*	SA
—Lemon-browed Flycatcher	*Conopias cinchoneti*	SA
—Golden-bellied Flycatcher	*Myiodynastes hemichrysus*	MA
—Golden-crowned Flycatcher	*Myiodynastes chrysocephalus*	SA
—Baird's Flycatcher	*Myiodynastes bairdii*	SA
—Sulphur-bellied Flycatcher	*Myiodynastes luteiventris*	NA, MA
—Streaked Flycatcher	*Myiodynastes maculatus*	LA
—Boat-billed Flycatcher	*Megarynchus pitangua*	LA
—Sulphury Flycatcher	*Tyrannopsis sulphurea*	SA
—Variegated Flycatcher	*Empidonomus varius*	SA
—Crowned Slaty Flycatcher	*Griseotyrannus aurantioatrocristatus*	SA
—Snowy-throated Kingbird	*Tyrannus niveigularis*	SA
—White-throated Kingbird	*Tyrannus albogularis*	SA
—Tropical Kingbird	*Tyrannus melancholicus*	NA, LA
—Couch's Kingbird	*Tyrannus couchii*	NA, MA
—Cassin's Kingbird	*Tyrannus vociferans*	NA, MA
—Thick-billed Kingbird	*Tyrannus crassirostris*	NA, MA
—Western Kingbird	*Tyrannus verticalis*	NA
—Scissor-tailed Flycatcher	*Tyrannus forficatus*	NA
—Fork-tailed Flycatcher	*Tyrannus savana*	LA
—Eastern Kingbird	*Tyrannus tyrannus*	NA
—Grey Kingbird	*Tyrannus dominicensis*	NA
—Giant Kingbird	*Tyrannus cubensis*	NA
—Loggerhead Kingbird	*Tyrannus caudifasciatus*	NA
—Greyish Mourner	*Rhytipterna simplex*	SA
—Pale-bellied Mourner	*Rhytipterna immunda*	SA
—Rufous Mourner	*Rhytipterna holerythra*	LA
—Eastern Sirystes	*Sirystes sibilator*	SA
—Western Sirystes	*Sirystes albogriseus*	LA
—Rufous Casiornis	*Casiornis rufus*	SA
—Ash-throated Casiornis	*Casiornis fuscus*	SA
—Rufous Flycatcher	*Myiarchus semirufus*	SA
—Yucatan Flycatcher	*Myiarchus yucatanensis*	MA
—Sad Flycatcher	*Myiarchus barbirostris*	NA
—Dusky-capped Flycatcher	*Myiarchus tuberculifer*	NA, LA
—Swainson's Flycatcher	*Myiarchus swainsoni*	SA
—Venezuelan Flycatcher	*Myiarchus venezuelensis*	SA
—Panamanian Flycatcher	*Myiarchus panamensis*	LA
—Short-crested Flycatcher	*Myiarchus ferox*	SA
—Apical Flycatcher	*Myiarchus apicalis*	SA
—Pale-edged Flycatcher	*Myiarchus cephalotes*	SA
—Sooty-crowned Flycatcher	*Myiarchus phaeocephalus*	SA
—Ash-throated Flycatcher	*Myiarchus cinerascens*	NA, MA
—Nutting's Flycatcher	*Myiarchus nuttingi*	MA

INTERNATIONAL ENGLISH NAME	SCIENTIFIC NAME	REGION(S)
—Great Crested Flycatcher	*Myiarchus crinitus*	NA
—Brown-crested Flycatcher	*Myiarchus tyrannulus*	NA, LA
—Galapagos Flycatcher	*Myiarchus magnirostris*	SA
—Grenada Flycatcher	*Myiarchus nugator*	NA
—Rufous-tailed Flycatcher	*Myiarchus validus*	NA
—La Sagra's Flycatcher	*Myiarchus sagrae*	NA
—Stolid Flycatcher	*Myiarchus stolidus*	NA
—Puerto Rican Flycatcher	*Myiarchus antillarum*	NA
—Lesser Antillean Flycatcher	*Myiarchus oberi*	NA
—Flammulated Flycatcher	*Deltarhynchus flammulatus*	MA
—Bamboo Flatbill	*Ramphotrigon megacephalum*	SA
—Rufous-tailed Flatbill	*Ramphotrigon ruficauda*	SA
—Dusky-tailed Flatbill	*Ramphotrigon fuscicauda*	SA
—Rufous-tailed Attila	*Attila phoenicurus*	SA
—Cinnamon Attila	*Attila cinnamomeus*	SA
—Ochraceous Attila	*Attila torridus*	SA
—Citron-bellied Attila	*Attila citriniventris*	SA
—White-eyed Attila	*Attila bolivianus*	SA
—Grey-hooded Attila	*Attila rufus*	SA
—Bright-rumped Attila	*Attila spadiceus*	LA

ANTBIRDS	**Family Thamnophilidae**	
—Fasciated Antshrike	*Cymbilaimus lineatus*	LA
—Bamboo Antshrike	*Cymbilaimus sanctaemariae*	SA
—Spot-backed Antshrike	*Hypoedaleus guttatus*	SA
—Giant Antshrike	*Batara cinerea*	SA
—Large-tailed Antshrike	*Mackenziaena leachii*	SA
—Tufted Antshrike	*Mackenziaena severa*	SA
—Black-throated Antshrike	*Frederickena viridis*	SA
—Undulated Antshrike	*Frederickena unduligera*	SA
—Great Antshrike	*Taraba major*	LA
—Black-crested Antshrike	*Sakesphorus canadensis*	SA
—Silvery-cheeked Antshrike	*Sakesphorus cristatus*	SA
—Collared Antshrike	*Sakesphorus bernardi*	SA
—Black-backed Antshrike	*Sakesphorus melanonotus*	SA
—Band-tailed Antshrike	*Sakesphorus melanothorax*	SA
—Glossy Antshrike	*Sakesphorus luctuosus*	SA
—White-bearded Antshrike	*Biatas nigropectus*	SA
—Barred Antshrike	*Thamnophilus doliatus*	LA
—Chapman's Antshrike	*Thamnophilus zarumae*	SA
—Bar-crested Antshrike	*Thamnophilus multistriatus*	SA
—Lined Antshrike	*Thamnophilus tenuepunctatus*	SA
—Chestnut-backed Antshrike	*Thamnophilus palliatus*	SA
—Black-hooded Antshrike	*Thamnophilus bridgesi*	MA
—Black Antshrike	*Thamnophilus nigriceps*	LA
—Cocha Antshrike	*Thamnophilus praecox*	SA
—Blackish-grey Antshrike	*Thamnophilus nigrocinereus*	SA
—Castelnau's Antshrike	*Thamnophilus cryptoleucus*	SA
—White-shouldered Antshrike	*Thamnophilus aethiops*	SA
—Uniform Antshrike	*Thamnophilus unicolor*	SA
—Plain-winged Antshrike	*Thamnophilus schistaceus*	SA
—Mouse-colored Antshrike	*Thamnophilus murinus*	SA
—Upland Antshrike	*Thamnophilus aroyae*	SA

INTERNATIONAL ENGLISH NAME	SCIENTIFIC NAME	REGION(S)
__Western Slaty Antshrike	*Thamnophilus atrinucha*	LA
__Northern Slaty Antshrike	*Thamnophilus punctatus*	SA
__Natterer's Slaty Antshrike	*Thamnophilus stictocephalus*	SA
__Bolivian Slaty Antshrike	*Thamnophilus sticturus*	SA
__Planalto Slaty Antshrike	*Thamnophilus pelzelni*	SA
__Sooretama Slaty Antshrike	*Thamnophilus ambiguus*	SA
__Amazonian Antshrike	*Thamnophilus amazonicus*	SA
__Acre Antshrike	*Thamnophilus divisorius*	SA
__Streak-backed Antshrike	*Thamnophilus insignis*	SA
__Variable Antshrike	*Thamnophilus caerulescens*	SA
__Rufous-winged Antshrike	*Thamnophilus torquatus*	SA
__Rufous-capped Antshrike	*Thamnophilus ruficapillus*	SA
__Pearly Antshrike	*Megastictus margaritatus*	SA
__Black Bushbird	*Neoctantes niger*	SA
__Recurve-billed Bushbird	*Clytoctantes alixii*	SA
__Rondonia Bushbird	*Clytoctantes atrogularis*	SA
__Speckled Antshrike	*Xenornis setifrons*	LA
__Russet Antshrike	*Thamnistes anabatinus*	LA
__Spot-breasted Antvireo	*Dysithamnus stictothorax*	SA
__Plain Antvireo	*Dysithamnus mentalis*	LA
__Streak-crowned Antvireo	*Dysithamnus striaticeps*	MA
__Spot-crowned Antvireo	*Dysithamnus puncticeps*	LA
__Rufous-backed Antvireo	*Dysithamnus xanthopterus*	SA
__Bicolored Antvireo	*Dysithamnus occidentalis*	SA
__Plumbeous Antvireo	*Dysithamnus plumbeus*	SA
__White-streaked Antvireo	*Dysithamnus leucostictus*	SA
__Venezuelan Antvireo	*Dysithamnus tucuyensis*	SA
__Dusky-throated Antshrike	*Thamnomanes ardesiacus*	SA
__Saturnine Antshrike	*Thamnomanes saturninus*	SA
__Cinereous Antshrike	*Thamnomanes caesius*	SA
__Bluish-slate Antshrike	*Thamnomanes schistogynus*	SA
__Spot-winged Antshrike	*Pygiptila stellaris*	SA
__Moustached Antwren	*Myrmotherula ignota*	LA
__Pygmy Antwren	*Myrmotherula brachyura*	SA
__Guianan Streaked Antwren	*Myrmotherula surinamensis*	SA
__Amazonian Streaked Antwren	*Myrmotherula multostriata*	SA
__Pacific Antwren	*Myrmotherula pacifica*	LA
__Cherrie's Antwren	*Myrmotherula cherriei*	SA
__Klages's Antwren	*Myrmotherula klagesi*	SA
__Stripe-chested Antwren	*Myrmotherula longicauda*	SA
__Yellow-throated Antwren	*Myrmotherula ambigua*	SA
__Sclater's Antwren	*Myrmotherula sclateri*	SA
__Plain-throated Antwren	*Myrmotherula hauxwelli*	SA
__Rufous-bellied Antwren	*Myrmotherula guttata*	SA
__Star-throated Antwren	*Myrmotherula gularis*	SA
__Checker-throated Antwren	*Myrmotherula fulviventris*	LA
__Brown-bellied Antwren	*Myrmotherula gutturalis*	SA
__White-eyed Antwren	*Myrmotherula leucophthalma*	SA
__Stipple-throated Antwren	*Myrmotherula haematonota*	SA
__Yasuni Antwren	*Myrmotherula fjeldsaai*	SA
__Foothill Antwren	*Myrmotherula spodionota*	SA
__Ornate Antwren	*Myrmotherula ornata*	SA
__Rufous-tailed Antwren	*Myrmotherula erythrura*	SA

INTERNATIONAL ENGLISH NAME	SCIENTIFIC NAME	REGION(S)
—White-flanked Antwren	*Myrmotherula axillaris*	LA
—Silvery-flanked Antwren	*Myrmotherula luctuosa*	SA
—Slaty Antwren	*Myrmotherula schisticolor*	LA
—Rio Suno Antwren	*Myrmotherula sunensis*	SA
—Salvadori's Antwren	*Myrmotherula minor*	SA
—Long-winged Antwren	*Myrmotherula longipennis*	SA
—Band-tailed Antwren	*Myrmotherula urosticta*	SA
—Ihering's Antwren	*Myrmotherula iheringi*	SA
—Rio de Janeiro Antwren	*Myrmotherula fluminensis*	SA
—Yungas Antwren	*Myrmotherula grisea*	SA
—Unicolored Antwren	*Myrmotherula unicolor*	SA
—Alagoas Antwren	*Myrmotherula snowi*	SA
—Plain-winged Antwren	*Myrmotherula behni*	SA
—Grey Antwren	*Myrmotherula menetriesii*	SA
—Leaden Antwren	*Myrmotherula assimilis*	SA
—Banded Antbird	*Dichrozona cincta*	SA
—Stripe-backed Antbird	*Myrmorchilus strigilatus*	SA
—Bahia Antwren	*Herpsilochmus pileatus*	SA
—Caatinga Antwren	*Herpsilochmus sellowi*	SA
—Black-capped Antwren	*Herpsilochmus atricapillus*	SA
—Creamy-bellied Antwren	*Herpsilochmus motacilloides*	SA
—Ash-throated Antwren	*Herpsilochmus parkeri*	SA
—Spot-tailed Antwren	*Herpsilochmus sticturus*	SA
—Dugand's Antwren	*Herpsilochmus dugandi*	SA
—Todd's Antwren	*Herpsilochmus stictocephalus*	SA
—Spot-backed Antwren	*Herpsilochmus dorsimaculatus*	SA
—Roraiman Antwren	*Herpsilochmus roraimae*	SA
—Pectoral Antwren	*Herpsilochmus pectoralis*	SA
—Large-billed Antwren	*Herpsilochmus longirostris*	SA
—Ancient Antwren	*Herpsilochmus gentryi*	SA
—Yellow-breasted Antwren	*Herpsilochmus axillaris*	SA
—Rufous-winged Antwren	*Herpsilochmus rufimarginatus*	LA
—Dot-winged Antwren	*Microrhopias quixensis*	LA
—Narrow-billed Antwren	*Formicivora iheringi*	SA
—Black-hooded Antwren	*Formicivora erythronotos*	SA
—Southern White-fringed Antwren	*Formicivora grisea*	SA
—Northern White-fringed Antwren	*Formicivora intermedia*	SA
—Serra Antwren	*Formicivora serrana*	SA
—Restinga Antwren	*Formicivora littoralis*	SA
—Black-bellied Antwren	*Formicivora melanogaster*	SA
—Rusty-backed Antwren	*Formicivora rufa*	SA
—Marsh Antwren	*Stymphalornis acutirostris*	SA
—Ferruginous Antbird	*Drymophila ferruginea*	SA
—Bertoni's Antbird	*Drymophila rubricollis*	SA
—Rufous-tailed Antbird	*Drymophila genei*	SA
—Ochre-rumped Antbird	*Drymophila ochropyga*	SA
—Dusky-tailed Antbird	*Drymophila malura*	SA
—Scaled Antbird	*Drymophila squamata*	SA
—Striated Antbird	*Drymophila devillei*	SA
—Long-tailed Antbird	*Drymophila caudata*	SA
—Streak-capped Antwren	*Terenura maculata*	SA
—Orange-bellied Antwren	*Terenura sicki*	SA
—Rufous-rumped Antwren	*Terenura callinota*	LA

INTERNATIONAL ENGLISH NAME	SCIENTIFIC NAME	REGION(S)
—Chestnut-shouldered Antwren	*Terenura humeralis*	SA
—Yellow-rumped Antwren	*Terenura sharpei*	SA
—Ash-winged Antwren	*Terenura spodioptila*	SA
—Grey Antbird	*Cercomacra cinerascens*	SA
—Rio de Janeiro Antbird	*Cercomacra brasiliana*	SA
—Dusky Antbird	*Cercomacra tyrannina*	LA
—Willis's Antbird	*Cercomacra laeta*	SA
—Parker's Antbird	*Cercomacra parkeri*	SA
—Blackish Antbird	*Cercomacra nigrescens*	SA
—Black Antbird	*Cercomacra serva*	SA
—Jet Antbird	*Cercomacra nigricans*	LA
—Rio Branco Antbird	*Cercomacra carbonaria*	SA
—Mato Grosso Antbird	*Cercomacra melanaria*	SA
—Manu Antbird	*Cercomacra manu*	SA
—Bananal Antbird	*Cercomacra ferdinandi*	SA
—White-backed Fire-eye	*Pyriglena leuconota*	SA
—Fringe-backed Fire-eye	*Pyriglena atra*	SA
—White-shouldered Fire-eye	*Pyriglena leucoptera*	SA
—Slender Antbird	*Rhopornis ardesiacus*	SA
—White-browed Antbird	*Myrmoborus leucophrys*	SA
—Ash-breasted Antbird	*Myrmoborus lugubris*	SA
—Black-faced Antbird	*Myrmoborus myotherinus*	SA
—Black-tailed Antbird	*Myrmoborus melanurus*	SA
—Warbling Antbird	*Hypocnemis cantator*	SA
—Yellow-browed Antbird	*Hypocnemis hypoxantha*	SA
—Black-chinned Antbird	*Hypocnemoides melanopogon*	SA
—Band-tailed Antbird	*Hypocnemoides maculicauda*	SA
—Black-and-white Antbird	*Myrmochanes hemileucus*	SA
—Bare-crowned Antbird	*Gymnocichla nudiceps*	LA
—Silvered Antbird	*Sclateria naevia*	SA
—Black-headed Antbird	*Percnostola rufifrons*	SA
—Allpahuayo Antbird	*Percnostola arenarum*	SA
—White-lined Antbird	*Percnostola lophotes*	SA
—Slate-colored Antbird	*Schistocichla schistacea*	SA
—Spot-winged Antbird	*Schistocichla leucostigma*	SA
—Caura Antbird	*Schistocichla caurensis*	SA
—Yapacana Antbird	*Myrmeciza disjuncta*	SA
—White-bellied Antbird	*Myrmeciza longipes*	SA
—Chestnut-backed Antbird	*Myrmeciza exsul*	LA
—Ferruginous-backed Antbird	*Myrmeciza ferruginea*	SA
—Scalloped Antbird	*Myrmeciza ruficauda*	SA
—White-bibbed Antbird	*Myrmeciza loricata*	SA
—Squamate Antbird	*Myrmeciza squamosa*	SA
—Dull-mantled Antbird	*Myrmeciza laemosticta*	LA
—Esmeraldas Antbird	*Myrmeciza nigricauda*	SA
—Stub-tailed Antbird	*Myrmeciza berlepschi*	SA
—Grey-bellied Antbird	*Myrmeciza pelzelni*	SA
—Northern Chestnut-tailed Antbird	*Myrmeciza castanea*	SA
—Southern Chestnut-tailed Antbird	*Myrmeciza hemimelaena*	SA
—Black-throated Antbird	*Myrmeciza atrothorax*	SA
—White-shouldered Antbird	*Myrmeciza melanoceps*	SA
—Goeldi's Antbird	*Myrmeciza goeldii*	SA
—Plumbeous Antbird	*Myrmeciza hyperythra*	SA

INTERNATIONAL ENGLISH NAME	SCIENTIFIC NAME	REGION(S)
—Sooty Antbird	*Myrmeciza fortis*	SA
—Immaculate Antbird	*Myrmeciza immaculata*	LA
—Grey-headed Antbird	*Myrmeciza griseiceps*	SA
—Wing-banded Antbird	*Myrmornis torquata*	LA
—White-plumed Antbird	*Pithys albifrons*	SA
—White-masked Antbird	*Pithys castaneus*	SA
—Bicolored Antbird	*Gymnopithys leucaspis*	LA
—Rufous-throated Antbird	*Gymnopithys rufigula*	SA
—White-throated Antbird	*Gymnopithys salvini*	SA
—Lunulated Antbird	*Gymnopithys lunulatus*	SA
—Bare-eyed Antbird	*Rhegmatorhina gymnops*	SA
—Harlequin Antbird	*Rhegmatorhina berlepschi*	SA
—White-breasted Antbird	*Rhegmatorhina hoffmannsi*	SA
—Chestnut-crested Antbird	*Rhegmatorhina cristata*	SA
—Hairy-crested Antbird	*Rhegmatorhina melanosticta*	SA
—Spotted Antbird	*Hylophylax naevioides*	LA
—Spot-backed Antbird	*Hylophylax naevius*	SA
—Dot-backed Antbird	*Hylophylax punctulatus*	SA
—Scale-backed Antbird	*Hylophylax poecilinotus*	SA
—Black-spotted Bare-eye	*Phlegopsis nigromaculata*	SA
—Reddish-winged Bare-eye	*Phlegopsis erythroptera*	SA
—Pale-faced Antbird	*Skutchia borbae*	SA
—Ocellated Antbird	*Phaenostictus mcleannani*	LA
GNATEATERS	**Family Conopophagidae**	
—Rufous Gnateater	*Conopophaga lineata*	SA
—Ceara Gnateater	*Conopophaga cearae*	SA
—Chestnut-belted Gnateater	*Conopophaga aurita*	SA
—Hooded Gnateater	*Conopophaga roberti*	SA
—Ash-throated Gnateater	*Conopophaga peruviana*	SA
—Slaty Gnateater	*Conopophaga ardesiaca*	SA
—Chestnut-crowned Gnateater	*Conopophaga castaneiceps*	SA
—Black-cheeked Gnateater	*Conopophaga melanops*	SA
—Black-bellied Gnateater	*Conopophaga melanogaster*	SA
TAPACULOS	**Family Rhinocryptidae**	
—Ocellated Tapaculo	*Acropternis orthonyx*	SA
—Chestnut-throated Huet-huet	*Pteroptochos castaneus*	SA
—Black-throated Huet-huet	*Pteroptochos tarnii*	SA
—Moustached Turca	*Pteroptochos megapodius*	SA
—White-throated Tapaculo	*Scelorchilus albicollis*	SA
—Chucao Tapaculo	*Scelorchilus rubecula*	SA
—Crested Gallito	*Rhinocrypta lanceolata*	SA
—Sandy Gallito	*Teledromas fuscus*	SA
—Rusty-belted Tapaculo	*Liosceles thoracicus*	SA
—Collared Crescentchest	*Melanopareia torquata*	SA
—Olive-crowned Crescentchest	*Melanopareia maximiliani*	SA
—Maranon Crescentchest	*Melanopareia maranonica*	SA
—Elegant Crescentchest	*Melanopareia elegans*	SA
—Spotted Bamboowren	*Psilorhamphus guttatus*	SA
—Slaty Bristlefront	*Merulaxis ater*	SA
—Stresemann's Bristlefront	*Merulaxis stresemanni*	SA
—Ochre-flanked Tapaculo	*Eugralla paradoxa*	SA

INTERNATIONAL ENGLISH NAME	SCIENTIFIC NAME	REGION(S)
—Ash-colored Tapaculo	*Myornis senilis*	SA
—Marsh Tapaculo	*Scytalopus iraiensis*	SA
—Mouse-colored Tapaculo	*Scytalopus speluncae*	SA
—Brasilia Tapaculo	*Scytalopus novacapitalis*	SA
—White-breasted Tapaculo	*Scytalopus indigoticus*	SA
—Bahia Tapaculo	*Scytalopus psychopompus*	SA
—Bolivian White-crowned Tapaculo	*Scytalopus bolivianus*	SA
—Northern White-crowned Tapaculo	*Scytalopus atratus*	SA
—Santa Marta Tapaculo	*Scytalopus sanctaemartae*	SA
—Rufous-vented Tapaculo	*Scytalopus femoralis*	SA
—Long-tailed Tapaculo	*Scytalopus micropterus*	SA
—Nariño Tapaculo	*Scytalopus vicinior*	SA
—El Oro Tapaculo	*Scytalopus robbinsi*	SA
—Choco Tapaculo	*Scytalopus chocoensis*	LA
—Tacarcuna Tapaculo	*Scytalopus panamensis*	MA
—Silvery-fronted Tapaculo	*Scytalopus argentifrons*	MA
—Caracas Tapaculo	*Scytalopus caracae*	SA
—Merida Tapaculo	*Scytalopus meridanus*	SA
—Brown-rumped Tapaculo	*Scytalopus latebricola*	SA
—Spillmann's Tapaculo	*Scytalopus spillmanni*	SA
—Chusquea Tapaculo	*Scytalopus parkeri*	SA
—Trilling Tapaculo	*Scytalopus parvirostris*	SA
—Tschudi's Tapaculo	*Scytalopus acutirostris*	SA
—Unicolored Tapaculo	*Scytalopus unicolor*	SA
—Lara Tapaculo	*Scytalopus fuscicauda*	SA
—Rufous-rumped Tapaculo	*Scytalopus griseicollis*	SA
—Paramo Tapaculo	*Scytalopus canus*	SA
—Ancash Tapaculo	*Scytalopus affinis*	SA
—Neblina Tapaculo	*Scytalopus altirostris*	SA
—Vilcabamba Tapaculo	*Scytalopus urubambae*	SA
—Diademed Tapaculo	*Scytalopus schulenbergi*	SA
—Puna Tapaculo	*Scytalopus simonsi*	SA
—Zimmer's Tapaculo	*Scytalopus zimmeri*	SA
—White-browed Tapaculo	*Scytalopus superciliaris*	SA
—Magellanic Tapaculo	*Scytalopus magellanicus*	SA
—Dusky Tapaculo	*Scytalopus fuscus*	SA
—Blackish Tapaculo	*Scytalopus latrans*	SA
—Large-footed Tapaculo	*Scytalopus macropus*	SA
—Cundinamarca Tapaculo	*Scytalopus infasciatus*	SA
ANTTHRUSHES, ANTPITTAS	**Family Formicariidae**	
—Rufous-capped Antthrush	*Formicarius colma*	SA
—Black-faced Antthrush	*Formicarius analis*	SA
—Mayan Antthrush	*Formicarius moniliger*	MA
—Panamanian Antthrush	*Formicarius hoffmanni*	LA
—Rufous-fronted Antthrush	*Formicarius rufifrons*	SA
—Black-headed Antthrush	*Formicarius nigricapillus*	LA
—Rufous-breasted Antthrush	*Formicarius rufipectus*	LA
—Short-tailed Antthrush	*Chamaeza campanisona*	SA
—Striated Antthrush	*Chamaeza nobilis*	SA
—Cryptic Antthrush	*Chamaeza meruloides*	SA
—Rufous-tailed Antthrush	*Chamaeza ruficauda*	SA
—Schwartz's Antthrush	*Chamaeza turdina*	SA

INTERNATIONAL ENGLISH NAME	SCIENTIFIC NAME	REGION(S)
—Barred Antthrush	*Chamaeza mollissima*	SA
—Black-crowned Antpitta	*Pittasoma michleri*	LA
—Rufous-crowned Antpitta	*Pittasoma rufopileatum*	SA
—Undulated Antpitta	*Grallaria squamigera*	SA
—Giant Antpitta	*Grallaria gigantea*	SA
—Great Antpitta	*Grallaria excelsa*	SA
—Variegated Antpitta	*Grallaria varia*	SA
—Moustached Antpitta	*Grallaria alleni*	SA
—Scaled Antpitta	*Grallaria guatimalensis*	LA
—Tachira Antpitta	*Grallaria chthonia*	SA
—Plain-backed Antpitta	*Grallaria haplonota*	SA
—Ochre-striped Antpitta	*Grallaria dignissima*	SA
—Elusive Antpitta	*Grallaria eludens*	SA
—Chestnut-crowned Antpitta	*Grallaria ruficapilla*	SA
—Watkins's Antpitta	*Grallaria watkinsi*	SA
—Santa Marta Antpitta	*Grallaria bangsi*	SA
—Cundinamarca Antpitta	*Grallaria kaestneri*	SA
—Stripe-headed Antpitta	*Grallaria andicolus*	SA
—Grey-naped Antpitta	*Grallaria griseonucha*	SA
—Bicolored Antpitta	*Grallaria rufocinerea*	SA
—Jocotoco Antpitta	*Grallaria ridgelyi*	SA
—Chestnut-naped Antpitta	*Grallaria nuchalis*	SA
—Pale-billed Antpitta	*Grallaria carrikeri*	SA
—White-throated Antpitta	*Grallaria albigula*	SA
—Yellow-breasted Antpitta	*Grallaria flavotincta*	SA
—White-bellied Antpitta	*Grallaria hypoleuca*	SA
—Rusty-tinged Antpitta	*Grallaria przewalskii*	SA
—Bay Antpitta	*Grallaria capitalis*	SA
—Red-and-white Antpitta	*Grallaria erythroleuca*	SA
—Rufous Antpitta	*Grallaria rufula*	SA
—Chestnut Antpitta	*Grallaria blakei*	SA
—Tawny Antpitta	*Grallaria quitensis*	SA
—Brown-banded Antpitta	*Grallaria milleri*	SA
—Rufous-faced Antpitta	*Grallaria erythrotis*	SA
—Streak-chested Antpitta	*Hylopezus perspicillatus*	LA
—Spotted Antpitta	*Hylopezus macularius*	SA
—Masked Antpitta	*Hylopezus auricularis*	SA
—Thicket Antpitta	*Hylopezus dives*	LA
—White-lored Antpitta	*Hylopezus fulviventris*	SA
—Amazonian Antpitta	*Hylopezus berlepschi*	SA
—White-browed Antpitta	*Hylopezus ochroleucus*	SA
—Speckle-breasted Antpitta	*Hylopezus nattereri*	SA
—Thrush-like Antpitta	*Myrmothera campanisona*	SA
—Tepui Antpitta	*Myrmothera simplex*	SA
—Ochre-breasted Antpitta	*Grallaricula flavirostris*	LA
—Scallop-breasted Antpitta	*Grallaricula loricata*	SA
—Hooded Antpitta	*Grallaricula cucullata*	SA
—Peruvian Antpitta	*Grallaricula peruviana*	SA
—Ochre-fronted Antpitta	*Grallaricula ochraceifrons*	SA
—Rusty-breasted Antpitta	*Grallaricula ferrugineipectus*	SA
—Leymebamba Antpitta	*Grallaricula leymebambae*	SA
—Slaty-crowned Antpitta	*Grallaricula nana*	SA
—Crescent-faced Antpitta	*Grallaricula lineifrons*	SA

INTERNATIONAL ENGLISH NAME	SCIENTIFIC NAME	REGION(S)
OVENBIRDS	**Family Furnariidae**	
—Campo Miner	*Geobates poecilopterus*	SA
—Common Miner	*Geositta cunicularia*	SA
—Puna Miner	*Geositta punensis*	SA
—Short-billed Miner	*Geositta antarctica*	SA
—Slender-billed Miner	*Geositta tenuirostris*	SA
—Greyish Miner	*Geositta maritima*	SA
—Coastal Miner	*Geositta peruviana*	SA
—Dark-winged Miner	*Geositta saxicolina*	SA
—Rufous-banded Miner	*Geositta rufipennis*	SA
—Creamy-rumped Miner	*Geositta isabellina*	SA
—Thick-billed Miner	*Geositta crassirostris*	SA
—Plain-breasted Earthcreeper	*Upucerthia jelskii*	SA
—Buff-breasted Earthcreeper	*Upucerthia validirostris*	SA
—White-throated Earthcreeper	*Upucerthia albigula*	SA
—Scaly-throated Earthcreeper	*Upucerthia dumetaria*	SA
—Striated Earthcreeper	*Upucerthia serrana*	SA
—Straight-billed Earthcreeper	*Upucerthia ruficaudus*	SA
—Rock Earthcreeper	*Upucerthia andaecola*	SA
—Bolivian Earthcreeper	*Upucerthia harterti*	SA
—Chaco Earthcreeper	*Upucerthia certhioides*	SA
—Band-tailed Eremobius	*Eremobius phoenicurus*	SA
—Crag Chilia	*Chilia melanura*	SA
—Stout-billed Cinclodes	*Cinclodes excelsior*	SA
—Royal Cinclodes	*Cinclodes aricomae*	SA
—Bar-winged Cinclodes	*Cinclodes fuscus*	SA
—Cordoba Cinclodes	*Cinclodes comechingonus*	SA
—Long-tailed Cinclodes	*Cinclodes pabsti*	SA
—Olrog's Cinclodes	*Cinclodes olrogi*	SA
—Grey-flanked Cinclodes	*Cinclodes oustaleti*	SA
—Dark-bellied Cinclodes	*Cinclodes patagonicus*	SA
—Blackish Cinclodes	*Cinclodes antarcticus*	SA
—Peruvian Seaside Cinclodes	*Cinclodes taczanowskii*	SA
—Chilean Seaside Cinclodes	*Cinclodes nigrofumosus*	SA
—White-winged Cinclodes	*Cinclodes atacamensis*	SA
—White-bellied Cinclodes	*Cinclodes palliatus*	SA
—Lesser Hornero	*Furnarius minor*	SA
—Band-tailed Hornero	*Furnarius figulus*	SA
—Pale-legged Hornero	*Furnarius leucopus*	SA
—Pacific Hornero	*Furnarius cinnamomeus*	SA
—Caribbean Hornero	*Furnarius longirostris*	SA
—Bay Hornero	*Furnarius torridus*	SA
—Rufous Hornero	*Furnarius rufus*	SA
—Crested Hornero	*Furnarius cristatus*	SA
Des Murs's Wiretail	*Sylviorthorhynchus desmursii*	SA
—Thorn-tailed Rayadito	*Aphrastura spinicauda*	SA
—Mas Afuera Rayadito	*Aphrastura masafuerae*	SA
—Brown-capped Tit-Spinetail	*Leptasthenura fuliginiceps*	SA
—Tawny Tit-Spinetail	*Leptasthenura yanacensis*	SA
—Tufted Tit-Spinetail	*Leptasthenura platensis*	SA
—Plain-mantled Tit-Spinetail	*Leptasthenura aegithaloides*	SA
—Striolated Tit-Spinetail	*Leptasthenura striolata*	SA
—Rusty-crowned Tit-Spinetail	*Leptasthenura pileata*	SA

INTERNATIONAL ENGLISH NAME	SCIENTIFIC NAME	REGION(S)
—White-browed Tit-Spinetail	*Leptasthenura xenothorax*	SA
—Streak-backed Tit-Spinetail	*Leptasthenura striata*	SA
—Andean Tit-Spinetail	*Leptasthenura andicola*	SA
—Araucaria Tit-Spinetail	*Leptasthenura setaria*	SA
—Perija Thistletail	*Schizoeaca perijana*	SA
—White-chinned Thistletail	*Schizoeaca fuliginosa*	SA
—Vilcabamba Thistletail	*Schizoeaca vilcabambae*	SA
—Ochre-browed Thistletail	*Schizoeaca coryi*	SA
—Mouse-colored Thistletail	*Schizoeaca griseomurina*	SA
—Eye-ringed Thistletail	*Schizoeaca palpebralis*	SA
—Puna Thistletail	*Schizoeaca helleri*	SA
—Black-throated Thistletail	*Schizoeaca harterti*	SA
—Itatiaia Spinetail	*Oreophylax moreirae*	SA
—Sharp-billed Canastero	*Asthenes pyrrholeuca*	SA
—Short-billed Canastero	*Asthenes baeri*	SA
—Dusky-tailed Canastero	*Asthenes humicola*	SA
—Patagonian Canastero	*Asthenes patagonica*	SA
—Canyon Canastero	*Asthenes pudibunda*	SA
—Rusty-fronted Canastero	*Asthenes ottonis*	SA
—Maquis Canastero	*Asthenes heterura*	SA
—Cordilleran Canastero	*Asthenes modesta*	SA
—Cactus Canastero	*Asthenes cactorum*	SA
—Streak-throated Canastero	*Asthenes humilis*	SA
—Rusty-vented Canastero	*Asthenes dorbignyi*	SA
—Dark-winged Canastero	*Asthenes arequipae*	SA
—Pale-tailed Canastero	*Asthenes huancavelicae*	SA
—Berlepsch's Canastero	*Asthenes berlepschi*	SA
—Steinbach's Canastero	*Asthenes steinbachi*	SA
—Cipo Canastero	*Asthenes luizae*	SA
—Streak-backed Canastero	*Asthenes wyatti*	SA
—Puna Canastero	*Asthenes sclateri*	SA
—Austral Canastero	*Asthenes anthoides*	SA
—Hudson's Canastero	*Asthenes hudsoni*	SA
—Line-fronted Canastero	*Asthenes urubambensis*	SA
—Many-striped Canastero	*Asthenes flammulata*	SA
—Junin Canastero	*Asthenes virgata*	SA
—Scribble-tailed Canastero	*Asthenes maculicauda*	SA
—Chotoy Spinetail	*Schoeniophylax phryganophilus*	SA
—White-whiskered Spinetail	*Synallaxis candei*	SA
—Hoary-throated Spinetail	*Synallaxis kollari*	SA
—Ochre-cheeked Spinetail	*Synallaxis scutata*	SA
—Rufous Spinetail	*Synallaxis unirufa*	SA
—Black-throated Spinetail	*Synallaxis castanea*	SA
—Rusty-headed Spinetail	*Synallaxis fuscorufa*	SA
—Rufous-capped Spinetail	*Synallaxis ruficapilla*	SA
—Bahia Spinetail	*Synallaxis cinerea*	SA
—Pinto's Spinetail	*Synallaxis infuscata*	SA
—Stripe-breasted Spinetail	*Synallaxis cinnamomea*	SA
—Grey-bellied Spinetail	*Synallaxis cinerascens*	SA
—Silvery-throated Spinetail	*Synallaxis subpudica*	SA
—Sooty-fronted Spinetail	*Synallaxis frontalis*	SA
—Azara's Spinetail	*Synallaxis azarae*	SA
—Apurimac Spinetail	*Synallaxis courseni*	SA

INTERNATIONAL ENGLISH NAME	SCIENTIFIC NAME	REGION(S)
__Pale-breasted Spinetail	*Synallaxis albescens*	LA
__Dark-breasted Spinetail	*Synallaxis albigularis*	SA
__Cinereous-breasted Spinetail	*Synallaxis hypospodia*	SA
__Spix's Spinetail	*Synallaxis spixi*	SA
__Ruddy Spinetail	*Synallaxis rutilans*	SA
__Chestnut-throated Spinetail	*Synallaxis cherriei*	SA
__Rufous-breasted Spinetail	*Synallaxis erythrothorax*	MA
__Slaty Spinetail	*Synallaxis brachyura*	LA
__Blackish-headed Spinetail	*Synallaxis tithys*	SA
__White-bellied Spinetail	*Synallaxis propinqua*	SA
__McConnell's Spinetail	*Synallaxis macconnelli*	SA
__Dusky Spinetail	*Synallaxis moesta*	SA
__Cabanis's Spinetail	*Synallaxis cabanisi*	SA
__Plain-crowned Spinetail	*Synallaxis gujanensis*	SA
__Maranon Spinetail	*Synallaxis maranonica*	SA
__White-lored Spinetail	*Synallaxis albilora*	SA
__Russet-bellied Spinetail	*Synallaxis zimmeri*	SA
__Necklaced Spinetail	*Synallaxis stictothorax*	SA
__Chinchipe Spinetail	*Synallaxis chinchipensis*	SA
__Great Spinetail	*Siptornopsis hypochondriaca*	SA
__Red-shouldered Spinetail	*Gyalophylax hellmayri*	SA
__White-browed Spinetail	*Hellmayrea gularis*	SA
__Marcapata Spinetail	*Cranioleuca marcapatae*	SA
__Light-crowned Spinetail	*Cranioleuca albiceps*	SA
__Rusty-backed Spinetail	*Cranioleuca vulpina*	SA
__Coiba Spinetail	*Cranioleuca dissita*	MA
__Parker's Spinetail	*Cranioleuca vulpecula*	SA
__Sulphur-bearded Spinetail	*Cranioleuca sulphurifera*	SA
__Crested Spinetail	*Cranioleuca subcristata*	SA
__Stripe-crowned Spinetail	*Cranioleuca pyrrhophia*	SA
__Inquisivi Spinetail	*Cranioleuca henricae*	SA
__Olive Spinetail	*Cranioleuca obsoleta*	SA
__Pallid Spinetail	*Cranioleuca pallida*	SA
__Grey-headed Spinetail	*Cranioleuca semicinerea*	SA
__Creamy-crested Spinetail	*Cranioleuca albicapilla*	SA
__Red-faced Spinetail	*Cranioleuca erythrops*	LA
__Tepui Spinetail	*Cranioleuca demissa*	SA
__Streak-capped Spinetail	*Cranioleuca hellmayri*	SA
__Ash-browed Spinetail	*Cranioleuca curtata*	SA
__Line-cheeked Spinetail	*Cranioleuca antisiensis*	SA
__Baron's Spinetail	*Cranioleuca baroni*	SA
__Speckled Spinetail	*Cranioleuca gutturata*	SA
__Scaled Spinetail	*Cranioleuca muelleri*	SA
__Yellow-chinned Spinetail	*Certhiaxis cinnamomeus*	SA
__Red-and-white Spinetail	*Certhiaxis mustelinus*	SA
__Orinoco Softtail	*Thripophaga cherriei*	SA
__Striated Softtail	*Thripophaga macroura*	SA
__Plain Softtail	*Thripophaga fusciceps*	SA
__Russet-mantled Softtail	*Thripophaga berlepschi*	SA
__Rufous-fronted Thornbird	*Phacellodomus rufifrons*	SA
__Plain Thornbird	*Phacellodomus inornatus*	SA
__Little Thornbird	*Phacellodomus sibilatrix*	SA
__Streak-fronted Thornbird	*Phacellodomus striaticeps*	SA

115

INTERNATIONAL ENGLISH NAME	SCIENTIFIC NAME	REGION(S)
—Freckle-breasted Thornbird	*Phacellodomus striaticollis*	SA
—Spot-breasted Thornbird	*Phacellodomus maculipectus*	SA
—Chestnut-backed Thornbird	*Phacellodomus dorsalis*	SA
—Greater Thornbird	*Phacellodomus ruber*	SA
—Orange-eyed Thornbird	*Phacellodomus erythrophthalmus*	SA
—Red-eyed Thornbird	*Phacellodomus ferrugineigula*	SA
—Canebrake Groundcreeper	*Clibanornis dendrocolaptoides*	SA
—Bay-capped Wren-Spinetail	*Spartonoica maluroides*	SA
—Wren-like Rushbird	*Phleocryptes melanops*	SA
—Curve-billed Reedhaunter	*Limnornis curvirostris*	SA
—Straight-billed Reedhaunter	*Limnoctites rectirostris*	SA
—Firewood-gatherer	*Anumbius annumbi*	SA
—Lark-like Brushrunner	*Coryphistera alaudina*	SA
—Spectacled Prickletail	*Siptornis striaticollis*	SA
—Orange-fronted Plushcrown	*Metopothrix aurantiaca*	SA
—Double-banded Greytail	*Xenerpestes minlosi*	LA
—Equatorial Greytail	*Xenerpestes singularis*	SA
—Rusty-winged Barbtail	*Premnornis guttuligera*	SA
—Spotted Barbtail	*Premnoplex brunnescens*	LA
—White-throated Barbtail	*Premnoplex tatei*	SA
—Roraiman Barbtail	*Roraimia adusta*	SA
—Pink-legged Graveteiro	*Acrobatornis fonsecai*	SA
—Ruddy Treerunner	*Margarornis rubiginosus*	MA
—Star-chested Treerunner	*Margarornis stellatus*	SA
—Beautiful Treerunner	*Margarornis bellulus*	MA
—Pearled Treerunner	*Margarornis squamiger*	SA
—Caatinga Cacholote	*Pseudoseisura cristata*	SA
—Grey-crested Cacholote	*Pseudoseisura unirufa*	SA
—Brown Cacholote	*Pseudoseisura lophotes*	SA
—White-throated Cacholote	*Pseudoseisura gutturalis*	SA
—Buffy Tuftedcheek	*Pseudocolaptes lawrencii*	MA
—Pacific Tuftedcheek	*Pseudocolaptes johnsoni*	SA
—Streaked Tuftedcheek	*Pseudocolaptes boissonneautii*	SA
—Point-tailed Palmcreeper	*Berlepschia rikeri*	SA
—Scaly-throated Foliage-gleaner	*Anabacerthia variegaticeps*	LA
—Montane Foliage-gleaner	*Anabacerthia striaticollis*	SA
—White-browed Foliage-gleaner	*Anabacerthia amaurotis*	SA
—Guttulated Foliage-gleaner	*Syndactyla guttulata*	SA
—Lineated Foliage-gleaner	*Syndactyla subalaris*	LA
—Buff-browed Foliage-gleaner	*Syndactyla rufosuperciliata*	SA
—Rufous-necked Foliage-gleaner	*Syndactyla ruficollis*	SA
—Peruvian Recurvebill	*Simoxenops ucayalae*	SA
—Bolivian Recurvebill	*Simoxenops striatus*	SA
—Chestnut-winged Hookbill	*Ancistrops strigilatus*	SA
—Eastern Woodhaunter	*Hyloctistes subulatus*	SA
—Western Woodhaunter	*Hyloctistes virgatus*	LA
—Rufous-tailed Foliage-gleaner	*Philydor ruficaudatum*	SA
—Slaty-winged Foliage-gleaner	*Philydor fuscipenne*	LA
—Rufous-rumped Foliage-gleaner	*Philydor erythrocercum*	SA
—Chestnut-winged Foliage-gleaner	*Philydor erythropterum*	SA
—Ochre-breasted Foliage-gleaner	*Philydor lichtensteini*	SA
—Alagoas Foliage-gleaner	*Philydor novaesi*	SA
—Black-capped Foliage-gleaner	*Philydor atricapillus*	SA

INTERNATIONAL ENGLISH NAME	SCIENTIFIC NAME	REGION(S)
__Buff-fronted Foliage-gleaner	*Philydor rufum*	LA
__Cinnamon-rumped Foliage-gleaner	*Philydor pyrrhodes*	SA
__Planalto Foliage-gleaner	*Philydor dimidiatum*	SA
__Bamboo Foliage-gleaner	*Anabazenops dorsalis*	SA
__White-collared Foliage-gleaner	*Anabazenops fuscus*	SA
__Pale-browed Treehunter	*Cichlocolaptes leucophrus*	SA
__Uniform Treehunter	*Thripadectes ignobilis*	SA
__Streak-breasted Treehunter	*Thripadectes rufobrunneus*	MA
__Black-billed Treehunter	*Thripadectes melanorhynchus*	SA
__Striped Treehunter	*Thripadectes holostictus*	SA
__Streak-capped Treehunter	*Thripadectes virgaticeps*	SA
__Flammulated Treehunter	*Thripadectes flammulatus*	SA
__Peruvian Treehunter	*Thripadectes scrutator*	SA
__Buff-throated Foliage-gleaner	*Automolus ochrolaemus*	LA
__Olive-backed Foliage-gleaner	*Automolus infuscatus*	SA
__Para Foliage-gleaner	*Automolus paraensis*	SA
__White-eyed Foliage-gleaner	*Automolus leucophthalmus*	SA
__Brown-rumped Foliage-gleaner	*Automolus melanopezus*	SA
__Tepui Foliage-gleaner	*Automolus roraimae*	SA
__Ruddy Foliage-gleaner	*Automolus rubiginosus*	LA
__Chestnut-crowned Foliage-gleaner	*Automolus rufipileatus*	SA
__Henna-hooded Foliage-gleaner	*Hylocryptus erythrocephalus*	SA
__Henna-capped Foliage-gleaner	*Hylocryptus rectirostris*	SA
__Tawny-throated Leaftosser	*Sclerurus mexicanus*	LA
__Short-billed Leaftosser	*Sclerurus rufigularis*	SA
__Grey-throated Leaftosser	*Sclerurus albigularis*	LA
__Black-tailed Leaftosser	*Sclerurus caudacutus*	SA
__Rufous-breasted Leaftosser	*Sclerurus scansor*	SA
__Scaly-throated Leaftosser	*Sclerurus guatemalensis*	LA
__Sharp-tailed Streamcreeper	*Lochmias nematura*	SA
__Sharp-billed Treehunter	*Heliobletus contaminatus*	SA
__Rufous-tailed Xenops	*Xenops milleri*	SA
__Slender-billed Xenops	*Xenops tenuirostris*	SA
__Plain Xenops	*Xenops minutus*	LA
__Streaked Xenops	*Xenops rutilans*	LA
__Great Xenops	*Megaxenops parnaguae*	SA
__White-throated Treerunner	*Pygarrhichas albogularis*	SA

WOODCREEPERS	**Family Dendrocolaptidae**	
__Tyrannine Woodcreeper	*Dendrocincla tyrannina*	SA
__Plain-brown Woodcreeper	*Dendrocincla fuliginosa*	LA
__Plain-winged Woodcreeper	*Dendrocincla turdina*	SA
__Tawny-winged Woodcreeper	*Dendrocincla anabatina*	MA
__White-chinned Woodcreeper	*Dendrocincla merula*	SA
__Ruddy Woodcreeper	*Dendrocincla homochroa*	LA
__Long-tailed Woodcreeper	*Deconychura longicauda*	LA
__Spot-throated Woodcreeper	*Deconychura stictolaema*	SA
__Olivaceous Woodcreeper	*Sittasomus griseicapillus*	LA
__Wedge-billed Woodcreeper	*Glyphorynchus spirurus*	LA
__Scimitar-billed Woodcreeper	*Drymornis bridgesii*	SA
__Long-billed Woodcreeper	*Nasica longirostris*	SA
__Cinnamon-throated Woodcreeper	*Dendrexetastes rufigula*	SA
__Red-billed Woodcreeper	*Hylexetastes perrotii*	SA

INTERNATIONAL ENGLISH NAME	SCIENTIFIC NAME	REGION(S)
—Uniform Woodcreeper	*Hylexetastes uniformis*	SA
—Bar-bellied Woodcreeper	*Hylexetastes stresemanni*	SA
—Strong-billed Woodcreeper	*Xiphocolaptes promeropirhynchus*	LA
—White-throated Woodcreeper	*Xiphocolaptes albicollis*	SA
—Moustached Woodcreeper	*Xiphocolaptes falcirostris*	SA
—Great Rufous Woodcreeper	*Xiphocolaptes major*	SA
—Northern Barred Woodcreeper	*Dendrocolaptes sanctithomae*	LA
—Amazonian Barred Woodcreeper	*Dendrocolaptes certhia*	SA
—Hoffman's Woodcreeper	*Dendrocolaptes hoffmannsi*	SA
—Black-banded Woodcreeper	*Dendrocolaptes picumnus*	LA
—Planalto Woodcreeper	*Dendrocolaptes platyrostris*	SA
—Straight-billed Woodcreeper	*Xiphorhynchus picus*	LA
—Zimmer's Woodcreeper	*Xiphorhynchus kienerii*	SA
—Striped Woodcreeper	*Xiphorhynchus obsoletus*	SA
—Lesser Woodcreeper	*Xiphorhynchus fuscus*	SA
—Ocellated Woodcreeper	*Xiphorhynchus ocellatus*	SA
—Elegant Woodcreeper	*Xiphorhynchus elegans*	SA
—Spix's Woodcreeper	*Xiphorhynchus spixii*	SA
—Chestnut-rumped Woodcreeper	*Xiphorhynchus pardalotus*	SA
—Buff-throated Woodcreeper	*Xiphorhynchus guttatus*	SA
—Cocoa Woodcreeper	*Xiphorhynchus susurrans*	LA
—Ivory-billed Woodcreeper	*Xiphorhynchus flavigaster*	MA
—Black-striped Woodcreeper	*Xiphorhynchus lachrymosus*	LA
—Spotted Woodcreeper	*Xiphorhynchus erythropygius*	LA
—Olive-backed Woodcreeper	*Xiphorhynchus triangularis*	SA
—White-striped Woodcreeper	*Lepidocolaptes leucogaster*	MA
—Streak-headed Woodcreeper	*Lepidocolaptes souleyetii*	LA
—Narrow-billed Woodcreeper	*Lepidocolaptes angustirostris*	SA
—Spot-crowned Woodcreeper	*Lepidocolaptes affinis*	MA
—Montane Woodcreeper	*Lepidocolaptes lacrymiger*	SA
—Scalloped Woodcreeper	*Lepidocolaptes squamatus*	SA
—Lineated Woodcreeper	*Lepidocolaptes albolineatus*	SA
—Greater Scythebill	*Campylorhamphus pucherani*	SA
—Red-billed Scythebill	*Campylorhamphus trochilirostris*	LA
—Black-billed Scythebill	*Campylorhamphus falcularius*	SA
—Brown-billed Scythebill	*Campylorhamphus pusillus*	LA
—Curve-billed Scythebill	*Campylorhamphus procurvoides*	SA

INTERNATIONAL ENGLISH NAME	SCIENTIFIC NAME	REGION(S)
	ORDER PASSERIFORMES	
LYREBIRDS	**Family Menuridae**	
—Albert's Lyrebird	*Menura alberti*	AU
—Superb Lyrebird	*Menura novaehollandiae*	AU
SCRUBBIRDS	**Family Atrichornithidae**	
—Rufous Scrubbird	*Atrichornis rufescens*	AU
—Noisy Scrubbird	*Atrichornis clamosus*	AU
BOWERBIRDS	**Family Ptilonorhynchidae**	
—White-eared Catbird	*Ailuroedus buccoides*	AU
—Green Catbird	*Ailuroedus crassirostris*	AU
—Tooth-billed Bowerbird	*Scenopoeetes dentirostris*	AU
—Archbold's Bowerbird	*Archboldia papuensis*	AU
—Vogelkop Bowerbird	*Amblyornis inornata*	AU
—Macgregor's Bowerbird	*Amblyornis macgregoriae*	AU
—Streaked Bowerbird	*Amblyornis subalaris*	AU
—Golden-fronted Bowerbird	*Amblyornis flavifrons*	AU
—Golden Bowerbird	*Prionodura newtoniana*	AU
—Masked Bowerbird	*Sericulus aureus*	AU
—Flame Bowerbird	*Sericulus ardens*	AU
—Fire-maned Bowerbird	*Sericulus bakeri*	AU
—Regent Bowerbird	*Sericulus chrysocephalus*	AU
—Satin Bowerbird	*Ptilonorhynchus violaceus*	AU
—Western Bowerbird	*Chlamydera guttata*	AU
—Great Bowerbird	*Chlamydera nuchalis*	AU
—Spotted Bowerbird	*Chlamydera maculata*	AU
—Yellow-breasted Bowerbird	*Chlamydera lauterbachi*	AU
—Fawn-breasted Bowerbird	*Chlamydera cerviniventris*	AU
AUSTRALASIAN TREECREEPERS	**Family Climacteridae**	
—White-throated Treecreeper	*Cormobates leucophaea*	AU
—Papuan Treecreeper	*Cormobates placens*	AU
—Red-browed Treecreeper	*Climacteris erythrops*	AU
—White-browed Treecreeper	*Climacteris affinis*	AU
—Rufous Treecreeper	*Climacteris rufus*	AU
—Brown Treecreeper	*Climacteris picumnus*	AU
—Black-tailed Treecreeper	*Climacteris melanurus*	AU
AUSTRALASIAN WRENS	**Family Maluridae**	
—Wallace's Fairywren	*Sipodotus wallacii*	AU
—Broad-billed Fairywren	*Malurus grayi*	AU
—Campbell's Fairywren	*Malurus campbelli*	AU
—Emperor Fairywren	*Malurus cyanocephalus*	AU
—Lovely Fairywren	*Malurus amabilis*	AU
—Variegated Fairywren	*Malurus lamberti*	AU
—Blue-breasted Fairywren	*Malurus pulcherrimus*	AU
—Red-winged Fairywren	*Malurus elegans*	AU
—Superb Fairywren	*Malurus cyaneus*	AU
—Splendid Fairywren	*Malurus splendens*	AU
—Purple-crowned Fairywren	*Malurus coronatus*	AU

INTERNATIONAL ENGLISH NAME	SCIENTIFIC NAME	REGION(S)
—White-shouldered Fairywren	*Malurus alboscapulatus*	AU
—Red-backed Fairywren	*Malurus melanocephalus*	AU
—White-winged Fairywren	*Malurus leucopterus*	AU
—Orange-crowned Fairywren	*Clytomyias insignis*	AU
—Southern Emu-wren	*Stipiturus malachurus*	AU
—Mallee Emu-wren	*Stipiturus mallee*	AU
—Rufous-crowned Emu-wren	*Stipiturus ruficeps*	AU
—Grey Grasswren	*Amytornis barbatus*	AU
—Black Grasswren	*Amytornis housei*	AU
—White-throated Grasswren	*Amytornis woodwardi*	AU
—Carpentarian Grasswren	*Amytornis dorotheae*	AU
—Short-tailed Grasswren	*Amytornis merrotsyi*	AU
—Striated Grasswren	*Amytornis striatus*	AU
—Eyrean Grasswren	*Amytornis goyderi*	AU
—Thick-billed Grasswren	*Amytornis textilis*	AU
—Dusky Grasswren	*Amytornis purnelli*	AU
—Kalkadoon Grasswren	*Amytornis ballarae*	AU

HONEYEATERS	**Family Meliphagidae**	
—Kauai Oo	*Moho braccatus*	PO
—Bishop's Oo	*Moho bishopi*	PO
—Stitchbird	*Notiomystis cincta*	AU
—Spotted Honeyeater	*Xanthotis polygrammus*	AU
—Macleay's Honeyeater	*Xanthotis macleayanus*	AU
—Tawny-breasted Honeyeater	*Xanthotis flaviventer*	AU
—Kadavu Honeyeater	*Xanthotis provocator*	PO
—Streak-breasted Honeyeater	*Lichenostomus reticulatus*	AU
—Black-throated Honeyeater	*Lichenostomus subfrenatus*	AU
—Obscure Honeyeater	*Lichenostomus obscurus*	AU
—Bridled Honeyeater	*Lichenostomus frenatus*	AU
—Eungella Honeyeater	*Lichenostomus hindwoodi*	AU
—Yellow-faced Honeyeater	*Lichenostomus chrysops*	AU
—Singing Honeyeater	*Lichenostomus virescens*	AU
—Varied Honeyeater	*Lichenostomus versicolor*	AU
—Mangrove Honeyeater	*Lichenostomus fasciogularis*	AU
—White-gaped Honeyeater	*Lichenostomus unicolor*	AU
—Yellow Honeyeater	*Lichenostomus flavus*	AU
—White-eared Honeyeater	*Lichenostomus leucotis*	AU
—Yellow-throated Honeyeater	*Lichenostomus flavicollis*	AU
—Yellow-tufted Honeyeater	*Lichenostomus melanops*	AU
—Purple-gaped Honeyeater	*Lichenostomus cratitius*	AU
—Grey-headed Honeyeater	*Lichenostomus keartlandi*	AU
—Yellow-plumed Honeyeater	*Lichenostomus ornatus*	AU
—Grey-fronted Honeyeater	*Lichenostomus plumulus*	AU
—Fuscous Honeyeater	*Lichenostomus fuscus*	AU
—Yellow-tinted Honeyeater	*Lichenostomus flavescens*	AU
—White-plumed Honeyeater	*Lichenostomus penicillatus*	AU
—Guadalcanal Honeyeater	*Guadalcanaria inexpectata*	AU
—Orange-cheeked Honeyeater	*Oreornis chrysogenys*	AU
—Mottle-breasted Honeyeater	*Meliphaga mimikae*	AU
—Forest Honeyeater	*Meliphaga montana*	AU
—Hill-forest Honeyeater	*Meliphaga orientalis*	AU
—Scrub Honeyeater	*Meliphaga albonotata*	AU

INTERNATIONAL ENGLISH NAME	SCIENTIFIC NAME	REGION(S)
—Mimic Honeyeater	*Meliphaga analoga*	AU
—Tagula Honeyeater	*Meliphaga vicina*	AU
—Graceful Honeyeater	*Meliphaga gracilis*	AU
—Yellow-gaped Honeyeater	*Meliphaga flavirictus*	AU
—White-lined Honeyeater	*Meliphaga albilineata*	AU
—Puff-backed Honeyeater	*Meliphaga aruensis*	AU
—Yellow-spotted Honeyeater	*Meliphaga notata*	AU
—Lewin's Honeyeater	*Meliphaga lewinii*	AU
—Wattled Honeyeater	*Foulehaio carunculatus*	PO
—Yodeling Honeyeater	*Gymnomyza viridis*	PO
—Mao	*Gymnomyza samoensis*	PO
—Crow Honeyeater	*Gymnomyza aubryana*	AU
—Bell Miner	*Manorina melanophrys*	AU
—Noisy Miner	*Manorina melanocephala*	AU
—Yellow-throated Miner	*Manorina flavigula*	AU
—Black-eared Miner	*Manorina melanotis*	AU
—Blue-faced Honeyeater	*Entomyzon cyanotis*	AU
—Black-chinned Honeyeater	*Melithreptus gularis*	AU
—Strong-billed Honeyeater	*Melithreptus validirostris*	AU
—Brown-headed Honeyeater	*Melithreptus brevirostris*	AU
—White-throated Honeyeater	*Melithreptus albogularis*	AU
—White-naped Honeyeater	*Melithreptus lunatus*	AU
—Black-headed Honeyeater	*Melithreptus affinis*	AU
—New Zealand Bellbird	*Anthornis melanura*	AU
—Tui	*Prosthemadera novaeseelandiae*	AU
—Plain Honeyeater	*Pycnopygius ixoides*	AU
—Marbled Honeyeater	*Pycnopygius cinereus*	AU
—Streak-headed Honeyeater	*Pycnopygius stictocephalus*	AU
—White-streaked Friarbird	*Melitograis gilolensis*	AU
—Meyer's Friarbird	*Philemon meyeri*	AU
—Brass's Friarbird	*Philemon brassi*	AU
—Little Friarbird	*Philemon citreogularis*	AU
—Grey Friarbird	*Philemon kisserensis*	AU
—Timor Friarbird	*Philemon inornatus*	AU
—Dusky Friarbird	*Philemon fuscicapillus*	AU
—Seram Friarbird	*Philemon subcorniculatus*	AU
—Black-faced Friarbird	*Philemon moluccensis*	AU
—Helmeted Friarbird	*Philemon buceroides*	AU
—Papuan Friarbird	*Philemon novaeguineae*	AU
—Hornbill Friarbird	*Philemon yorki*	AU
—New Britain Friarbird	*Philemon cockerelli*	AU
—New Ireland Friarbird	*Philemon eichhorni*	AU
—White-naped Friarbird	*Philemon albitorques*	AU
—Silver-crowned Friarbird	*Philemon argenticeps*	AU
—Noisy Friarbird	*Philemon corniculatus*	AU
—New Caledonian Friarbird	*Philemon diemenensis*	AU
—Striped Honeyeater	*Plectorhyncha lanceolata*	AU
—Spiny-cheeked Honeyeater	*Acanthagenys rufogularis*	AU
—Little Wattlebird	*Anthochaera chrysoptera*	AU
—Western Wattlebird	*Anthochaera lunulata*	AU
—Red Wattlebird	*Anthochaera carunculata*	AU
—Yellow Wattlebird	*Anthochaera paradoxa*	AU
—Regent Honeyeater	*Xanthomyza phrygia*	AU

INTERNATIONAL ENGLISH NAME	SCIENTIFIC NAME	REGION(S)
—Bare-eyed Honeyeater	*Melipotes gymnops*	AU
—Smoky Honeyeater	*Melipotes fumigatus*	AU
—Spangled Honeyeater	*Melipotes ater*	AU
—Macgregor's Lappetface	*Macgregoria pulchra*	AU
—Sooty Honeyeater	*Melidectes fuscus*	AU
—Gilliard's Honeyeater	*Melidectes whitemanensis*	AU
—Short-bearded Honeyeater	*Melidectes nouhuysi*	AU
—Long-bearded Honeyeater	*Melidectes princeps*	AU
—Cinnamon-browed Honeyeater	*Melidectes ochromelas*	AU
—White-capped Honeyeater	*Melidectes leucostephes*	AU
—Yellow-browed Honeyeater	*Melidectes rufocrissalis*	AU
—Huon Honeyeater	*Melidectes foersteri*	AU
—Belford's Honeyeater	*Melidectes belfordi*	AU
—Ornate Honeyeater	*Melidectes torquatus*	AU
—Graceless Honeyeater	*Meliarchus sclateri*	AU
—Leaden Honeyeater	*Ptiloprora plumbea*	AU
—Olive-streaked Honeyeater	*Ptiloprora meekiana*	AU
—Rufous-sided Honeyeater	*Ptiloprora erythropleura*	AU
—Rufous-backed Honeyeater	*Ptiloprora guisei*	AU
—Mayr's Honeyeater	*Ptiloprora mayri*	AU
—Grey-streaked Honeyeater	*Ptiloprora perstriata*	AU
—Dark-eared Myza	*Myza celebensis*	AU
—White-eared Myza	*Myza sarasinorum*	AU
—Long-billed Honeyeater	*Melilestes megarhynchus*	AU
—Bougainville Honeyeater	*Stresemannia bougainvillei*	AU
—Barred Honeyeater	*Glycifohia undulata*	AU
—White-bellied Honeyeater	*Glycifohia notabilis*	PO
—Scaly-crowned Honeyeater	*Lichmera lombokia*	AU
—Olive Honeyeater	*Lichmera argentauris*	AU
—Brown Honeyeater	*Lichmera indistincta*	AU
—Grey-eared Honeyeater	*Lichmera incana*	PO
—Silver-eared Honeyeater	*Lichmera alboauricularis*	AU
—Scaly-breasted Honeyeater	*Lichmera squamata*	AU
—Buru Honeyeater	*Lichmera deningeri*	AU
—Seram Honeyeater	*Lichmera monticola*	AU
—Flame-eared Honeyeater	*Lichmera flavicans*	AU
—Black-necklaced Honeyeater	*Lichmera notabilis*	AU
—White-streaked Honeyeater	*Trichodere cockerelli*	AU
—Painted Honeyeater	*Grantiella picta*	AU
—Crescent Honeyeater	*Phylidonyris pyrrhopterus*	AU
—New Holland Honeyeater	*Phylidonyris novaehollandiae*	AU
—White-cheeked Honeyeater	*Phylidonyris niger*	AU
—White-fronted Honeyeater	*Phylidonyris albifrons*	AU
—Tawny-crowned Honeyeater	*Glyciphila melanops*	AU
—Brown-backed Honeyeater	*Ramsayornis modestus*	AU
—Bar-breasted Honeyeater	*Ramsayornis fasciatus*	AU
—Rufous-banded Honeyeater	*Conopophila albogularis*	AU
—Rufous-throated Honeyeater	*Conopophila rufogularis*	AU
—Grey Honeyeater	*Conopophila whitei*	AU
—Eastern Spinebill	*Acanthorhynchus tenuirostris*	AU
—Western Spinebill	*Acanthorhynchus superciliosus*	AU
—Pied Honeyeater	*Certhionyx variegatus*	AU
—Banded Honeyeater	*Certhionyx pectoralis*	AU

INTERNATIONAL ENGLISH NAME	SCIENTIFIC NAME	REGION(S)
—Black Honeyeater	*Certhionyx niger*	AU
—Drab Myzomela	*Myzomela blasii*	AU
—White-chinned Myzomela	*Myzomela albigula*	AU
—Ashy Myzomela	*Myzomela cineracea*	AU
—Ruby-throated Myzomela	*Myzomela eques*	AU
—Dusky Myzomela	*Myzomela obscura*	AU
—Red Myzomela	*Myzomela cruentata*	AU
—Black Myzomela	*Myzomela nigrita*	AU
—Crimson-fronted Myzomela	*Myzomela pulchella*	AU
—Crimson-hooded Myzomela	*Myzomela kuehni*	AU
—Red-headed Myzomela	*Myzomela erythrocephala*	AU
—Midget Myzomela	*Myzomela adolphinae*	AU
—Banda Myzomela	*Myzomela boiei*	AU
—Sulawesi Myzomela	*Myzomela chloroptera*	AU
—Wakolo Myzomela	*Myzomela wakoloensis*	AU
—Scarlet Myzomela	*Myzomela sanguinolenta*	AU
—Cardinal Myzomela	*Myzomela cardinalis*	AU
—Rotuma Myzomela	*Myzomela chermesina*	PO
—Micronesian Myzomela	*Myzomela rubratra*	PO
—Scarlet-bibbed Myzomela	*Myzomela sclateri*	AU
—Ebony Myzomela	*Myzomela pammelaena*	AU
—Red-capped Myzomela	*Myzomela lafargei*	AU
—Crimson-rumped Myzomela	*Myzomela eichhorni*	AU
—Red-vested Myzomela	*Myzomela malaitae*	AU
—Black-headed Myzomela	*Myzomela melanocephala*	AU
—Sooty Myzomela	*Myzomela tristrami*	AU
—Sulphur-breasted Myzomela	*Myzomela jugularis*	PO
—Splendid Myzomela	*Myzomela erythromelas*	AU
—Black-breasted Myzomela	*Myzomela vulnerata*	AU
—Red-collared Myzomela	*Myzomela rosenbergii*	AU
—Olive Straightbill	*Timeliopsis fulvigula*	AU
—Tawny Straightbill	*Timeliopsis griseigula*	AU
—Green-backed Honeyeater	*Timeliopsis fallax*	AU
—Crimson Chat	*Epthianura tricolor*	AU
—Orange Chat	*Epthianura aurifrons*	AU
—Yellow Chat	*Epthianura crocea*	AU
—White-fronted Chat	*Epthianura albifrons*	AU
—Gibberbird	*Ashbyia lovensis*	AU
BRISTLEBIRDS	**Family Dasyornithidae**	
—Eastern Bristlebird	*Dasyornis brachypterus*	AU
—Western Bristlebird	*Dasyornis longirostris*	AU
—Rufous Bristlebird	*Dasyornis broadbenti*	AU
PARDALOTES	**Family Pardalotidae**	
—Spotted Pardalote	*Pardalotus punctatus*	AU
—Forty-spotted Pardalote	*Pardalotus quadragintus*	AU
—Red-browed Pardalote	*Pardalotus rubricatus*	AU
—Striated Pardalote	*Pardalotus striatus*	AU
AUSTRALASIAN WARBLERS	**Family Acanthizidae**	
—Pilotbird	*Pycnoptilus floccosus*	AU
—Scrubtit	*Acanthornis magna*	AU

INTERNATIONAL ENGLISH NAME	SCIENTIFIC NAME	REGION(S)
—Rockwarbler	*Origma solitaria*	AU
—Chestnut-rumped Heathwren	*Calamanthus pyrrhopygius*	AU
—Shy Heathwren	*Calamanthus cautus*	AU
—Striated Fieldwren	*Calamanthus fuliginosus*	AU
—Western Fieldwren	*Calamanthus montanellus*	AU
—Rufous Fieldwren	*Calamanthus campestris*	AU
—Redthroat	*Pyrrholaemus brunneus*	AU
—Speckled Warbler	*Pyrrholaemus sagittatus*	AU
—Fernwren	*Oreoscopus gutturalis*	AU
—Rusty Mouse Warbler	*Crateroscelis murina*	AU
—Bicolored Mouse Warbler	*Crateroscelis nigrorufa*	AU
—Mountain Mouse Warbler	*Crateroscelis robusta*	AU
—Pale-billed Scrubwren	*Sericornis spilodera*	AU
—Papuan Scrubwren	*Sericornis papuensis*	AU
—Atherton Scrubwren	*Sericornis keri*	AU
—White-browed Scrubwren	*Sericornis frontalis*	AU
—Yellow-throated Scrubwren	*Sericornis citreogularis*	AU
—Large-billed Scrubwren	*Sericornis magnirostra*	AU
—Large Scrubwren	*Sericornis nouhuysi*	AU
—Buff-faced Scrubwren	*Sericornis perspicillatus*	AU
—Vogelkop Scrubwren	*Sericornis rufescens*	AU
—Grey-green Scrubwren	*Sericornis arfakianus*	AU
—Weebill	*Smicrornis brevirostris*	AU
—Brown Gerygone	*Gerygone mouki*	AU
—Grey Gerygone	*Gerygone igata*	AU
—Norfolk Gerygone	*Gerygone modesta*	AU
—Chatham Gerygone	*Gerygone albofrontata*	AU
—Fan-tailed Gerygone	*Gerygone flavolateralis*	PO
—Treefern Gerygone	*Gerygone ruficollis*	AU
—Golden-bellied Gerygone	*Gerygone sulphurea*	OR
—Rufous-sided Gerygone	*Gerygone dorsalis*	AU
—Mangrove Gerygone	*Gerygone levigaster*	AU
—Plain Gerygone	*Gerygone inornata*	AU
—Western Gerygone	*Gerygone fusca*	AU
—Dusky Gerygone	*Gerygone tenebrosa*	AU
—Large-billed Gerygone	*Gerygone magnirostris*	AU
—Yellow-bellied Gerygone	*Gerygone chrysogaster*	AU
—Ashy Gerygone	*Gerygone cinerea*	AU
—Green-backed Gerygone	*Gerygone chloronota*	AU
—White-throated Gerygone	*Gerygone olivacea*	AU
—Fairy Gerygone	*Gerygone palpebrosa*	AU
—Mountain Thornbill	*Acanthiza katherina*	AU
—Brown Thornbill	*Acanthiza pusilla*	AU
—Inland Thornbill	*Acanthiza apicalis*	AU
—Tasmanian Thornbill	*Acanthiza ewingii*	AU
—Papuan Thornbill	*Acanthiza murina*	AU
—Chestnut-rumped Thornbill	*Acanthiza uropygialis*	AU
—Buff-rumped Thornbill	*Acanthiza reguloides*	AU
—Western Thornbill	*Acanthiza inornata*	AU
—Slender-billed Thornbill	*Acanthiza iredalei*	AU
—Yellow-rumped Thornbill	*Acanthiza chrysorrhoa*	AU
—Yellow Thornbill	*Acanthiza nana*	AU
—Striated Thornbill	*Acanthiza lineata*	AU

INTERNATIONAL ENGLISH NAME	SCIENTIFIC NAME	REGION(S)
—Slaty-backed Thornbill	*Acanthiza robustirostris*	AU
—Southern Whiteface	*Aphelocephala leucopsis*	AU
—Chestnut-breasted Whiteface	*Aphelocephala pectoralis*	AU
—Banded Whiteface	*Aphelocephala nigricincta*	AU
—Yellowhead	*Mohoua ochrocephala*	AU
—Whitehead	*Mohoua albicilla*	AU
—Pipipi	*Finschia novaeseelandiae*	AU
AUSTRALASIAN BABBLERS	**Family Pomatostomidae**	
—Papuan Babbler	*Garritornis isidorei*	AU
—Grey-crowned Babbler	*Pomatostomus temporalis*	AU
—Hall's Babbler	*Pomatostomus halli*	AU
—White-browed Babbler	*Pomatostomus superciliosus*	AU
—Chestnut-crowned Babbler	*Pomatostomus ruficeps*	AU
LOGRUNNERS	**Family Orthonychidae**	
—Papuan Logrunner	*Orthonyx novaeguineae*	AU
—Australian Logrunner	*Orthonyx temminckii*	AU
—Chowchilla	*Orthonyx spaldingii*	AU
SATINBIRDS	**Family Cnemophilidae**	
—Velvet Satinbird	*Cnemophilus loriae*	AU
—Antenna Satinbird	*Cnemophilus macgregorii*	AU
—Silken Satinbird	*Loboparadisea sericea*	AU
BERRYPECKERS	**Family Melanocharitidae**	
Obscure Berrypecker	*Melanocharis arfakiana*	AU
—Black Berrypecker	*Melanocharis nigra*	AU
—Lemon-breasted Berrypecker	*Melanocharis longicauda*	AU
—Fan-tailed Berrypecker	*Melanocharis versteri*	AU
—Streaked Berrypecker	*Melanocharis striativentris*	AU
—Spotted Berrypecker	*Rhamphocharis crassirostris*	AU
—Plumed Longbill	*Oedistoma iliolophum*	AU
—Pygmy Longbill	*Oedistoma pygmaeum*	AU
—Green-crowned Longbill	*Toxorhamphus novaeguineae*	AU
—Slaty-headed Longbill	*Toxorhamphus poliopterus*	AU
—Tit Berrypecker	*Oreocharis arfaki*	AU
—Crested Berrypecker	*Paramythia montium*	AU
WATTLED CROWS	**Family Callaeatidae**	
—Kokako	*Callaeas cinerea*	AU
—Saddleback	*Philesturnus carunculatus*	AU
WHIPBIRDS, JEWEL-BABBLERS	**Family Eupetidae**	
—Papuan Whipbird	*Androphobus viridis*	AU
—Eastern Whipbird	*Psophodes olivaceus*	AU
—Western Whipbird	*Psophodes nigrogularis*	AU
—Mallee Whipbird	*Psophodes leucogaster*	AU
—Chirruping Wedgebill	*Psophodes cristatus*	AU
—Chiming Wedgebill	*Psophodes occidentalis*	AU
—Spotted Jewel-babbler	*Ptilorrhoa leucosticta*	AU
—Blue Jewel-babbler	*Ptilorrhoa caerulescens*	AU
—Chestnut-backed Jewel-babbler	*Ptilorrhoa castanonota*	AU
—Malaysian Rail-babbler	*Eupetes macrocerus*	OR

INTERNATIONAL ENGLISH NAME	SCIENTIFIC NAME	REGION(S)
QUAIL-THRUSHES	**Family Cinclosomatidae**	
—Spotted Quail-thrush	*Cinclosoma punctatum*	AU
—Chestnut-backed Quail-thrush	*Cinclosoma castanotum*	AU
—Cinnamon Quail-thrush	*Cinclosoma cinnamomeum*	AU
—Chestnut-breasted Quail-thrush	*Cinclosoma castaneothorax*	AU
—Painted Quail-thrush	*Cinclosoma ajax*	AU
WATTLE-EYES, BATISES	**Family Platysteiridae**	
—Shrike-flycatcher	*Megabyas flammulatus*	AF
—Black-and-white Flycatcher	*Bias musicus*	AF
—Chestnut Wattle-eye	*Dyaphorophyia castanea*	AF
—White-spotted Wattle-eye	*Dyaphorophyia tonsa*	AF
—Red-cheeked Wattle-eye	*Dyaphorophyia blissetti*	AF
—Black-necked Wattle-eye	*Dyaphorophyia chalybea*	AF
—Jameson's Wattle-eye	*Dyaphorophyia jamesoni*	AF
—Yellow-bellied Wattle-eye	*Dyaphorophyia concreta*	AF
—Ruwenzori Batis	*Batis diops*	AF
—Margaret's Batis	*Batis margaritae*	AF
—Forest Batis	*Batis mixta*	AF
—Cape Batis	*Batis capensis*	AF
—Woodward's Batis	*Batis fratrum*	AF
—Chinspot Batis	*Batis molitor*	AF
—Senegal Batis	*Batis senegalensis*	AF
—Grey-headed Batis	*Batis orientalis*	AF
—Pale Batis	*Batis soror*	AF
—Pririt Batis	*Batis pririt*	AF
—Black-headed Batis	*Batis minor*	AF
—Pygmy Batis	*Batis perkeo*	AF
—Angola Batis	*Batis minulla*	AF
—Gabon Batis	*Batis minima*	AF
—Ituri Batis	*Batis ituriensis*	AF
—Fernando Po Batis	*Batis poensis*	AF
—White-tailed Shrike	*Lanioturdus torquatus*	AF
—Brown-throated Wattle-eye	*Platysteira cyanea*	AF
—White-fronted Wattle-eye	*Platysteira albifrons*	AF
—Black-throated Wattle-eye	*Platysteira peltata*	AF
—Banded Wattle-eye	*Platysteira laticincta*	AF
FAMILY UNCERTAIN	**Incertae Sedis**	
—Large Woodshrike	*Tephrodornis virgatus*	OR
—Common Woodshrike	*Tephrodornis pondicerianus*	OR
—Rufous-winged Philentoma	*Philentoma pyrhoptera*	OR
—Maroon-breasted Philentoma	*Philentoma velata*	OR
HELMETSHRIKES, BUSHSHRIKES	**Family Malaconotidae**	
—White-crested Helmetshrike	*Prionops plumatus*	AF
—Grey-crested Helmetshrike	*Prionops poliolophus*	AF
—Yellow-crested Helmetshrike	*Prionops alberti*	AF
—Red-billed Helmetshrike	*Prionops caniceps*	AF
—Rufous-bellied Helmetshrike	*Prionops rufiventris*	AF
—Retz's Helmetshrike	*Prionops retzii*	AF
—Gabela Helmetshrike	*Prionops gabela*	AF

INTERNATIONAL ENGLISH NAME	SCIENTIFIC NAME	REGION(S)
__Chestnut-fronted Helmetshrike	*Prionops scopifrons*	AF
__Fiery-breasted Bushshrike	*Malaconotus cruentus*	AF
__Monteiro's Bushshrike	*Malaconotus monteiri*	AF
__Grey-headed Bushshrike	*Malaconotus blanchoti*	AF
__Lagden's Bushshrike	*Malaconotus lagdeni*	AF
__Green-breasted Bushshrike	*Malaconotus gladiator*	AF
__Uluguru Bushshrike	*Malaconotus alius*	AF
__Mount Kupe Bushshrike	*Chlorophoneus kupeensis*	AF
__Many-colored Bushshrike	*Chlorophoneus multicolor*	AF
__Black-fronted Bushshrike	*Chlorophoneus nigrifrons*	AF
__Olive Bushshrike	*Chlorophoneus olivaceus*	AF
__Bocage's Bushshrike	*Chlorophoneus bocagei*	AF
__Orange-breasted Bushshrike	*Chlorophoneus sulfureopectus*	AF
__Gorgeous Bushshrike	*Chlorophoneus viridis*	AF
__Four-colored Bushshrike	*Chlorophoneus quadricolor*	AF
__Doherty's Bushshrike	*Chlorophoneus dohertyi*	AF
__Bokmakierie	*Telophorus zeylonus*	AF
__Rosy-patched Bushshrike	*Rhodophoneus cruentus*	AF
__Marsh Tchagra	*Bocagia minuta*	AF
__Brown-crowned Tchagra	*Tchagra australis*	AF
__Three-streaked Tchagra	*Tchagra jamesi*	AF
__Southern Tchagra	*Tchagra tchagra*	AF
__Black-crowned Tchagra	*Tchagra senegalus*	AF
__Sabine's Puffback	*Dryoscopus sabini*	AF
__Pink-footed Puffback	*Dryoscopus angolensis*	AF
__Red-eyed Puffback	*Dryoscopus senegalensis*	AF
__Black-backed Puffback	*Dryoscopus cubla*	AF
__Northern Puffback	*Dryoscopus gambensis*	AF
__Pringle's Puffback	*Dryoscopus pringlii*	AF
__Lowland Sooty Boubou	*Laniarius leucorhynchus*	AF
__Mountain Sooty Boubou	*Laniarius poensis*	AF
__Fülleborn's Boubou	*Laniarius fuelleborni*	AF
__Slate-colored Boubou	*Laniarius funebris*	AF
__Lühder's Bushshrike	*Laniarius luehderi*	AF
__Braun's Bushshrike	*Laniarius brauni*	AF
__Gabela Bushshrike	*Laniarius amboimensis*	AF
__Red-naped Bushshrike	*Laniarius ruficeps*	AF
__Bulo Burti Boubou	*Laniarius liberatus*	AF
__Tropical Boubou	*Laniarius aethiopicus*	AF
__Southern Boubou	*Laniarius ferrugineus*	AF
__Swamp Boubou	*Laniarius bicolor*	AF
__Turati's Boubou	*Laniarius turatii*	AF
__Yellow-crowned Gonolek	*Laniarius barbarus*	AF
__Papyrus Gonolek	*Laniarius mufumbiri*	AF
__Black-headed Gonolek	*Laniarius erythrogaster*	AF
__Crimson-breasted Shrike	*Laniarius atrococcineus*	AF
__Yellow-breasted Boubou	*Laniarius atroflavus*	AF
__Brubru	*Nilaus afer*	AF
BOATBILLS	**Family Machaerirhynchidae**	
__Yellow-breasted Boatbill	*Machaerirhynchus flaviventer*	AU
__Black-breasted Boatbill	*Machaerirhynchus nigripectus*	AU

INTERNATIONAL ENGLISH NAME	SCIENTIFIC NAME	REGION(S)
VANGAS	**Family Vangidae**	
—Red-tailed Vanga	*Calicalicus madagascariensis*	AF
—Red-shouldered Vanga	*Calicalicus rufocarpalis*	AF
—Hook-billed Vanga	*Vanga curvirostris*	AF
—Bernier's Vanga	*Oriolia bernieri*	AF
—Lafresnaye's Vanga	*Xenopirostris xenopirostris*	AF
—Van Dam's Vanga	*Xenopirostris damii*	AF
—Pollen's Vanga	*Xenopirostris polleni*	AF
—Sickle-billed Vanga	*Falculea palliata*	AF
—White-headed Vanga	*Artamella viridis*	AF
—Chabert's Vanga	*Leptopterus chabert*	AF
—Blue Vanga	*Cyanolanius madagascarinus*	AF
—Rufous Vanga	*Schetba rufa*	AF
—Helmet Vanga	*Euryceros prevostii*	AF
—Tylas Vanga	*Tylas eduardi*	AF
—Nuthatch Vanga	*Hypositta corallirostris*	AF
—Dark Newtonia	*Newtonia amphichroa*	AF
—Common Newtonia	*Newtonia brunneicauda*	AF
—Archbold's Newtonia	*Newtonia archboldi*	AF
—Red-tailed Newtonia	*Newtonia fanovanae*	AF
—Ward's Flycatcher	*Pseudobias wardi*	AF
—Crossley's Babbler	*Mystacornis crossleyi*	AF
BUTCHERBIRDS & ALLIES	**Family Cracticidae**	
—Black Butcherbird	*Cracticus quoyi*	AU
—Grey Butcherbird	*Cracticus torquatus*	AU
—Silver-backed Butcherbird	*Cracticus argenteus*	AU
—Black-backed Butcherbird	*Cracticus mentalis*	AU
—Pied Butcherbird	*Cracticus nigrogularis*	AU
—Hooded Butcherbird	*Cracticus cassicus*	AU
—Tagula Butcherbird	*Cracticus louisiadensis*	AU
—Australian Magpie	*Gymnorhina tibicen*	AU
—Pied Currawong	*Strepera graculina*	AU
—Black Currawong	*Strepera fuliginosa*	AU
—Grey Currawong	*Strepera versicolor*	AU
—Clicking Shieldbill	*Peltops blainvillii*	AU
—Tinkling Shieldbill	*Peltops montanus*	AU
—Bornean Bristlehead	*Pityriasis gymnocephala*	OR
WOODSWALLOWS	**Family Artamidae**	
—Ashy Woodswallow	*Artamus fuscus*	OR
—White-breasted Woodswallow	*Artamus leucorynchus*	AU
—Fiji Woodswallow	*Artamus mentalis*	PO
—Ivory-backed Woodswallow	*Artamus monachus*	AU
—Great Woodswallow	*Artamus maximus*	AU
—White-backed Woodswallow	*Artamus insignis*	AU
—Masked Woodswallow	*Artamus personatus*	AU
—White-browed Woodswallow	*Artamus superciliosus*	AU
—Black-faced Woodswallow	*Artamus cinereus*	AU
—Dusky Woodswallow	*Artamus cyanopterus*	AU
—Little Woodswallow	*Artamus minor*	AU

INTERNATIONAL ENGLISH NAME	SCIENTIFIC NAME	REGION(S)
IORAS	**Family Aegithinidae**	
__Common Iora	*Aegithina tiphia*	OR
__Marshall's Iora	*Aegithina nigrolutea*	OR
__Green Iora	*Aegithina viridissima*	OR
__Great Iora	*Aegithina lafresnayei*	OR
CUCKOOSHRIKES	**Family Campephagidae**	
__Ground Cuckooshrike	*Coracina maxima*	AU
__Large Cuckooshrike	*Coracina macei*	OR
__Javan Cuckooshrike	*Coracina javensis*	OR
__Black-faced Cuckooshrike	*Coracina novaehollandiae*	AU
__Wallacean Cuckooshrike	*Coracina personata*	AU
__Buru Cuckooshrike	*Coracina fortis*	AU
__Moluccan Cuckooshrike	*Coracina atriceps*	AU
__Slaty Cuckooshrike	*Coracina schistacea*	AU
__Melanesian Cuckooshrike	*Coracina caledonica*	AU
__Stout-billed Cuckooshrike	*Coracina caeruleogrisea*	AU
__Cerulean Cuckooshrike	*Coracina temminckii*	AU
__Sunda Cuckooshrike	*Coracina larvata*	OR
__Bar-bellied Cuckooshrike	*Coracina striata*	OR
__Pied Cuckooshrike	*Coracina bicolor*	AU
__Barred Cuckooshrike	*Coracina lineata*	AU
__Boyer's Cuckooshrike	*Coracina boyeri*	AU
__White-rumped Cuckooshrike	*Coracina leucopygia*	AU
__White-bellied Cuckooshrike	*Coracina papuensis*	AU
__Manus Cuckooshrike	*Coracina ingens*	AU
__Hooded Cuckooshrike	*Coracina longicauda*	AU
__Halmahera Cuckooshrike	*Coracina parvula*	AU
__Pygmy Cuckooshrike	*Coracina abbotti*	AU
__New Caledonian Cuckooshrike	*Coracina analis*	AU
__Grey Cuckooshrike	*Coracina caesia*	AF
__White-breasted Cuckooshrike	*Coracina pectoralis*	AF
__Grauer's Cuckooshrike	*Coracina graueri*	AF
__Madagascar Cuckooshrike	*Coracina cinerea*	AF
__Comoros Cuckooshrike	*Coracina cucullata*	AF
__Blue Cuckooshrike	*Coracina azurea*	AF
__Mauritius Cuckooshrike	*Coracina typica*	IO
__Reunion Cuckooshrike	*Coracina newtoni*	IO
__Blackish Cuckooshrike	*Coracina coerulescens*	OR
__Pale-shouldered Cicadabird	*Coracina dohertyi*	AU
__Kai Cicadabird	*Coracina dispar*	AU
__Common Cicadabird	*Coracina tenuirostris*	AU
__Palau Cicadabird	*Coracina monacha*	AU
__Yap Cicadabird	*Coracina nesiotis*	PO
__Pohnpei Cicadabird	*Coracina insperata*	PO
__Grey-capped Cicadabird	*Coracina remota*	AU
__Makira Cicadabird	*Coracina salomonis*	AU
__Black-bibbed Cicadabird	*Coracina mindanensis*	OR
__Sulawesi Cicadabird	*Coracina morio*	AU
__Sula Cicadabird	*Coracina sula*	AU
__Pale Cicadabird	*Coracina ceramensis*	AU
__Black-shouldered Cicadabird	*Coracina incerta*	AU
__Black-tipped Cicadabird	*Coracina schisticeps*	AU

INTERNATIONAL ENGLISH NAME	SCIENTIFIC NAME	REGION(S)
—Black Cicadabird	*Coracina melas*	AU
—Black-bellied Cuckooshrike	*Coracina montana*	AU
—Black-bellied Cicadabird	*Coracina holopolia*	AU
—White-winged Cuckooshrike	*Coracina ostenta*	OR
—McGregor's Cuckooshrike	*Coracina mcgregori*	OR
—Indochinese Cuckooshrike	*Coracina polioptera*	OR
—Black-winged Cuckooshrike	*Coracina melaschistos*	OR
—Lesser Cuckooshrike	*Coracina fimbriata*	OR
—Black-headed Cuckooshrike	*Coracina melanoptera*	OR
—Golden Cuckooshrike	*Campochaera sloetii*	AU
—Black-and-white Triller	*Lalage melanoleuca*	OR
—Pied Triller	*Lalage nigra*	OR
—White-rumped Triller	*Lalage leucopygialis*	AU
—White-shouldered Triller	*Lalage sueurii*	AU
—White-winged Triller	*Lalage tricolor*	AU
—Rufous-bellied Triller	*Lalage aurea*	AU
—Black-browed Triller	*Lalage atrovirens*	AU
—White-browed Triller	*Lalage moesta*	AU
—Varied Triller	*Lalage leucomela*	AU
—Polynesian Triller	*Lalage maculosa*	PO
—Samoan Triller	*Lalage sharpei*	PO
—Long-tailed Triller	*Lalage leucopyga*	PO
—Black Cuckooshrike	*Campephaga flava*	AF
—Red-shouldered Cuckooshrike	*Campephaga phoenicea*	AF
—Petit's Cuckooshrike	*Campephaga petiti*	AF
—Purple-throated Cuckooshrike	*Campephaga quiscalina*	AF
—Western Wattled Cuckooshrike	*Lobotos lobatus*	AF
—Eastern Wattled Cuckooshrike	*Lobotos oriolinus*	AF
—Rosy Minivet	*Pericrocotus roseus*	OR
—Swinhoe's Minivet	*Pericrocotus cantonensis*	EU
—Ashy Minivet	*Pericrocotus divaricatus*	EU
—Ryukyu Minivet	*Pericrocotus tegimae*	EU
—Small Minivet	*Pericrocotus cinnamomeus*	OR
—Fiery Minivet	*Pericrocotus igneus*	OR
—Little Minivet	*Pericrocotus lansbergei*	AU
—White-bellied Minivet	*Pericrocotus erythropygius*	OR
—Grey-chinned Minivet	*Pericrocotus solaris*	OR
—Long-tailed Minivet	*Pericrocotus ethologus*	OR
—Short-billed Minivet	*Pericrocotus brevirostris*	OR
—Sunda Minivet	*Pericrocotus miniatus*	OR
—Scarlet Minivet	*Pericrocotus flammeus*	OR
—Bar-winged Flycatcher-shrike	*Hemipus picatus*	OR
—Black-winged Flycatcher-shrike	*Hemipus hirundinaceus*	OR

SITTELLAS — Family Neosittidae

—Varied Sittella	*Daphoenositta chrysoptera*	AU
—Papuan Sittella	*Daphoenositta papuensis*	AU
—Black Sittella	*Daphoenositta miranda*	AU

SHRIKETITS — Family Falcunculidae

—Wattled Ploughbill	*Eulacestoma nigropectus*	AU
—Northern Shriketit	*Falcunculus whitei*	AU
—Western Shriketit	*Falcunculus leucogaster*	AU
—Crested Shriketit	*Falcunculus frontatus*	AU

INTERNATIONAL ENGLISH NAME	SCIENTIFIC NAME	REGION(S)
FAMILY UNCERTAIN	**Incertae Sedis**	
—Piopio	*Turnagra capensis*	AU
WHISTLERS	**Family Pachycephalidae**	
—Goldenface	*Pachycare flavogriseum*	AU
—Mottled Whistler	*Rhagologus leucostigma*	AU
—Yellow-flanked Whistler	*Hylocitrea bonensis*	AU
—Maroon-backed Whistler	*Coracornis raveni*	AU
—Rufous-naped Whistler	*Aleadryas rufinucha*	AU
—Olive Whistler	*Pachycephala olivacea*	AU
—Red-lored Whistler	*Pachycephala rufogularis*	AU
—Gilbert's Whistler	*Pachycephala inornata*	AU
—Mangrove Whistler	*Pachycephala grisola*	OR
—Green-backed Whistler	*Pachycephala albiventris*	OR
—White-vented Whistler	*Pachycephala homeyeri*	OR
—Island Whistler	*Pachycephala phaionota*	AU
—Rusty Whistler	*Pachycephala hyperythra*	AU
—Brown-backed Whistler	*Pachycephala modesta*	AU
—Yellow-bellied Whistler	*Pachycephala philippinensis*	OR
—Sulphur-vented Whistler	*Pachycephala sulfuriventer*	AU
—Bornean Whistler	*Pachycephala hypoxantha*	OR
—Vogelkop Whistler	*Pachycephala meyeri*	AU
—Grey Whistler	*Pachycephala simplex*	AU
—Fawn-breasted Whistler	*Pachycephala orpheus*	AU
—Sclater's Whistler	*Pachycephala soror*	AU
—Rusty-breasted Whistler	*Pachycephala fulvotincta*	AU
—Yellow-throated Whistler	*Pachycephala macrorhyncha*	AU
—Black-chinned Whistler	*Pachycephala mentalis*	AU
—Australian Golden Whistler	*Pachycephala pectoralis*	AU
—Bismarck Whistler	*Pachycephala citreogaster*	AU
—Oriole Whistler	*Pachycephala orioloides*	AU
—Melanesian Whistler	*Pachycephala caledonica*	AU
—White-throated Whistler	*Pachycephala vitiensis*	PO
—Fiji Whistler	*Pachycephala graeffii*	PO
—Tongan Whistler	*Pachycephala jacquinoti*	PO
—Mangrove Golden Whistler	*Pachycephala melanura*	AU
—Samoan Whistler	*Pachycephala flavifrons*	PO
—Hooded Whistler	*Pachycephala implicata*	AU
—Bare-throated Whistler	*Pachycephala nudigula*	AU
—Lorentz's Whistler	*Pachycephala lorentzi*	AU
—Regent Whistler	*Pachycephala schlegelii*	AU
—Golden-backed Whistler	*Pachycephala aurea*	AU
—Rufous Whistler	*Pachycephala rufiventris*	AU
—Black-headed Whistler	*Pachycephala monacha*	AU
—Wallacean Whistler	*Pachycephala arctitorquis*	AU
—Drab Whistler	*Pachycephala griseonota*	AU
—Cinnamon-breasted Whistler	*Pachycephala johni*	AU
—White-breasted Whistler	*Pachycephala lanioides*	AU
SHRIKES	**Family Laniidae**	
—Yellow-billed Shrike	*Corvinella corvina*	AF
—Magpie Shrike	*Urolestes melanoleucus*	AF
—Northern White-crowned Shrike	*Eurocephalus rueppelli*	AF

INTERNATIONAL ENGLISH NAME	SCIENTIFIC NAME	REGION(S)
—Southern White-crowned Shrike	*Eurocephalus anguitimens*	AF
—Tiger Shrike	*Lanius tigrinus*	EU
—Souza's Shrike	*Lanius souzae*	AF
—Bull-headed Shrike	*Lanius bucephalus*	EU
—Brown Shrike	*Lanius cristatus*	EU
—Red-backed Shrike	*Lanius collurio*	EU
—Isabelline Shrike	*Lanius isabellinus*	EU
—Burmese Shrike	*Lanius collurioides*	OR
—Emin's Shrike	*Lanius gubernator*	AF
—Bay-backed Shrike	*Lanius vittatus*	EU
—Long-tailed Shrike	*Lanius schach*	OR
—Grey-backed Shrike	*Lanius tephronotus*	EU
—Mountain Shrike	*Lanius validirostris*	OR
—Mackinnon's Shrike	*Lanius mackinnoni*	AF
—Lesser Grey Shrike	*Lanius minor*	EU
—Loggerhead Shrike	*Lanius ludovicianus*	NA, MA
—Great Grey Shrike	*Lanius excubitor*	NA, EU
—Southern Grey Shrike	*Lanius meridionalis*	EU, AF
—Chinese Grey Shrike	*Lanius sphenocercus*	EU
—Grey-backed Fiscal	*Lanius excubitoroides*	AF
—Long-tailed Fiscal	*Lanius cabanisi*	AF
—Taita Fiscal	*Lanius dorsalis*	AF
—Somali Fiscal	*Lanius somalicus*	AF
—Common Fiscal	*Lanius collaris*	AF
—Uhehe Fiscal	*Lanius marwitzi*	AF
—Sao Tome Fiscal	*Lanius newtoni*	AF
—Woodchat Shrike	*Lanius senator*	EU
—Masked Shrike	*Lanius nubicus*	EU
VIREOS, GREENLETS	**Family Vireonidae**	
—Rufous-browed Peppershrike	*Cyclarhis gujanensis*	LA
—Black-billed Peppershrike	*Cyclarhis nigrirostris*	SA
—Chestnut-sided Shrike-Vireo	*Vireolanius melitophrys*	MA
—Green Shrike-Vireo	*Vireolanius pulchellus*	MA
—Yellow-browed Shrike-Vireo	*Vireolanius eximius*	SA
—Slaty-capped Shrike-Vireo	*Vireolanius leucotis*	SA
—Slaty Vireo	*Vireo brevipennis*	SA
—White-eyed Vireo	*Vireo griseus*	NA, MA
—Thick-billed Vireo	*Vireo crassirostris*	NA
—Mangrove Vireo	*Vireo pallens*	MA
—Providencia Vireo	*Vireo approximans*	MA
—Cozumel Vireo	*Vireo bairdi*	MA
—San Andres Vireo	*Vireo caribaeus*	MA
—Jamaican Vireo	*Vireo modestus*	NA
—Cuban Vireo	*Vireo gundlachii*	NA
—Puerto Rican Vireo	*Vireo latimeri*	NA
—Flat-billed Vireo	*Vireo nanus*	NA
—Bell's Vireo	*Vireo bellii*	NA, MA
—Black-capped Vireo	*Vireo atricapilla*	NA, MA
—Dwarf Vireo	*Vireo nelsoni*	MA
—Grey Vireo	*Vireo vicinior*	NA, MA
—Blue Mountain Vireo	*Vireo osburni*	NA
—Yellow-throated Vireo	*Vireo flavifrons*	NA

INTERNATIONAL ENGLISH NAME	SCIENTIFIC NAME	REGION(S)
__Plumbeous Vireo	*Vireo plumbeus*	NA, MA
__Cassin's Vireo	*Vireo cassinii*	NA
__Blue-headed Vireo	*Vireo solitarius*	NA
__Yellow-winged Vireo	*Vireo carmioli*	MA
__Choco Vireo	*Vireo masteri*	SA
__Hutton's Vireo	*Vireo huttoni*	NA, MA
__Golden Vireo	*Vireo hypochryseus*	MA
__Warbling Vireo	*Vireo gilvus*	NA, MA
__Brown-capped Vireo	*Vireo leucophrys*	LA
__Philadelphia Vireo	*Vireo philadelphicus*	NA
__Red-eyed Vireo	*Vireo olivaceus*	NA, LA
__Noronha Vireo	*Vireo gracilirostris*	SA
__Yellow-green Vireo	*Vireo flavoviridis*	MA
__Black-whiskered Vireo	*Vireo altiloquus*	NA
__Yucatan Vireo	*Vireo magister*	MA
__Rufous-crowned Greenlet	*Hylophilus poicilotis*	SA
__Grey-eyed Greenlet	*Hylophilus amaurocephalus*	SA
__Lemon-chested Greenlet	*Hylophilus thoracicus*	SA
__Grey-chested Greenlet	*Hylophilus semicinereus*	SA
__Ashy-headed Greenlet	*Hylophilus pectoralis*	SA
__Tepui Greenlet	*Hylophilus sclateri*	SA
__Brown-headed Greenlet	*Hylophilus brunneiceps*	SA
__Rufous-naped Greenlet	*Hylophilus semibrunneus*	SA
__Golden-fronted Greenlet	*Hylophilus aurantiifrons*	SA
__Dusky-capped Greenlet	*Hylophilus hypoxanthus*	SA
__Buff-cheeked Greenlet	*Hylophilus muscicapinus*	SA
__Scrub Greenlet	*Hylophilus flavipes*	LA
__Olivaceous Greenlet	*Hylophilus olivaceus*	SA
__Tawny-crowned Greenlet	*Hylophilus ochraceiceps*	LA
__Lesser Greenlet	*Hylophilus decurtatus*	LA

FIGBIRDS, ORIOLES

Family Oriolidae

__Green Figbird	*Sphecotheres viridis*	AU
__Wetar Figbird	*Sphecotheres hypoleucus*	AU
__Australasian Figbird	*Sphecotheres vieilloti*	AU
__Brown Oriole	*Oriolus szalayi*	AU
__Dusky-brown Oriole	*Oriolus phaeochromus*	AU
__Grey-collared Oriole	*Oriolus forsteni*	AU
__Black-eared Oriole	*Oriolus bouroensis*	AU
__Olive-brown Oriole	*Oriolus melanotis*	AU
__Olive-backed Oriole	*Oriolus sagittatus*	AU
__Green Oriole	*Oriolus flavocinctus*	AU
__Dark-throated Oriole	*Oriolus xanthonotus*	OR
__Philippine Oriole	*Oriolus steerii*	OR
__White-lored Oriole	*Oriolus albiloris*	OR
__Isabella Oriole	*Oriolus isabellae*	OR
__Eurasian Golden Oriole	*Oriolus oriolus*	EU
__African Golden Oriole	*Oriolus auratus*	AF
__Slender-billed Oriole	*Oriolus tenuirostris*	OR
__Black-naped Oriole	*Oriolus chinensis*	OR
__Green-headed Oriole	*Oriolus chlorocephalus*	AF
__Sao Tome Oriole	*Oriolus crassirostris*	AF
__Western Oriole	*Oriolus brachyrhynchus*	AF

INTERNATIONAL ENGLISH NAME	SCIENTIFIC NAME	REGION(S)
—Ethiopian Oriole	*Oriolus monacha*	AF
—Mountain Oriole	*Oriolus percivali*	AF
—Black-headed Oriole	*Oriolus larvatus*	AF
—Black-winged Oriole	*Oriolus nigripennis*	AF
—Black-hooded Oriole	*Oriolus xanthornus*	OR
—Black Oriole	*Oriolus hosii*	OR
—Black-and-crimson Oriole	*Oriolus cruentus*	OR
—Maroon Oriole	*Oriolus traillii*	OR
—Silver Oriole	*Oriolus mellianus*	OR
SHRIKETHRUSHES, PITOHUIS	**Family Colluricinclidae**	
—Bower's Shrikethrush	*Colluricincla boweri*	AU
—Sooty Shrikethrush	*Colluricincla umbrina*	AU
—Little Shrikethrush	*Colluricincla megarhyncha*	AU
—Sangihe Shrikethrush	*Colluricincla sanghirensis*	AU
—Morningbird	*Colluricincla tenebrosa*	AU
—Grey Shrikethrush	*Colluricincla harmonica*	AU
—Sandstone Shrikethrush	*Colluricincla woodwardi*	AU
—Variable Pitohui	*Pitohui kirhocephalus*	AU
—Hooded Pitohui	*Pitohui dichrous*	AU
—White-belled Pitohui	*Pitohui incertus*	AU
—Rusty Pitohui	*Pitohui ferrugineus*	AU
—Crested Pitohui	*Pitohui cristatus*	AU
—Black Pitohui	*Pitohui nigrescens*	AU
—Crested Bellbird	*Oreoica gutturalis*	AU
DRONGOS	**Family Dicruridae**	
—Pygmy Drongo	*Chaetorhynchus papuensis*	AU
—Square-tailed Drongo	*Dicrurus ludwigii*	AF
—Shining Drongo	*Dicrurus atripennis*	AF
—Fork-tailed Drongo	*Dicrurus adsimilis*	AF
—Velvet-mantled Drongo	*Dicrurus modestus*	AF
—Grand Comoro Drongo	*Dicrurus fuscipennis*	AF
—Aldabra Drongo	*Dicrurus aldabranus*	AF
—Crested Drongo	*Dicrurus forficatus*	AF
—Mayotte Drongo	*Dicrurus waldenii*	AF
—Black Drongo	*Dicrurus macrocercus*	OR
—Ashy Drongo	*Dicrurus leucophaeus*	OR
—White-bellied Drongo	*Dicrurus caerulescens*	OR
—Crow-billed Drongo	*Dicrurus annectans*	OR
—Bronzed Drongo	*Dicrurus aeneus*	OR
—Lesser Racket-tailed Drongo	*Dicrurus remifer*	OR
—Balicassiao	*Dicrurus balicassius*	OR
—Hair-crested Drongo	*Dicrurus hottentottus*	OR
—Sulawesi Drongo	*Dicrurus montanus*	AU
—Spangled Drongo	*Dicrurus bracteatus*	AU
—Ribbon-tailed Drongo	*Dicrurus megarhynchus*	AU
—Andaman Drongo	*Dicrurus andamanensis*	OR
—Greater Racket-tailed Drongo	*Dicrurus paradiseus*	OR
FANTAILS	**Family Rhipiduridae**	
—Yellow-bellied Fantail	*Rhipidura hypoxantha*	OR
—Blue Fantail	*Rhipidura superciliaris*	OR

INTERNATIONAL ENGLISH NAME	SCIENTIFIC NAME	REGION(S)
—Blue-headed Fantail	*Rhipidura cyaniceps*	OR
—White-throated Fantail	*Rhipidura albicollis*	OR
—White-bellied Fantail	*Rhipidura euryura*	OR
—White-browed Fantail	*Rhipidura aureola*	OR
—Pied Fantail	*Rhipidura javanica*	OR
—Spotted Fantail	*Rhipidura perlata*	OR
—Willie Wagtail	*Rhipidura leucophrys*	AU
—Brown-capped Fantail	*Rhipidura diluta*	AU
—Cinnamon-tailed Fantail	*Rhipidura fuscorufa*	AU
—Northern Fantail	*Rhipidura rufiventris*	AU
—White-winged Fantail	*Rhipidura cockerelli*	AU
—Sooty Thicket Fantail	*Rhipidura threnothorax*	AU
—Black Thicket Fantail	*Rhipidura maculipectus*	AU
—White-bellied Thicket Fantail	*Rhipidura leucothorax*	AU
—Black Fantail	*Rhipidura atra*	AU
—Chestnut-bellied Fantail	*Rhipidura hyperythra*	AU
—Friendly Fantail	*Rhipidura albolimbata*	AU
—Grey Fantail	*Rhipidura albiscapa*	AU
—New Zealand Fantail	*Rhipidura fuliginosa*	AU
—Mangrove Fantail	*Rhipidura phasiana*	AU
—Brown Fantail	*Rhipidura drownei*	AU
—Makira Fantail	*Rhipidura tenebrosa*	AU
—Rennell Fantail	*Rhipidura rennelliana*	AU
—Streaked Fantail	*Rhipidura spilodera*	PO
—Kadavu Fantail	*Rhipidura personata*	PO
—Samoan Fantail	*Rhipidura nebulosa*	PO
—Rufous-tailed Fantail	*Rhipidura phoenicura*	OR
—Black-and-cinnamon Fantail	*Rhipidura nigrocinnamomea*	OR
—Dimorphic Fantail	*Rhipidura brachyrhyncha*	AU
—Palau Fantail	*Rhipidura lepida*	AU
—Streak-breasted Fantail	*Rhipidura dedemi*	AU
—Tawny-backed Fantail	*Rhipidura superflua*	AU
—Rusty-bellied Fantail	*Rhipidura teysmanni*	AU
—Long-tailed Fantail	*Rhipidura opistherythra*	AU
—Rufous-backed Fantail	*Rhipidura rufidorsa*	AU
—Bismarck Fantail	*Rhipidura dahli*	AU
—Mussau Fantail	*Rhipidura matthiae*	AU
—Malaita Fantail	*Rhipidura malaitae*	AU
—Manus Fantail	*Rhipidura semirubra*	AU
—Rufous Fantail	*Rhipidura rufifrons*	AU
—Pohnpei Fantail	*Rhipidura kubaryi*	PO
—Arafura Fantail	*Rhipidura dryas*	AU
MONARCHS	**Family Monarchidae**	
—Black-naped Monarch	*Hypothymis azurea*	OR
—Short-crested Monarch	*Hypothymis helenae*	OR
—Celestial Monarch	*Hypothymis coelestis*	OR
—Cerulean Paradise Flycatcher	*Eutrichomyias rowleyi*	AU
—Blue-mantled Crested Flycatcher	*Trochocercus cyanomelas*	AF
—Blue-headed Crested Flycatcher	*Trochocercus nitens*	AF
—Dusky Crested Flycatcher	*Trochocercus nigromitratus*	AF
—White-bellied Crested Flycatcher	*Trochocercus albiventris*	AF
—White-tailed Crested Flycatcher	*Trochocercus albicaudatus*	AF

INTERNATIONAL ENGLISH NAME	SCIENTIFIC NAME	REGION(S)
—Bedford's Paradise Flycatcher	*Terpsiphone bedfordi*	AF
—Rufous-vented Paradise Flycatcher	*Terpsiphone rufocinerea*	AF
—Bates's Paradise Flycatcher	*Terpsiphone batesi*	AF
—African Paradise Flycatcher	*Terpsiphone viridis*	AF
—Asian Paradise Flycatcher	*Terpsiphone paradisi*	OR
—Japanese Paradise Flycatcher	*Terpsiphone atrocaudata*	EU
—Blue Paradise Flycatcher	*Terpsiphone cyanescens*	OR
—Rufous Paradise Flycatcher	*Terpsiphone cinnamomea*	OR
—Sao Tome Paradise Flycatcher	*Terpsiphone atrochalybeia*	AF
—Malagasy Paradise Flycatcher	*Terpsiphone mutata*	AF
—Seychelles Paradise Flycatcher	*Terpsiphone corvina*	IO
—Mascarene Paradise Flycatcher	*Terpsiphone bourbonnensis*	IO
—Elepaio	*Chasiempis sandwichensis*	PO
—Rarotonga Monarch	*Pomarea dimidiata*	PO
—Tahiti Monarch	*Pomarea nigra*	PO
—Marquesan Monarch	*Pomarea mendozae*	PO
—Iphis Monarch	*Pomarea iphis*	PO
—Fatuhiva Monarch	*Pomarea whitneyi*	PO
—Vanikolo Monarch	*Mayrornis schistaceus*	PO
—Versicolored Monarch	*Mayrornis versicolor*	PO
—Slaty Monarch	*Mayrornis lessoni*	PO
—Buff-bellied Monarch	*Neolalage banksiana*	PO
—Southern Shrikebill	*Clytorhynchus pachycephaloides*	PO
—Fiji Shrikebill	*Clytorhynchus vitiensis*	PO
—Black-throated Shrikebill	*Clytorhynchus nigrogularis*	PO
—Rennell Shrikebill	*Clytorhynchus hamlini*	AU
—Chuuk Monarch	*Metabolus rugensis*	PO
—Black Monarch	*Monarcha axillaris*	AU
—Rufous Monarch	*Monarcha rubiensis*	AU
—Island Monarch	*Monarcha cinerascens*	AU
—Black-faced Monarch	*Monarcha melanopsis*	AU
—Black-winged Monarch	*Monarcha frater*	AU
—Bougainville Monarch	*Monarcha erythrostictus*	AU
—Chestnut-bellied Monarch	*Monarcha castaneiventris*	AU
—White-capped Monarch	*Monarcha richardsii*	AU
—White-eared Monarch	*Monarcha leucotis*	AU
—White-naped Monarch	*Monarcha pileatus*	AU
—Spot-winged Monarch	*Monarcha guttulus*	AU
—Black-bibbed Monarch	*Monarcha mundus*	AU
—Flores Monarch	*Monarcha sacerdotum*	AU
—Black-chinned Monarch	*Monarcha boanensis*	AU
—Spectacled Monarch	*Monarcha trivirgatus*	AU
—Moluccan Monarch	*Monarcha bimaculatus*	AU
—White-tailed Monarch	*Monarcha leucurus*	AU
—White-tipped Monarch	*Monarcha everetti*	AU
—Black-tipped Monarch	*Monarcha loricatus*	AU
—Kofiau Monarch	*Monarcha julianae*	AU
—Biak Monarch	*Monarcha brehmii*	AU
—Hooded Monarch	*Monarcha manadensis*	AU
—Manus Monarch	*Monarcha infelix*	AU
—Mussau Monarch	*Monarcha menckei*	AU
—Black-tailed Monarch	*Monarcha verticalis*	AU
—Solomons Monarch	*Monarcha barbatus*	AU

INTERNATIONAL ENGLISH NAME	SCIENTIFIC NAME	REGION(S)
—Kulambangra Monarch	*Monarcha browni*	AU
—White-collared Monarch	*Monarcha viduus*	AU
—Yap Monarch	*Monarcha godeffroyi*	PO
—Tinian Monarch	*Monarcha takatsukasae*	PO
—Golden Monarch	*Monarcha chrysomela*	AU
—Rufous-collared Monarch	*Arses insularis*	AU
—Frilled Monarch	*Arses telescopthalmus*	AU
—Frill-necked Monarch	*Arses lorealis*	AU
—Pied Monarch	*Arses kaupi*	AU
—Magpielark	*Grallina cyanoleuca*	AU
—Torrentlark	*Grallina bruijni*	AU
—Oceanic Flycatcher	*Myiagra oceanica*	PO
—Palau Flycatcher	*Myiagra erythrops*	PO
—Guam Flycatcher	*Myiagra freycineti*	PO
—Pohnpei Flycatcher	*Myiagra pluto*	PO
—Moluccan Flycatcher	*Myiagra galeata*	AU
—Biak Black Flycatcher	*Myiagra atra*	AU
—Leaden Flycatcher	*Myiagra rubecula*	AU
—Steel-blue Flycatcher	*Myiagra ferrocyanea*	AU
—Makira Flycatcher	*Myiagra cervinicauda*	AU
—Melanesian Flycatcher	*Myiagra caledonica*	AU
—Vanikoro Flycatcher	*Myiagra vanikorensis*	PO
—Samoan Flycatcher	*Myiagra albiventris*	PO
—Azure-crested Flycatcher	*Myiagra azureocapilla*	PO
—Broad-billed Flycatcher	*Myiagra ruficollis*	AU
—Tanimbar Flycatcher	*Myiagra fulviventris*	AU
—Satin Flycatcher	*Myiagra cyanoleuca*	AU
—Shining Flycatcher	*Myiagra alecto*	AU
—Velvet Flycatcher	*Myiagra hebetior*	AU
—Paperbark Flycatcher	*Myiagra nana*	AU
—Restless Flycatcher	*Myiagra inquieta*	AU
—Silktail	*Lamprolia victoriae*	PO

CROWS, JAYS	**Family Corvidae**	
—Crested Jay	*Platylophus galericulatus*	OR
—Black Magpie	*Platysmurus leucopterus*	OR
—Siberian Jay	*Perisoreus infaustus*	EU
—Sichuan Jay	*Perisoreus internigrans*	EU
—Grey Jay	*Perisoreus canadensis*	NA
—Black-collared Jay	*Cyanolyca armillata*	SA
—White-collared Jay	*Cyanolyca viridicyanus*	SA
—Turquoise Jay	*Cyanolyca turcosa*	SA
—Beautiful Jay	*Cyanolyca pulchra*	SA
—Azure-hooded Jay	*Cyanolyca cucullata*	MA
—Black-throated Jay	*Cyanolyca pumilo*	MA
—Dwarf Jay	*Cyanolyca nana*	MA
—White-throated Jay	*Cyanolyca mirabilis*	MA
—Silvery-throated Jay	*Cyanolyca argentigula*	MA
—Bushy-crested Jay	*Cyanocorax melanocyaneus*	MA
—San Blas Jay	*Cyanocorax sanblasianus*	MA
—Yucatan Jay	*Cyanocorax yucatanicus*	MA
—Purplish-backed Jay	*Cyanocorax beecheii*	MA
—Violaceous Jay	*Cyanocorax violaceus*	SA

INTERNATIONAL ENGLISH NAME	SCIENTIFIC NAME	REGION(S)
—Azure Jay	*Cyanocorax caeruleus*	SA
—Purplish Jay	*Cyanocorax cyanomelas*	SA
—Curl-crested Jay	*Cyanocorax cristatellus*	SA
—Tufted Jay	*Cyanocorax dickeyi*	MA
—Black-chested Jay	*Cyanocorax affinis*	LA
—White-tailed Jay	*Cyanocorax mystacalis*	SA
—Cayenne Jay	*Cyanocorax cayanus*	SA
—Azure-naped Jay	*Cyanocorax heilprini*	SA
—Plush-crested Jay	*Cyanocorax chrysops*	SA
—White-naped Jay	*Cyanocorax cyanopogon*	SA
—Green Jay	*Cyanocorax luxuosus*	MA
—Inca Jay	*Cyanocorax yncas*	SA
—Brown Jay	*Cyanocorax morio*	MA
—Black-throated Magpie-Jay	*Calocitta colliei*	MA
—White-throated Magpie-Jay	*Calocitta formosa*	MA
—Blue Jay	*Cyanocitta cristata*	NA
—Steller's Jay	*Cyanocitta stelleri*	NA, MA
—Mexican Jay	*Aphelocoma ultramarina*	NA, MA
—Unicolored Jay	*Aphelocoma unicolor*	MA
—Western Scrub Jay	*Aphelocoma californica*	NA, MA
—Island Scrub Jay	*Aphelocoma insularis*	NA
—Florida Scrub Jay	*Aphelocoma coerulescens*	NA
—Pinyon Jay	*Gymnorhinus cyanocephalus*	NA
—Eurasian Jay	*Garrulus glandarius*	EU, OR
—Black-headed Jay	*Garrulus lanceolatus*	EU
—Lidth's Jay	*Garrulus lidthi*	EU
—Azure-winged Magpie	*Cyanopica cyanus*	EU
—Iberian Magpie	*Cyanopica cooki*	EU
—Sri Lanka Blue Magpie	*Urocissa ornata*	OR
—Taiwan Blue Magpie	*Urocissa caerulea*	OR
—Yellow-billed Blue Magpie	*Urocissa flavirostris*	OR
—Red-billed Blue Magpie	*Urocissa erythrorhyncha*	OR
—White-winged Magpie	*Urocissa whiteheadi*	OR
—Common Green Magpie	*Cissa chinensis*	OR
—Indochinese Green Magpie	*Cissa hypoleuca*	OR
—Short-tailed Green Magpie	*Cissa thalassina*	OR
—Rufous Treepie	*Dendrocitta vagabunda*	OR
—Sumatran Treepie	*Dendrocitta occipitalis*	OR
—Bornean Treepie	*Dendrocitta cinerascens*	OR
—Grey Treepie	*Dendrocitta formosae*	OR
—White-bellied Treepie	*Dendrocitta leucogastra*	OR
—Collared Treepie	*Dendrocitta frontalis*	OR
—Andaman Treepie	*Dendrocitta bayleyi*	OR
—Racket-tailed Treepie	*Crypsirina temia*	OR
—Hooded Treepie	*Crypsirina cucullata*	OR
—Ratchet-tailed Treepie	*Temnurus temnurus*	OR
—Eurasian Magpie	*Pica pica*	EU
—Black-billed Magpie	*Pica hudsonia*	NA
—Yellow-billed Magpie	*Pica nuttalli*	NA
—Stresemann's Bush Crow	*Zavattariornis stresemanni*	AF
—Henderson's Ground Jay	*Podoces hendersoni*	EU
—Biddulph's Ground Jay	*Podoces biddulphi*	EU

INTERNATIONAL ENGLISH NAME	SCIENTIFIC NAME	REGION(S)
__Pander's Ground Jay	*Podoces panderi*	EU
__Pleske's Ground Jay	*Podoces pleskei*	EU
__Clark's Nutcracker	*Nucifraga columbiana*	NA
__Spotted Nutcracker	*Nucifraga caryocatactes*	EU
__Red-billed Chough	*Pyrrhocorax pyrrhocorax*	EU
__Alpine Chough	*Pyrrhocorax graculus*	EU
__Piapiac	*Ptilostomus afer*	AF
__Western Jackdaw	*Corvus monedula*	EU
__Daurian Jackdaw	*Corvus dauuricus*	EU
__House Crow	*Corvus splendens*	OR
__New Caledonian Crow	*Corvus moneduloides*	AU
__Banggai Crow	*Corvus unicolor*	AU
__Slender-billed Crow	*Corvus enca*	OR
__Violet Crow	*Corvus violaceus*	AU
__Piping Crow	*Corvus typicus*	AU
__Flores Crow	*Corvus florensis*	AU
__Mariana Crow	*Corvus kubaryi*	PO
__Long-billed Crow	*Corvus validus*	AU
__White-billed Crow	*Corvus woodfordi*	AU
__Brown-headed Crow	*Corvus fuscicapillus*	AU
__Grey Crow	*Corvus tristis*	AU
__Cape Crow	*Corvus capensis*	AF
__Rook	*Corvus frugilegus*	EU
__American Crow	*Corvus brachyrhynchos*	NA
__Northwestern Crow	*Corvus caurinus*	NA
__Tamaulipas Crow	*Corvus imparatus*	NA, MA
__Sinaloa Crow	*Corvus sinaloae*	MA
__Fish Crow	*Corvus ossifragus*	NA
__Hispaniolan Palm Crow	*Corvus palmarum*	NA
__Cuban Palm Crow	*Corvus minutus*	NA
__Jamaican Crow	*Corvus jamaicensis*	NA
__Cuban Crow	*Corvus nasicus*	NA
__White-necked Crow	*Corvus leucognaphalus*	NA
__Hawaiian Crow	*Corvus hawaiiensis*	PO
__Carrion Crow	*Corvus corone*	EU
__Hooded Crow	*Corvus cornix*	EU
__Collared Crow	*Corvus pectoralis*	EU
__Large-billed Crow	*Corvus macrorhynchos*	EU
__Jungle Crow	*Corvus levaillantii*	OR
__Torresian Crow	*Corvus orru*	AU
__Little Crow	*Corvus bennetti*	AU
__Forest Raven	*Corvus tasmanicus*	AU
__Little Raven	*Corvus mellori*	AU
__Australian Raven	*Corvus coronoides*	AU
__Pied Crow	*Corvus albus*	AF
__Brown-necked Raven	*Corvus ruficollis*	EU
__Somali Crow	*Corvus edithae*	AF
__Northern Raven	*Corvus corax*	NA, MA, EU
__Chihuahuan Raven	*Corvus cryptoleucus*	NA, MA
__Fan-tailed Raven	*Corvus rhipidurus*	EU
__White-necked Raven	*Corvus albicollis*	AF
__Thick-billed Raven	*Corvus crassirostris*	AF

INTERNATIONAL ENGLISH NAME	SCIENTIFIC NAME	REGION(S)
AUSTRALIAN MUDNESTERS	**Family Corcoracidae**	
—White-winged Chough	*Corcorax melanorhamphos*	AU
—Apostlebird	*Struthidea cinerea*	AU
FAMILY UNCERTAIN	**Incertae Sedis**	
—Lesser Melampitta	*Melampitta lugubris*	AU
—Greater Melampitta	*Melampitta gigantea*	AU
—Ifrit	*Ifrita kowaldi*	AU
BIRDS-OF-PARADISE	**Family Paradisaeidae**	
—Paradise-crow	*Lycocorax pyrrhopterus*	AU
—Glossy-mantled Manucode	*Manucodia ater*	AU
—Jobi Manucode	*Manucodia jobiensis*	AU
—Crinkle-collared Manucode	*Manucodia chalybatus*	AU
—Curl-crested Manucode	*Manucodia comrii*	AU
—Trumpet Manucode	*Phonygammus keraudrenii*	AU
—Long-tailed Paradigalla	*Paradigalla carunculata*	AU
—Short-tailed Paradigalla	*Paradigalla brevicauda*	AU
—Arfak Astrapia	*Astrapia nigra*	AU
—Splendid Astrapia	*Astrapia splendidissima*	AU
—Ribbon-tailed Astrapia	*Astrapia mayeri*	AU
—Princess Stephanie's Astrapia	*Astrapia stephaniae*	AU
—Huon Astrapia	*Astrapia rothschildi*	AU
—Western Parotia	*Parotia sefilata*	AU
—Carola's Parotia	*Parotia carolae*	AU
—Bronze Parotia	*Parotia berlepschi*	AU
—Lawes's Parotia	*Parotia lawesii*	AU
—Eastern Parotia	*Parotia helenae*	AU
—Wahnes's Parotia	*Parotia wahnesi*	AU
—King of Saxony Bird-of-Paradise	*Pteridophora alberti*	AU
—Superb Bird-of-Paradise	*Lophorina superba*	AU
—Paradise Riflebird	*Ptiloris paradiseus*	AU
—Victoria's Riflebird	*Ptiloris victoriae*	AU
—Magnificent Riflebird	*Ptiloris magnificus*	AU
—Growling Riflebird	*Ptiloris intercedens*	AU
—Black Sicklebill	*Epimachus fastuosus*	AU
—Brown Sicklebill	*Epimachus meyeri*	AU
—Black-billed Sicklebill	*Drepanornis albertisi*	AU
—Pale-billed Sicklebill	*Drepanornis bruijnii*	AU
—Magnificent Bird-of-Paradise	*Diphyllodes magnificus*	AU
—Wilson's Bird-of-Paradise	*Diphyllodes respublica*	AU
—King Bird-of-Paradise	*Cicinnurus regius*	AU
—Standardwing	*Semioptera wallacii*	AU
—Twelve-wired Bird-of-Paradise	*Seleucidis melanoleucus*	AU
—Greater Bird-of-Paradise	*Paradisaea apoda*	AU
—Raggiana Bird-of-Paradise	*Paradisaea raggiana*	AU
—Lesser Bird-of-Paradise	*Paradisaea minor*	AU
—Goldie's Bird-of-Paradise	*Paradisaea decora*	AU
—Red Bird-of-Paradise	*Paradisaea rubra*	AU
—Emperor Bird-of-Paradise	*Paradisaea guilielmi*	AU
—Blue Bird-of-Paradise	*Paradisaea rudolphi*	AU
AUSTRALASIAN ROBINS	**Family Petroicidae**	
—Ashy Robin	*Poecilodryas albispecularis*	AU
—Grey-headed Robin	*Poecilodryas cinereifrons*	AU

INTERNATIONAL ENGLISH NAME	SCIENTIFIC NAME	REGION(S)
_Black-chinned Robin	*Poecilodryas brachyura*	AU
_Black-sided Robin	*Poecilodryas hypoleuca*	AU
_White-browed Robin	*Poecilodryas superciliosa*	AU
_Buff-sided Robin	*Poecilodryas cerviniventris*	AU
_Olive-yellow Robin	*Poecilodryas placens*	AU
_Black-throated Robin	*Poecilodryas albonotata*	AU
_White-winged Robin	*Peneothello sigillata*	AU
_Smoky Robin	*Peneothello cryptoleuca*	AU
_Slaty Robin	*Peneothello cyanus*	AU
_White-rumped Robin	*Peneothello bimaculata*	AU
_Mangrove Robin	*Peneoenanthe pulverulenta*	AU
_White-faced Robin	*Tregellasia leucops*	AU
_Pale-yellow Robin	*Tregellasia capito*	AU
_Eastern Yellow Robin	*Eopsaltria australis*	AU
_Western Yellow Robin	*Eopsaltria griseogularis*	AU
_White-breasted Robin	*Eopsaltria georgiana*	AU
_Yellow-bellied Robin	*Eopsaltria flaviventris*	AU
_Hooded Robin	*Melanodryas cucullata*	AU
_Dusky Robin	*Melanodryas vittata*	AU
_Green-backed Robin	*Pachycephalopsis hattamensis*	AU
_White-eyed Robin	*Pachycephalopsis poliosoma*	AU
_Torrent Flyrobin	*Monachella muelleriana*	AU
_Canary Flyrobin	*Microeca papuana*	AU
_Yellow-legged Flyrobin	*Microeca griseoceps*	AU
_Olive Flyrobin	*Microeca flavovirescens*	AU
_Lemon-bellied Flyrobin	*Microeca flavigaster*	AU
_Golden-bellied Flyrobin	*Microeca hemixantha*	AU
_Jacky Winter	*Microeca fascinans*	AU
_Garnet Robin	*Eugerygone rubra*	AU
_Rose Robin	*Petroica rosea*	AU
_Pink Robin	*Petroica rodinogaster*	AU
_Snow Mountains Robin	*Petroica archboldi*	AU
_Cloud-forest Robin	*Petroica bivittata*	AU
_Flame Robin	*Petroica phoenicea*	AU
_Pacific Robin	*Petroica multicolor*	PO
_Scarlet Robin	*Petroica boodang*	AU
_Red-capped Robin	*Petroica goodenovii*	AU
_Tomtit	*Petroica macrocephala*	AU
_New Zealand Robin	*Petroica australis*	AU
_Black Robin	*Petroica traversi*	AU
_Northern Scrub Robin	*Drymodes superciliaris*	AU
_Southern Scrub Robin	*Drymodes brunneopygia*	AU
_Greater Ground Robin	*Amalocichla sclateriana*	AU
_Lesser Ground Robin	*Amalocichla incerta*	AU
BALD CROWS	**Family Picathartidae**	
_White-necked Picathartes	*Picathartes gymnocephalus*	AF
_Grey-necked Picathartes	*Picathartes oreas*	AF
ROCKJUMPERS	**Family Chaetopidae**	
_Cape Rockjumper	*Chaetops frenatus*	AF
_Drakensburg Rockjumper	*Chaetops aurantius*	AF

INTERNATIONAL ENGLISH NAME	SCIENTIFIC NAME	REGION(S)
WAXWINGS & ALLIES	**Family Bombycillidae**	
—Bohemian Waxwing	*Bombycilla garrulus*	EU, NA
—Japanese Waxwing	*Bombycilla japonica*	EU
—Cedar Waxwing	*Bombycilla cedrorum*	NA, LA
—Black-and-yellow Phainoptila	*Phainoptila melanoxantha*	MA
—Grey Silky-flycatcher	*Ptilogonys cinereus*	MA
—Long-tailed Silky-flycatcher	*Ptilogonys caudatus*	MA
—Phainopepla	*Phainopepla nitens*	NA, MA
—Hypocolius	*Hypocolius ampelinus*	EU
PALMCHAT	**Family Dulidae**	
—Palmchat	*Dulus dominicus*	NA
TITS, CHICKADEES	**Family Paridae**	
—Marsh Tit	*Poecile palustris*	EU
—Sombre Tit	*Poecile lugubris*	EU
—Willow Tit	*Poecile montana*	EU
—Carolina Chickadee	*Poecile carolinensis*	NA
—Black-capped Chickadee	*Poecile atricapillus*	NA
—Mountain Chickadee	*Poecile gambeli*	NA
—Mexican Chickadee	*Poecile sclateri*	NA, MA
—White-browed Tit	*Poecile superciliosa*	EU
—Pere David's Tit	*Poecile davidi*	EU
—Grey-headed Chickadee	*Poecile cincta*	EU
—Boreal Chickadee	*Poecile hudsonica*	NA
—Chestnut-backed Chickadee	*Poecile rufescens*	NA
—Varied Tit	*Poecile varia*	EU
—Rufous-naped Tit	*Periparus rufonuchalis*	EU
—Rufous-vented Tit	*Periparus rubidiventris*	OR
—Spot-winged Tit	*Periparus melanolophus*	EU
—Coal Tit	*Periparus ater*	EU
—Yellow-bellied Tit	*Periparus venustulus*	EU
—Elegant Tit	*Periparus elegans*	OR
—Palawan Tit	*Periparus amabilis*	OR
—European Crested Tit	*Lophophanes cristatus*	EU
—Grey Crested Tit	*Lophophanes dichrous*	OR
—White-shouldered Black Tit	*Parus guineensis*	AF
—White-winged Black Tit	*Parus leucomelas*	AF
—Carp's Black Tit	*Parus carpi*	AF
—Southern Black Tit	*Parus niger*	AF
—White-bellied Tit	*Parus albiventris*	AF
—White-backed Black Tit	*Parus leuconotus*	AF
—Dusky Tit	*Parus funereus*	AF
—Rufous-bellied Tit	*Parus rufiventris*	AF
—Cinnamon-breasted Tit	*Parus pallidiventris*	AF
—Red-throated Tit	*Parus fringillinus*	AF
—Stripe-breasted Tit	*Parus fasciiventer*	AF
—Acacia Tit	*Parus thruppi*	AF
—Miombo Tit	*Parus griseiventris*	AF
—Ashy Tit	*Parus cinerascens*	AF
—Grey Tit	*Parus afer*	AF
—Great Tit	*Parus major*	EU, OR
—Turkestan Tit	*Parus bokharensis*	EU

INTERNATIONAL ENGLISH NAME	SCIENTIFIC NAME	REGION(S)
__Green-backed Tit	*Parus monticolus*	EU, OR
__White-naped Tit	*Parus nuchalis*	OR
__Black-lored Tit	*Parus xanthogenys*	OR
__Yellow-cheeked Tit	*Parus spilonotus*	OR
__Yellow Tit	*Parus holsti*	OR
__White-fronted Tit	*Parus semilarvatus*	OR
__Groundpecker	*Parus humilis*	EU
__Blue Tit	*Cyanistes caeruleus*	EU
__Azure Tit	*Cyanistes cyanus*	EU
__Bridled Titmouse	*Baeolophus wollweberi*	NA, MA
__Oak Titmouse	*Baeolophus inornatus*	NA, MA
__Juniper Titmouse	*Baeolophus ridgwayi*	NA, MA
__Tufted Titmouse	*Baeolophus bicolor*	NA
__Black-crested Titmouse	*Baeolophus atricristatus*	NA, MA
__Yellow-browed Tit	*Sylviparus modestus*	OR
__Sultan Tit	*Melanochlora sultanea*	OR

PENDULINE TITS	**Family Remizidae**	
__Eurasian Penduline Tit	*Remiz pendulinus*	EU
__White-crowned Penduline Tit	*Remiz coronatus*	EU
__Chinese Penduline Tit	*Remiz consobrinus*	EU
__Sennar Penduline Tit	*Anthoscopus punctifrons*	AF
__Yellow Penduline Tit	*Anthoscopus parvulus*	AF
__Mouse-colored Penduline Tit	*Anthoscopus musculus*	AF
__Forest Penduline Tit	*Anthoscopus flavifrons*	AF
__Grey Penduline Tit	*Anthoscopus caroli*	AF
__Cape Penduline Tit	*Anthoscopus minutus*	AF
__Verdin	*Auriparus flaviceps*	NA, MA
__Fire-capped Tit	*Cephalopyrus flammiceps*	OR

SWALLOWS, MARTINS	**Family Hirundinidae**	
__African River Martin	*Pseudochelidon eurystomina*	AF
__White-eyed River Martin	*Pseudochelidon sirintarae*	OR
__Square-tailed Saw-wing	*Psalidoprocne nitens*	AF
__Mountain Saw-wing	*Psalidoprocne fuliginosa*	AF
__White-headed Saw-wing	*Psalidoprocne albiceps*	AF
__Black Saw-wing	*Psalidoprocne pristoptera*	AF
__Fanti Saw-wing	*Psalidoprocne obscura*	AF
__Grey-rumped Swallow	*Pseudhirundo griseopyga*	AF
__White-backed Swallow	*Cheramoeca leucosterna*	AU
__Mascarene Martin	*Phedina borbonica*	AF
__Brazza's Martin	*Phedina brazzae*	AF
__Brown-throated Martin	*Riparia paludicola*	AF, OR
__Congo Martin	*Riparia congica*	AF
__Sand Martin	*Riparia riparia*	Worldwide
__Pale Martin	*Riparia diluta*	EU
__Banded Martin	*Riparia cincta*	AF
__Tree Swallow	*Tachycineta bicolor*	NA
__Mangrove Swallow	*Tachycineta albilinea*	MA
__Tumbes Swallow	*Tachycineta stolzmanni*	SA
__White-winged Swallow	*Tachycineta albiventer*	SA
__White-rumped Swallow	*Tachycineta leucorrhoa*	SA
__Chilean Swallow	*Tachycineta meyeni*	SA

INTERNATIONAL ENGLISH NAME	SCIENTIFIC NAME	REGION(S)
—Golden Swallow	*Tachycineta euchrysea*	NA
—Violet-green Swallow	*Tachycineta thalassina*	NA, MA
—Bahama Swallow	*Tachycineta cyaneoviridis*	NA
—Purple Martin	*Progne subis*	NA, MA
—Cuban Martin	*Progne cryptoleuca*	NA
—Caribbean Martin	*Progne dominicensis*	NA
—Sinaloa Martin	*Progne sinaloae*	MA
—Grey-breasted Martin	*Progne chalybea*	LA
—Galapagos Martin	*Progne modesta*	SA
—Peruvian Martin	*Progne murphyi*	SA
—Southern Martin	*Progne elegans*	SA
—Brown-chested Martin	*Progne tapera*	SA
—Blue-and-white Swallow	*Notiochelidon cyanoleuca*	SA
—Brown-bellied Swallow	*Notiochelidon murina*	SA
—Pale-footed Swallow	*Notiochelidon flavipes*	SA
—Black-capped Swallow	*Notiochelidon pileata*	MA
—Andean Swallow	*Haplochelidon andecola*	SA
—White-banded Swallow	*Atticora fasciata*	SA
—Black-collared Swallow	*Atticora melanoleuca*	SA
—White-thighed Swallow	*Neochelidon tibialis*	LA
—Northern Rough-winged Swallow	*Stelgidopteryx serripennis*	NA, MA
—Ridgway's Rough-winged Swallow	*Stelgidopteryx ridgwayi*	MA
—Southern Rough-winged Swallow	*Stelgidopteryx ruficollis*	LA
—Tawny-headed Swallow	*Alopochelidon fucata*	SA
—Barn Swallow	*Hirundo rustica*	Worldwide
—Red-chested Swallow	*Hirundo lucida*	AF
—Angola Swallow	*Hirundo angolensis*	AF
—Pacific Swallow	*Hirundo tahitica*	OR, AU
—Welcome Swallow	*Hirundo neoxena*	AU
—White-throated Swallow	*Hirundo albigularis*	AF
—Ethiopian Swallow	*Hirundo aethiopica*	AF
—Wire-tailed Swallow	*Hirundo smithii*	AF, OR
—Blue Swallow	*Hirundo atrocaerulea*	AF
—White-bibbed Swallow	*Hirundo nigrita*	AF
—Pied-winged Swallow	*Hirundo leucosoma*	AF
—White-tailed Swallow	*Hirundo megaensis*	AF
—Black-and-rufous Swallow	*Hirundo nigrorufa*	AF
—Pearl-breasted Swallow	*Hirundo dimidiata*	AF
—Eurasian Crag Martin	*Ptyonoprogne rupestris*	EU
—Pale Crag Martin	*Ptyonoprogne obsoleta*	EU
—Rock Martin	*Ptyonoprogne fuligula*	AF
—Dusky Crag Martin	*Ptyonoprogne concolor*	OR
—Common House Martin	*Delichon urbicum*	EU
—Asian House Martin	*Delichon dasypus*	EU
—Nepal House Martin	*Delichon nipalensis*	OR
—Greater Striped Swallow	*Cecropis cucullata*	AF
—Lesser Striped Swallow	*Cecropis abyssinica*	AF
—Red-breasted Swallow	*Cecropis semirufa*	AF
—Mosque Swallow	*Cecropis senegalensis*	AF
—Red-rumped Swallow	*Cecropis daurica*	EU, OR, AF
—West African Swallow	*Cecropis domicella*	AF
—Striated Swallow	*Cecropis striolata*	OR
—Rufous-bellied Swallow	*Cecropis badia*	OR

INTERNATIONAL ENGLISH NAME	SCIENTIFIC NAME	REGION(S)
__Red-throated Cliff Swallow	*Petrochelidon rufigula*	AF
__Preuss's Cliff Swallow	*Petrochelidon preussi*	AF
__Red Sea Cliff Swallow	*Petrochelidon perdita*	AF
__South African Cliff Swallow	*Petrochelidon spilodera*	AF
__Forest Swallow	*Petrochelidon fuliginosa*	AF
__Streak-throated Swallow	*Petrochelidon fluvicola*	OR
__Fairy Martin	*Petrochelidon ariel*	AU
__Tree Martin	*Petrochelidon nigricans*	AU
__American Cliff Swallow	*Petrochelidon pyrrhonota*	NA, MA
__Cave Swallow	*Petrochelidon fulva*	NA, MA
__Chestnut-collared Swallow	*Petrochelidon rufocollaris*	SA
BUSHTITS	**Family Aegithalidae**	
__Long-tailed Bushtit	*Aegithalos caudatus*	EU
__White-cheeked Bushtit	*Aegithalos leucogenys*	EU
__Black-throated Bushtit	*Aegithalos concinnus*	OR
__White-throated Bushtit	*Aegithalos niveogularis*	EU
__Rufous-fronted Bushtit	*Aegithalos iouschistos*	OR
__Black-browed Bushtit	*Aegithalos bonvaloti*	OR
__Sooty Bushtit	*Aegithalos fuliginosus*	EU
__White-browed Tit-warbler	*Leptopoecile sophiae*	EU
__Crested Tit-warbler	*Leptopoecile elegans*	EU
__Pygmy Bushtit	*Psaltria exilis*	OR
__American Bushtit	*Psaltriparus minimus*	NA, MA
LARKS	**Family Alaudidae**	
__Singing Bush Lark	*Mirafra cantillans*	AF
__Horsfield's Bush Lark	*Mirafra javanica*	OR, AU
__Madagascar Lark	*Mirafra hova*	AF
__Monotonous Lark	*Mirafra passerina*	AF
__White-tailed Lark	*Mirafra albicauda*	AF
__Melodious Lark	*Mirafra cheniana*	AF
__Kordofan Lark	*Mirafra cordofanica*	AF
__Williams's Lark	*Mirafra williamsi*	AF
__Friedmann's Lark	*Mirafra pulpa*	AF
__Rufous-naped Lark	*Mirafra africana*	AF
__Red-winged Lark	*Mirafra hypermetra*	AF
__Somali Lark	*Mirafra somalica*	AF
__Ash's Lark	*Mirafra ashi*	AF
__Angola Lark	*Mirafra angolensis*	AF
__Flappet Lark	*Mirafra rufocinnamomea*	AF
__Clapper Lark	*Mirafra apiata*	AF
__Fawn-colored Lark	*Mirafra africanoides*	AF
__Foxy Lark	*Mirafra alopex*	AF
__Collared Lark	*Mirafra collaris*	AF
__Bengal Bush Lark	*Mirafra assamica*	OR
__Jerdon's Bush Lark	*Mirafra affinis*	OR
__Burmese Bush Lark	*Mirafra microptera*	OR
__Indochinese Bush Lark	*Mirafra erythrocephala*	OR
__Rusty Bush Lark	*Mirafra rufa*	AF
__Gillett's Lark	*Mirafra gilletti*	AF
__Degodi Lark	*Mirafra degodiensis*	AF
__Pink-breasted Lark	*Mirafra poecilosterna*	AF

INTERNATIONAL ENGLISH NAME	SCIENTIFIC NAME	REGION(S)
—Sabota Lark	*Mirafra sabota*	AF
—Indian Bush Lark	*Mirafra erythroptera*	OR
—Rudd's Lark	*Heteromirafra ruddi*	AF
—Archer's Lark	*Heteromirafra archeri*	AF
—Sidamo Lark	*Heteromirafra sidamoensis*	AF
—Benguela Long-billed Lark	*Certhilauda benguelensis*	AF
—Karoo Long-billed Lark	*Certhilauda subcoronata*	AF
—Eastern Long-billed Lark	*Certhilauda semitorquata*	AF
—Cape Long-billed Lark	*Certhilauda curvirostris*	AF
—Agulhas Long-billed Lark	*Certhilauda brevirostris*	AF
—Short-clawed Lark	*Certhilauda chuana*	AF
—Karoo Lark	*Certhilauda albescens*	AF
—Dune Lark	*Certhilauda erythrochlamys*	AF
—Barlow's Lark	*Certhilauda barlowi*	AF
—Red Lark	*Certhilauda burra*	AF
—Dusky Lark	*Pinarocorys nigricans*	AF
—Rufous-rumped Lark	*Pinarocorys erythropygia*	AF
—Spike-heeled Lark	*Chersomanes albofasciata*	AF
—Greater Hoopoe-Lark	*Alaemon alaudipes*	AF, EU
—Lesser Hoopoe-Lark	*Alaemon hamertoni*	AF
—Thick-billed Lark	*Ramphocoris clotbey*	AF
—Calandra Lark	*Melanocorypha calandra*	EU
—Bimaculated Lark	*Melanocorypha bimaculata*	EU
—Mongolian Lark	*Melanocorypha mongolica*	EU
—Tibetan Lark	*Melanocorypha maxima*	EU
—White-winged Lark	*Melanocorypha leucoptera*	EU
—Black Lark	*Melanocorypha yeltoniensis*	EU
—Bar-tailed Lark	*Ammomanes cinctura*	AF, EU
—Rufous-tailed Lark	*Ammomanes phoenicura*	OR
—Desert Lark	*Ammomanes deserti*	AF, EU
—Gray's Lark	*Ammomanes grayi*	AF
—Greater Short-toed Lark	*Calandrella brachydactyla*	EU
—Blanford's Short-toed Lark	*Calandrella blanfordi*	AF
—Erlanger's Lark	*Calandrella erlangeri*	AF
—Red-capped Lark	*Calandrella cinerea*	AF
—Hume's Short-toed Lark	*Calandrella acutirostris*	EU
—Sand Lark	*Calandrella raytal*	OR
—Lesser Short-toed Lark	*Calandrella rufescens*	EU
—Asian Short-toed Lark	*Calandrella cheleensis*	EU
—Somali Short-toed Lark	*Calandrella somalica*	AF
—Athi Short-toed Lark	*Calandrella athensis*	AF
—Pink-billed Lark	*Spizocorys conirostris*	AF
—Botha's Lark	*Spizocorys fringillaris*	AF
—Sclater's Lark	*Spizocorys sclateri*	AF
—Obbia Lark	*Spizocorys obbiensis*	AF
—Masked Lark	*Spizocorys personata*	AF
—Dunn's Lark	*Eremalauda dunni*	AF
—Stark's Lark	*Eremalauda starki*	AF
—Dupont's Lark	*Chersophilus duponti*	AF
—Short-tailed Lark	*Pseudalaemon fremantlii*	AF
—Crested Lark	*Galerida cristata*	EU, AF
—Thekla Lark	*Galerida theklae*	AF
—Malabar Lark	*Galerida malabarica*	OR

INTERNATIONAL ENGLISH NAME	SCIENTIFIC NAME	REGION(S)
—Sykes's Lark	*Galerida deva*	OR
—Sun Lark	*Galerida modesta*	AF
—Large-billed Lark	*Galerida magnirostris*	AF
—Woodlark	*Lullula arborea*	EU
—Eurasian Skylark	*Alauda arvensis*	EU
—Oriental Skylark	*Alauda gulgula*	OR
—Raso Lark	*Alauda razae*	AF
—Black-eared Sparrow-Lark	*Eremopterix australis*	AF
—Chestnut-backed Sparrow-Lark	*Eremopterix leucotis*	AF
—Chestnut-headed Sparrow-Lark	*Eremopterix signatus*	AF
—Grey-backed Sparrow-Lark	*Eremopterix verticalis*	AF
—Black-crowned Sparrow-Lark	*Eremopterix nigriceps*	AF, EU
—Ashy-crowned Sparrow-Lark	*Eremopterix griseus*	OR
—Fischer's Sparrow-Lark	*Eremopterix leucopareia*	AF
—Horned Lark	*Eremophila alpestris*	NA, MA, EU
—Temminck's Lark	*Eremophila bilopha*	AF

CISTICOLAS & ALLIES

	Family Cisticolidae	
—Red-faced Cisticola	*Cisticola erythrops*	
—Lepe Cisticola	*Cisticola lepe*	AF
—Singing Cisticola	*Cisticola cantans*	AF
—Whistling Cisticola	*Cisticola lateralis*	AF
—Trilling Cisticola	*Cisticola woosnami*	AF
—Chattering Cisticola	*Cisticola anonymus*	AF
—Bubbling Cisticola	*Cisticola bulliens*	AF
—Chubb's Cisticola	*Cisticola chubbi*	AF
—Hunter's Cisticola	*Cisticola hunteri*	AF
—Black-lored Cisticola	*Cisticola nigriloris*	AF
—Lazy Cisticola	*Cisticola aberrans*	AF
—Rock-loving Cisticola	*Cisticola emini*	AF
—Rattling Cisticola	*Cisticola chiniana*	AF
—Boran Cisticola	*Cisticola bodessa*	AF
—Churring Cisticola	*Cisticola njombe*	AF
—Ashy Cisticola	*Cisticola cinereolus*	AF
—Tana River Cisticola	*Cisticola restrictus*	AF
—Tinkling Cisticola	*Cisticola rufilatus*	AF
—Grey-backed Cisticola	*Cisticola subruficapilla*	AF
—Wailing Cisticola	*Cisticola lais*	AF
—Lynes's Cisticola	*Cisticola distinctus*	AF
—Rufous-winged Cisticola	*Cisticola galactotes*	AF
—Winding Cisticola	*Cisticola marginatus*	AF
—Coastal Cisticola	*Cisticola haematocephalus*	AF
—Ethiopian Cisticola	*Cisticola lugubris*	AF
—Luapula Cisticola	*Cisticola luapula*	AF
—Chirping Cisticola	*Cisticola pipiens*	AF
—Carruthers's Cisticola	*Cisticola carruthersi*	AF
—Levaillant's Cisticola	*Cisticola tinniens*	AF
—Stout Cisticola	*Cisticola robustus*	AF
—Aberdare Cisticola	*Cisticola aberdare*	AF
—Croaking Cisticola	*Cisticola natalensis*	AF
—Red-pate Cisticola	*Cisticola ruficeps*	AF
—Dorst's Cisticola	*Cisticola dorsti*	AF
—Tiny Cisticola	*Cisticola nana*	AF

INTERNATIONAL ENGLISH NAME	SCIENTIFIC NAME	REGION(S)
—Short-winged Cisticola	*Cisticola brachypterus*	AF
—Rufous Cisticola	*Cisticola rufus*	AF
—Foxy Cisticola	*Cisticola troglodytes*	AF
—Neddicky	*Cisticola fulvicapilla*	AF
—Long-tailed Cisticola	*Cisticola angusticauda*	AF
—Black-tailed Cisticola	*Cisticola melanurus*	AF
—Zitting Cisticola	*Cisticola juncidis*	EU, OR, AU, AF
—Socotra Cisticola	*Cisticola haesitatus*	EU
—Madagascar Cisticola	*Cisticola cherina*	AF
—Desert Cisticola	*Cisticola aridulus*	AF
—Cloud Cisticola	*Cisticola textrix*	AF
—Black-backed Cisticola	*Cisticola eximius*	AF
—Dambo Cisticola	*Cisticola dambo*	AF
—Pectoral-patch Cisticola	*Cisticola brunnescens*	AF
—Pale-crowned Cisticola	*Cisticola cinnamomeus*	AF
—Wing-snapping Cisticola	*Cisticola ayresii*	AF
—Golden-headed Cisticola	*Cisticola exilis*	OR, AU
—Socotra Warbler	*Incana incana*	EU
—Scrub Warbler	*Scotocerca inquieta*	EU
—Chinese Hill Warbler	*Rhopophilus pekinensis*	EU
—Rufous-eared Warbler	*Malcorus pectoralis*	AF
—Rufous-vented Prinia	*Prinia burnesii*	OR
—Striated Prinia	*Prinia crinigera*	EU
—Brown Prinia	*Prinia polychroa*	OR
—Hill Prinia	*Prinia atrogularis*	OR
—Grey-crowned Prinia	*Prinia cinereocapilla*	OR
—Rufous-fronted Prinia	*Prinia buchanani*	OR
—Rufescent Prinia	*Prinia rufescens*	OR
—Grey-breasted Prinia	*Prinia hodgsonii*	OR
—Graceful Prinia	*Prinia gracilis*	EU
—Jungle Prinia	*Prinia sylvatica*	OR
—Bar-winged Prinia	*Prinia familiaris*	OR
—Yellow-bellied Prinia	*Prinia flaviventris*	OR
—Ashy Prinia	*Prinia socialis*	OR
—Tawny-flanked Prinia	*Prinia subflava*	AF
—Plain Prinia	*Prinia inornata*	OR
—Pale Prinia	*Prinia somalica*	AF
—River Prinia	*Prinia fluviatilis*	AF
—Black-chested Prinia	*Prinia flavicans*	AF
—Karoo Prinia	*Prinia maculosa*	AF
—Drakensburg Prinia	*Prinia hypoxantha*	AF
—Sao Tome Prinia	*Prinia molleri*	AF
—Banded Prinia	*Prinia bairdii*	AF
—Black-faced Prinia	*Prinia melanops*	AF
—White-chinned Prinia	*Schistolais leucopogon*	AF
—Sierra Leone Prinia	*Schistolais leontica*	AF
—Namaqua Warbler	*Phragmacia substriata*	AF
—Roberts's Warbler	*Oreophilais robertsi*	AF
—Red-winged Warbler	*Heliolais erythropterus*	AF
—Green Longtail	*Urolais epichlorus*	AF
—Red-winged Grey Warbler	*Drymocichla incana*	AF
—Cricket Longtail	*Spiloptila clamans*	AF
—Buff-bellied Warbler	*Phyllolais pulchella*	AF

INTERNATIONAL ENGLISH NAME	SCIENTIFIC NAME	REGION(S)
—Bar-throated Apalis	*Apalis thoracica*	AF
—Yellow-throated Apalis	*Apalis flavigularis*	AF
—Taita Apalis	*Apalis fuscigularis*	AF
—Namuli Apalis	*Apalis lynesi*	AF
—Black-collared Apalis	*Apalis pulchra*	AF
—Ruwenzori Apalis	*Apalis ruwenzorii*	AF
—Rudd's Apalis	*Apalis ruddi*	AF
—Yellow-breasted Apalis	*Apalis flavida*	AF
—Lowland Masked Apalis	*Apalis binotata*	AF
—Mountain Masked Apalis	*Apalis personata*	AF
—Black-throated Apalis	*Apalis jacksoni*	AF
—White-winged Apalis	*Apalis chariessa*	AF
—Black-capped Apalis	*Apalis nigriceps*	AF
—Black-headed Apalis	*Apalis melanocephala*	AF
—Chirinda Apalis	*Apalis chirindensis*	AF
—Chestnut-throated Apalis	*Apalis porphyrolaema*	AF
—Kabobo Apalis	*Apalis kaboboensis*	AF
—Chapin's Apalis	*Apalis chapini*	AF
—Sharpe's Apalis	*Apalis sharpei*	AF
—Buff-throated Apalis	*Apalis rufogularis*	AF
—Kungwe Apalis	*Apalis argentea*	AF
—Karamoja Apalis	*Apalis karamojae*	AF
—Bamenda Apalis	*Apalis bamendae*	AF
—Gosling's Apalis	*Apalis goslingi*	AF
—Grey Apalis	*Apalis cinerea*	AF
—Brown-headed Apalis	*Apalis alticola*	AF
—Red-fronted Apalis	*Urorhipis rufifrons*	AF
—Oriole Warbler	*Hypergerus atriceps*	AF
—Grey-capped Warbler	*Eminia lepida*	AF
—Green-backed Camaroptera	*Camaroptera brachyura*	AF
—Grey-backed Camaroptera	*Camaroptera brevicaudata*	AF
—Hartert's Camaroptera	*Camaroptera harterti*	AF
—Yellow-browed Camaroptera	*Camaroptera superciliaris*	AF
—Olive-green Camaroptera	*Camaroptera chloronota*	AF
—Grey Wren-Warbler	*Calamonastes simplex*	AF
—Miombo Wren-Warbler	*Calamonastes undosus*	AF
—Stierling's Wren-Warbler	*Calamonastes stierlingi*	AF
—Barred Wren-Warbler	*Calamonastes fasciolatus*	AF
—Cinnamon-breasted Warbler	*Euryptila subcinnamomea*	AF

FAMILY UNCERTAIN	**Incertae Sedis**	
—Common Jery	*Neomixis tenella*	AF
—Green Jery	*Neomixis viridis*	AF
—Stripe-throated Jery	*Neomixis striatigula*	AF
—Fairy Warbler	*Stenostira scita*	AF
—Mountain Tailorbird	*Orthotomus cucullatus*	OR
—Common Tailorbird	*Orthotomus sutorius*	OR
—Dark-necked Tailorbird	*Orthotomus atrogularis*	OR
—Philippine Tailorbird	*Orthotomus castaneiceps*	OR
—Grey-backed Tailorbird	*Orthotomus derbianus*	OR
—Rufous-tailed Tailorbird	*Orthotomus sericeus*	OR
—Ashy Tailorbird	*Orthotomus ruficeps*	OR
—Olive-backed Tailorbird	*Orthotomus sepium*	OR

INTERNATIONAL ENGLISH NAME	SCIENTIFIC NAME	REGION(S)
—White-eared Tailorbird	*Orthotomus cinereiceps*	OR
—Black-headed Tailorbird	*Orthotomus nigriceps*	OR
—Yellow-breasted Tailorbird	*Orthotomus samarensis*	OR
—Long-billed Forest Warbler	*Artisornis moreaui*	AF
—Red-capped Forest Warbler	*Artisornis metopias*	AF
—White-tailed Warbler	*Poliolais lopezi*	AF
BULBULS	**Family Pycnonotidae**	
—Crested Finchbill	*Spizixos canifrons*	OR
—Collared Finchbill	*Spizixos semitorques*	OR
—Straw-headed Bulbul	*Pycnonotus zeylanicus*	OR
—Striated Bulbul	*Pycnonotus striatus*	OR
—Cream-striped Bulbul	*Pycnonotus leucogrammicus*	OR
—Spot-necked Bulbul	*Pycnonotus tympanistrigus*	OR
—Black-and-white Bulbul	*Pycnonotus melanoleucus*	OR
—Grey-headed Bulbul	*Pycnonotus priocephalus*	OR
—Black-headed Bulbul	*Pycnonotus atriceps*	OR
—Black-crested Bulbul	*Pycnonotus melanicterus*	OR
—Scaly-breasted Bulbul	*Pycnonotus squamatus*	OR
—Grey-bellied Bulbul	*Pycnonotus cyaniventris*	OR
—Red-whiskered Bulbul	*Pycnonotus jocosus*	OR
—Brown-breasted Bulbul	*Pycnonotus xanthorrhous*	OR
—Light-vented Bulbul	*Pycnonotus sinensis*	OR
—Styan's Bulbul	*Pycnonotus taivanus*	OR
—Himalayan Bulbul	*Pycnonotus leucogenys*	EU
—White-eared Bulbul	*Pycnonotus leucotis*	EU
—Red-vented Bulbul	*Pycnonotus cafer*	OR
—Sooty-headed Bulbul	*Pycnonotus aurigaster*	OR
—White-spectacled Bulbul	*Pycnonotus xanthopygos*	EU
—African Red-eyed Bulbul	*Pycnonotus nigricans*	AF
—Cape Bulbul	*Pycnonotus capensis*	AF
—Common Bulbul	*Pycnonotus barbatus*	AF
—Somali Bulbul	*Pycnonotus somaliensis*	AF
—Dodson's Bulbul	*Pycnonotus dodsoni*	AF
—Dark-capped Bulbul	*Pycnonotus tricolor*	AF
—Puff-backed Bulbul	*Pycnonotus eutilotus*	OR
—Blue-wattled Bulbul	*Pycnonotus nieuwenhuisii*	OR
—Yellow-wattled Bulbul	*Pycnonotus urostictus*	OR
—Orange-spotted Bulbul	*Pycnonotus bimaculatus*	OR
—Stripe-throated Bulbul	*Pycnonotus finlaysoni*	OR
—Yellow-throated Bulbul	*Pycnonotus xantholaemus*	OR
—Yellow-eared Bulbul	*Pycnonotus penicillatus*	OR
—Flavescent Bulbul	*Pycnonotus flavescens*	OR
—Yellow-vented Bulbul	*Pycnonotus goiavier*	OR
—White-browed Bulbul	*Pycnonotus luteolus*	OR
—Olive-winged Bulbul	*Pycnonotus plumosus*	OR
—Streak-eared Bulbul	*Pycnonotus blanfordi*	OR
—Cream-vented Bulbul	*Pycnonotus simplex*	OR
—Asian Red-eyed Bulbul	*Pycnonotus brunneus*	OR
—Spectacled Bulbul	*Pycnonotus erythropthalmos*	OR
—Shelley's Greenbul	*Andropadus masukuensis*	AF
—Kakamega Greenbul	*Andropadus kakamegae*	AF
—Cameroon Greenbul	*Andropadus montanus*	AF

INTERNATIONAL ENGLISH NAME	SCIENTIFIC NAME	REGION(S)
__Western Greenbul	*Andropadus tephrolaemus*	AF
__Olive-breasted Greenbul	*Andropadus kikuyuensis*	AF
__Mountain Greenbul	*Andropadus nigriceps*	AF
__Black-browed Greenbul	*Andropadus fusciceps*	AF
__Yellow-throated Greenbul	*Andropadus chlorigula*	AF
__Stripe-cheeked Greenbul	*Andropadus milanjensis*	AF
__Olive-headed Greenbul	*Andropadus olivaceiceps*	AF
__Stripe-faced Greenbul	*Andropadus striifacies*	AF
__Little Greenbul	*Andropadus virens*	AF
__Little Grey Greenbul	*Andropadus gracilis*	AF
__Ansorge's Greenbul	*Andropadus ansorgei*	AF
__Plain Greenbul	*Andropadus curvirostris*	AF
__Slender-billed Greenbul	*Andropadus gracilirostris*	AF
__Yellow-whiskered Greenbul	*Andropadus latirostris*	AF
__Sombre Greenbul	*Andropadus importunus*	AF
__Golden Greenbul	*Calyptocichla serina*	AF
__Honeyguide Greenbul	*Baeopogon indicator*	AF
__Sjostedt's Greenbul	*Baeopogon clamans*	AF
__Spotted Greenbul	*Ixonotus guttatus*	AF
__Joyful Greenbul	*Chlorocichla laetissima*	AF
__Prigogine's Greenbul	*Chlorocichla prigoginei*	AF
__Yellow-bellied Greenbul	*Chlorocichla flaviventris*	AF
__Falkenstein's Greenbul	*Chlorocichla falkensteini*	AF
__Simple Greenbul	*Chlorocichla simplex*	AF
__Yellow-throated Leaflove	*Chlorocichla flavicollis*	AF
__Swamp Palm Bulbul	*Thescelocichla leucopleura*	AF
__Red-tailed Leaflove	*Phyllastrephus scandens*	AF
__Terrestrial Brownbul	*Phyllastrephus terrestris*	AF
__Northern Brownbul	*Phyllastrephus strepitans*	AF
__Grey-olive Bulbul	*Phyllastrephus cerviniventris*	AF
__Pale-olive Bulbul	*Phyllastrephus fulviventris*	AF
__Baumann's Olive Greenbul	*Phyllastrephus baumanni*	AF
__Toro Olive Greenbul	*Phyllastrephus hypochloris*	AF
__Sassi's Olive Greenbul	*Phyllastrephus lorenzi*	AF
__Fischer's Greenbul	*Phyllastrephus fischeri*	AF
__Cabanis's Greenbul	*Phyllastrephus cabanisi*	AF
__Placid Greenbul	*Phyllastrephus placidus*	AF
__Cameroon Olive Greenbul	*Phyllastrephus poensis*	AF
__Icterine Greenbul	*Phyllastrephus icterinus*	AF
__Xavier's Greenbul	*Phyllastrephus xavieri*	AF
__Liberian Greenbul	*Phyllastrephus leucolepis*	AF
__White-throated Greenbul	*Phyllastrephus albigularis*	AF
__Yellow-streaked Greenbul	*Phyllastrephus flavostriatus*	AF
__Sharpe's Greenbul	*Phyllastrephus alfredi*	AF
__Grey-headed Greenbul	*Phyllastrephus poliocephalus*	AF
__Tiny Greenbul	*Phyllastrephus debilis*	AF
__Red-tailed Bristlebill	*Bleda syndactylus*	AF
__Green-tailed Bristlebill	*Bleda eximius*	AF
__Yellow-lored Bristlebill	*Bleda notatus*	AF
__Grey-headed Bristlebill	*Bleda canicapillus*	AF
__Western Bearded Greenbul	*Criniger barbatus*	AF
__Eastern Bearded Greenbul	*Criniger chloronotus*	AF
__Red-tailed Greenbul	*Criniger calurus*	AF

INTERNATIONAL ENGLISH NAME	SCIENTIFIC NAME	REGION(S)
—White-bearded Greenbul	*Criniger ndussumensis*	AF
—Yellow-bearded Greenbul	*Criniger olivaceus*	AF
—Finsch's Bulbul	*Criniger finschii*	OR
—White-throated Bulbul	*Criniger flaveolus*	OR
—Puff-throated Bulbul	*Criniger pallidus*	OR
—Ochraceous Bulbul	*Criniger ochraceus*	OR
—Grey-cheeked Bulbul	*Criniger bres*	OR
—Yellow-bellied Bulbul	*Criniger phaeocephalus*	OR
—Yellow-browed Bulbul	*Acritillas indica*	OR
—Hook-billed Bulbul	*Setornis criniger*	OR
—Hairy-backed Bulbul	*Tricholestes criniger*	OR
—Olive Bulbul	*Iole virescens*	OR
—Grey-eyed Bulbul	*Iole propinqua*	OR
—Buff-vented Bulbul	*Iole olivacea*	OR
—Sulphur-bellied Bulbul	*Iole palawanensis*	OR
—Nicobar Bulbul	*Ixos nicobariensis*	OR
—Mountain Bulbul	*Ixos mcclellandii*	OR
—Streaked Bulbul	*Ixos malaccensis*	OR
—Sunda Bulbul	*Ixos virescens*	OR
—Philippine Bulbul	*Ixos philippinus*	OR
—Zamboanga Bulbul	*Ixos rufigularis*	OR
—Streak-breasted Bulbul	*Ixos siquijorensis*	OR
—Yellowish Bulbul	*Ixos everetti*	OR
—Golden Bulbul	*Thapsinillas affinis*	AU
—Brown-eared Bulbul	*Microscelis amaurotis*	EU
—Ashy Bulbul	*Hemixos flavala*	OR
—Chestnut Bulbul	*Hemixos castanonotus*	OR
—Seychelles Bulbul	*Hypsipetes crassirostris*	IO
—Reunion Bulbul	*Hypsipetes borbonicus*	IO
—Mauritius Bulbul	*Hypsipetes olivaceus*	IO
—Malagasy Bulbul	*Hypsipetes madagascariensis*	AF
—Comoros Bulbul	*Hypsipetes parvirostris*	AF
—Black Bulbul	*Hypsipetes leucocephalus*	OR
—White-headed Bulbul	*Cerasophila thompsoni*	OR
FAMILY UNCERTAIN	**Incertae Sedis**	
—Black-collared Bulbul	*Neolestes torquatus*	AF
—Western Nicator	*Nicator chloris*	AF
—Eastern Nicator	*Nicator gularis*	AF
—Yellow-throated Nicator	*Nicator vireo*	AF
—Little Yellow Flycatcher	*Erythrocercus holochlorus*	AF
—Chestnut-capped Flycatcher	*Erythrocercus mccallii*	AF
—Livingstone's Flycatcher	*Erythrocercus livingstonei*	AF
—African Blue Flycatcher	*Elminia longicauda*	AF
—White-tailed Blue Flycatcher	*Elminia albicauda*	AF
OLD WORLD WARBLERS	**Family Sylviidae**	
—Grey Emutail	*Amphilais seebohmi*	AF
—Brown Emutail	*Dromaeocercus brunneus*	AF
—Tawny Grassbird	*Megalurus timoriensis*	AU
—Papuan Grassbird	*Megalurus macrurus*	AU
—Striated Grassbird	*Megalurus palustris*	OR
—Fly River Grassbird	*Megalurus albolimbatus*	AU

INTERNATIONAL ENGLISH NAME	SCIENTIFIC NAME	REGION(S)
__Little Grassbird	*Megalurus gramineus*	AU
__New Zealand Fernbird	*Megalurus punctatus*	AU
__Rufous Songlark	*Cincloramphus mathewsi*	AU
__Brown Songlark	*Cincloramphus cruralis*	AU
__Spinifexbird	*Eremiornis carteri*	AU
__Buff-banded Thicketbird	*Buettikoferella bivittata*	AU
__New Caledonian Thicketbird	*Megalurulus mariei*	AU
__Vanuatu Thicketbird	*Megalurulus whitneyi*	AU
__Melanesian Thicketbird	*Megalurulus llaneae*	AU
__Rusty Thicketbird	*Megalurulus rubiginosus*	AU
__Long-legged Thicketbird	*Megalurulus rufa*	PO
__Bristled Grassbird	*Chaetornis striata*	OR
__Rufous-rumped Grassbird	*Graminicola bengalensis*	OR
__Broad-tailed Grassbird	*Schoenicola platyurus*	OR
__Fan-tailed Grassbird	*Schoenicola brevirostris*	AF
__Neumann's Warbler	*Hemitesia neumanni*	AF
__Chestnut-headed Tesia	*Oligura castaneocoronata*	OR
__Slaty-bellied Tesia	*Tesia olivea*	OR
__Grey-bellied Tesia	*Tesia cyaniventer*	OR
__Javan Tesia	*Tesia superciliaris*	OR
__Russet-capped Tesia	*Tesia everetti*	AU
__Asian Stubtail	*Urosphena squameiceps*	EU
__Bornean Stubtail	*Urosphena whiteheadi*	OR
__Timor Stubtail	*Urosphena subulata*	AU
__Pale-footed Bush Warbler	*Cettia pallidipes*	OR
__Japanese Bush Warbler	*Cettia diphone*	EU
__Philippine Bush Warbler	*Cettia seebohmi*	OR
__Palau Bush Warbler	*Cettia annae*	AU
__Shade Bush Warbler	*Cettia parens*	AU
__Fiji Bush Warbler	*Cettia ruficapilla*	PO
__Brown-flanked Bush Warbler	*Cettia fortipes*	OR
__Sunda Bush Warbler	*Cettia vulcania*	OR
__Chestnut-crowned Bush Warbler	*Cettia major*	OR
__Tanimbar Bush Warbler	*Cettia carolinae*	AU
__Aberrant Bush Warbler	*Cettia flavolivacea*	OR
__Yellow-bellied Bush Warbler	*Cettia acanthizoides*	OR
__Hume's Bush Warbler	*Cettia brunnescens*	OR
__Grey-sided Bush Warbler	*Cettia brunnifrons*	OR
__Cetti's Warbler	*Cettia cetti*	EU
__Victorin's Warbler	*Cryptillas victorini*	AF
__Little Rush Warbler	*Bradypterus baboecala*	AF
__Grauer's Swamp Warbler	*Bradypterus graueri*	AF
__Ja River Scrub Warbler	*Bradypterus grandis*	AF
__White-winged Swamp Warbler	*Bradypterus carpalis*	AF
__Bamboo Warbler	*Bradypterus alfredi*	AF
__Knysna Warbler	*Bradypterus sylvaticus*	AF
__Evergreen Forest Warbler	*Bradypterus lopezi*	AF
__Barratt's Warbler	*Bradypterus barratti*	AF
__Cinnamon Bracken Warbler	*Bradypterus cinnamomeus*	AF
__Spotted Bush Warbler	*Bradypterus thoracicus*	OR
__Baikal Bush Warbler	*Bradypterus davidi*	EU
__Long-billed Bush Warbler	*Bradypterus major*	EU, OR
__Chinese Bush Warbler	*Bradypterus tacsanowskius*	EU

INTERNATIONAL ENGLISH NAME	SCIENTIFIC NAME	REGION(S)
—Brown Bush Warbler	*Bradypterus luteoventris*	OR
—Taiwan Bush Warbler	*Bradypterus alishanensis*	OR
—Russet Bush Warbler	*Bradypterus mandelli*	OR
—Benguet Bush Warbler	*Bradypterus seebohmi*	OR
—Javan Bush Warbler	*Bradypterus montis*	OR
—Timor Bush Warbler	*Bradypterus timorensis*	AU
—Long-tailed Bush Warbler	*Bradypterus caudatus*	OR
—Friendly Bush Warbler	*Bradypterus accentor*	OR
—Chestnut-backed Bush Warbler	*Bradypterus castaneus*	AU
—Sri Lanka Bush Warbler	*Elaphrornis palliseri*	OR
—Black-headed Rufous Warbler	*Bathmocercus cerviniventris*	AF
—Black-faced Rufous Warbler	*Bathmocercus rufus*	AF
—Winifred's Warbler	*Bathmocercus winifredae*	AF
—Malagasy Brush Warbler	*Nesillas typica*	AF
—Subdesert Brush Warbler	*Nesillas lantzii*	AF
—Anjouan Brush Warbler	*Nesillas longicaudata*	AF
—Grand Comoro Brush Warbler	*Nesillas brevicaudata*	AF
—Moheli Brush Warbler	*Nesillas mariae*	AF
—Aldabra Brush Warbler	*Nesillas aldabrana*	AF
—Moustached Grass Warbler	*Melocichla mentalis*	AF
—Cape Grassbird	*Sphenoeacus afer*	AF
—Rockrunner	*Achaetops pycnopygius*	AF
—Lanceolated Warbler	*Locustella lanceolata*	EU
—Common Grasshopper Warbler	*Locustella naevia*	EU
—Pallas's Grasshopper Warbler	*Locustella certhiola*	EU
—Middendorff's Grasshopper Warbler	*Locustella ochotensis*	EU
—Styan's Grasshopper Warbler	*Locustella pleskei*	EU
—River Warbler	*Locustella fluviatilis*	EU
—Savi's Warbler	*Locustella luscinioides*	EU
—Gray's Grasshopper Warbler	*Locustella fasciolata*	EU
—Marsh Grassbird	*Locustella pryeri*	EU
—Thick-billed Warbler	*Acrocephalus aedon*	EU
—Basra Reed Warbler	*Acrocephalus griseldis*	EU
—Cape Verde Warbler	*Acrocephalus brevipennis*	AF
—Greater Swamp Warbler	*Acrocephalus rufescens*	AF
—Lesser Swamp Warbler	*Acrocephalus gracilirostris*	AF
—Madagascar Swamp Warbler	*Acrocephalus newtoni*	AF
—Seychelles Warbler	*Acrocephalus sechellensis*	IO
—Rodrigues Warbler	*Acrocephalus rodericanus*	IO
—Great Reed Warbler	*Acrocephalus arundinaceus*	EU
—Oriental Reed Warbler	*Acrocephalus orientalis*	EU
—Clamorous Reed Warbler	*Acrocephalus stentoreus*	EU, OR
—Australian Reed Warbler	*Acrocephalus australis*	AU
—Millerbird	*Acrocephalus familiaris*	PO
—Nightingale Reed Warbler	*Acrocephalus luscinius*	PO
—Nauru Reed Warbler	*Acrocephalus rehsei*	PO
—Carolinian Reed Warbler	*Acrocephalus syrinx*	PO
—Bokikokiko	*Acrocephalus aequinoctialis*	PO
—Tahiti Reed Warbler	*Acrocephalus caffer*	PO
—Marquesan Reed Warbler	*Acrocephalus mendanae*	PO
—Tuamotu Reed Warbler	*Acrocephalus atyphus*	PO
—Cook Reed Warbler	*Acrocephalus kerearako*	PO
—Rimatara Reed Warbler	*Acrocephalus rimitarae*	PO

INTERNATIONAL ENGLISH NAME	SCIENTIFIC NAME	REGION(S)
__Henderson Reed Warbler	*Acrocephalus taiti*	PO
__Pitcairn Reed Warbler	*Acrocephalus vaughani*	PO
__Black-browed Reed Warbler	*Acrocephalus bistrigiceps*	EU
__Moustached Warbler	*Acrocephalus melanopogon*	EU
__Aquatic Warbler	*Acrocephalus paludicola*	EU
__Sedge Warbler	*Acrocephalus schoenobaenus*	EU
__Speckled Reed Warbler	*Acrocephalus sorghophilus*	EU
__Blunt-winged Warbler	*Acrocephalus concinens*	EU
__Manchurian Reed Warbler	*Acrocephalus tangorum*	EU
__Large-billed Reed Warbler	*Acrocephalus orinus*	OR
__Paddyfield Warbler	*Acrocephalus agricola*	EU
__Blyth's Reed Warbler	*Acrocephalus dumetorum*	EU
__Eurasian Reed Warbler	*Acrocephalus scirpaceus*	EU
__African Reed Warbler	*Acrocephalus baeticatus*	AF
__Marsh Warbler	*Acrocephalus palustris*	EU
__Booted Warbler	*Hippolais caligata*	EU
__Sykes's Warbler	*Hippolais rama*	EU
__Eastern Olivaceous Warbler	*Hippolais pallida*	EU
__Western Olivaceous Warbler	*Hippolais opaca*	EU
__Upcher's Warbler	*Hippolais languida*	EU
__Olive-tree Warbler	*Hippolais olivetorum*	EU
__Melodious Warbler	*Hippolais polyglotta*	EU
__Icterine Warbler	*Hippolais icterina*	EU
__Dark-capped Yellow Warbler	*Chloropeta natalensis*	AF
__Mountain Yellow Warbler	*Chloropeta similis*	AF
__Papyrus Yellow Warbler	*Chloropeta gracilirostris*	AF
__Yellow Longbill	*Macrosphenus flavicans*	AF
__Kemp's Longbill	*Macrosphenus kempi*	AF
__Grey Longbill	*Macrosphenus concolor*	AF
__Pulitzer's Longbill	*Macrosphenus pulitzeri*	AF
__Kretschmer's Longbill	*Macrosphenus kretschmeri*	AF
__Yellow-bellied Hyliota	*Hyliota flavigaster*	AF
__Southern Hyliota	*Hyliota australis*	AF
__Usambara Hyliota	*Hyliota usambarae*	AF
__Violet-backed Hyliota	*Hyliota violacea*	AF
__Green Hylia	*Hylia prasina*	AF
__Sao Tome Shorttail	*Amaurocichla bocagii*	AF
__White-throated Oxylabes	*Oxylabes madagascariensis*	AF
__Long-billed Bernieria	*Bernieria madagascariensis*	AF
__Cryptic Warbler	*Cryptosylvicola randrianasoloi*	AF
__Wedge-tailed Jery	*Hartertula flavoviridis*	AF
__Thamnornis	*Thamnornis chloropetoides*	AF
__Spectacled Tetraka	*Xanthomixis zosterops*	AF
__Appert's Tetraka	*Xanthomixis apperti*	AF
__Dusky Tetraka	*Xanthomixis tenebrosa*	AF
__Grey-crowned Tetraka	*Xanthomixis cinereiceps*	AF
__Madagascar Yellowbrow	*Crossleyia xanthophrys*	AF
__Rand's Warbler	*Randia pseudozosterops*	AF
__Yellow-throated Woodland Warbler	*Phylloscopus ruficapilla*	AF
__Laura's Woodland Warbler	*Phylloscopus laurae*	AF
__Red-faced Woodland Warbler	*Phylloscopus laetus*	AF
__Black-capped Woodland Warbler	*Phylloscopus herberti*	AF
__Uganda Woodland Warbler	*Phylloscopus budongoensis*	AF

INTERNATIONAL ENGLISH NAME	SCIENTIFIC NAME	REGION(S)
—Brown Woodland Warbler	*Phylloscopus umbrovirens*	AF
—Willow Warbler	*Phylloscopus trochilus*	EU
—Common Chiffchaff	*Phylloscopus collybita*	EU
—Iberian Chiffchaff	*Phylloscopus ibericus*	EU
—Canary Islands Chiffchaff	*Phylloscopus canariensis*	AF
—Mountain Chiffchaff	*Phylloscopus sindianus*	EU
—Plain Leaf Warbler	*Phylloscopus neglectus*	EU
—Western Bonelli's Warbler	*Phylloscopus bonelli*	EU
—Eastern Bonelli's Warbler	*Phylloscopus orientalis*	EU
—Wood Warbler	*Phylloscopus sibilatrix*	EU
—Dusky Warbler	*Phylloscopus fuscatus*	EU
—Smoky Warbler	*Phylloscopus fuligiventer*	EU
—Tickell's Leaf Warbler	*Phylloscopus affinis*	EU
—Buff-throated Warbler	*Phylloscopus subaffinis*	OR
—Sulphur-bellied Warbler	*Phylloscopus griseolus*	EU
—Yellow-streaked Warbler	*Phylloscopus armandii*	EU
—Radde's Warbler	*Phylloscopus schwarzi*	EU
—Buff-barred Warbler	*Phylloscopus pulcher*	OR
—Ashy-throated Warbler	*Phylloscopus maculipennis*	OR
—Gansu Leaf Warbler	*Phylloscopus kansuensis*	EU
—Chinese Leaf Warbler	*Phylloscopus yunnanensis*	EU
—Pallas's Leaf Warbler	*Phylloscopus proregulus*	EU
—Lemon-rumped Warbler	*Phylloscopus chloronotus*	EU
—Brooks's Leaf Warbler	*Phylloscopus subviridis*	EU
—Yellow-browed Warbler	*Phylloscopus inornatus*	EU
—Hume's Leaf Warbler	*Phylloscopus humei*	EU
—Arctic Warbler	*Phylloscopus borealis*	EU
—Green Warbler	*Phylloscopus nitidus*	EU
—Greenish Warbler	*Phylloscopus trochiloides*	EU
—Two-barred Warbler	*Phylloscopus plumbeitarsus*	EU
—Pale-legged Leaf Warbler	*Phylloscopus tenellipes*	EU
—Sakhalin Leaf Warbler	*Phylloscopus borealoides*	EU
—Large-billed Leaf Warbler	*Phylloscopus magnirostris*	OR
—Tytler's Leaf Warbler	*Phylloscopus tytleri*	EU
—Western Crowned Warbler	*Phylloscopus occipitalis*	EU
—Eastern Crowned Warbler	*Phylloscopus coronatus*	EU
—Ijima's Leaf Warbler	*Phylloscopus ijimae*	EU
—Blyth's Leaf Warbler	*Phylloscopus reguloides*	EU
—Emei Leaf Warbler	*Phylloscopus emeiensis*	OR
—White-tailed Leaf Warbler	*Phylloscopus davisoni*	OR
—Hainan Leaf Warbler	*Phylloscopus hainanus*	OR
—Sichuan Leaf Warbler	*Phylloscopus forresti*	OR
—Yellow-vented Warbler	*Phylloscopus cantator*	OR
—Sulphur-breasted Warbler	*Phylloscopus ricketti*	OR
—Philippine Leaf Warbler	*Phylloscopus olivaceus*	OR
—Lemon-throated Leaf Warbler	*Phylloscopus cebuensis*	OR
—Mountain Leaf Warbler	*Phylloscopus trivirgatus*	OR
—Sulawesi Leaf Warbler	*Phylloscopus sarasinorum*	AU
—Timor Leaf Warbler	*Phylloscopus presbytes*	AU
—Island Leaf Warbler	*Phylloscopus poliocephalus*	AU
—Makira Leaf Warbler	*Phylloscopus makirensis*	AU
—Kolombangara Leaf Warbler	*Phylloscopus amoenus*	AU
—Grey-hooded Warbler	*Phylloscopus xanthoschistos*	OR

INTERNATIONAL ENGLISH NAME	SCIENTIFIC NAME	REGION(S)
__White-spectacled Warbler	*Seicercus affinis*	OR
__Green-crowned Warbler	*Seicercus burkii*	EU
__Grey-crowned Warbler	*Seicercus tephrocephalus*	OR
__Whistler's Warbler	*Seicercus whistleri*	OR
__Bianchi's Warbler	*Seicercus valentini*	EU
__Omei Warbler	*Seicercus omeiensis*	EU
__Plain-tailed Warbler	*Seicercus soror*	EU
__Grey-cheeked Warbler	*Seicercus poliogenys*	OR
__Chestnut-crowned Warbler	*Seicercus castaniceps*	OR
Yellow-breasted Warbler	*Seicercus montis*	OR
__Sunda Warbler	*Seicercus grammiceps*	OR
__Broad-billed Warbler	*Tickellia hodgsoni*	OR
__Rufous-faced Warbler	*Abroscopus albogularis*	OR
__Black-faced Warbler	*Abroscopus schisticeps*	OR
__Yellow-belled Warbler	*Abroscopus superciliaris*	OR
__Grauer's Warbler	*Graueria vittata*	AF
__Yellow-bellied Eremomela	*Eremomela icteropygialis*	AF
__Salvadori's Eremomela	*Eremomela salvadorii*	AF
__Yellow-vented Eremomela	*Eremomela flavicrissalis*	AF
__Senegal Eremomela	*Eremomela pusilla*	AF
__Green-backed Eremomela	*Eremomela canescens*	AF
__Green-capped Eremomela	*Eremomela scotops*	AF
__Karoo Eremomela	*Eremomela gregalis*	AF
__Burnt-neck Eremomela	*Eremomela usticollis*	AF
__Rufous-crowned Eremomela	*Eremomela badiceps*	AF
__Turner's Eremomela	*Eremomela turneri*	AF
__Black-necked Eremomela	*Eremomela atricollis*	AF
__Tit-Hylia	*Pholidornis rushiae*	AF
__Northern Crombec	*Sylvietta brachyura*	AF
__Red-faced Crombec	*Sylvietta whytii*	AF
__Philippa's Crombec	*Sylvietta philippae*	AF
__Long-billed Crombec	*Sylvietta rufescens*	AF
__Somali Crombec	*Sylvietta isabellina*	AF
__Red-capped Crombec	*Sylvietta ruficapilla*	AF
__Green Crombec	*Sylvietta virens*	AF
__Lemon-bellied Crombec	*Sylvietta denti*	AF
__White-browed Crombec	*Sylvietta leucophrys*	AF
__Eurasian Blackcap	*Sylvia atricapilla*	EU
__Garden Warbler	*Sylvia borin*	EU
__Barred Warbler	*Sylvia nisoria*	EU
__Lesser Whitethroat	*Sylvia curruca*	EU
__Desert Whitethroat	*Sylvia minula*	EU
__Hume's Whitethroat	*Sylvia althaea*	EU
__Orphean Warbler	*Sylvia hortensis*	EU
__Arabian Warbler	*Sylvia leucomelaena*	AF
__Asian Desert Warbler	*Sylvia nana*	EU
__African Desert Warbler	*Sylvia deserti*	EU
__Common Whitethroat	*Sylvia communis*	EU
__Dartford Warbler	*Sylvia undata*	EU
__Marmora's Warbler	*Sylvia sarda*	EU
__Tristram's Warbler	*Sylvia deserticola*	AF
__Spectacled Warbler	*Sylvia conspicillata*	EU
__Subalpine Warbler	*Sylvia cantillans*	EU

INTERNATIONAL ENGLISH NAME	SCIENTIFIC NAME	REGION(S)
__Sardinian Warbler	*Sylvia melanocephala*	EU
__Menetries's Warbler	*Sylvia mystacea*	EU
__Rüppell's Warbler	*Sylvia rueppelli*	EU
__Cyprus Warbler	*Sylvia melanothorax*	EU
__Balearic Warbler	*Sylvia balearica*	EU
__Yemen Warbler	*Parisoma buryi*	EU
__Brown Parisoma	*Parisoma lugens*	AF
__Chestnut-vented Tit-babbler	*Parisoma subcaeruleum*	AF
__Layard's Tit-babbler	*Parisoma layardi*	AF
__Banded Parisoma	*Parisoma boehmi*	AF
BABBLERS, PARROTBILLS	**Family Timaliidae**	
__Bagobo Babbler	*Leonardina woodi*	OR
__Spot-throated Babbler	*Pellorneum albiventre*	OR
__Marsh Babbler	*Pellorneum palustre*	OR
__Puff-throated Babbler	*Pellorneum ruficeps*	OR
__Brown-capped Babbler	*Pellorneum fuscocapillus*	OR
__Buff-breasted Babbler	*Pellorneum tickelli*	OR
__Sumatran Babbler	*Pellorneum buettikoferi*	OR
__Temminck's Babbler	*Pellorneum pyrrogenys*	OR
__Black-capped Babbler	*Pellorneum capistratum*	OR
__White-chested Babbler	*Trichastoma rostratum*	OR
__Sulawesi Babbler	*Trichastoma celebense*	OR
__Ferruginous Babbler	*Trichastoma bicolor*	OR
__Abbott's Babbler	*Malacocincla abbotti*	OR
__Horsfield's Babbler	*Malacocincla sepiaria*	OR
__Black-browed Babbler	*Malacocincla perspicillata*	OR
__Short-tailed Babbler	*Malacocincla malaccensis*	OR
__Ashy-headed Babbler	*Malacocincla cinereiceps*	OR
__Moustached Babbler	*Malacopteron magnirostre*	OR
__Sooty-capped Babbler	*Malacopteron affine*	OR
__Scaly-crowned Babbler	*Malacopteron cinereum*	OR
__Rufous-crowned Babbler	*Malacopteron magnum*	OR
__Melodious Babbler	*Malacopteron palawanense*	OR
__Grey-breasted Babbler	*Malacopteron albogulare*	OR
__Blackcap Illadopsis	*Illadopsis cleaveri*	AF
__Scaly-breasted Illadopsis	*Illadopsis albipectus*	AF
__Rufous-winged Illadopsis	*Illadopsis rufescens*	AF
__Puvel's Illadopsis	*Illadopsis puveli*	AF
__Pale-breasted Illadopsis	*Illadopsis rufipennis*	AF
__Brown Illadopsis	*Illadopsis fulvescens*	AF
__Mountain Illadopsis	*Illadopsis pyrrhoptera*	AF
__Grey-chested Babbler	*Kakamega poliothorax*	AF
__African Hill Babbler	*Pseudoalcippe abyssinica*	AF
__Spotted Thrush-Babbler	*Ptyrticus turdinus*	AF
__Large Scimitar Babbler	*Pomatorhinus hypoleucos*	OR
__Rusty-cheeked Scimitar Babbler	*Pomatorhinus erythrogenys*	OR
__Spot-breasted Scimitar Babbler	*Pomatorhinus erythrocnemis*	OR
__Indian Scimitar Babbler	*Pomatorhinus horsfieldii*	OR
__White-browed Scimitar Babbler	*Pomatorhinus schisticeps*	OR
__Chestnut-backed Scimitar Babbler	*Pomatorhinus montanus*	OR
__Streak-breasted Scimitar Babbler	*Pomatorhinus ruficollis*	OR
__Red-billed Scimitar Babbler	*Pomatorhinus ochraceiceps*	OR

INTERNATIONAL ENGLISH NAME	SCIENTIFIC NAME	REGION(S)
__Coral-billed Scimitar Babbler	*Pomatorhinus ferruginosus*	OR
__Slender-billed Scimitar Babbler	*Xiphirhynchus superciliaris*	OR
__Short-tailed Scimitar Babbler	*Jabouilleia danjoui*	OR
__Long-billed Wren-Babbler	*Rimator malacoptilus*	OR
__Bornean Wren-Babbler	*Ptilocichla leucogrammica*	OR
__Striated Wren-Babbler	*Ptilocichla mindanensis*	OR
__Falcated Wren-Babbler	*Ptilocichla falcata*	OR
__Striped Wren-Babbler	*Kenopia striata*	OR
__Rusty-breasted Wren-Babbler	*Napothera rufipectus*	OR
__Black-throated Wren-Babbler	*Napothera atrigularis*	OR
__Large Wren-Babbler	*Napothera macrodactyla*	OR
__Marbled Wren-Babbler	*Napothera marmorata*	OR
__Limestone Wren-Babbler	*Napothera crispifrons*	OR
__Streaked Wren-Babbler	*Napothera brevicaudata*	OR
__Mountain Wren-Babbler	*Napothera crassa*	OR
__Rabor's Wren-Babbler	*Napothera rabori*	OR
__Eyebrowed Wren-Babbler	*Napothera epilepidota*	OR
__Scaly-breasted Wren-Babbler	*Pnoepyga albiventer*	OR
__Nepal Wren-Babbler	*Pnoepyga immaculata*	OR
__Pygmy Wren-Babbler	*Pnoepyga pusilla*	OR
__Rufous-throated Wren-Babbler	*Spelaeornis caudatus*	OR
__Rusty-throated Wren-Babbler	*Spelaeornis badeigularis*	OR
__Bar-winged Wren-Babbler	*Spelaeornis troglodytoides*	OR
__Spotted Wren-Babbler	*Spelaeornis formosus*	OR
__Long-tailed Wren-Babbler	*Spelaeornis chocolatinus*	OR
__Tawny-breasted Wren-Babbler	*Spelaeornis longicaudatus*	OR
__Wedge-billed Wren-Babbler	*Sphenocichla humei*	OR
__Deignan's Babbler	*Stachyris rodolphei*	OR
__Rufous-fronted Babbler	*Stachyris rufifrons*	OR
__Buff-chested Babbler	*Stachyris ambigua*	OR
__Rufous-capped Babbler	*Stachyris ruficeps*	OR
__Black-chinned Babbler	*Stachyris pyrrhops*	OR
__Golden Babbler	*Stachyris chrysaea*	OR
__Pygmy Babbler	*Stachyris plateni*	OR
__Golden-crowned Babbler	*Stachyris dennistouni*	OR
__Black-crowned Babbler	*Stachyris nigrocapitata*	OR
__Rusty-crowned Babbler	*Stachyris capitalis*	OR
__Flame-templed Babbler	*Stachyris speciosa*	OR
__Chestnut-faced Babbler	*Stachyris whiteheadi*	OR
__Luzon Striped Babbler	*Stachyris striata*	OR
__Panay Striped Babbler	*Stachyris latistriata*	OR
__Negros Striped Babbler	*Stachyris nigrorum*	OR
__Palawan Striped Babbler	*Stachyris hypogrammica*	OR
__White-breasted Babbler	*Stachyris grammiceps*	OR
__Sooty Babbler	*Stachyris herberti*	OR
__Grey-throated Babbler	*Stachyris nigriceps*	OR
__Grey-headed Babbler	*Stachyris poliocephala*	OR
__Spot-necked Babbler	*Stachyris striolata*	OR
__Snowy-throated Babbler	*Stachyris oglei*	OR
__Chestnut-rumped Babbler	*Stachyris maculata*	OR
__White-necked Babbler	*Stachyris leucotis*	OR
__Black-throated Babbler	*Stachyris nigricollis*	OR
__White-bibbed Babbler	*Stachyris thoracica*	OR

INTERNATIONAL ENGLISH NAME	SCIENTIFIC NAME	REGION(S)
—Chestnut-winged Babbler	*Stachyris erythroptera*	OR
—Crescent-chested Babbler	*Stachyris melanothorax*	OR
—Tawny-bellied Babbler	*Dumetia hyperythra*	OR
—Dark-fronted Babbler	*Rhopocichla atriceps*	OR
—Striped Tit-Babbler	*Macronous gularis*	OR
—Grey-cheeked Tit-Babbler	*Macronous flavicollis*	OR
—Grey-faced Tit-Babbler	*Macronous kelleyi*	OR
—Brown Tit-Babbler	*Macronous striaticeps*	OR
—Fluffy-backed Tit-Babbler	*Macronous ptilosus*	OR
—Miniature Tit-Babbler	*Micromacronus leytensis*	OR
—Chestnut-capped Babbler	*Timalia pileata*	OR
—Yellow-eyed Babbler	*Chrysomma sinense*	OR
—Jerdon's Babbler	*Moupinia altirostris*	OR
—Rufous-tailed Babbler	*Moupinia poecilotis*	EU
—Wrentit	*Chamaea fasciata*	NA
—Spiny Babbler	*Turdoides nipalensis*	OR
—Iraq Babbler	*Turdoides altirostris*	EU
—Common Babbler	*Turdoides caudata*	EU
—Striated Babbler	*Turdoides earlei*	OR
—White-throated Babbler	*Turdoides gularis*	OR
—Slender-billed Babbler	*Turdoides longirostris*	OR
—Large Grey Babbler	*Turdoides malcolmi*	OR
—Arabian Babbler	*Turdoides squamiceps*	EU
—Fulvous Babbler	*Turdoides fulva*	AF
—Scaly Chatterer	*Turdoides aylmeri*	AF
—Rufous Chatterer	*Turdoides rubiginosa*	AF
—Rufous Babbler	*Turdoides subrufa*	OR
—Jungle Babbler	*Turdoides striata*	OR
—Orange-billed Babbler	*Turdoides rufescens*	OR
—Yellow-billed Babbler	*Turdoides affinis*	OR
—Black-faced Babbler	*Turdoides melanops*	AF
—Black-lored Babbler	*Turdoides sharpei*	AF
—Dusky Babbler	*Turdoides tenebrosa*	AF
—Blackcap Babbler	*Turdoides reinwardtii*	AF
—Brown Babbler	*Turdoides plebejus*	AF
—White-headed Babbler	*Turdoides leucocephala*	AF
—Arrow-marked Babbler	*Turdoides jardineii*	AF
—Scaly Babbler	*Turdoides squamulata*	AF
—White-rumped Babbler	*Turdoides leucopygia*	AF
—Hartlaub's Babbler	*Turdoides hartlaubii*	AF
—Hinde's Babbler	*Turdoides hindei*	AF
—Northern Pied Babbler	*Turdoides hypoleuca*	AF
—Southern Pied Babbler	*Turdoides bicolor*	AF
—Bare-cheeked Babbler	*Turdoides gymnogenys*	AF
—Chinese Babax	*Babax lanceolatus*	OR
—Giant Babax	*Babax waddelli*	EU
—Tibetan Babax	*Babax koslowi*	EU
—Ashy-headed Laughingthrush	*Garrulax cinereifrons*	OR
—Sunda Laughingthrush	*Garrulax palliatus*	OR
—Rufous-fronted Laughingthrush	*Garrulax rufifrons*	OR
—Masked Laughingthrush	*Garrulax perspicillatus*	OR
—White-throated Laughingthrush	*Garrulax albogularis*	OR
—White-crested Laughingthrush	*Garrulax leucolophus*	OR

INTERNATIONAL ENGLISH NAME	SCIENTIFIC NAME	REGION(S)
__Lesser Necklaced Laughingthrush	*Garrulax monileger*	OR
__Greater Necklaced Laughingthrush	*Garrulax pectoralis*	OR
__Black Laughingthrush	*Garrulax lugubris*	OR
__Striated Laughingthrush	*Garrulax striatus*	OR
__White-necked Laughingthrush	*Garrulax strepitans*	OR
__Black-hooded Laughingthrush	*Garrulax milleti*	OR
__Grey Laughingthrush	*Garrulax maesi*	OR
__Chestnut-backed Laughingthrush	*Garrulax nuchalis*	OR
__Black-throated Laughingthrush	*Garrulax chinensis*	OR
__White-cheeked Laughingthrush	*Garrulax vassali*	OR
__Yellow-throated Laughingthrush	*Garrulax galbanus*	OR
__Wynaad Laughingthrush	*Garrulax delesserti*	OR
__Rufous-vented Laughingthrush	*Garrulax gularis*	OR
__Variegated Laughingthrush	*Garrulax variegatus*	EU
__Plain Laughingthrush	*Garrulax davidi*	EU
__Snowy-cheeked Laughingthrush	*Garrulax sukatschewi*	EU
__Moustached Laughingthrush	*Garrulax cineraceus*	OR
__Rufous-chinned Laughingthrush	*Garrulax rufogularis*	OR
__Chestnut-eared Laughingthrush	*Garrulax konkakinhensis*	OR
__Barred Laughingthrush	*Garrulax lunulatus*	EU
__White-speckled Laughingthrush	*Garrulax bieti*	OR
__Giant Laughingthrush	*Garrulax maximus*	EU
__Spotted Laughingthrush	*Garrulax ocellatus*	OR
__Grey-sided Laughingthrush	*Garrulax caerulatus*	OR
__Rusty Laughingthrush	*Garrulax poecilorhynchus*	OR
__Chestnut-capped Laughingthrush	*Garrulax mitratus*	OR
__Rufous-necked Laughingthrush	*Garrulax ruficollis*	OR
__Spot-breasted Laughingthrush	*Garrulax merulinus*	OR
__Hwamei	*Garrulax canorus*	OR
__White-browed Laughingthrush	*Garrulax sannio*	OR
__Nilgiri Laughingthrush	*Garrulax cachinnans*	OR
__Grey-breasted Laughingthrush	*Garrulax jerdoni*	OR
__Streaked Laughingthrush	*Garrulax lineatus*	EU
__Striped Laughingthrush	*Garrulax virgatus*	OR
__Brown-capped Laughingthrush	*Garrulax austeni*	OR
__Blue-winged Laughingthrush	*Garrulax squamatus*	OR
__Scaly Laughingthrush	*Garrulax subunicolor*	OR
__Elliot's Laughingthrush	*Garrulax elliotii*	EU
__Brown-cheeked Laughingthrush	*Garrulax henrici*	EU
__Black-faced Laughingthrush	*Garrulax affinis*	OR
__White-whiskered Laughingthrush	*Garrulax morrisonianus*	OR
__Chestnut-crowned Laughingthrush	*Garrulax erythrocephalus*	OR
__Collared Laughingthrush	*Garrulax yersini*	OR
__Red-winged Laughingthrush	*Garrulax formosus*	OR
__Red-tailed Laughingthrush	*Garrulax milnei*	OR
__Red-faced Liocichla	*Liocichla phoenicea*	OR
__Emei Shan Liocichla	*Liocichla omeiensis*	OR
__Steere's Liocichla	*Liocichla steerii*	OR
__Silver-eared Leiothrix	*Leiothrix argentauris*	OR
__Red-billed Leiothrix	*Leiothrix lutea*	OR
__Cutia	*Cutia nipalensis*	OR
__Black-headed Shrike-Babbler	*Pteruthius rufiventer*	OR
__White-browed Shrike-Babbler	*Pteruthius flaviscapis*	OR

INTERNATIONAL ENGLISH NAME	SCIENTIFIC NAME	REGION(S)
—Green Shrike-Babbler	*Pteruthius xanthochlorus*	OR
—Black-eared Shrike-Babbler	*Pteruthius melanotis*	OR
—Chestnut-fronted Shrike-Babbler	*Pteruthius aenobarbus*	OR
—White-hooded Babbler	*Gampsorhynchus rufulus*	OR
—Rusty-fronted Barwing	*Actinodura egertoni*	OR
—Spectacled Barwing	*Actinodura ramsayi*	OR
—Black-crowned Barwing	*Actinodura sodangorum*	OR
—Hoary-throated Barwing	*Actinodura nipalensis*	OR
—Streak-throated Barwing	*Actinodura waldeni*	OR
—Streaked Barwing	*Actinodura souliei*	OR
—Taiwan Barwing	*Actinodura morrisoniana*	OR
—Blue-winged Minla	*Minla cyanouroptera*	OR
—Chestnut-tailed Minla	*Minla strigula*	OR
—Red-tailed Minla	*Minla ignotincta*	OR
—Golden-breasted Fulvetta	*Alcippe chrysotis*	OR
—Golden-fronted Fulvetta	*Alcippe variegaticeps*	OR
—Yellow-throated Fulvetta	*Alcippe cinerea*	OR
—Rufous-winged Fulvetta	*Alcippe castaneceps*	OR
—White-browed Fulvetta	*Alcippe vinipectus*	OR
—Chinese Fulvetta	*Alcippe striaticollis*	EU
—Spectacled Fulvetta	*Alcippe ruficapilla*	OR
—Brown-throated Fulvetta	*Alcippe ludlowi*	OR
—Streak-throated Fulvetta	*Alcippe cinereiceps*	OR
—Rufous-throated Fulvetta	*Alcippe rufogularis*	OR
—Rusty-capped Fulvetta	*Alcippe dubia*	OR
—Dusky Fulvetta	*Alcippe brunnea*	OR
—Brown Fulvetta	*Alcippe brunneicauda*	OR
—Brown-cheeked Fulvetta	*Alcippe poioicephala*	OR
—Javan Fulvetta	*Alcippe pyrrhoptera*	OR
—Mountain Fulvetta	*Alcippe peracensis*	OR
—Grey-cheeked Fulvetta	*Alcippe morrisonia*	OR
—Nepal Fulvetta	*Alcippe nipalensis*	OR
—Bush Blackcap	*Lioptilus nigricapillus*	AF
—White-throated Mountain Babbler	*Kupeornis gilberti*	AF
—Red-collared Babbler	*Kupeornis rufocinctus*	AF
—Chapin's Babbler	*Kupeornis chapini*	AF
—Dohrn's Thrush-Babbler	*Horizorhinus dohrni*	AF
—Abyssinian Catbird	*Parophasma galinieri*	AF
—Capuchin Babbler	*Phyllanthus atripennis*	AF
—Grey-crowned Crocias	*Crocias langbianis*	OR
—Spotted Crocias	*Crocias albonotatus*	OR
—Rufous-backed Sibia	*Heterophasia annectens*	OR
—Rufous Sibia	*Heterophasia capistrata*	OR
—Grey Sibia	*Heterophasia gracilis*	OR
—Dark-backed Sibia	*Heterophasia melanoleuca*	OR
—Black-headed Sibia	*Heterophasia desgodinsi*	OR
—White-eared Sibia	*Heterophasia auricularis*	OR
—Beautiful Sibia	*Heterophasia pulchella*	OR
—Long-tailed Sibia	*Heterophasia picaoides*	OR
—Striated Yuhina	*Yuhina castaniceps*	OR
—Chestnut-crested Yuhina	*Yuhina everetti*	OR
—White-naped Yuhina	*Yuhina bakeri*	OR
—Whiskered Yuhina	*Yuhina flavicollis*	OR

162

INTERNATIONAL ENGLISH NAME	SCIENTIFIC NAME	REGION(S)
—Burmese Yuhina	*Yuhina humilis*	OR
—Stripe-throated Yuhina	*Yuhina gularis*	OR
—White-collared Yuhina	*Yuhina diademata*	OR
—Rufous-vented Yuhina	*Yuhina occipitalis*	OR
—Taiwan Yuhina	*Yuhina brunneiceps*	OR
—Black-chinned Yuhina	*Yuhina nigrimenta*	OR
—White-bellied Yuhina	*Erpornis zantholeuca*	OR
—Bearded Reedling	*Panurus biarmicus*	EU
—Great Parrotbill	*Conostoma oemodium*	OR
—Three-toed Parrotbill	*Paradoxornis paradoxus*	OR
—Brown Parrotbill	*Paradoxornis unicolor*	OR
—Black-breasted Parrotbill	*Paradoxornis flavirostris*	OR
—Spot-breasted Parrotbill	*Paradoxornis guttaticollis*	OR
—Spectacled Parrotbill	*Paradoxornis conspicillatus*	EU
—Vinous-throated Parrotbill	*Paradoxornis webbianus*	EU
—Ashy-throated Parrotbill	*Paradoxornis alphonsianus*	OR
—Brown-winged Parrotbill	*Paradoxornis brunneus*	OR
—Grey-hooded Parrotbill	*Paradoxornis zappeyi*	OR
—Przevalski's Parrotbill	*Paradoxornis przewalskii*	OR
—Fulvous Parrotbill	*Paradoxornis fulvifrons*	OR
—Black-throated Parrotbill	*Paradoxornis nipalensis*	OR
—Golden Parrotbill	*Paradoxornis verreauxi*	OR
—Short-tailed Parrotbill	*Paradoxornis davidianus*	OR
—Lesser Rufous-headed Parrotbill	*Paradoxornis atrosuperciliaris*	OR
—Greater Rufous-headed Parrotbill	*Paradoxornis ruficeps*	OR
—Grey-headed Parrotbill	*Paradoxornis gularis*	OR
—Northern Parrotbill	*Paradoxornis polivanovi*	EU
—Reed Parrotbill	*Paradoxornis heudei*	EU
FAMILY UNCERTAIN	**Incertae Sedis**	
—Fire-tailed Myzornis	*Myzornis pyrrhoura*	OR
—Malia	*Malia grata*	AU
—Spot-throat	*Modulatrix stictigula*	AF
—Dappled Mountain-robin	*Modulatrix orostruthus*	AF
SUGARBIRDS	**Family Promeropidae**	
—Cape Sugarbird	*Promerops cafer*	AF
—Gurney's Sugarbird	*Promerops gurneyi*	AF
WHITE-EYES	**Family Zosteropidae**	
—Chestnut-flanked White-eye	*Zosterops erythropleurus*	EU
—Japanese White-eye	*Zosterops japonicus*	EU
—Lowland White-eye	*Zosterops meyeni*	OR
—Oriental White-eye	*Zosterops palpebrosus*	OR
—Sri Lanka White-eye	*Zosterops ceylonensis*	OR
—Rota White-eye	*Zosterops rotensis*	PO
—Bridled White-eye	*Zosterops conspicillatus*	PO
—Citrine White-eye	*Zosterops semperi*	PO
—Plain White-eye	*Zosterops hypolais*	PO
—Enggano White-eye	*Zosterops salvadorii*	OR
—Black-capped White-eye	*Zosterops atricapilla*	OR
—Everett's White-eye	*Zosterops everetti*	OR
—Yellowish White-eye	*Zosterops nigrorum*	OR

INTERNATIONAL ENGLISH NAME	SCIENTIFIC NAME	REGION(S)
—Mountain White-eye	*Zosterops montanus*	OR
—Yellow-ringed White-eye	*Zosterops wallacei*	AU
—Javan White-eye	*Zosterops flavus*	OR
—Lemon-bellied White-eye	*Zosterops chloris*	AU
—Ashy-bellied White-eye	*Zosterops citrinella*	AU
—Pale-bellied White-eye	*Zosterops consobrinorum*	AU
—Pearl-bellied White-eye	*Zosterops grayi*	AU
—Golden-bellied White-eye	*Zosterops uropygialis*	AU
—Black-ringed White-eye	*Zosterops anomalus*	AU
—Cream-throated White-eye	*Zosterops atriceps*	AU
—Sangihe White-eye	*Zosterops nehrkorni*	AU
—Black-crowned White-eye	*Zosterops atrifrons*	AU
—Seram White-eye	*Zosterops stalkeri*	AU
—Black-fronted White-eye	*Zosterops minor*	AU
—Tagula White-eye	*Zosterops meeki*	AU
—Bismarck White-eye	*Zosterops hypoxanthus*	AU
—Biak White-eye	*Zosterops mysorensis*	AU
—Capped White-eye	*Zosterops fuscicapilla*	AU
—Buru White-eye	*Zosterops buruensis*	AU
—Ambon White-eye	*Zosterops kuehni*	AU
—Papuan White-eye	*Zosterops novaeguineae*	AU
—Yellow-throated White-eye	*Zosterops metcalfii*	AU
—Christmas White-eye	*Zosterops natalis*	IO
—Canary White-eye	*Zosterops luteus*	AU
—Islet White-eye	*Zosterops griseotinctus*	AU
—Bare-ringed White-eye	*Zosterops rennellianus*	AU
—Belted White-eye	*Zosterops vellalavella*	AU
—Yellow-billed White-eye	*Zosterops luteirostris*	AU
—Splendid White-eye	*Zosterops splendidus*	AU
—New Georgia White-eye	*Zosterops kulambangrae*	AU
—Hermit White-eye	*Zosterops murphyi*	AU
—Grey-throated White-eye	*Zosterops ugiensis*	AU
—Malaita White-eye	*Zosterops stresemanni*	AU
—Santa Cruz White-eye	*Zosterops sanctaecrucis*	PO
—Samoan White-eye	*Zosterops samoensis*	PO
—Fiji White-eye	*Zosterops explorator*	PO
—Vanuatu White-eye	*Zosterops flavifrons*	PO
—Sulphur White-eye	*Zosterops minutus*	PO
—Green-backed White-eye	*Zosterops xanthochroa*	AU
—Silvereye	*Zosterops lateralis*	AU
—Slender-billed White-eye	*Zosterops tenuirostris*	AU
—White-chested White-eye	*Zosterops albogularis*	AU
—Forest White-eye	*Zosterops inornatus*	PO
—Grey-brown White-eye	*Zosterops cinereus*	PO
—Dusky White-eye	*Zosterops finschii*	PO
—Abyssinian White-eye	*Zosterops abyssinicus*	AF
—Cape White-eye	*Zosterops pallidus*	AF
—African Yellow White-eye	*Zosterops senegalensis*	AF
—Montane White-eye	*Zosterops poliogastrus*	AF
—Reunion Grey White-eye	*Zosterops borbonicus*	IO
—Mauritius Grey White-eye	*Zosterops mauritianus*	IO
—Principe White-eye	*Zosterops ficedulinus*	AF
—Annobon White-eye	*Zosterops griseovirescens*	AF

INTERNATIONAL ENGLISH NAME	SCIENTIFIC NAME	REGION(S)
—Madagascar White-eye	*Zosterops maderaspatanus*	AF
—Kirk's White-eye	*Zosterops kirki*	AF
—Mayotte White-eye	*Zosterops mayottensis*	AF
—Seychelles White-eye	*Zosterops modestus*	IO
—Karthala White-eye	*Zosterops mouroniensis*	AF
—Reunion Olive White-eye	*Zosterops olivaceus*	IO
—Mauritius Olive White-eye	*Zosterops chloronothos*	IO
—Pemba White-eye	*Zosterops vaughani*	IO
—Olive-colored White-eye	*Zosterops oleagineus*	PO
—Bare-eyed White-eye	*Woodfordia superciliosa*	AU
—Sanford's White-eye	*Woodfordia lacertosa*	PO
—Teardrop White-eye	*Rukia ruki*	PO
—Long-billed White-eye	*Rukia longirostra*	PO
—Golden White-eye	*Cleptornis marchei*	PO
—Bonin White-eye	*Apalopteron familiare*	EU
—Rufescent Darkeye	*Tephrozosterops stalkeri*	AU
—Madanga	*Madanga ruficollis*	AU
—Grey-hooded Ibon	*Lophozosterops pinaiae*	AU
—Mindanao Ibon	*Lophozosterops goodfellowi*	OR
—Streak-headed Ibon	*Lophozosterops squamiceps*	AU
—Grey-throated Ibon	*Lophozosterops javanicus*	OR
—Cream-browed Ibon	*Lophozosterops superciliaris*	AU
—Crested Ibon	*Lophozosterops dohertyi*	AU
—Pygmy Ibon	*Oculocincta squamifrons*	AU
—Spot-breasted Heleia	*Heleia muelleri*	AU
—Thick-billed Heleia	*Heleia crassirostris*	AU
—Mountain Blackeye	*Chlorocharis emiliae*	OR
—Giant White-eye	*Megazosterops palauensis*	AU
—Cinnamon Ibon	*Hypocryptadius cinnamomeus*	OR
—Fernando Po Speirops	*Speirops brunneus*	AF
—Principe Speirops	*Speirops leucophoeus*	AF
—Black-capped Speirops	*Speirops lugubris*	AF
—Mount Cameroon Speirops	*Speirops melanocephalus*	AF
FAIRY-BLUEBIRDS	**Family Irenidae**	
—Asian Fairy-bluebird	*Irena puella*	OR
—Philippine Fairy-bluebird	*Irena cyanogastra*	OR
GOLDCRESTS, KINGLETS	**Family Regulidae**	
—Firecrest	*Regulus ignicapilla*	EU
—Flamecrest	*Regulus goodfellowi*	OR
—Goldcrest	*Regulus regulus*	EU
—Madeiracrest	*Regulus madeirae*	EU
—Golden-crowned Kinglet	*Regulus satrapa*	NA, MA
—Ruby-crowned Kinglet	*Regulus calendula*	NA
WRENS, DONACOBIUS	**Family Troglodytidae**	
—White-headed Wren	*Campylorhynchus albobrunneus*	LA
—Band-backed Wren	*Campylorhynchus zonatus*	LA
—Grey-barred Wren	*Campylorhynchus megalopterus*	MA
—Stripe-backed Wren	*Campylorhynchus nuchalis*	SA
—Fasciated Wren	*Campylorhynchus fasciatus*	SA

INTERNATIONAL ENGLISH NAME	SCIENTIFIC NAME	REGION(S)
—Giant Wren	*Campylorhynchus chiapensis*	MA
—Bicolored Wren	*Campylorhynchus griseus*	SA
—Rufous-naped Wren	*Campylorhynchus rufinucha*	MA
—Spotted Wren	*Campylorhynchus gularis*	MA
—Boucard's Wren	*Campylorhynchus jocosus*	MA
—Yucatan Wren	*Campylorhynchus yucatanicus*	MA
—Cactus Wren	*Campylorhynchus brunneicapillus*	NA, MA
—Thrush-like Wren	*Campylorhynchus turdinus*	SA
—Grey-mantled Wren	*Odontorchilus branickii*	SA
—Tooth-billed Wren	*Odontorchilus cinereus*	SA
—Rock Wren	*Salpinctes obsoletus*	NA, MA
—Canyon Wren	*Catherpes mexicanus*	NA, MA
—Sumichrast's Wren	*Hylorchilus sumichrasti*	MA
—Nava's Wren	*Hylorchilus nava*	MA
—Rufous Wren	*Cinnycerthia unirufa*	SA
—Sepia-brown Wren	*Cinnycerthia olivascens*	SA
—Peruvian Wren	*Cinnycerthia peruana*	SA
—Fulvous Wren	*Cinnycerthia fulva*	SA
—Sedge Wren	*Cistothorus platensis*	NA, LA
—Merida Wren	*Cistothorus meridae*	SA
—Apolinar's Wren	*Cistothorus apolinari*	SA
—Marsh Wren	*Cistothorus palustris*	NA
—Bewick's Wren	*Thryomanes bewickii*	NA
—Socorro Wren	*Thryomanes sissonii*	MA
—Zapata Wren	*Ferminia cerverai*	NA
—Black-throated Wren	*Thryothorus atrogularis*	MA
—Sooty-headed Wren	*Thryothorus spadix*	LA
—Black-bellied Wren	*Thryothorus fasciatoventris*	LA
—Plain-tailed Wren	*Thryothorus euophrys*	SA
—Inca Wren	*Thryothorus eisenmanni*	SA
—Moustached Wren	*Thryothorus genibarbis*	SA
—Whiskered Wren	*Thryothorus mystacalis*	SA
—Coraya Wren	*Thryothorus coraya*	SA
—Happy Wren	*Thryothorus felix*	MA
—Spot-breasted Wren	*Thryothorus maculipectus*	MA
—Rufous-breasted Wren	*Thryothorus rutilus*	LA
—Speckle-breasted Wren	*Thryothorus sclateri*	SA
—Riverside Wren	*Thryothorus semibadius*	MA
—Bay Wren	*Thryothorus nigricapillus*	LA
—Stripe-breasted Wren	*Thryothorus thoracicus*	MA
—Stripe-throated Wren	*Thryothorus leucopogon*	LA
—Banded Wren	*Thryothorus pleurostictus*	MA
—Carolina Wren	*Thryothorus ludovicianus*	NA, MA
—Rufous-and-white Wren	*Thryothorus rufalbus*	LA
—Niceforo's Wren	*Thryothorus nicefori*	SA
—Sinaloa Wren	*Thryothorus sinaloa*	MA
—Plain Wren	*Thryothorus modestus*	MA
—Buff-breasted Wren	*Thryothorus leucotis*	LA
—Superciliated Wren	*Thryothorus superciliaris*	SA
—Fawn-breasted Wren	*Thryothorus guarayanus*	SA
—Long-billed Wren	*Thryothorus longirostris*	SA
—Grey Wren	*Thryothorus griseus*	SA

INTERNATIONAL ENGLISH NAME	SCIENTIFIC NAME	REGION(S)
__Winter Wren	*Troglodytes troglodytes*	NA, EU
__Clarion Wren	*Troglodytes tanneri*	MA
__House Wren	*Troglodytes aedon*	NA, LA
__Cobb's Wren	*Troglodytes cobbi*	SA
__Rufous-browed Wren	*Troglodytes rufociliatus*	MA
__Ochraceous Wren	*Troglodytes ochraceus*	MA
__Mountain Wren	*Troglodytes solstitialis*	SA
__Santa Marta Wren	*Troglodytes monticola*	SA
__Tepui Wren	*Troglodytes rufulus*	SA
__Timberline Wren	*Thryorchilus browni*	MA
__White-bellied Wren	*Uropsila leucogastra*	MA
__White-breasted Wood Wren	*Henicorhina leucosticta*	LA
__Grey-breasted Wood Wren	*Henicorhina leucophrys*	LA
__Bar-winged Wood Wren	*Henicorhina leucoptera*	SA
__Munchique Wood Wren	*Henicorhina negreti*	SA
__Northern Nightingale-Wren	*Microcerculus philomela*	MA
__Southern Nightingale-Wren	*Microcerculus marginatus*	LA
__Flutist Wren	*Microcerculus ustulatus*	SA
__Wing-banded Wren	*Microcerculus bambla*	SA
__Chestnut-breasted Wren	*Cyphorhinus thoracicus*	SA
__Musician Wren	*Cyphorhinus arada*	SA
__Song Wren	*Cyphorhinus phaeocephalus*	LA
__Black-capped Donacobius	*Donacobius atricapilla*	LA
GNATCATCHERS	**Family Polioptilidae**	
__Collared Gnatwren	*Microbates collaris*	SA
__Tawny-faced Gnatwren	*Microbates cinereiventris*	LA
__Long-billed Gnatwren	*Ramphocaenus melanurus*	LA
__Blue-grey Gnatcatcher	*Polioptila caerulea*	NA, MA
__Black-tailed Gnatcatcher	*Polioptila melanura*	NA, MA
__California Gnatcatcher	*Polioptila californica*	NA, MA
__Cuban Gnatcatcher	*Polioptila lembeyei*	NA
__White-lored Gnatcatcher	*Polioptila albiloris*	MA
__Black-capped Gnatcatcher	*Polioptila nigriceps*	MA
__Tropical Gnatcatcher	*Polioptila plumbea*	LA
__Maranon Gnatcatcher	*Polioptila maior*	SA
__Creamy-bellied Gnatcatcher	*Polioptila lactea*	SA
__Guianan Gnatcatcher	*Polioptila guianensis*	SA
__Slate-throated Gnatcatcher	*Polioptila schistaceigula*	LA
__Masked Gnatcatcher	*Polioptila dumicola*	SA
NUTHATCHES, WALLCREEPER	**Family Sittidae**	
__Eurasian Nuthatch	*Sitta europaea*	EU
__Chestnut-vented Nuthatch	*Sitta nagaensis*	OR
__Kashmir Nuthatch	*Sitta cashmirensis*	EU
__Chestnut-bellied Nuthatch	*Sitta castanea*	OR
__White-tailed Nuthatch	*Sitta himalayensis*	OR
__White-browed Nuthatch	*Sitta victoriae*	OR
__Pygmy Nuthatch	*Sitta pygmaea*	NA, MA
__Brown-headed Nuthatch	*Sitta pusilla*	NA
__Corsican Nuthatch	*Sitta whiteheadi*	EU
__Algerian Nuthatch	*Sitta ledanti*	AF

INTERNATIONAL ENGLISH NAME	SCIENTIFIC NAME	REGION(S)
—Krüper's Nuthatch	*Sitta krueperi*	EU
—Yunnan Nuthatch	*Sitta yunnanensis*	OR
—Red-breasted Nuthatch	*Sitta canadensis*	NA
—Chinese Nuthatch	*Sitta villosa*	EU
—White-cheeked Nuthatch	*Sitta leucopsis*	EU
—White-breasted Nuthatch	*Sitta carolinensis*	NA
—Western Rock Nuthatch	*Sitta neumayer*	EU
—Eastern Rock Nuthatch	*Sitta tephronota*	EU
—Velvet-fronted Nuthatch	*Sitta frontalis*	OR
—Yellow-billed Nuthatch	*Sitta solangiae*	OR
—Sulphur-billed Nuthatch	*Sitta oenochlamys*	OR
—Blue Nuthatch	*Sitta azurea*	OR
—Giant Nuthatch	*Sitta magna*	OR
—Beautiful Nuthatch	*Sitta formosa*	OR
—Wallcreeper	*Tichodroma muraria*	EU
TREECREEPERS	**Family Certhiidae**	
—Eurasian Treecreeper	*Certhia familiaris*	EU
—Brown Creeper	*Certhia americana*	NA, MA
—Short-toed Treecreeper	*Certhia brachydactyla*	EU
—Bar-tailed Treecreeper	*Certhia himalayana*	EU
—Rusty-flanked Treecreeper	*Certhia nipalensis*	OR
—Brown-throated Treecreeper	*Certhia discolor*	OR
—Sichuan Treecreeper	*Certhia tianquanensis*	OR
—Spotted Creeper	*Salpornis spilonotus*	AF
MOCKINGBIRDS, THRASHERS	**Family Mimidae**	
—Grey Catbird	*Dumetella carolinensis*	NA
—Black Catbird	*Melanoptila glabrirostris*	MA
—Northern Mockingbird	*Mimus polyglottos*	NA, MA
—Tropical Mockingbird	*Mimus gilvus*	LA
—Bahama Mockingbird	*Mimus gundlachii*	NA
—Chilean Mockingbird	*Mimus thenca*	SA
—Long-tailed Mockingbird	*Mimus longicaudatus*	SA
—Chalk-browed Mockingbird	*Mimus saturninus*	SA
—Patagonian Mockingbird	*Mimus patagonicus*	SA
—White-banded Mockingbird	*Mimus triurus*	SA
—Brown-backed Mockingbird	*Mimus dorsalis*	SA
—Galapagos Mockingbird	*Nesomimus parvulus*	SA
—Floreana Mockingbird	*Nesomimus trifasciatus*	SA
—Hood Mockingbird	*Nesomimus macdonaldi*	SA
—San Cristobal Mockingbird	*Nesomimus melanotis*	SA
—Sage Thrasher	*Oreoscoptes montanus*	NA
—Socorro Mockingbird	*Mimodes graysoni*	MA
—Brown Thrasher	*Toxostoma rufum*	NA
—Long-billed Thrasher	*Toxostoma longirostre*	NA, MA
—Cozumel Thrasher	*Toxostoma guttatum*	MA
—Grey Thrasher	*Toxostoma cinereum*	MA
—Bendire's Thrasher	*Toxostoma bendirei*	NA, MA
—Ocellated Thrasher	*Toxostoma ocellatum*	MA
—Curve-billed Thrasher	*Toxostoma curvirostre*	NA, MA
—California Thrasher	*Toxostoma redivivum*	NA
—Crissal Thrasher	*Toxostoma crissale*	NA, MA

INTERNATIONAL ENGLISH NAME	SCIENTIFIC NAME	REGION(S)
__Le Conte's Thrasher	*Toxostoma lecontei*	NA, MA
__White-breasted Thrasher	*Ramphocinclus brachyurus*	NA
__Blue Mockingbird	*Melanotis caerulescens*	MA
__Blue-and-white Mockingbird	*Melanotis hypoleucus*	MA
__Scaly-breasted Thrasher	*Allenia fusca*	NA
__Pearly-eyed Thrasher	*Margarops fuscatus*	NA
__Brown Trembler	*Cinclocerthia ruficauda*	NA
__Grey Trembler	*Cinclocerthia gutturalis*	NA

PHILIPPINE CREEPERS — **Family Rhabdornithidae**

__Stripe-headed Creeper	*Rhabdornis mystacalis*	OR
__Stripe-breasted Creeper	*Rhabdornis inornatus*	OR
__Long-billed Creeper	*Rhabdornis grandis*	OR

STARLINGS — **Family Sturnidae**

__Metallic Starling	*Aplonis metallica*	AU
__Violet-hooded Starling	*Aplonis circumscripta*	AU
__Yellow-eyed Starling	*Aplonis mystacea*	AU
__Singing Starling	*Aplonis cantoroides*	AU
__Tanimbar Starling	*Aplonis crassa*	AU
__Atoll Starling	*Aplonis feadensis*	AU
__Rennell Starling	*Aplonis insularis*	AU
__Long-tailed Starling	*Aplonis magna*	AU
__White-eyed Starling	*Aplonis brunneicapillus*	AU
__Brown-winged Starling	*Aplonis grandis*	AU
__Makira Starling	*Aplonis dichroa*	AU
__Rusty-winged Starling	*Aplonis zelandica*	PO
__Striated Starling	*Aplonis striata*	PO
__Vanuatu Starling	*Aplonis santovestris*	PO
__Asian Glossy Starling	*Aplonis panayensis*	OR
__Moluccan Starling	*Aplonis mysolensis*	AU
__Short-tailed Starling	*Aplonis minor*	AU
__Micronesian Starling	*Aplonis opaca*	PO
__Pohnpei Starling	*Aplonis pelzelni*	PO
__Polynesian Starling	*Aplonis tabuensis*	PO
__Samoan Starling	*Aplonis atrifusca*	PO
__Rarotonga Starling	*Aplonis cinerascens*	PO
__Yellow-faced Myna	*Mino dumontii*	AU
__Long-tailed Myna	*Mino kreffti*	AU
__Golden Myna	*Mino anais*	AU
__Sulawesi Myna	*Basilornis celebensis*	AU
__Helmeted Myna	*Basilornis galeatus*	AU
__Long-crested Myna	*Basilornis corythaix*	AU
__Apo Myna	*Basilornis mirandus*	OR
__Coleto	*Sarcops calvus*	OR
__White-necked Myna	*Streptocitta albicollis*	AU
__Bare-eyed Myna	*Streptocitta albertinae*	AU
__Fiery-browed Starling	*Enodes erythrophris*	AU
__Grosbeak Starling	*Scissirostrum dubium*	AU
__Spot-winged Starling	*Saroglossa spiloptera*	OR
__Madagascar Starling	*Saroglossa aurata*	AF
__Golden-crested Myna	*Ampeliceps coronatus*	OR
__Sri Lanka Hill Myna	*Gracula ptilogenys*	OR

INTERNATIONAL ENGLISH NAME	SCIENTIFIC NAME	REGION(S)
—Common Hill Myna	*Gracula religiosa*	OR
—Southern Hill Myna	*Gracula indica*	OR
—Nias Hill Myna	*Gracula robusta*	AU
—Enggano Hill Myna	*Gracula enganensis*	AU
—Great Myna	*Acridotheres grandis*	OR
—Crested Myna	*Acridotheres cristatellus*	OR
—White-vented Myna	*Acridotheres javanicus*	OR
—Pale-bellied Myna	*Acridotheres cinereus*	AU
—Jungle Myna	*Acridotheres fuscus*	OR
—Collared Myna	*Acridotheres albocinctus*	OR
—Bank Myna	*Acridotheres ginginianus*	OR
—Common Myna	*Acridotheres tristis*	OR
—Black-winged Starling	*Acridotheres melanopterus*	OR
—Bali Myna	*Leucopsar rothschildi*	OR
—Vinous-breasted Starling	*Sturnus burmannicus*	OR
—Black-collared Starling	*Sturnus nigricollis*	OR
—Pied Myna	*Sturnus contra*	OR
—Daurian Starling	*Sturnus sturninus*	EU
—Chestnut-cheeked Starling	*Sturnus philippensis*	EU
—White-shouldered Starling	*Sturnus sinensis*	OR
—Chestnut-tailed Starling	*Sturnus malabaricus*	OR
—White-headed Starling	*Sturnus erythropygius*	OR
—White-faced Starling	*Sturnus albofrontatus*	OR
—Brahminy Starling	*Sturnus pagodarum*	OR
—Rosy Starling	*Sturnus roseus*	EU
—Red-billed Starling	*Sturnus sericeus*	OR
—White-cheeked Starling	*Sturnus cineraceus*	EU
—Common Starling	*Sturnus vulgaris*	EU
—Spotless Starling	*Sturnus unicolor*	EU
—Wattled Starling	*Creatophora cinerea*	AF
—Cape Starling	*Lamprotornis nitens*	AF
—Greater Blue-eared Starling	*Lamprotornis chalybaeus*	AF
—Lesser Blue-eared Starling	*Lamprotornis chloropterus*	AF
—Miombo Blue-eared Starling	*Lamprotornis elisabeth*	AF
—Bronze-tailed Starling	*Lamprotornis chalcurus*	AF
—Splendid Starling	*Lamprotornis splendidus*	AF
—Principe Starling	*Lamprotornis ornatus*	AF
—Emerald Starling	*Lamprotornis iris*	AF
—Purple Starling	*Lamprotornis purpureus*	AF
—Rüppell's Starling	*Lamprotornis purpuroptera*	AF
—Long-tailed Glossy Starling	*Lamprotornis caudatus*	AF
—Golden-breasted Starling	*Lamprotornis regius*	AF
—Meves's Starling	*Lamprotornis mevesii*	AF
—Burchell's Starling	*Lamprotornis australis*	AF
—Sharp-tailed Starling	*Lamprotornis acuticaudus*	AF
—Black-bellied Starling	*Lamprotornis corruscus*	AF
—Superb Starling	*Lamprotornis superbus*	AF
—Hildebrandt's Starling	*Lamprotornis hildebrandti*	AF
—Shelley's Starling	*Lamprotornis shelleyi*	AF
—Chestnut-bellied Starling	*Lamprotornis pulcher*	AF
—Purple-headed Starling	*Lamprotornis purpureiceps*	AF
—Copper-tailed Starling	*Lamprotornis cupreocauda*	AF
—Ashy Starling	*Lamprotornis unicolor*	AF

INTERNATIONAL ENGLISH NAME	SCIENTIFIC NAME	REGION(S)
__Abbott's Starling	*Cinnyricinclus femoralis*	AF
__Violet-backed Starling	*Cinnyricinclus leucogaster*	AF
__Fischer's Starling	*Spreo fischeri*	AF
__Pied Starling	*Spreo bicolor*	AF
__White-crowned Starling	*Spreo albicapillus*	AF
__Red-winged Starling	*Onychognathus morio*	AF
__Slender-billed Starling	*Onychognathus tenuirostris*	AF
__Chestnut-winged Starling	*Onychognathus fulgidus*	AF
__Waller's Starling	*Onychognathus walleri*	AF
Somali Starling	*Onychognathus blythii*	AF
__Socotra Starling	*Onychognathus frater*	EU
__Tristram's Starling	*Onychognathus tristramii*	EU
__Pale-winged Starling	*Onychognathus nabouroup*	AF
__Bristle-crowned Starling	*Onychognathus salvadorii*	AF
__White-billed Starling	*Onychognathus albirostris*	AF
__Neumann's Starling	*Onychognathus neumanni*	AF
__Stuhlmann's Starling	*Poeoptera stuhlmanni*	AF
__Kenrick's Starling	*Poeoptera kenricki*	AF
__Narrow-tailed Starling	*Poeoptera lugubris*	AF
__Sharpe's Starling	*Pholia sharpii*	AF
__White-collared Starling	*Grafisia torquata*	AF
__Magpie Starling	*Speculipastor bicolor*	AF
__Babbling Starling	*Neocichla gutturalis*	AF
__Yellow-billed Oxpecker	*Buphagus africanus*	AF
__Red-billed Oxpecker	*Buphagus erythrorhynchus*	AF
THRUSHES	**Family Turdidae**	
__Red-tailed Rufous Thrush	*Neocossyphus rufus*	AF
__White-tailed Rufous Thrush	*Neocossyphus poensis*	AF
__Fraser's Rufous Thrush	*Stizorhina fraseri*	AF
__Finsch's Rufous Thrush	*Stizorhina finschii*	AF
__Sri Lanka Whistling Thrush	*Myophonus blighi*	OR
__Shiny Whistling Thrush	*Myophonus melanurus*	OR
__Sunda Whistling Thrush	*Myophonus glaucinus*	OR
__Brown-winged Whistling Thrush	*Myophonus castaneus*	OR
__Malayan Whistling Thrush	*Myophonus robinsoni*	OR
__Malabar Whistling Thrush	*Myophonus horsfieldii*	OR
__Taiwan Whistling Thrush	*Myophonus insularis*	OR
__Blue Whistling Thrush	*Myophonus caeruleus*	OR
__Geomalia	*Geomalia heinrichi*	AU
__Slaty-backed Thrush	*Zoothera schistacea*	AU
__Moluccan Thrush	*Zoothera dumasi*	AU
__Chestnut-capped Thrush	*Zoothera interpres*	OR
__Red-backed Thrush	*Zoothera erythronota*	AU
__Peleng Thrush	*Zoothera mendeni*	AU
__Chestnut-backed Thrush	*Zoothera dohertyi*	AU
__Pied Thrush	*Zoothera wardii*	OR
__Ashy Thrush	*Zoothera cinerea*	OR
__Orange-sided Thrush	*Zoothera peronii*	AU
__Orange-headed Thrush	*Zoothera citrina*	OR
__Everett's Thrush	*Zoothera everetti*	OR
__Siberian Thrush	*Zoothera sibirica*	EU
__Abyssinian Ground Thrush	*Zoothera piaggiae*	AF

INTERNATIONAL ENGLISH NAME	SCIENTIFIC NAME	REGION(S)
—Crossley's Ground Thrush	*Zoothera crossleyi*	AF
—Orange Ground Thrush	*Zoothera gurneyi*	AF
—Öberländer's Ground Thrush	*Zoothera oberlaenderi*	AF
—Black-eared Ground Thrush	*Zoothera cameronensis*	AF
—Kibale Ground Thrush	*Zoothera kibalensis*	AF
—Grey Ground Thrush	*Zoothera princei*	AF
—Spotted Ground Thrush	*Zoothera guttata*	AF
—Spot-winged Thrush	*Zoothera spiloptera*	OR
—Sunda Thrush	*Zoothera andromedae*	OR
—Plain-backed Thrush	*Zoothera mollissima*	OR
—Long-tailed Thrush	*Zoothera dixoni*	OR
—White's Thrush	*Zoothera aurea*	EU
—Amami Thrush	*Zoothera major*	EU
—Scaly Thrush	*Zoothera dauma*	OR
—Nilgiri Thrush	*Zoothera neilgherriensis*	OR
—Sri Lanka Thrush	*Zoothera imbricata*	OR
—Fawn-breasted Thrush	*Zoothera machiki*	OR
—Russet-tailed Thrush	*Zoothera heinei*	AU
—Bassian Thrush	*Zoothera lunulata*	AU
—Black-backed Thrush	*Zoothera talaseae*	AU
—White-bellied Thrush	*Zoothera margaretae*	AU
—Long-billed Thrush	*Zoothera monticola*	OR
—Dark-sided Thrush	*Zoothera marginata*	OR
—Varied Thrush	*Ixoreus naevia*	NA
—Aztec Thrush	*Ridgwayia pinicola*	MA
—Sulawesi Thrush	*Cataponera turdoides*	OR
—Eastern Bluebird	*Sialia sialis*	NA, MA
—Western Bluebird	*Sialia mexicana*	NA, MA
—Mountain Bluebird	*Sialia currucoides*	NA
—Omao	*Myadestes obscurus*	PO
—Kamao	*Myadestes myadestinus*	PO
—Puaiohi	*Myadestes palmeri*	PO
—Olomao	*Myadestes lanaiensis*	PO
—Townsend's Solitaire	*Myadestes townsendi*	NA, MA
—Brown-backed Solitaire	*Myadestes occidentalis*	MA
—Cuban Solitaire	*Myadestes elisabeth*	NA
—Rufous-throated Solitaire	*Myadestes genibarbis*	NA
—Black-faced Solitaire	*Myadestes melanops*	MA
—St. Vincent Solitaire	*Myadestes sibilans*	NA
—Varied Solitaire	*Myadestes coloratus*	MA
—Andean Solitaire	*Myadestes ralloides*	SA
—Slate-colored Solitaire	*Myadestes unicolor*	MA
—Rufous-brown Solitaire	*Cichlopsis leucogenys*	SA
—Black-billed Nightingale-Thrush	*Catharus gracilirostris*	MA
—Orange-billed Nightingale-Thrush	*Catharus aurantiirostris*	LA
—Slaty-backed Nightingale-Thrush	*Catharus fuscater*	LA
—Russet Nightingale-Thrush	*Catharus occidentalis*	MA
—Ruddy-capped Nightingale-Thrush	*Catharus frantzii*	MA
—Black-headed Nightingale-Thrush	*Catharus mexicanus*	MA
—Spotted Nightingale-Thrush	*Catharus dryas*	LA
—Veery	*Catharus fuscescens*	NA
—Grey-cheeked Thrush	*Catharus minimus*	NA
—Bicknell's Thrush	*Catharus bicknelli*	NA

INTERNATIONAL ENGLISH NAME	SCIENTIFIC NAME	REGION(S)
__Swainson's Thrush	*Catharus ustulatus*	NA
__Hermit Thrush	*Catharus guttatus*	NA
__Wood Thrush	*Hylocichla mustelina*	NA
__Black Solitaire	*Entomodestes coracinus*	SA
__White-eared Solitaire	*Entomodestes leucotis*	SA
__Yellow-legged Thrush	*Platycichla flavipes*	SA
__Pale-eyed Thrush	*Platycichla leucops*	SA
__Groundscraper Thrush	*Psophocichla litsitsirupa*	AF
__African Thrush	*Turdus pelios*	AF
__African Bare-eyed Thrush	*Turdus tephronotus*	AF
__Kurrichane Thrush	*Turdus libonyanus*	AF
__Gulf of Guinea Thrush	*Turdus olivaceofuscus*	AF
__Olive Thrush	*Turdus olivaceus*	AF
__Karoo Thrush	*Turdus smithii*	AF
__Somali Thrush	*Turdus ludoviciae*	AF
__Taita Thrush	*Turdus helleri*	AF
__Yemen Thrush	*Turdus menachensis*	EU
__Comoros Thrush	*Turdus bewsheri*	AF
__Grey-backed Thrush	*Turdus hortulorum*	EU
__Tickell's Thrush	*Turdus unicolor*	EU
__Black-breasted Thrush	*Turdus dissimilis*	OR
__Japanese Thrush	*Turdus cardis*	EU
__White-collared Blackbird	*Turdus albocinctus*	OR
__Ring Ouzel	*Turdus torquatus*	EU
__Grey-winged Blackbird	*Turdus boulboul*	OR
__Common Blackbird	*Turdus merula*	EU, OR
__Island Thrush	*Turdus poliocephalus*	OR, AU, PO
__Chestnut Thrush	*Turdus rubrocanus*	OR
__Kessler's Thrush	*Turdus kessleri*	OR
__Grey-sided Thrush	*Turdus feae*	EU
__Eyebrowed Thrush	*Turdus obscurus*	EU
__Pale Thrush	*Turdus pallidus*	EU
__Brown-headed Thrush	*Turdus chrysolaus*	EU
__Izu Thrush	*Turdus celaenops*	EU
__Black-throated Thrush	*Turdus atrogularis*	EU
__Red-throated Thrush	*Turdus ruficollis*	EU
__Naumann's Thrush	*Turdus naumanni*	EU
__Dusky Thrush	*Turdus eunomus*	EU
__Fieldfare	*Turdus pilaris*	EU
__Redwing	*Turdus iliacus*	EU
__Song Thrush	*Turdus philomelos*	EU
__Chinese Thrush	*Turdus mupinensis*	EU
__Mistle Thrush	*Turdus viscivorus*	EU
__Great Thrush	*Turdus fuscater*	SA
__Chiguanco Thrush	*Turdus chiguanco*	SA
__Sooty Thrush	*Turdus nigrescens*	MA
__Black Thrush	*Turdus infuscatus*	MA
__Glossy-black Thrush	*Turdus serranus*	SA
__Andean Slaty Thrush	*Turdus nigriceps*	SA
__Eastern Slaty Thrush	*Turdus subalaris*	SA
__Plumbeous-backed Thrush	*Turdus reevei*	SA
__Black-hooded Thrush	*Turdus olivater*	SA
__Maranon Thrush	*Turdus maranonicus*	SA

INTERNATIONAL ENGLISH NAME	SCIENTIFIC NAME	REGION(S)
—Chestnut-bellied Thrush	*Turdus fulviventris*	SA
—Rufous-bellied Thrush	*Turdus rufiventris*	SA
—Austral Thrush	*Turdus falcklandii*	SA
—Pale-breasted Thrush	*Turdus leucomelas*	SA
—Creamy-bellied Thrush	*Turdus amaurochalinus*	SA
—Mountain Thrush	*Turdus plebejus*	MA
—Black-billed Thrush	*Turdus ignobilis*	SA
—Lawrence's Thrush	*Turdus lawrencii*	SA
—Cocoa Thrush	*Turdus fumigatus*	SA
—Lesser Antillean Thrush	*Turdus personus*	NA
—Pale-vented Thrush	*Turdus obsoletus*	LA
—Hauxwell's Thrush	*Turdus hauxwelli*	SA
—Unicolored Thrush	*Turdus haplochrous*	SA
—Clay-colored Thrush	*Turdus grayi*	LA
—American Bare-eyed Thrush	*Turdus nudigenis*	NA, SA
—Ecuadorian Thrush	*Turdus maculirostris*	SA
—White-eyed Thrush	*Turdus jamaicensis*	NA
—White-throated Thrush	*Turdus assimilis*	MA
—Dagua Thrush	*Turdus daguae*	LA
—White-necked Thrush	*Turdus albicollis*	SA
—Rufous-backed Robin	*Turdus rufopalliatus*	MA
—Grayson's Thrush	*Turdus graysoni*	MA
—Rufous-collared Thrush	*Turdus rufitorques*	MA
—American Robin	*Turdus migratorius*	NA, MA
—La Selle Thrush	*Turdus swalesi*	NA
—White-chinned Thrush	*Turdus aurantius*	NA
—Red-legged Thrush	*Turdus plumbeus*	NA
—Tristan Thrush	*Nesocichla eremita*	AO
—Forest Thrush	*Cichlherminia lherminieri*	NA
—Purple Cochoa	*Cochoa purpurea*	OR
—Green Cochoa	*Cochoa viridis*	OR
—Sumatran Cochoa	*Cochoa beccarii*	OR
—Javan Cochoa	*Cochoa azurea*	OR
—Fruithunter	*Chlamydochaera jefferyi*	OR
—Gould's Shortwing	*Brachypteryx stellata*	OR
—Rusty-bellied Shortwing	*Brachypteryx hyperythra*	OR
—White-bellied Shortwing	*Brachypteryx major*	OR
—Lesser Shortwing	*Brachypteryx leucophrys*	OR
—White-browed Shortwing	*Brachypteryx montana*	OR
—Great Shortwing	*Heinrichia calligyna*	AU
—Fire-crested Alethe	*Alethe diademata*	AF
—Red-throated Alethe	*Alethe poliophrys*	AF
—Brown-chested Alethe	*Alethe poliocephala*	AF
—White-chested Alethe	*Alethe fuelleborni*	AF
—Thyolo Alethe	*Alethe choloensis*	AF

CHATS, OLD WORLD FLYCATCHERS	**Family Muscicapidae**	
—White-starred Robin	*Pogonocichla stellata*	AF
—Swynnerton's Robin	*Swynnertonia swynnertoni*	AF
—Western Forest Robin	*Stiphrornis erythrothorax*	AF
—Gabon Forest Robin	*Stiphrornis gabonensis*	AF
—Eastern Forest Robin	*Stiphrornis xanthogaster*	AF
—Sangha Forest Robin	*Stiphrornis sanghensis*	AF

INTERNATIONAL ENGLISH NAME	SCIENTIFIC NAME	REGION(S)
__Bocage's Robin	*Sheppardia bocagei*	AF
__Alexander's Robin	*Sheppardia poensis*	AF
__Lowland Akalat	*Sheppardia cyornithopsis*	AF
__Equatorial Akalat	*Sheppardia aequatorialis*	AF
__Sharpe's Akalat	*Sheppardia sharpei*	AF
__East Coast Akalat	*Sheppardia gunningi*	AF
__Gabela Akalat	*Sheppardia gabela*	AF
__Rubeho Akalat	*Sheppardia aurantiithorax*	AF
__Usambara Akalat	*Sheppardia montana*	AF
__Iringa Akalat	*Sheppardia lowei*	AF
__European Robin	*Erithacus rubecula*	EU
__Japanese Robin	*Erithacus akahige*	EU
__Ryukyu Robin	*Erithacus komadori*	EU
__Bluethroat	*Luscinia svecica*	EU
__Siberian Rubythroat	*Luscinia calliope*	EU
__White-tailed Rubythroat	*Luscinia pectoralis*	OR
__Rufous-headed Robin	*Luscinia ruficeps*	EU
__Blackthroat	*Luscinia obscura*	EU
__Firethroat	*Luscinia pectardens*	EU
__Indian Blue Robin	*Luscinia brunnea*	OR
__Siberian Blue Robin	*Luscinia cyane*	EU
__Rufous-tailed Robin	*Luscinia sibilans*	EU
__Thrush Nightingale	*Luscinia luscinia*	EU
__Common Nightingale	*Luscinia megarhynchos*	EU
__White-browed Bush Robin	*Tarsiger indicus*	OR
__Rufous-breasted Bush Robin	*Tarsiger hyperythrus*	OR
__Collared Bush Robin	*Tarsiger johnstoniae*	OR
__Red-flanked Bluetail	*Tarsiger cyanurus*	EU, OR
__Golden Bush Robin	*Tarsiger chrysaeus*	OR
__White-throated Robin	*Irania gutturalis*	EU
__White-bellied Robin-Chat	*Cossyphicula roberti*	AF
__Cameroon Mountain Robin	*Cossypha isabellae*	AF
__Archer's Ground Robin	*Cossypha archeri*	AF
__Olive-flanked Ground Robin	*Cossypha anomala*	AF
__Cape Robin-Chat	*Cossypha caffra*	AF
__White-throated Robin-Chat	*Cossypha humeralis*	AF
__Grey-winged Robin-Chat	*Cossypha polioptera*	AF
__Blue-shouldered Robin-Chat	*Cossypha cyanocampter*	AF
__Rüppell's Robin-Chat	*Cossypha semirufa*	AF
__White-browed Robin-Chat	*Cossypha heuglini*	AF
__Red-capped Robin-Chat	*Cossypha natalensis*	AF
__Chorister Robin-Chat	*Cossypha dichroa*	AF
__White-headed Robin-Chat	*Cossypha heinrichi*	AF
__Snowy-crowned Robin-Chat	*Cossypha niveicapilla*	AF
__White-crowned Robin-Chat	*Cossypha albicapilla*	AF
__Angola Cave Chat	*Xenocopsychus ansorgei*	AF
__Collared Palm Thrush	*Cichladusa arquata*	AF
__Rufous-tailed Palm Thrush	*Cichladusa ruficauda*	AF
__Spotted Palm Thrush	*Cichladusa guttata*	AF
__Forest Scrub Robin	*Cercotrichas leucosticta*	AF
__Miombo Scrub Robin	*Cercotrichas barbata*	AF
__Bearded Scrub Robin	*Cercotrichas quadrivirgata*	AF
__Brown Scrub Robin	*Cercotrichas signata*	AF

INTERNATIONAL ENGLISH NAME	SCIENTIFIC NAME	REGION(S)
—Brown-backed Scrub Robin	*Cercotrichas hartlaubi*	AF
—White-browed Scrub Robin	*Cercotrichas leucophrys*	AF
—Rufous-tailed Scrub Robin	*Cercotrichas galactotes*	EU
—Kalahari Scrub Robin	*Cercotrichas paena*	AF
—Karoo Scrub Robin	*Cercotrichas coryphaeus*	AF
—Black Scrub Robin	*Cercotrichas podobe*	AF
—Herero Chat	*Namibornis herero*	AF
—Madagascar Magpie-Robin	*Copsychus albospecularis*	AF
—Seychelles Magpie-Robin	*Copsychus sechellarum*	IO
—Oriental Magpie-Robin	*Copsychus saularis*	OR
—White-rumped Shama	*Copsychus malabaricus*	OR
—White-crowned Shama	*Copsychus stricklandii*	OR
—White-browed Shama	*Copsychus luzoniensis*	OR
—White-vented Shama	*Copsychus niger*	OR
—Black Shama	*Copsychus cebuensis*	OR
—Rufous-tailed Shama	*Trichixos pyrropygus*	OR
—Indian Robin	*Saxicoloides fulicatus*	OR
—Przevalski's Redstart	*Phoenicurus alaschanicus*	EU
—Eversmann's Redstart	*Phoenicurus erythronotus*	EU
—Blue-capped Redstart	*Phoenicurus caeruleocephala*	EU
—Black Redstart	*Phoenicurus ochruros*	EU, OR
—Common Redstart	*Phoenicurus phoenicurus*	EU
—Hodgson's Redstart	*Phoenicurus hodgsoni*	OR
—White-throated Redstart	*Phoenicurus schisticeps*	EU
—Daurian Redstart	*Phoenicurus auroreus*	EU
—Moussier's Redstart	*Phoenicurus moussieri*	AF
—Güldenstädt's Redstart	*Phoenicurus erythrogastrus*	EU
—Blue-fronted Redstart	*Phoenicurus frontalis*	OR
—White-bellied Redstart	*Hodgsonius phaenicuroides*	OR
—Plumbeous Water Redstart	*Rhyacornis fuliginosa*	OR
—Luzon Water Redstart	*Rhyacornis bicolor*	OR
—White-capped Redstart	*Chaimarrornis leucocephalus*	EU
—White-tailed Robin	*Myiomela leucura*	OR
—Sunda Robin	*Myiomela diana*	OR
—Blue-fronted Robin	*Cinclidium frontale*	OR
—Grandala	*Grandala coelicolor*	OR
—Little Forktail	*Enicurus scouleri*	OR
—Sunda Forktail	*Enicurus velatus*	OR
—Chestnut-naped Forktail	*Enicurus ruficapillus*	OR
—Black-backed Forktail	*Enicurus immaculatus*	OR
—Slaty-backed Forktail	*Enicurus schistaceus*	OR
—White-crowned Forktail	*Enicurus leschenaulti*	OR
—Spotted Forktail	*Enicurus maculatus*	OR
—Whinchat	*Saxicola rubetra*	EU
—White-browed Bush Chat	*Saxicola macrorhynchus*	OR
—White-throated Bush Chat	*Saxicola insignis*	EU
—Canary Islands Bush Chat	*Saxicola dacotiae*	AF
—Eurasian Stone Chat	*Saxicola torquatus*	EU, AF
—Reunion Stone Chat	*Saxicola tectes*	IO
—White-tailed Stone Chat	*Saxicola leucurus*	OR
—Pied Bush Chat	*Saxicola caprata*	EU, OR, AU
—Jerdon's Bush Chat	*Saxicola jerdoni*	OR
—Grey Bush Chat	*Saxicola ferreus*	OR

INTERNATIONAL ENGLISH NAME	SCIENTIFIC NAME	REGION(S)
—White-bellied Bush Chat	*Saxicola gutturalis*	AU
—Buff-streaked Chat	*Saxicola bifasciata*	AF
—Red-rumped Wheatear	*Oenanthe moesta*	EU, AF
—Capped Wheatear	*Oenanthe pileata*	AF
—Red-breasted Wheatear	*Oenanthe bottae*	EU, AF
—Heuglin's Wheatear	*Oenanthe heuglini*	AF
—Isabelline Wheatear	*Oenanthe isabellina*	EU
—Northern Wheatear	*Oenanthe oenanthe*	EU
—Somali Wheatear	*Oenanthe phillipsi*	AF
—Kurdistan Wheatear	*Oenanthe xanthoprymna*	EU
—Red-tailed Wheatear	*Oenanthe chrysopygia*	EU
—Pied Wheatear	*Oenanthe pleschanka*	EU
—Cyprus Wheatear	*Oenanthe cypriaca*	EU
—Black-eared Wheatear	*Oenanthe hispanica*	EU
—Desert Wheatear	*Oenanthe deserti*	EU
—Mourning Wheatear	*Oenanthe lugens*	EU, AF
—Abyssinian Wheatear	*Oenanthe lugubris*	AF
—Arabian Wheatear	*Oenanthe lugentoides*	EU
—Finsch's Wheatear	*Oenanthe finschii*	EU
—Variable Wheatear	*Oenanthe picata*	EU
—Mountain Wheatear	*Oenanthe monticola*	AF
—Hume's Wheatear	*Oenanthe albonigra*	EU
—White-crowned Wheatear	*Oenanthe leucopyga*	AF, EU
—Black Wheatear	*Oenanthe leucura*	EU
—Hooded Wheatear	*Oenanthe monacha*	EU
—Sickle-winged Chat	*Cercomela sinuata*	AF
—Karoo Chat	*Cercomela schlegelii*	AF
—Brown Rock Chat	*Cercomela fusca*	OR
—Tractrac Chat	*Cercomela tractrac*	AF
—Familiar Chat	*Cercomela familiaris*	AF
—Brown-tailed Rock Chat	*Cercomela scotocerca*	AF
—Sombre Rock Chat	*Cercomela dubia*	AF
—Blackstart	*Cercomela melanura*	EU, AF
—Moorland Chat	*Cercomela sordida*	AF
—Congo Moor Chat	*Myrmecocichla tholloni*	AF
—Anteater Chat	*Myrmecocichla aethiops*	AF
—Ant-eating Chat	*Myrmecocichla formicivora*	AF
—Sooty Chat	*Myrmecocichla nigra*	AF
—Rüppell's Black Chat	*Myrmecocichla melaena*	AF
—White-fronted Black Chat	*Myrmecocichla albifrons*	AF
—Arnot's Chat	*Myrmecocichla arnotti*	AF
—Mocking Cliff Chat	*Thamnolaea cinnamomeiventris*	AF
—White-crowned Cliff Chat	*Thamnolaea coronata*	AF
—White-winged Cliff Chat	*Thamnolaea semirufa*	AF
—Boulder Chat	*Pinarornis plumosus*	AF
—Cape Rock Thrush	*Monticola rupestris*	AF
—Sentinel Rock Thrush	*Monticola explorator*	AF
—Short-toed Rock Thrush	*Monticola brevipes*	AF
—Miombo Rock Thrush	*Monticola angolensis*	AF
—Pretoria Rock Thrush	*Monticola pretoriae*	AF
—Rufous-tailed Rock Thrush	*Monticola saxatilis*	EU
—Little Rock Thrush	*Monticola rufocinereus*	AF
—Blue Rock Thrush	*Monticola solitarius*	EU, OR

INTERNATIONAL ENGLISH NAME	SCIENTIFIC NAME	REGION(S)
—Chestnut-bellied Rock Thrush	*Monticola rufiventris*	OR
—Blue-capped Rock Thrush	*Monticola cinclorhynchus*	OR
—White-throated Rock Thrush	*Monticola gularis*	EU
—Littoral Rock Thrush	*Pseudocossyphus imerina*	AF
—Forest Rock Thrush	*Pseudocossyphus sharpei*	AF
—Benson's Rock Thrush	*Pseudocossyphus bensoni*	AF
—Fraser's Forest Flycatcher	*Fraseria ocreata*	AF
—White-browed Forest Flycatcher	*Fraseria cinerascens*	AF
—Angola Slaty Flycatcher	*Dioptrornis brunneus*	AF
—White-eyed Slaty Flycatcher	*Dioptrornis fischeri*	AF
—Abyssinian Slaty Flycatcher	*Dioptrornis chocolatinus*	AF
—Nimba Flycatcher	*Melaenornis annamarulae*	AF
—Yellow-eyed Black Thrush	*Melaenornis ardesiacus*	AF
—Northern Black Flycatcher	*Melaenornis edolioides*	AF
—Southern Black Flycatcher	*Melaenornis pammelaina*	AF
—Pale Flycatcher	*Bradornis pallidus*	AF
—Chat Flycatcher	*Bradornis infuscatus*	AF
—African Grey Flycatcher	*Bradornis microrhynchus*	AF
—Ethiopian Grey Flycatcher	*Bradornis pumilus*	AF
—Marico Flycatcher	*Bradornis mariquensis*	AF
—Fiscal Flycatcher	*Sigelus silens*	AF
—Silverbird	*Empidornis semipartitus*	AF
—Streak-breasted Jungle Flycatcher	*Rhinomyias additus*	AU
—Russet-backed Jungle Flycatcher	*Rhinomyias oscillans*	AU
—Brown-chested Jungle Flycatcher	*Rhinomyias brunneatus*	OR
—Fulvous-chested Jungle Flycatcher	*Rhinomyias olivaceus*	OR
—Grey-chested Jungle Flycatcher	*Rhinomyias umbratilis*	OR
—Rufous-tailed Jungle Flycatcher	*Rhinomyias ruficauda*	OR
—Henna-tailed Jungle Flycatcher	*Rhinomyias colonus*	AU
—Eyebrowed Jungle Flycatcher	*Rhinomyias gularis*	OR
—White-throated Jungle Flycatcher	*Rhinomyias albigularis*	OR
—White-browed Jungle Flycatcher	*Rhinomyias insignis*	OR
—Slaty-backed Jungle Flycatcher	*Rhinomyias goodfellowi*	OR
—Spotted Flycatcher	*Muscicapa striata*	EU
—Gambaga Flycatcher	*Muscicapa gambagae*	AF
—Grey-streaked Flycatcher	*Muscicapa griseisticta*	EU
—Dark-sided Flycatcher	*Muscicapa sibirica*	EU, OR
—Asian Brown Flycatcher	*Muscicapa dauurica*	EU, OR
—Ashy-breasted Flycatcher	*Muscicapa randi*	OR
—Sumba Brown Flycatcher	*Muscicapa segregata*	AU
—Brown-breasted Flycatcher	*Muscicapa muttui*	OR
—Rusty-tailed Flycatcher	*Muscicapa ruficauda*	EU
—Ferruginous Flycatcher	*Muscicapa ferruginea*	OR
—Ashy Flycatcher	*Muscicapa caerulescens*	AF
—Swamp Flycatcher	*Muscicapa aquatica*	AF
—Cassin's Flycatcher	*Muscicapa cassini*	AF
—Olivaceous Flycatcher	*Muscicapa olivascens*	AF
—Chapin's Flycatcher	*Muscicapa lendu*	AF
—Itombwe Flycatcher	*Muscicapa itombwensis*	AF
—African Dusky Flycatcher	*Muscicapa adusta*	AF
—Little Grey Flycatcher	*Muscicapa epulata*	AF
—Yellow-footed Flycatcher	*Muscicapa sethsmithi*	AF
—Dusky-blue Flycatcher	*Muscicapa comitata*	AF

INTERNATIONAL ENGLISH NAME	SCIENTIFIC NAME	REGION(S)
—Tessmann's Flycatcher	*Muscicapa tessmanni*	AF
—Sooty Flycatcher	*Muscicapa infuscata*	AF
—Ussher's Flycatcher	*Muscicapa ussheri*	AF
—Böhm's Flycatcher	*Muscicapa boehmi*	AF
—Grey-throated Tit-Flycatcher	*Myioparus griseigularis*	AF
—Grey Tit-Flycatcher	*Myioparus plumbeus*	AF
—Fairy Flycatcher	*Stenostira scita*	AF
—Humblot's Flycatcher	*Humblotia flavirostris*	AF
—European Pied Flycatcher	*Ficedula hypoleuca*	EU
—Atlas Pied Flycatcher	*Ficedula speculigera*	AF
—Collared Flycatcher	*Ficedula albicollis*	EU
—Semicollared Flycatcher	*Ficedula semitorquata*	EU
—Yellow-rumped Flycatcher	*Ficedula zanthopygia*	EU
—Narcissus Flycatcher	*Ficedula narcissina*	EU
—Chinese Flycatcher	*Ficedula elisae*	EU
—Mugimaki Flycatcher	*Ficedula mugimaki*	EU
—Slaty-backed Flycatcher	*Ficedula hodgsonii*	OR
—Rufous-chested Flycatcher	*Ficedula dumetoria*	OR
—Rufous-gorgeted Flycatcher	*Ficedula strophiata*	OR
—Red-breasted Flycatcher	*Ficedula parva*	EU
—Taiga Flycatcher	*Ficedula albicilla*	EU
—Kashmir Flycatcher	*Ficedula subrubra*	OR
—White-gorgeted Flycatcher	*Ficedula monileger*	OR
—Rufous-browed Flycatcher	*Ficedula solitaris*	OR
—Snowy-browed Flycatcher	*Ficedula hyperythra*	OR
—Little Slaty Flycatcher	*Ficedula basilanica*	OR
—Rufous-throated Flycatcher	*Ficedula rufigula*	AU
—Cinnamon-chested Flycatcher	*Ficedula buruensis*	AU
—Damar Flycatcher	*Ficedula henrici*	AU
—Sumba Flycatcher	*Ficedula harterti*	AU
—Palawan Flycatcher	*Ficedula platenae*	OR
—Cryptic Flycatcher	*Ficedula crypta*	OR
—Furtive Flycatcher	*Ficedula disposita*	OR
—Lompobattang Flycatcher	*Ficedula bonthaina*	AU
—Little Pied Flycatcher	*Ficedula westermanni*	OR
—Ultramarine Flycatcher	*Ficedula superciliaris*	OR
—Slaty-blue Flycatcher	*Ficedula tricolor*	OR
—Sapphire Flycatcher	*Ficedula sapphira*	OR
—Black-and-orange Flycatcher	*Ficedula nigrorufa*	OR
—Black-banded Flycatcher	*Ficedula timorensis*	AU
—Blue-and-white Flycatcher	*Cyanoptila cyanomelana*	EU
—Dull-blue Flycatcher	*Eumyias sordidus*	OR
—Verditer Flycatcher	*Eumyias thalassinus*	OR
—Turquoise Flycatcher	*Eumyias panayensis*	AU
—Nilgiri Flycatcher	*Eumyias albicaudatus*	OR
—Indigo Flycatcher	*Eumyias indigo*	OR
—Hainan Blue Flycatcher	*Cyornis hainanus*	OR
—Pale Blue Flycatcher	*Cyornis unicolor*	OR
—Rück's Blue Flycatcher	*Cyornis rucki*	OR
—Blue-breasted Blue Flycatcher	*Cyornis herioti*	OR
—White-bellied Blue Flycatcher	*Cyornis pallipes*	OR
—Pale-chinned Blue Flycatcher	*Cyornis poliogenys*	OR
—Hill Blue Flycatcher	*Cyornis banyumas*	OR

INTERNATIONAL ENGLISH NAME	SCIENTIFIC NAME	REGION(S)
—Palawan Blue Flycatcher	*Cyornis lemprieri*	OR
—Tickell's Blue Flycatcher	*Cyornis tickelliae*	OR
—Sunda Blue Flycatcher	*Cyornis caerulatus*	OR
—Bornean Blue Flycatcher	*Cyornis superbus*	OR
—Blue-throated Blue Flycatcher	*Cyornis rubeculoides*	OR
—Chinese Blue Flycatcher	*Cyornis glaucicomans*	OR
—Malaysian Blue Flycatcher	*Cyornis turcosus*	OR
—Mangrove Blue Flycatcher	*Cyornis rufigastra*	OR
—Tanahjampea Blue Flycatcher	*Cyornis djampeanus*	AU
—Sulawesi Blue Flycatcher	*Cyornis omissus*	AU
—Timor Blue Flycatcher	*Cyornis hyacinthinus*	AU
—Blue-fronted Blue Flycatcher	*Cyornis hoevelli*	AU
—Matinan Blue Flycatcher	*Cyornis sanfordi*	AU
—White-tailed Flycatcher	*Cyornis concretus*	OR
—Fujian Niltava	*Niltava davidi*	OR
—Rufous-bellied Niltava	*Niltava sundara*	OR
—Rufous-vented Niltava	*Niltava sumatrana*	OR
—Vivid Niltava	*Niltava vivida*	OR
—Large Niltava	*Niltava grandis*	OR
—Small Niltava	*Niltava macgrigoriae*	OR
—Pygmy Flycatcher	*Muscicapella hodgsoni*	OR
—Grey-headed Canary-Flycatcher	*Culicicapa ceylonensis*	OR
—Citrine Canary-Flycatcher	*Culicicapa helianthea*	OR
DIPPERS	**Family Cinclidae**	
—White-throated Dipper	*Cinclus cinclus*	EU
—Brown Dipper	*Cinclus pallasii*	EU
—American Dipper	*Cinclus mexicanus*	NA, MA
—White-capped Dipper	*Cinclus leucocephalus*	SA
—Rufous-throated Dipper	*Cinclus schulzi*	SA
LEAFBIRDS	**Family Chloropseidae**	
—Philippine Leafbird	*Chloropsis flavipennis*	OR
—Yellow-throated Leafbird	*Chloropsis palawanensis*	OR
—Greater Green Leafbird	*Chloropsis sonnerati*	OR
—Lesser Green Leafbird	*Chloropsis cyanopogon*	OR
—Blue-winged Leafbird	*Chloropsis cochinchinensis*	OR
—Golden-fronted Leafbird	*Chloropsis aurifrons*	OR
—Orange-bellied Leafbird	*Chloropsis hardwickii*	OR
—Blue-masked Leafbird	*Chloropsis venusta*	OR
FLOWERPECKERS	**Family Dicaeidae**	
—Olive-backed Flowerpecker	*Prionochilus olivaceus*	OR
—Yellow-breasted Flowerpecker	*Prionochilus maculatus*	OR
—Crimson-breasted Flowerpecker	*Prionochilus percussus*	OR
—Palawan Flowerpecker	*Prionochilus plateni*	OR
—Yellow-rumped Flowerpecker	*Prionochilus xanthopygius*	OR
—Scarlet-breasted Flowerpecker	*Prionochilus thoracicus*	OR
—Golden-rumped Flowerpecker	*Dicaeum annae*	AU
—Thick-billed Flowerpecker	*Dicaeum agile*	OR
—Striped Flowerpecker	*Dicaeum aeruginosum*	OR
—Brown-backed Flowerpecker	*Dicaeum everetti*	OR
—Whiskered Flowerpecker	*Dicaeum proprium*	OR

INTERNATIONAL ENGLISH NAME	SCIENTIFIC NAME	REGION(S)
__Yellow-vented Flowerpecker	*Dicaeum chrysorrheum*	OR
__Yellow-bellied Flowerpecker	*Dicaeum melanoxanthum*	OR
__Legge's Flowerpecker	*Dicaeum vincens*	OR
__Yellow-sided Flowerpecker	*Dicaeum aureolimbatum*	AU
__Olive-capped Flowerpecker	*Dicaeum nigrilore*	OR
__Flame-crowned Flowerpecker	*Dicaeum anthonyi*	OR
__Bicolored Flowerpecker	*Dicaeum bicolor*	OR
__Red-keeled Flowerpecker	*Dicaeum australe*	OR
__Black-belted Flowerpecker	*Dicaeum haematostictum*	OR
__Scarlet-collared Flowerpecker	*Dicaeum retrocinctum*	OR
__Cebu Flowerpecker	*Dicaeum quadricolor*	OR
__Orange-bellied Flowerpecker	*Dicaeum trigonostigma*	OR
__Buzzing Flowerpecker	*Dicaeum hypoleucum*	OR
__Pale-billed Flowerpecker	*Dicaeum erythrorhynchos*	OR
__Plain Flowerpecker	*Dicaeum concolor*	OR
__Pygmy Flowerpecker	*Dicaeum pygmaeum*	OR
__Crimson-crowned Flowerpecker	*Dicaeum nehrkorni*	AU
__Flame-breasted Flowerpecker	*Dicaeum erythrothorax*	AU
__Ashy Flowerpecker	*Dicaeum vulneratum*	AU
__Olive-crowned Flowerpecker	*Dicaeum pectorale*	AU
__Red-capped Flowerpecker	*Dicaeum geelvinkianum*	AU
__Louisiade Flowerpecker	*Dicaeum nitidum*	AU
__Red-banded Flowerpecker	*Dicaeum eximium*	AU
__Midget Flowerpecker	*Dicaeum aeneum*	AU
__White-mottled Flowerpecker	*Dicaeum tristrami*	AU
__Black-fronted Flowerpecker	*Dicaeum igniferum*	AU
__Blue-cheeked Flowerpecker	*Dicaeum maugei*	AU
__Mistletoebird	*Dicaeum hirundinaceum*	AU
__Grey-sided Flowerpecker	*Dicaeum celebicum*	AU
__Black-sided Flowerpecker	*Dicaeum monticolum*	OR
__Fire-breasted Flowerpecker	*Dicaeum ignipectus*	OR
__Blood-breasted Flowerpecker	*Dicaeum sanguinolentum*	OR
__Scarlet-backed Flowerpecker	*Dicaeum cruentatum*	OR
__Scarlet-headed Flowerpecker	*Dicaeum trochileum*	OR
SUNBIRDS	**Family Nectariniidae**	
__Ruby-cheeked Sunbird	*Chalcoparia singalensis*	OR
__Fraser's Sunbird	*Deleornis fraseri*	AF
__Grey-headed Sunbird	*Deleornis axillaris*	AF
__Plain-backed Sunbird	*Anthreptes reichenowi*	AF
__Anchieta's Sunbird	*Anthreptes anchietae*	AF
__Plain Sunbird	*Anthreptes simplex*	OR
__Brown-throated Sunbird	*Anthreptes malacensis*	OR
__Red-throated Sunbird	*Anthreptes rhodolaemus*	OR
__Mangrove Sunbird	*Anthreptes gabonicus*	AF
__Western Violet-backed Sunbird	*Anthreptes longuemarei*	AF
__Eastern Violet-backed Sunbird	*Anthreptes orientalis*	AF
__Uluguru Violet-backed Sunbird	*Anthreptes neglectus*	AF
__Violet-tailed Sunbird	*Anthreptes aurantium*	AF
__Little Green Sunbird	*Anthreptes seimundi*	AF
__Grey-chinned Sunbird	*Anthreptes rectirostris*	AF
__Banded Green Sunbird	*Anthreptes rubritorques*	AF
__Collared Sunbird	*Hedydipna collaris*	AF

INTERNATIONAL ENGLISH NAME	SCIENTIFIC NAME	REGION(S)
—Pygmy Sunbird	*Hedydipna platura*	AF
—Nile Valley Sunbird	*Hedydipna metallica*	AF
—Amani Sunbird	*Hedydipna pallidigaster*	AF
—Purple-naped Sunbird	*Hypogramma hypogrammicum*	OR
—Reichenbach's Sunbird	*Anabathmis reichenbachii*	AF
—Principe Sunbird	*Anabathmis hartlaubii*	AF
—Newton's Sunbird	*Anabathmis newtonii*	AF
—Giant Sunbird	*Dreptes thomensis*	AF
—Orange-breasted Sunbird	*Anthobaphes violacea*	AF
—Green-headed Sunbird	*Cyanomitra verticalis*	AF
—Bannerman's Sunbird	*Cyanomitra bannermani*	AF
—Blue-throated Brown Sunbird	*Cyanomitra cyanolaema*	AF
—Cameroon Sunbird	*Cyanomitra oritis*	AF
—Blue-headed Sunbird	*Cyanomitra alinae*	AF
—Eastern Olive Sunbird	*Cyanomitra olivacea*	AF
—Western Olive Sunbird	*Cyanomitra obscura*	AF
—Grey Sunbird	*Cyanomitra veroxii*	AF
—Buff-throated Sunbird	*Chalcomitra adelberti*	AF
—Carmelite Sunbird	*Chalcomitra fuliginosa*	AF
—Green-throated Sunbird	*Chalcomitra rubescens*	AF
—Amethyst Sunbird	*Chalcomitra amethystina*	AF
—Scarlet-chested Sunbird	*Chalcomitra senegalensis*	AF
—Hunter's Sunbird	*Chalcomitra hunteri*	AF
—Socotra Sunbird	*Chalcomitra balfouri*	EU
—Purple-rumped Sunbird	*Leptocoma zeylonica*	OR
—Crimson-backed Sunbird	*Leptocoma minima*	OR
—Purple-throated Sunbird	*Leptocoma sperata*	OR
—Black Sunbird	*Leptocoma sericea*	AU
—Copper-throated Sunbird	*Leptocoma calcostetha*	OR
—Bocage's Sunbird	*Nectarinia bocagii*	AF
—Purple-breasted Sunbird	*Nectarinia purpureiventris*	AF
—Tacazze Sunbird	*Nectarinia tacazze*	AF
—Bronzy Sunbird	*Nectarinia kilimensis*	AF
—Malachite Sunbird	*Nectarinia famosa*	AF
—Scarlet-tufted Sunbird	*Nectarinia johnstoni*	AF
—Golden-winged Sunbird	*Drepanorhynchus reichenowi*	AF
—Olive-bellied Sunbird	*Cinnyris chloropygius*	AF
—Tiny Sunbird	*Cinnyris minullus*	AF
—Miombo Double-collared Sunbird	*Cinnyris manoensis*	AF
—Southern Double-collared Sunbird	*Cinnyris chalybeus*	AF
—Neergaard's Sunbird	*Cinnyris neergaardi*	AF
—Ruwenzori Double-collared Sunbird	*Cinnyris stuhlmanni*	AF
—Prigogine's Double-collared Sunbird	*Cinnyris prigoginei*	AF
—Ludwig's Double-collared Sunbird	*Cinnyris ludovicensis*	AF
—Northern Double-collared Sunbird	*Cinnyris reichenowi*	AF
—Greater Double-collared Sunbird	*Cinnyris afer*	AF
—Regal Sunbird	*Cinnyris regius*	AF
—Rockefeller's Sunbird	*Cinnyris rockefelleri*	AF
—Eastern Double-collared Sunbird	*Cinnyris mediocris*	AF
—Moreau's Sunbird	*Cinnyris moreaui*	AF
—Loveridge's Sunbird	*Cinnyris loveridgei*	AF
—Beautiful Sunbird	*Cinnyris pulchellus*	AF
—Marico Sunbird	*Cinnyris mariquensis*	AF

INTERNATIONAL ENGLISH NAME	SCIENTIFIC NAME	REGION(S)
—Shelley's Sunbird	*Cinnyris shelleyi*	AF
—Congo Sunbird	*Cinnyris congensis*	AF
—Red-chested Sunbird	*Cinnyris erythrocercus*	AF
—Black-bellied Sunbird	*Cinnyris nectarinioides*	AF
—Purple-banded Sunbird	*Cinnyris bifasciatus*	AF
—Tsavo Sunbird	*Cinnyris tsavoensis*	AF
—Violet-breasted Sunbird	*Cinnyris chalcomelas*	AF
—Pemba Sunbird	*Cinnyris pembae*	IO
—Orange-tufted Sunbird	*Cinnyris bouvieri*	AF
—Palestine Sunbird	*Cinnyris osea*	AF
—Shining Sunbird	*Cinnyris habessinicus*	AF
—Splendid Sunbird	*Cinnyris coccinigastrus*	AF
—Johanna's Sunbird	*Cinnyris johannae*	AF
—Superb Sunbird	*Cinnyris superbus*	AF
—Rufous-winged Sunbird	*Cinnyris rufipennis*	AF
—Oustalet's Sunbird	*Cinnyris oustaleti*	AF
—White-bellied Sunbird	*Cinnyris talatala*	AF
—Variable Sunbird	*Cinnyris venustus*	AF
—Dusky Sunbird	*Cinnyris fuscus*	AF
—Ursula's Sunbird	*Cinnyris ursulae*	AF
—Bates's Sunbird	*Cinnyris batesi*	AF
—Copper Sunbird	*Cinnyris cupreus*	AF
—Purple Sunbird	*Cinnyris asiaticus*	EU, OR
—Olive-backed Sunbird	*Cinnyris jugularis*	OR, AU
—Apricot-breasted Sunbird	*Cinnyris buettikoferi*	AU
—Flame-breasted Sunbird	*Cinnyris solaris*	AU
—Souimanga Sunbird	*Cinnyris souimanga*	AF
—Abbott's Sunbird	*Cinnyris abbotti*	AF
—Malagasy Green Sunbird	*Cinnyris notatus*	AF
—Seychelles Sunbird	*Cinnyris dussumieri*	IO
—Humblot's Sunbird	*Cinnyris humbloti*	AF
—Anjouan Sunbird	*Cinnyris comorensis*	AF
—Mayotte Sunbird	*Cinnyris coquerellii*	AF
—Loten's Sunbird	*Cinnyris lotenius*	OR
—Grey-hooded Sunbird	*Aethopyga primigenia*	OR
—Apo Sunbird	*Aethopyga boltoni*	OR
—Lina's Sunbird	*Aethopyga linaraborae*	OR
—Flaming Sunbird	*Aethopyga flagrans*	OR
—Metallic-winged Sunbird	*Aethopyga pulcherrima*	OR
—Elegant Sunbird	*Aethopyga duyvenbodei*	AU
—Lovely Sunbird	*Aethopyga shelleyi*	OR
—Handsome Sunbird	*Aethopyga bella*	OR
—Mrs. Gould's Sunbird	*Aethopyga gouldiae*	OR
—Green-tailed Sunbird	*Aethopyga nipalensis*	OR
—White-flanked Sunbird	*Aethopyga eximia*	OR
—Fork-tailed Sunbird	*Aethopyga christinae*	OR
—Black-throated Sunbird	*Aethopyga saturata*	OR
—Crimson Sunbird	*Aethopyga siparaja*	OR
—Javan Sunbird	*Aethopyga mystacalis*	OR
—Temminck's Sunbird	*Aethopyga temminckii*	OR
—Fire-tailed Sunbird	*Aethopyga ignicauda*	OR
—Little Spiderhunter	*Arachnothera longirostra*	OR
—Thick-billed Spiderhunter	*Arachnothera crassirostris*	OR

INTERNATIONAL ENGLISH NAME	SCIENTIFIC NAME	REGION(S)
—Long-billed Spiderhunter	*Arachnothera robusta*	OR
—Spectacled Spiderhunter	*Arachnothera flavigaster*	OR
—Yellow-eared Spiderhunter	*Arachnothera chrysogenys*	OR
—Naked-faced Spiderhunter	*Arachnothera clarae*	OR
—Grey-breasted Spiderhunter	*Arachnothera modesta*	OR
—Streaky-breasted Spiderhunter	*Arachnothera affinis*	OR
—Streaked Spiderhunter	*Arachnothera magna*	OR
—Whitehead's Spiderhunter	*Arachnothera juliae*	OR

OLD WORLD SPARROWS, SNOWFINCHES	**Family Passeridae**	
—White-browed Sparrow-Weaver	*Plocepasser mahali*	AF
—Chestnut-crowned Sparrow-Weaver	*Plocepasser superciliosus*	AF
—Donaldson-Smith's Sparrow-Weaver	*Plocepasser donaldsoni*	AF
—Chestnut-backed Sparrow-Weaver	*Plocepasser rufoscapulatus*	AF
—Rufous-tailed Weaver	*Histurgops ruficauda*	AF
—Grey-capped Social Weaver	*Pseudonigrita arnaudi*	AF
—Black-capped Social Weaver	*Pseudonigrita cabanisi*	AF
—Sociable Weaver	*Philetairus socius*	AF
—Saxaul Sparrow	*Passer ammodendri*	EU
—House Sparrow	*Passer domesticus*	EU, OR, AF
—Spanish Sparrow	*Passer hispaniolensis*	EU
—Jungle Sparrow	*Passer pyrrhonotus*	EU
—Somali Sparrow	*Passer castanopterus*	AF
—Russet Sparrow	*Passer rutilans*	EU, OR
—Plain-backed Sparrow	*Passer flaveolus*	OR
—Dead Sea Sparrow	*Passer moabiticus*	EU
—Iago Sparrow	*Passer iagoensis*	AF
—Great Sparrow	*Passer motitensis*	AF
—Socotra Sparrow	*Passer insularis*	EU
—Kenya Sparrow	*Passer rufocinctus*	AF
—Cape Sparrow	*Passer melanurus*	AF
—Northern Grey-headed Sparrow	*Passer griseus*	AF
—Swainson's Sparrow	*Passer swainsonii*	AF
—Parrot-billed Sparrow	*Passer gongonensis*	AF
—Swahili Sparrow	*Passer suahelicus*	AF
—Southern Grey-headed Sparrow	*Passer diffusus*	AF
—Desert Sparrow	*Passer simplex*	EU, AF
—Eurasian Tree Sparrow	*Passer montanus*	EU, OR
—Sudan Golden Sparrow	*Passer luteus*	AF
—Arabian Golden Sparrow	*Passer euchlorus*	EU
—Chestnut Sparrow	*Passer eminibey*	AF
—Pale Rockfinch	*Carpospiza brachydactyla*	EU
—Rock Sparrow	*Petronia petronia*	EU
—Yellow-throated Petronia	*Gymnoris superciliaris*	AF
—Bush Petronia	*Gymnoris dentata*	AF
—Yellow-spotted Petronia	*Gymnoris pyrgita*	AF
—Yellow-throated Sparrow	*Gymnoris xanthocollis*	EU, OR
—White-winged Snowfinch	*Montifringilla nivalis*	EU
—Henri's Snowfinch	*Montifringilla henrici*	EU
—Tibetan Snowfinch	*Montifringilla adamsi*	EU
—White-rumped Snowfinch	*Onychostruthus taczanowskii*	EU
—Pere David's Snowfinch	*Pyrgilauda davidiana*	EU
—Rufous-necked Snowfinch	*Pyrgilauda ruficollis*	EU

INTERNATIONAL ENGLISH NAME	SCIENTIFIC NAME	REGION(S)
__Blanford's Snowfinch	*Pyrgilauda blanfordi*	EU
__Afghan Snowfinch	*Pyrgilauda theresae*	EU
WEAVERS, WIDOWBIRDS	**Family Ploceidae**	
__White-billed Buffalo Weaver	*Bubalornis albirostris*	AF
__Red-billed Buffalo Weaver	*Bubalornis niger*	AF
__White-headed Buffalo Weaver	*Dinemellia dinemelli*	AF
__Scaly-feathered Weaver	*Sporopipes squamifrons*	AF
__Speckle-fronted Weaver	*Sporopipes frontalis*	AF
__Thick-billed Weaver	*Amblyospiza albifrons*	AF
__Baglafecht Weaver	*Ploceus baglafecht*	AF
__Bannerman's Weaver	*Ploceus bannermani*	AF
__Bates's Weaver	*Ploceus batesi*	AF
__Black-chinned Weaver	*Ploceus nigrimentus*	AF
__Bertram's Weaver	*Ploceus bertrandi*	AF
__Slender-billed Weaver	*Ploceus pelzelni*	AF
__Loango Weaver	*Ploceus subpersonatus*	AF
__Little Weaver	*Ploceus luteolus*	AF
__Spectacled Weaver	*Ploceus ocularis*	AF
__Black-necked Weaver	*Ploceus nigricollis*	AF
__Strange Weaver	*Ploceus alienus*	AF
__Black-billed Weaver	*Ploceus melanogaster*	AF
__Cape Weaver	*Ploceus capensis*	AF
__Bocage's Weaver	*Ploceus temporalis*	AF
__Yellow Weaver	*Ploceus subaureus*	AF
__African Golden Weaver	*Ploceus xanthops*	AF
__Orange Weaver	*Ploceus aurantius*	AF
__Heuglin's Masked Weaver	*Ploceus heuglini*	AF
__Golden Palm Weaver	*Ploceus bojeri*	AF
__Taveta Weaver	*Ploceus castaneiceps*	AF
__Principe Weaver	*Ploceus princeps*	AF
__Northern Brown-throated Weaver	*Ploceus castanops*	AF
__Southern Brown-throated Weaver	*Ploceus xanthopterus*	AF
__Kilombero Weaver	*Ploceus burnieri*	AF
__Rüppell's Weaver	*Ploceus galbula*	AF
__Northern Masked Weaver	*Ploceus taeniopterus*	AF
__Lesser Masked Weaver	*Ploceus intermedius*	AF
__Southern Masked Weaver	*Ploceus velatus*	AF
__Katanga Masked Weaver	*Ploceus katangae*	AF
__Lufira Masked Weaver	*Ploceus ruweti*	AF
__Tanzania Masked Weaver	*Ploceus reichardi*	AF
__Vitelline Masked Weaver	*Ploceus vitellinus*	AF
__Speke's Weaver	*Ploceus spekei*	AF
__Fox's Weaver	*Ploceus spekeoides*	AF
__Village Weaver	*Ploceus cucullatus*	AF
__Giant Weaver	*Ploceus grandis*	AF
__Vieillot's Black Weaver	*Ploceus nigerrimus*	AF
__Weyns's Weaver	*Ploceus weynsi*	AF
__Clarke's Weaver	*Ploceus golandi*	AF
__Juba Weaver	*Ploceus dicrocephalus*	AF
__Black-headed Weaver	*Ploceus melanocephalus*	AF
__Golden-backed Weaver	*Ploceus jacksoni*	AF
__Cinnamon Weaver	*Ploceus badius*	AF

INTERNATIONAL ENGLISH NAME	SCIENTIFIC NAME	REGION(S)
—Chestnut Weaver	*Ploceus rubiginosus*	AF
—Golden-naped Weaver	*Ploceus aureonucha*	AF
—Yellow-mantled Weaver	*Ploceus tricolor*	AF
—Maxwell's Black Weaver	*Ploceus albinucha*	AF
—Nelicourvi Weaver	*Ploceus nelicourvi*	AF
—Sakalava Weaver	*Ploceus sakalava*	AF
—Asian Golden Weaver	*Ploceus hypoxanthus*	OR
—Compact Weaver	*Ploceus superciliosus*	AF
—Black-breasted Weaver	*Ploceus benghalensis*	OR
—Streaked Weaver	*Ploceus manyar*	OR
—Baya Weaver	*Ploceus philippinus*	OR
—Finn's Weaver	*Ploceus megarhynchus*	OR
—Dark-backed Weaver	*Ploceus bicolor*	AF
—Preuss's Weaver	*Ploceus preussi*	AF
—Yellow-capped Weaver	*Ploceus dorsomaculatus*	AF
—Olive-headed Weaver	*Ploceus olivaceiceps*	AF
—Usambara Weaver	*Ploceus nicolli*	AF
—Brown-capped Weaver	*Ploceus insignis*	AF
—Bar-winged Weaver	*Ploceus angolensis*	AF
—Sao Tome Weaver	*Ploceus sanctithomae*	AF
—Yellow-legged Weaver	*Ploceus flavipes*	AF
—Red-crowned Malimbe	*Malimbus coronatus*	AF
—Cassin's Malimbe	*Malimbus cassini*	AF
—Rachel's Malimbe	*Malimbus racheliae*	AF
—Gola Malimbe	*Malimbus ballmanni*	AF
—Red-vented Malimbe	*Malimbus scutatus*	AF
—Ibadan Malimbe	*Malimbus ibadanensis*	AF
—Blue-billed Malimbe	*Malimbus nitens*	AF
—Red-headed Malimbe	*Malimbus rubricollis*	AF
—Red-bellied Malimbe	*Malimbus erythrogaster*	AF
—Crested Malimbe	*Malimbus malimbicus*	AF
—Red-headed Weaver	*Anaplectes melanotis*	AF
—Cardinal Quelea	*Quelea cardinalis*	AF
—Red-headed Quelea	*Quelea erythrops*	AF
—Red-billed Quelea	*Quelea quelea*	AF
—Red Fody	*Foudia madagascariensis*	AF
—Comoros Fody	*Foudia eminentissima*	AF
—Aldabra Fody	*Foudia aldabrana*	AF
—Forest Fody	*Foudia omissa*	AF
—Mauritius Fody	*Foudia rubra*	IO
—Seychelles Fody	*Foudia sechellarum*	IO
—Rodrigues Fody	*Foudia flavicans*	IO
—Bob-tailed Weaver	*Brachycope anomala*	AF
—Yellow-crowned Bishop	*Euplectes afer*	AF
—Fire-fronted Bishop	*Euplectes diadematus*	AF
—Black Bishop	*Euplectes gierowii*	AF
—Zanzibar Red Bishop	*Euplectes nigroventris*	AF
—Black-winged Red Bishop	*Euplectes hordeaceus*	AF
—Southern Red Bishop	*Euplectes orix*	AF
—Northern Red Bishop	*Euplectes franciscanus*	AF
—Golden-backed Bishop	*Euplectes aureus*	AF
—Yellow Bishop	*Euplectes capensis*	AF
—Fan-tailed Widowbird	*Euplectes axillaris*	AF

INTERNATIONAL ENGLISH NAME	SCIENTIFIC NAME	REGION(S)
__Yellow-mantled Widowbird	*Euplectes macroura*	AF
__Marsh Widowbird	*Euplectes hartlaubi*	AF
__Montane Widowbird	*Euplectes psammocromius*	AF
__White-winged Widowbird	*Euplectes albonotatus*	AF
__Red-collared Widowbird	*Euplectes ardens*	AF
__Long-tailed Widowbird	*Euplectes progne*	AF
__Jackson's Widowbird	*Euplectes jacksoni*	AF
WAXBILLS, MUNIAS & ALLIES	**Family Estrildidae**	
__Woodhouse's Antpecker	*Parmoptila woodhousei*	AF
__Red-fronted Antpecker	*Parmoptila rubrifrons*	AF
__Jameson's Antpecker	*Parmoptila jamesoni*	AF
__White-breasted Nigrita	*Nigrita fusconotus*	AF
__Chestnut-breasted Nigrita	*Nigrita bicolor*	AF
__Pale-fronted Nigrita	*Nigrita luteifrons*	AF
__Grey-headed Nigrita	*Nigrita canicapillus*	AF
__Shelley's Oliveback	*Nesocharis shelleyi*	AF
__White-collared Oliveback	*Nesocharis ansorgei*	AF
__Grey-headed Oliveback	*Nesocharis capistrata*	AF
__Red-billed Pytilia	*Pytilia lineata*	AF
__Red-winged Pytilia	*Pytilia phoenicoptera*	AF
__Yellow-winged Pytilia	*Pytilia hypogrammica*	AF
__Orange-winged Pytilia	*Pytilia afra*	AF
__Green-winged Pytilia	*Pytilia melba*	AF
__Red-headed Finch	*Amadina erythrocephala*	AF
__Cut-throat Finch	*Amadina fasciata*	AF
__Green Twinspot	*Mandingoa nitidula*	AF
__Red-faced Crimsonwing	*Cryptospiza reichenovii*	AF
__Abyssinian Crimsonwing	*Cryptospiza salvadorii*	AF
__Dusky Crimsonwing	*Cryptospiza jacksoni*	AF
__Shelley's Crimsonwing	*Cryptospiza shelleyi*	AF
__Black-bellied Seedcracker	*Pyrenestes ostrinus*	AF
__Crimson Seedcracker	*Pyrenestes sanguineus*	AF
__Lesser Seedcracker	*Pyrenestes minor*	AF
__Grant's Bluebill	*Spermophaga poliogenys*	AF
__Western Bluebill	*Spermophaga haematina*	AF
__Red-headed Bluebill	*Spermophaga ruficapilla*	AF
__Brown Twinspot	*Clytospiza monteiri*	AF
__Pink-throated Twinspot	*Hypargos margaritatus*	AF
__Red-throated Twinspot	*Hypargos niveoguttatus*	AF
__Dybowski's Twinspot	*Euschistospiza dybowskii*	AF
__Dusky Twinspot	*Euschistospiza cinereovinacea*	AF
__Black-bellied Firefinch	*Lagonosticta rara*	AF
__Bar-breasted Firefinch	*Lagonosticta rufopicta*	AF
__Brown Firefinch	*Lagonosticta nitidula*	AF
__Red-billed Firefinch	*Lagonosticta senegala*	AF
__Rock Firefinch	*Lagonosticta sanguinodorsalis*	AF
__Chad Firefinch	*Lagonosticta umbrinodorsalis*	AF
__Mali Firefinch	*Lagonosticta virata*	AF
__African Firefinch	*Lagonosticta rubricata*	AF
__Landana Firefinch	*Lagonosticta landanae*	AF
__Jameson's Firefinch	*Lagonosticta rhodopareia*	AF
__Black-throated Firefinch	*Lagonosticta larvata*	AF

INTERNATIONAL ENGLISH NAME	SCIENTIFIC NAME	REGION(S)
—Black-faced Firefinch	*Lagonosticta vinacea*	AF
—Blue Waxbill	*Uraeginthus angolensis*	AF
—Red-cheeked Cordon-bleu	*Uraeginthus bengalus*	AF
—Blue-capped Cordon-bleu	*Uraeginthus cyanocephalus*	AF
—Violet-eared Waxbill	*Uraeginthus granatinus*	AF
—Purple Grenadier	*Uraeginthus ianthinogaster*	AF
—Lavender Waxbill	*Estrilda caerulescens*	AF
—Grey Waxbill	*Estrilda perreini*	AF
—Cinderella Waxbill	*Estrilda thomensis*	AF
—Swee Waxbill	*Estrilda melanotis*	AF
—Yellow-bellied Waxbill	*Estrilda quartinia*	AF
—Anambra Waxbill	*Estrilda poliopareia*	AF
—Fawn-breasted Waxbill	*Estrilda paludicola*	AF
—Abyssinian Waxbill	*Estrilda ochrogaster*	AF
—Orange-cheeked Waxbill	*Estrilda melpoda*	AF
—Crimson-rumped Waxbill	*Estrilda rhodopyga*	AF
—Arabian Waxbill	*Estrilda rufibarba*	EU
—Black-rumped Waxbill	*Estrilda troglodytes*	AF
—Common Waxbill	*Estrilda astrild*	AF
—Black-lored Waxbill	*Estrilda nigriloris*	AF
—Black-crowned Waxbill	*Estrilda nonnula*	AF
—Black-headed Waxbill	*Estrilda atricapilla*	AF
—Black-faced Waxbill	*Estrilda erythronotos*	AF
—Black-cheeked Waxbill	*Estrilda charmosyna*	AF
—Red Avadavat	*Amandava amandava*	OR
—Green Avadavat	*Amandava formosa*	OR
—Orange-breasted Waxbill	*Amandava subflava*	AF
—Black-faced Quail-Finch	*Ortygospiza atricollis*	AF
—African Quail-Finch	*Ortygospiza fuscocrissa*	AF
—Black-chinned Quail-Finch	*Ortygospiza gabonensis*	AF
—Locust Finch	*Ortygospiza locustella*	AF
—Painted Finch	*Emblema pictum*	AU
—Beautiful Firetail	*Stagonopleura bella*	AU
—Red-eared Firetail	*Stagonopleura oculata*	AU
—Diamond Firetail	*Stagonopleura guttata*	AU
—Mountain Firetail	*Oreostruthus fuliginosus*	AU
—Red-browed Finch	*Neochmia temporalis*	AU
—Crimson Finch	*Neochmia phaeton*	AU
—Star Finch	*Neochmia ruficauda*	AU
—Plum-headed Finch	*Neochmia modesta*	AU
—Masked Finch	*Poephila personata*	AU
—Long-tailed Finch	*Poephila acuticauda*	AU
—Black-throated Finch	*Poephila cincta*	AU
—Zebra Finch	*Taeniopygia guttata*	AU
—Double-barred Finch	*Taeniopygia bichenovii*	AU
—Tawny-breasted Parrot-Finch	*Erythrura hyperythra*	OR, AU
—Pin-tailed Parrot-Finch	*Erythrura prasina*	OR
—Green-faced Parrot-Finch	*Erythrura viridifacies*	OR
—Tricolored Parrot-Finch	*Erythrura tricolor*	AU
—Red-eared Parrot-Finch	*Erythrura coloria*	OR
—Blue-faced Parrot-Finch	*Erythrura trichroa*	AU
—Papuan Parrot-Finch	*Erythrura papuana*	AU
—Red-throated Parrot-Finch	*Erythrura psittacea*	AU

INTERNATIONAL ENGLISH NAME	SCIENTIFIC NAME	REGION(S)
__Red-headed Parrot-Finch	*Erythrura cyaneovirens*	PO
__Pink-billed Parrot-Finch	*Erythrura kleinschmidti*	PO
__Gouldian Finch	*Erythrura gouldiae*	AU
__Madagascar Mannikin	*Lemuresthes nana*	AF
__African Silverbill	*Lonchura cantans*	AF
__Indian Silverbill	*Lonchura malabarica*	OR
__Grey-headed Silverbill	*Lonchura griseicapilla*	AF
__Bronze Mannikin	*Lonchura cucullata*	AF
__Black-and-white Mannikin	*Lonchura bicolor*	AF
__Red-backed Mannikin	*Lonchura nigriceps*	AF
__Magpie Mannikin	*Lonchura fringilloides*	AF
__White-rumped Munia	*Lonchura striata*	OR
__Javan Munia	*Lonchura leucogastroides*	OR
__Dusky Munia	*Lonchura fuscans*	OR
__Black-faced Munia	*Lonchura molucca*	AU
__Scaly-breasted Munia	*Lonchura punctulata*	OR
__Black-throated Munia	*Lonchura kelaarti*	OR
__White-bellied Munia	*Lonchura leucogastra*	OR
__Streak-headed Munia	*Lonchura tristissima*	AU
__White-spotted Munia	*Lonchura leucosticta*	AU
__Five-colored Munia	*Lonchura quinticolor*	AU
__Black-headed Munia	*Lonchura malacca*	OR
__White-headed Munia	*Lonchura maja*	OR
__Pale-headed Munia	*Lonchura pallida*	AU
__Great-billed Munia	*Lonchura grandis*	AU
__Grey-banded Munia	*Lonchura vana*	AU
__Grey-headed Munia	*Lonchura caniceps*	AU
__Grey-crowned Munia	*Lonchura nevermanni*	AU
__Hooded Munia	*Lonchura spectabilis*	AU
__New Ireland Munia	*Lonchura forbesi*	AU
__Mottled Munia	*Lonchura hunsteini*	AU
__Yellow-rumped Munia	*Lonchura flaviprymna*	AU
__Chestnut-breasted Munia	*Lonchura castaneothorax*	AU
__Black Munia	*Lonchura stygia*	AU
__Black-breasted Munia	*Lonchura teerinki*	AU
__Eastern Alpine Munia	*Lonchura monticola*	AU
__Western Alpine Munia	*Lonchura montana*	AU
__Sooty Munia	*Lonchura melaena*	AU
__Timor Sparrow	*Lonchura fuscata*	AU
__Java Sparrow	*Lonchura oryzivora*	OR
__Pictorella Munia	*Heteromunia pectoralis*	AU

INDIGOBIRDS, WHYDAHS	**Family Viduidae**	
__Village Indigobird	*Vidua chalybeata*	AF
__Purple Indigobird	*Vidua purpurascens*	AF
__Jambandu Indigobird	*Vidua raricola*	AF
__Barka Indigobird	*Vidua larvaticola*	AF
__Dusky Indigobird	*Vidua funerea*	AF
__Zambezi Indigobird	*Vidua codringtoni*	AF
__Wilson's Indigobird	*Vidua wilsoni*	AF
__Quailfinch Indigobird	*Vidua nigeriae*	AF
__Jos Plateau Indigobird	*Vidua maryae*	AF
__Camcroon Indigobird	*Vidua camerunensis*	AF

INTERNATIONAL ENGLISH NAME	SCIENTIFIC NAME	REGION(S)
—Pin-tailed Whydah	*Vidua macroura*	AF
—Steel-blue Whydah	*Vidua hypocherina*	AF
—Straw-tailed Whydah	*Vidua fischeri*	AF
—Shaft-tailed Whydah	*Vidua regia*	AF
—Long-tailed Paradise Whydah	*Vidua paradisaea*	AF
—Sahel Paradise Whydah	*Vidua orientalis*	AF
—Exclamatory Paradise Whydah	*Vidua interjecta*	AF
—Togo Paradise Whydah	*Vidua togoensis*	AF
—Broad-tailed Paradise Whydah	*Vidua obtusa*	AF
—Cuckoo Weaver	*Anomalospiza imberbis*	AF
ACCENTORS	**Family Prunellidae**	
—Alpine Accentor	*Prunella collaris*	EU
—Altai Accentor	*Prunella himalayana*	EU
—Robin Accentor	*Prunella rubeculoides*	OR
—Rufous-breasted Accentor	*Prunella strophiata*	OR
—Siberian Accentor	*Prunella montanella*	EU
—Brown Accentor	*Prunella fulvescens*	EU
—Radde's Accentor	*Prunella ocularis*	EU
—Arabian Accentor	*Prunella fagani*	EU
—Black-throated Accentor	*Prunella atrogularis*	EU
—Kozlov's Accentor	*Prunella koslowi*	EU
—Dunnock	*Prunella modularis*	EU
—Japanese Accentor	*Prunella rubida*	EU
—Maroon-backed Accentor	*Prunella immaculata*	OR
WAGTAILS, PIPITS	**Family Motacillidae**	
—Forest Wagtail	*Dendronanthus indicus*	EU
—Western Yellow Wagtail	*Motacilla flava*	EU
—Eastern Yellow Wagtail	*Motacilla tschutschensis*	EU, NA
—Citrine Wagtail	*Motacilla citreola*	EU
—Cape Wagtail	*Motacilla capensis*	AF
—Madagascar Wagtail	*Motacilla flaviventris*	AF
—Grey Wagtail	*Motacilla cinerea*	EU
—Mountain Wagtail	*Motacilla clara*	AF
—White Wagtail	*Motacilla alba*	EU
—African Pied Wagtail	*Motacilla aguimp*	AF
—Mekong Wagtail	*Motacilla samveasnae*	OR
—Japanese Wagtail	*Motacilla grandis*	EU
—White-browed Wagtail	*Motacilla madaraspatensis*	OR
—Golden Pipit	*Tmetothylacus tenellus*	AF
—Sharpe's Longclaw	*Macronyx sharpei*	AF
—Abyssinian Longclaw	*Macronyx flavicollis*	AF
—Fülleborn's Longclaw	*Macronyx fuellebornii*	AF
—Cape Longclaw	*Macronyx capensis*	AF
—Yellow-throated Longclaw	*Macronyx croceus*	AF
—Pangani Longclaw	*Macronyx aurantiigula*	AF
—Rosy-throated Longclaw	*Macronyx ameliae*	AF
—Grimwood's Longclaw	*Macronyx grimwoodi*	AF
—Richard's Pipit	*Anthus richardi*	EU
—Paddyfield Pipit	*Anthus rufulus*	OR
—Australian Pipit	*Anthus australis*	AU
—New Zealand Pipit	*Anthus novaeseelandiae*	AU

INTERNATIONAL ENGLISH NAME	SCIENTIFIC NAME	REGION(S)
__African Pipit	*Anthus cinnamomeus*	AF
__Jackson's Pipit	*Anthus latistriatus*	AF
__Mountain Pipit	*Anthus hoeschi*	AF
__Blyth's Pipit	*Anthus godlewskii*	EU
__Tawny Pipit	*Anthus campestris*	EU
__Long-billed Pipit	*Anthus similis*	AF, OR
__Wood Pipit	*Anthus nyassae*	AF
__Buffy Pipit	*Anthus vaalensis*	AF
__Long-tailed Pipit	*Anthus longicaudatus*	AF
__Plain-backed Pipit	*Anthus leucophrys*	AF
__Long-legged Pipit	*Anthus pallidiventris*	AF
__Meadow Pipit	*Anthus pratensis*	EU
__Tree Pipit	*Anthus trivialis*	EU
__Olive-backed Pipit	*Anthus hodgsoni*	EU
__Pechora Pipit	*Anthus gustavi*	EU
__Rosy Pipit	*Anthus roseatus*	EU
__Red-throated Pipit	*Anthus cervinus*	EU
__Buff-bellied Pipit	*Anthus rubescens*	NA, EU
__Water Pipit	*Anthus spinoletta*	EU
__Eurasian Rock Pipit	*Anthus petrosus*	EU
__Nilgiri Pipit	*Anthus nilghiriensis*	OR
__Upland Pipit	*Anthus sylvanus*	OR
__Berthelot's Pipit	*Anthus berthelotii*	AF
__Striped Pipit	*Anthus lineiventris*	AF
__African Rock Pipit	*Anthus crenatus*	AF
__Short-tailed Pipit	*Anthus brachyurus*	AF
__Bushveld Pipit	*Anthus caffer*	AF
__Sokoke Pipit	*Anthus sokokensis*	AF
__Malindi Pipit	*Anthus melindae*	AF
__Kimberly Pipit	*Anthus pseudosimilis*	AF
__Yellow-breasted Pipit	*Anthus chloris*	AF
__Alpine Pipit	*Anthus gutturalis*	AU
__Sprague's Pipit	*Anthus spragueii*	NA
__Yellowish Pipit	*Anthus lutescens*	SA
__Short-billed Pipit	*Anthus furcatus*	SA
__Campo Pipit	*Anthus chacoensis*	SA
__Correndera Pipit	*Anthus correndera*	SA
__South Georgia Pipit	*Anthus antarcticus*	AO
__Ochre-breasted Pipit	*Anthus nattereri*	SA
__Hellmayr's Pipit	*Anthus hellmayri*	SA
__Paramo Pipit	*Anthus bogotensis*	SA

OLIVE WARBLER — **Family Peucedramidae**

__Olive Warbler	*Peucedramus taeniatus*	NA, MA

FINCHES — **Family Fringillidae**

__Common Chaffinch	*Fringilla coelebs*	EU
__Blue Chaffinch	*Fringilla teydea*	AF
__Brambling	*Fringilla montifringilla*	EU
__Red-fronted Serin	*Serinus pusillus*	EU
__European Serin	*Serinus serinus*	EU
__Syrian Serin	*Serinus syriacus*	EU, AF
__Atlantic Canary	*Serinus canaria*	AF

INTERNATIONAL ENGLISH NAME	SCIENTIFIC NAME	REGION(S)
—Tibetan Serin	*Serinus thibetanus*	OR
—Cape Canary	*Serinus canicollis*	AF
—Yellow-crowned Canary	*Serinus flavivertex*	AF
—Ethiopian Siskin	*Serinus nigriceps*	AF
—African Citril	*Crithagra citrinelloides*	AF
—Western Citril	*Crithagra frontalis*	AF
—Southern Citril	*Crithagra hyposticta*	AF
—Black-faced Canary	*Crithagra capistrata*	AF
—Papyrus Canary	*Crithagra koliensis*	AF
—Forest Canary	*Crithagra scotops*	AF
—White-rumped Seedeater	*Crithagra leucopygia*	AF
—Black-throated Canary	*Crithagra atrogularis*	AF
—Yellow-rumped Seedeater	*Crithagra xanthopygia*	AF
—Reichenow's Seedeater	*Crithagra reichenowi*	AF
—Arabian Serin	*Crithagra rothschildi*	EU
—Yellow-throated Seedeater	*Crithagra flavigula*	AF
—Salvadori's Seedeater	*Crithagra xantholaema*	AF
—Lemon-breasted Canary	*Crithagra citrinipecta*	AF
—Yellow-fronted Canary	*Crithagra mozambica*	AF
—Northern Grosbeak-Canary	*Crithagra donaldsoni*	AF
—Southern Grosbeak-Canary	*Crithagra buchanani*	AF
—Yellow Canary	*Crithagra flaviventris*	AF
—White-bellied Canary	*Crithagra dorsostriata*	AF
—Brimstone Canary	*Crithagra sulphurata*	AF
—White-throated Canary	*Crithagra albogularis*	AF
—Reichard's Seedeater	*Crithagra reichardi*	AF
—Streaky-headed Seedeater	*Crithagra gularis*	AF
—West African Seedeater	*Crithagra canicapilla*	AF
—Black-eared Seedeater	*Crithagra mennelli*	AF
—Brown-rumped Seedeater	*Crithagra tristriata*	AF
—Ankober Serin	*Crithagra ankoberensis*	AF
—Yemen Serin	*Crithagra menachensis*	EU
—Streaky Seedeater	*Crithagra striolata*	AF
—Yellow-browed Seedeater	*Crithagra whytii*	AF
—Thick-billed Seedeater	*Crithagra burtoni*	AF
—Kipengere Seedeater	*Crithagra melanochroa*	AF
—Principe Seedeater	*Crithagra rufobrunnea*	AF
—Protea Canary	*Crithagra leucoptera*	AF
—Cape Siskin	*Crithagra totta*	AF
—Drakensberg Siskin	*Crithagra symonsi*	AF
—Black-headed Canary	*Crithagra alario*	AF
—Mountain Serin	*Serinus estherae*	OR
—Sao Tome Grosbeak	*Neospiza concolor*	AF
—Oriole Finch	*Linurgus olivaceus*	AF
—Socotra Golden-winged Grosbeak	*Rhynchostruthus socotranus*	EU
—Somali Golden-winged Grosbeak	*Rhynchostruthus louisae*	AF
—Jamaican Euphonia	*Euphonia jamaica*	NA
—Plumbeous Euphonia	*Euphonia plumbea*	SA
—Scrub Euphonia	*Euphonia affinis*	MA
—Godman's Euphonia	*Euphonia godmani*	MA
—Yellow-crowned Euphonia	*Euphonia luteicapilla*	MA
—Purple-throated Euphonia	*Euphonia chlorotica*	SA
—Trinidad Euphonia	*Euphonia trinitatis*	SA

INTERNATIONAL ENGLISH NAME	SCIENTIFIC NAME	REGION(S)
__Velvet-fronted Euphonia	*Euphonia concinna*	SA
__Orange-crowned Euphonia	*Euphonia saturata*	SA
__Finsch's Euphonia	*Euphonia finschi*	SA
__Violaceous Euphonia	*Euphonia violacea*	SA
__Thick-billed Euphonia	*Euphonia laniirostris*	LA
__Yellow-throated Euphonia	*Euphonia hirundinacea*	MA
__Green-chinned Euphonia	*Euphonia chalybea*	SA
__Elegant Euphonia	*Euphonia elegantissima*	MA
__Golden-rumped Euphonia	*Euphonia cyanocephala*	SA
__Antillean Euphonia	*Euphonia musica*	NA
__Fulvous-vented Euphonia	*Euphonia fulvicrissa*	LA
__Spot-crowned Euphonia	*Euphonia imitans*	MA
__Olive-backed Euphonia	*Euphonia gouldi*	MA
__White-lored Euphonia	*Euphonia chrysopasta*	SA
__Bronze-green Euphonia	*Euphonia mesochrysa*	SA
__White-vented Euphonia	*Euphonia minuta*	LA
__Tawny-capped Euphonia	*Euphonia anneae*	LA
__Orange-bellied Euphonia	*Euphonia xanthogaster*	LA
__Rufous-bellied Euphonia	*Euphonia rufiventris*	SA
__Chestnut-bellied Euphonia	*Euphonia pectoralis*	SA
__Golden-sided Euphonia	*Euphonia cayennensis*	SA
__Yellow-collared Chlorophonia	*Chlorophonia flavirostris*	SA
__Blue-naped Chlorophonia	*Chlorophonia cyanea*	SA
__Chestnut-breasted Chlorophonia	*Chlorophonia pyrrhophrys*	SA
__Blue-crowned Chlorophonia	*Chlorophonia occipitalis*	MA
__Golden-browed Chlorophonia	*Chlorophonia callophrys*	MA
__European Greenfinch	*Carduelis chloris*	EU
__Grey-capped Greenfinch	*Carduelis sinica*	EU
__Yellow-breasted Greenfi.nch	*Carduelis spinoides*	OR
__Vietnamese Greenfinch	*Carduelis monguilloti*	OR
__Black-headed Greenfinch	*Carduelis ambigua*	OR
__Eurasian Siskin	*Carduelis spinus*	EU
__Pine Siskin	*Carduelis pinus*	NA, MA
__Black-capped Siskin	*Carduelis atriceps*	MA
__Andean Siskin	*Carduelis spinescens*	SA
__Yellow-faced Siskin	*Carduelis yarrellii*	SA
__Red Siskin	*Carduelis cucullata*	SA
__Thick-billed Siskin	*Carduelis crassirostris*	SA
__Hooded Siskin	*Carduelis magellanica*	SA
__Antillean Siskin	*Carduelis dominicensis*	NA
__Saffron Siskin	*Carduelis siemiradzkii*	SA
__Olivaceous Siskin	*Carduelis olivacea*	SA
__Black-headed Siskin	*Carduelis notata*	MA
__Yellow-bellied Siskin	*Carduelis xanthogastra*	LA
__Black Siskin	*Carduelis atrata*	SA
__Yellow-rumped Siskin	*Carduelis uropygialis*	SA
__Black-chinned Siskin	*Carduelis barbata*	SA
__American Goldfinch	*Carduelis tristis*	NA, MA
__Lesser Goldfinch	*Carduelis psaltria*	NA, LA
__Lawrence's Goldfinch	*Carduelis lawrencei*	NA, MA
__European Goldfinch	*Carduelis carduelis*	EU
__Citril Finch	*Carduelis citrinella*	EU
__Corsican Finch	*Carduelis corsicana*	EU

INTERNATIONAL ENGLISH NAME	SCIENTIFIC NAME	REGION(S)
—Common Redpoll	*Carduelis flammea*	EU, NA
—Arctic Redpoll	*Carduelis hornemanni*	EU, NA
—Twite	*Carduelis flavirostris*	EU
—Common Linnet	*Carduelis cannabina*	EU
—Yemen Linnet	*Carduelis yemenensis*	EU
—Warsangli Linnet	*Carduelis johannis*	AF
—Plain Mountain Finch	*Leucosticte nemoricola*	OR
—Brandt's Mountain Finch	*Leucosticte brandti*	OR
—Sillem's Mountain Finch	*Leucosticte sillemi*	OR
—Asian Rosy Finch	*Leucosticte arctoa*	EU
—Grey-crowned Rosy Finch	*Leucosticte tephrocotis*	NA
—Black Rosy Finch	*Leucosticte atrata*	NA
—Brown-capped Rosy Finch	*Leucosticte australis*	NA
—Spectacled Finch	*Callacanthis burtoni*	OR
—Crimson-winged Finch	*Rhodopechys sanguineus*	EU
—Trumpeter Finch	*Bucanetes githagineus*	EU
—Mongolian Finch	*Bucanetes mongolicus*	EU
—Desert Finch	*Rhodospiza obsoleta*	EU
—Long-tailed Rosefinch	*Uragus sibiricus*	EU
—Pink-tailed Rosefinch	*Urocynchramus pylzowi*	OR
—Blanford's Rosefinch	*Carpodacus rubescens*	OR
—Dark-breasted Rosefinch	*Carpodacus nipalensis*	OR
—Common Rosefinch	*Carpodacus erythrinus*	EU
—Purple Finch	*Carpodacus purpureus*	NA
—Cassin's Finch	*Carpodacus cassinii*	NA
—House Finch	*Carpodacus mexicanus*	NA, MA
—Beautiful Rosefinch	*Carpodacus pulcherrimus*	OR
—Streseman's Rosefinch	*Carpodacus eos*	OR
—Pink-browed Rosefinch	*Carpodacus rodochroa*	OR
—Vinaceous Rosefinch	*Carpodacus vinaceus*	OR
—Dark-rumped Rosefinch	*Carpodacus edwardsii*	OR
—Sinai Rosefinch	*Carpodacus synoicus*	EU
—Pallas's Rosefinch	*Carpodacus roseus*	EU
—Three-banded Rosefinch	*Carpodacus trifasciatus*	EU
—Spot-winged Rosefinch	*Carpodacus rodopeplus*	OR
—White-browed Rosefinch	*Carpodacus thura*	OR
—Red-mantled Rosefinch	*Carpodacus rhodochlamys*	OR
—Blyth's Rosefinch	*Carpodacus grandis*	OR
—Streaked Rosefinch	*Carpodacus rubicilloides*	OR
—Great Rosefinch	*Carpodacus rubicilla*	EU
—Red-fronted Rosefinch	*Carpodacus puniceus*	OR
—Tibetan Rosefinch	*Kozlowia roborowskii*	OR
—Pine Grosbeak	*Pinicola enucleator*	EU, NA
—Crimson-browed Finch	*Pinicola subhimachala*	EU
—Scarlet Finch	*Haematospiza sipahi*	OR
—Parrot Crossbill	*Loxia pytyopsittacus*	EU
—Scottish Crossbill	*Loxia scotica*	EU
—Red Crossbill	*Loxia curvirostra*	EU, OR, NA, MA
—Two-barred Crossbill	*Loxia leucoptera*	EU, NA
—Hispaniolan Crossbill	*Loxia megaplaga*	NA
—Brown Bullfinch	*Pyrrhula nipalensis*	OR
—White-cheeked Bullfinch	*Pyrrhula leucogenis*	OR
—Orange Bullfinch	*Pyrrhula aurantiaca*	OR

INTERNATIONAL ENGLISH NAME	SCIENTIFIC NAME	REGION(S)
__Red-headed Bullfinch	*Pyrrhula erythrocephala*	OR
__Grey-headed Bullfinch	*Pyrrhula erythaca*	OR
__Eurasian Bullfinch	*Pyrrhula pyrrhula*	EU
__Hawfinch	*Coccothraustes coccothraustes*	EU
__Yellow-billed Grosbeak	*Eophona migratoria*	EU
__Japanese Grosbeak	*Eophona personata*	EU
__Black-and-yellow Grosbeak	*Mycerobas icterioides*	OR
__Collared Grosbeak	*Mycerobas affinis*	OR
__Spot-winged Grosbeak	*Mycerobas melanozanthos*	OR
__White-winged Grosbeak	*Mycerobas carnipes*	EU
__Evening Grosbeak	*Hesperiphona vespertina*	NA, MA
__Hooded Grosbeak	*Hesperiphona abeillei*	MA
__Golden-naped Finch	*Pyrrhoplectes epauletta*	OR

HAWAIIAN HONEYCREEPERS	**Family Drepanididae**	
__Laysan Finch	*Telespiza cantans*	PO
__Nihoa Finch	*Telespiza ultima*	PO
__Ou	*Psittirostra psittacea*	PO
__Palila	*Loxioides bailleui*	PO
__Maui Parrotbill	*Pseudonestor xanthophrys*	PO
__Hawaii Amakihi	*Hemignathus virens*	PO
__Oahu Amakihi	*Hemignathus flavus*	PO
__Kauai Amakihi	*Hemignathus kauaiensis*	PO
__Anianiau	*Hemignathus parvus*	PO
__Greater Akialoa	*Hemignathus ellisianus*	PO
__Nukupuu	*Hemignathus lucidus*	PO
__Akiapolaau	*Hemignathus munroi*	PO
__Akikiki	*Oreomystis bairdi*	PO
__Hawaii Creeper	*Oreomystis mana*	PO
__Oahu Alauahio	*Paroreomyza maculata*	PO
__Kakawahie	*Paroreomyza flammea*	PO
__Maui Alauahio	*Paroreomyza montana*	PO
__Akekee	*Loxops caeruleirostris*	PO
__Akepa	*Loxops coccineus*	PO
__Iiwi	*Vestiaria coccinea*	PO
__Akohekohe	*Palmeria dolei*	PO
__Apapane	*Himatione sanguinea*	PO
__Poo-uli	*Melamprosops phaeosoma*	PO

NEW WORLD WARBLERS	**Family Parulidae**	
__Bachman's Warbler	*Vermivora bachmanii*	NA
__Golden-winged Warbler	*Vermivora chrysoptera*	NA
__Blue-winged Warbler	*Vermivora pinus*	NA
__Tennessee Warbler	*Vermivora peregrina*	NA
__Orange-crowned Warbler	*Vermivora celata*	NA
__Nashville Warbler	*Vermivora ruficapilla*	NA
__Virginia's Warbler	*Vermivora virginiae*	NA
__Colima Warbler	*Vermivora crissalis*	NA
__Lucy's Warbler	*Vermivora luciae*	NA, MA
__Flame-throated Warbler	*Parula gutturalis*	MA
__Crescent-chested Warbler	*Parula superciliosa*	MA
__Northern Parula	*Parula americana*	NA

INTERNATIONAL ENGLISH NAME	SCIENTIFIC NAME	REGION(S)
—Tropical Parula	*Parula pitiayumi*	LA
—Chestnut-sided Warbler	*Dendroica pensylvanica*	NA
—American Yellow Warbler	*Dendroica petechia*	NA, MA
—Mangrove Warbler	*Dendroica erithachorides*	LA
—Blackpoll Warbler	*Dendroica striata*	NA
—Bay-breasted Warbler	*Dendroica castanea*	NA
—Blackburnian Warbler	*Dendroica fusca*	NA
—Magnolia Warbler	*Dendroica magnolia*	NA
—Cerulean Warbler	*Dendroica cerulea*	NA
—Cape May Warbler	*Dendroica tigrina*	NA
—Black-throated Blue Warbler	*Dendroica caerulescens*	NA
—Yellow-rumped Warbler	*Dendroica coronata*	NA
—Black-throated Grey Warbler	*Dendroica nigrescens*	NA
—Golden-cheeked Warbler	*Dendroica chrysoparia*	NA
—Black-throated Green Warbler	*Dendroica virens*	NA
—Townsend's Warbler	*Dendroica townsendi*	NA
—Hermit Warbler	*Dendroica occidentalis*	NA
—Yellow-throated Warbler	*Dendroica dominica*	NA
—Grace's Warbler	*Dendroica graciae*	NA
—Prairie Warbler	*Dendroica discolor*	NA
—Vitelline Warbler	*Dendroica vitellina*	NA
—Adelaide's Warbler	*Dendroica adelaidae*	NA
—Barbuda Warbler	*Dendroica subita*	NA
—St. Lucia Warbler	*Dendroica delicata*	NA
—Olive-capped Warbler	*Dendroica pityophila*	NA
—Pine Warbler	*Dendroica pinus*	NA
—Kirtland's Warbler	*Dendroica kirtlandii*	NA
—Palm Warbler	*Dendroica palmarum*	NA
—Plumbeous Warbler	*Dendroica plumbea*	NA
—Arrowhead Warbler	*Dendroica pharetra*	NA
—Elfin Woods Warbler	*Dendroica angelae*	NA
—Whistling Warbler	*Catharopeza bishopi*	NA
—Black-and-white Warbler	*Mniotilta varia*	NA
—American Redstart	*Setophaga ruticilla*	NA
—Prothonotary Warbler	*Protonotaria citrea*	NA
—Worm-eating Warbler	*Helmitheros vermivorum*	NA
—Swainson's Warbler	*Limnothlypis swainsonii*	NA
—Ovenbird	*Seiurus aurocapilla*	NA
—Northern Waterthrush	*Seiurus noveboracensis*	NA
—Louisiana Waterthrush	*Seiurus motacilla*	NA
—Kentucky Warbler	*Oporornis formosus*	NA
—Connecticut Warbler	*Oporornis agilis*	NA
—Mourning Warbler	*Oporornis philadelphia*	NA
—MacGillivray's Warbler	*Oporornis tolmiei*	NA
—Common Yellowthroat	*Geothlypis trichas*	NA, MA
—Belding's Yellowthroat	*Geothlypis beldingi*	MA
—Altamira Yellowthroat	*Geothlypis flavovelata*	MA
—Bahama Yellowthroat	*Geothlypis rostrata*	NA
—Olive-crowned Yellowthroat	*Geothlypis semiflava*	LA
—Black-polled Yellowthroat	*Geothlypis speciosa*	MA
—Hooded Yellowthroat	*Geothlypis nelsoni*	MA
—Masked Yellowthroat	*Geothlypis aequinoctialis*	SA
—Chiriqui Yellowthroat	*Geothlypis chiriquensis*	MA

INTERNATIONAL ENGLISH NAME	SCIENTIFIC NAME	REGION(S)
—Black-lored Yellowthroat	*Geothlypis auricularis*	SA
—Southern Yellowthroat	*Geothlypis velata*	SA
—Grey-crowned Yellowthroat	*Chamaethlypis poliocephala*	MA
—Green-tailed Warbler	*Microligea palustris*	NA
—Yellow-headed Warbler	*Teretistris fernandinae*	NA
—Oriente Warbler	*Teretistris fornsi*	NA
—Semper's Warbler	*Leucopeza semperi*	NA
—Hooded Warbler	*Wilsonia citrina*	NA
—Wilson's Warbler	*Wilsonia pusilla*	NA
—Canada Warbler	*Wilsonia canadensis*	NA
—Red-faced Warbler	*Cardellina rubrifrons*	NA, MA
—Red Warbler	*Ergaticus ruber*	MA
—Pink-headed Warbler	*Ergaticus versicolor*	MA
—Painted Whitestart	*Myioborus pictus*	NA, MA
—Slate-throated Whitestart	*Myioborus miniatus*	LA
—Brown-capped Whitestart	*Myioborus brunniceps*	SA
—Tepui Whitestart	*Myioborus castaneocapillus*	SA
—Paria Whitestart	*Myioborus pariae*	SA
—Guaiquinima Whitestart	*Myioborus cardonai*	SA
—Collared Whitestart	*Myioborus torquatus*	MA
—Golden-fronted Whitestart	*Myioborus ornatus*	SA
—Spectacled Whitestart	*Myioborus melanocephalus*	SA
—White-fronted Whitestart	*Myioborus albifrons*	SA
—Yellow-crowned Whitestart	*Myioborus flavivertex*	SA
—White-faced Whitestart	*Myioborus albifacies*	SA
—Fan-tailed Warbler	*Euthlypis lachrymosa*	MA
—Grey-and-gold Warbler	*Basileuterus fraseri*	SA
—Two-banded Warbler	*Basileuterus bivittatus*	SA
—Roraiman Warbler	*Basileuterus roraimae*	SA
—Cuzco Warbler	*Basileuterus chrysogaster*	SA
—Choco Warbler	*Basileuterus chlorophrys*	SA
—Flavescent Warbler	*Basileuterus flaveolus*	SA
—Citrine Warbler	*Basileuterus luteoviridis*	SA
—Pale-legged Warbler	*Basileuterus signatus*	SA
—Black-crested Warbler	*Basileuterus nigrocristatus*	SA
—Grey-headed Warbler	*Basileuterus griseiceps*	SA
—Santa Marta Warbler	*Basileuterus basilicus*	SA
—Grey-throated Warbler	*Basileuterus cinereicollis*	SA
—White-lored Warbler	*Basileuterus conspicillatus*	SA
—Russet-crowned Warbler	*Basileuterus coronatus*	SA
—Stripe-crowned Warbler	*Basileuterus culicivorus*	LA
—White-bellied Warbler	*Basileuterus hypoleucus*	SA
—Rufous-capped Warbler	*Basileuterus rufifrons*	MA
—Chestnut-capped Warbler	*Basileuterus delattrii*	LA
—Golden-browed Warbler	*Basileuterus belli*	MA
—Black-cheeked Warbler	*Basileuterus melanogenys*	MA
—Pirre Warbler	*Basileuterus ignotus*	LA
—Three-striped Warbler	*Basileuterus tristriatus*	LA
—Three-banded Warbler	*Basileuterus trifasciatus*	SA
—White-rimmed Warbler	*Basileuterus leucoblepharus*	SA
—White-striped Warbler	*Basileuterus leucophrys*	SA
—Buff-rumped Warbler	*Phaeothlypis fulvicauda*	LA
—Riverbank Warbler	*Phaeothlypis rivularis*	SA

INTERNATIONAL ENGLISH NAME	SCIENTIFIC NAME	REGION(S)
FAMILY UNCERTAIN	**Incertae Sedis**	
—Wrenthrush	*Zeledonia coronata*	MA
—Yellow-breasted Chat	*Icteria virens*	NA, MA
—Red-breasted Chat	*Granatellus venustus*	MA
—Grey-throated Chat	*Granatellus sallaei*	MA
—Rose-breasted Chat	*Granatellus pelzelni*	SA
—White-winged Warbler	*Xenoligea montana*	NA
NEW WORLD BLACKBIRDS	**Family Icteridae**	
—Casqued Oropendola	*Clypicterus oseryi*	SA
—Chestnut-headed Oropendola	*Zarhynchus wagleri*	LA
—Crested Oropendola	*Psarocolius decumanus*	SA
—Green Oropendola	*Psarocolius viridis*	SA
—Dusky-green Oropendola	*Psarocolius atrovirens*	SA
—Russet-backed Oropendola	*Psarocolius angustifrons*	SA
—Montezuma Oropendola	*Psarocolius montezuma*	MA
—Baudo Oropendola	*Psarocolius cassini*	SA
—Para Oropendola	*Psarocolius bifasciatus*	SA
—Olive Oropendola	*Psarocolius yuracares*	SA
—Black Oropendola	*Psarocolius guatimozinus*	LA
—Band-tailed Oropendola	*Ocyalus latirostris*	SA
—Yellow-rumped Cacique	*Cacicus cela*	LA
—Red-rumped Cacique	*Cacicus haemorrhous*	SA
—Subtropical Cacique	*Cacicus uropygialis*	LA
—Scarlet-rumped Cacique	*Cacicus microrhynchus*	MA
—Golden-winged Cacique	*Cacicus chrysopterus*	SA
—Southern Mountain Cacique	*Cacicus chrysonotus*	SA
—Northern Mountain Cacique	*Cacicus leucoramphus*	SA
—Ecuadorian Cacique	*Cacicus sclateri*	SA
—Selva Cacique	*Cacicus koepckeae*	SA
—Solitary Cacique	*Cacicus solitarius*	SA
—Mexican Cacique	*Cacicus melanicterus*	SA
—Yellow-billed Cacique	*Amblycercus holosericeus*	LA
—Venezuelan Troupial	*Icterus icterus*	SA
—Orange-backed Troupial	*Icterus croconotus*	SA
—Campo Troupial	*Icterus jamaicaii*	SA
—Spot-breasted Oriole	*Icterus pectoralis*	MA
—White-edged Oriole	*Icterus graceannae*	SA
—Yellow-tailed Oriole	*Icterus mesomelas*	LA
—Epaulet Oriole	*Icterus cayanensis*	SA
—Moriche Oriole	*Icterus chrysocephalus*	SA
—Martinique Oriole	*Icterus bonana*	NA
—St. Lucia Oriole	*Icterus laudabilis*	NA
—Montserrat Oriole	*Icterus oberi*	NA
—Greater Antillean Oriole	*Icterus dominicensis*	NA
—Black-cowled Oriole	*Icterus prosthemelas*	MA
—Orchard Oriole	*Icterus spurius*	NA, MA
—Ochre Oriole	*Icterus fuertesi*	MA
—Hooded Oriole	*Icterus cucullatus*	NA, MA
—Black-vented Oriole	*Icterus wagleri*	MA
—Bar-winged Oriole	*Icterus maculialatus*	MA
—Scott's Oriole	*Icterus parisorum*	NA, MA
—Orange-crowned Oriole	*Icterus auricapillus*	LA

INTERNATIONAL ENGLISH NAME	SCIENTIFIC NAME	REGION(S)
—Yellow-backed Oriole	*Icterus chrysater*	LA
—Audubon's Oriole	*Icterus graduacauda*	NA, MA
—Baltimore Oriole	*Icterus galbula*	NA
—Black-backed Oriole	*Icterus abeillei*	MA
—Bullock's Oriole	*Icterus bullockii*	NA
—Streak-backed Oriole	*Icterus pustulatus*	MA
—Jamaican Oriole	*Icterus leucopteryx*	NA
—Orange Oriole	*Icterus auratus*	MA
—Yellow Oriole	*Icterus nigrogularis*	SA
—Altamira Oriole	*Icterus gularis*	NA, MA
—Jamaican Blackbird	*Nesopsar nigerrimus*	NA
—Oriole Blackbird	*Gymnomystax mexicanus*	SA
—Colombian Mountain Grackle	*Macroagelaius subalaris*	SA
—Golden-tufted Mountain Grackle	*Macroagelaius imthurni*	SA
—Red-bellied Grackle	*Hypopyrrhus pyrohypogaster*	SA
—Velvet-fronted Grackle	*Lampropsar tanagrinus*	SA
—Chopi Blackbird	*Gnorimopsar chopi*	SA
—Austral Blackbird	*Curaeus curaeus*	SA
—Forbes's Blackbird	*Curaeus forbesi*	SA
—Scarlet-headed Blackbird	*Amblyramphus holosericeus*	SA
—Pale-eyed Blackbird	*Agelasticus xanthophthalmus*	SA
—Unicolored Blackbird	*Agelasticus cyanopus*	SA
—Yellow-winged Blackbird	*Agelasticus thilius*	SA
—Chestnut-capped Blackbird	*Chrysomus ruficapillus*	SA
—Yellow-hooded Blackbird	*Chrysomus icterocephalus*	SA
—Saffron-cowled Blackbird	*Xanthopsar flavus*	SA
—Yellow-rumped Marshbird	*Pseudoleistes guirahuro*	SA
—Brown-and-yellow Marshbird	*Pseudoleistes virescens*	SA
—Bolivian Blackbird	*Agelaioides oreopsar*	SA
—Baywing	*Agelaioides badius*	SA
—Screaming Cowbird	*Molothrus rufoaxillaris*	SA
—Giant Cowbird	*Molothrus oryzivorus*	LA
—Bronzed Cowbird	*Molothrus aeneus*	NA, MA
—Bronze-brown Cowbird	*Molothrus armenti*	SA
—Shiny Cowbird	*Molothrus bonariensis*	NA, SA
—Brown-headed Cowbird	*Molothrus ater*	NA, MA
—Cuban Blackbird	*Dives atroviolaceus*	NA
—Melodious Blackbird	*Dives dives*	MA
—Scrub Blackbird	*Dives warszewiczi*	SA
—Red-winged Blackbird	*Agelaius phoeniceus*	NA, MA
—Red-shouldered Blackbird	*Agelaius assimilis*	NA
—Tricolored Blackbird	*Agelaius tricolor*	NA
—Tawny-shouldered Blackbird	*Agelaius humeralis*	NA
—Yellow-shouldered Blackbird	*Agelaius xanthomus*	NA
—Rusty Blackbird	*Euphagus carolinus*	NA
—Brewer's Blackbird	*Euphagus cyanocephalus*	NA
—Common Grackle	*Quiscalus quiscula*	NA
—Carib Grackle	*Quiscalus lugubris*	NA, SA
—Great-tailed Grackle	*Quiscalus mexicanus*	NA, LA
—Boat-tailed Grackle	*Quiscalus major*	NA
—Nicaraguan Grackle	*Quiscalus nicaraguensis*	MA
—Greater Antillean Grackle	*Quiscalus niger*	NA
—Red-breasted Blackbird	*Sturnella militaris*	LA

INTERNATIONAL ENGLISH NAME	SCIENTIFIC NAME	REGION(S)
_White-browed Blackbird	*Sturnella superciliaris*	SA
_Peruvian Meadowlark	*Sturnella bellicosa*	SA
_Pampas Meadowlark	*Sturnella defilippii*	SA
_Long-tailed Meadowlark	*Sturnella loyca*	SA
_Eastern Meadowlark	*Sturnella magna*	NA, LA
_Western Meadowlark	*Sturnella neglecta*	NA, MA
_Yellow-headed Blackbird	*Xanthocephalus xanthocephalus*	NA, MA
_Bobolink	*Dolichonyx oryzivorus*	NA
BANANAQUIT	**Family Coerebidae**	
_Bananaquit	*Coereba flaveola*	LA
BUNTINGS, NEW WORLD SPARROWS & ALLIES	**Family Emberizidae**	
_Crested Bunting	*Melophus lathami*	OR
_Slaty Bunting	*Latoucheornis siemsseni*	EU
_Corn Bunting	*Emberiza calandra*	EU
_Yellowhammer	*Emberiza citrinella*	EU
_Pine Bunting	*Emberiza leucocephalos*	EU
_Rock Bunting	*Emberiza cia*	EU
_Godlewski's Bunting	*Emberiza godlewskii*	EU
_Meadow Bunting	*Emberiza cioides*	EU
_White-capped Bunting	*Emberiza stewarti*	OR
_Jankowski's Bunting	*Emberiza jankowskii*	EU
_Grey-necked Bunting	*Emberiza buchanani*	EU
_Cinereous Bunting	*Emberiza cineracea*	EU
_Ortolan Bunting	*Emberiza hortulana*	EU
_Cretzschmar's Bunting	*Emberiza caesia*	EU
_Cirl Bunting	*Emberiza cirlus*	EU
_House Bunting	*Emberiza striolata*	AF
_Lark-like Bunting	*Emberiza impetuani*	AF
_Cinnamon-breasted Bunting	*Emberiza tahapisi*	AF
_Socotra Bunting	*Emberiza socotrana*	EU
_Cape Bunting	*Emberiza capensis*	AF
_Vincent's Bunting	*Emberiza vincenti*	AF
_Tristram's Bunting	*Emberiza tristrami*	EU
_Chestnut-eared Bunting	*Emberiza fucata*	EU
_Little Bunting	*Emberiza pusilla*	EU
_Yellow-browed Bunting	*Emberiza chrysophrys*	EU
_Rustic Bunting	*Emberiza rustica*	EU
_Yellow-throated Bunting	*Emberiza elegans*	EU
_Yellow-breasted Bunting	*Emberiza aureola*	EU
_Somali Bunting	*Emberiza poliopleura*	AF
_Golden-breasted Bunting	*Emberiza flaviventris*	AF
_Brown-rumped Bunting	*Emberiza affinis*	AF
_Cabanis's Bunting	*Emberiza cabanisi*	AF
_Chestnut Bunting	*Emberiza rutila*	EU
_Tibetan Bunting	*Emberiza koslowi*	EU
_Black-headed Bunting	*Emberiza melanocephala*	EU
_Red-headed Bunting	*Emberiza bruniceps*	EU
_Yellow Bunting	*Emberiza sulphurata*	EU
_Black-faced Bunting	*Emberiza spodocephala*	EU
_Grey Bunting	*Emberiza variabilis*	EU
_Pallas's Reed Bunting	*Emberiza pallasi*	EU

INTERNATIONAL ENGLISH NAME	SCIENTIFIC NAME	REGION(S)
—Japanese Reed Bunting	*Emberiza yessoensis*	EU
—Common Reed Bunting	*Emberiza schoeniclus*	EU
—McCown's Longspur	*Calcarius mccownii*	NA
—Lapland Longspur	*Calcarius lapponicus*	NA, EU
—Smith's Longspur	*Calcarius pictus*	NA
—Chestnut-collared Longspur	*Calcarius ornatus*	NA
—Snow Bunting	*Plectrophenax nivalis*	NA, EU
—McKay's Bunting	*Plectrophenax hyperboreus*	NA
—Lark Bunting	*Calamospiza melanocorys*	NA
—Fox Sparrow	*Passerella iliaca*	NA
—Song Sparrow	*Melospiza melodia*	NA
—Lincoln's Sparrow	*Melospiza lincolnii*	NA
—Swamp Sparrow	*Melospiza georgiana*	NA
—Rufous-collared Sparrow	*Zonotrichia capensis*	LA
—Harris's Sparrow	*Zonotrichia querula*	NA
—White-crowned Sparrow	*Zonotrichia leucophrys*	NA
—White-throated Sparrow	*Zonotrichia albicollis*	NA
—Golden-crowned Sparrow	*Zonotrichia atricapilla*	NA
—Volcano Junco	*Junco vulcani*	MA
—Dark-eyed Junco	*Junco hyemalis*	NA
—Guadalupe Junco	*Junco insularis*	MA
—Yellow-eyed Junco	*Junco phaeonotus*	NA, MA
—Savannah Sparrow	*Passerculus sandwichensis*	NA, MA
—Large-billed Sparrow	*Passerculus rostratus*	MA
—Seaside Sparrow	*Ammodramus maritimus*	NA
—Nelson's Sparrow	*Ammodramus nelsoni*	NA
—Saltmarsh Sparrow	*Ammodramus caudacutus*	NA
—Le Conte's Sparrow	*Ammodramus leconteii*	NA
—Baird's Sparrow	*Ammodramus bairdii*	NA
—Henslow's Sparrow	*Ammodramus henslowii*	NA
—Grasshopper Sparrow	*Ammodramus savannarum*	NA, MA
—Sierra Madre Sparrow	*Xenospiza baileyi*	MA
—Grassland Sparrow	*Myospiza humeralis*	SA
—Yellow-browed Sparrow	*Myospiza aurifrons*	SA
—American Tree Sparrow	*Spizella arborea*	NA
—Chipping Sparrow	*Spizella passerina*	NA, MA
—Field Sparrow	*Spizella pusilla*	NA
—Worthen's Sparrow	*Spizella wortheni*	MA
—Black-chinned Sparrow	*Spizella atrogularis*	NA, MA
—Clay-colored Sparrow	*Spizella pallida*	NA
—Brewer's Sparrow	*Spizella breweri*	NA
—Timberline Sparrow	*Spizella taverneri*	NA
—Vesper Sparrow	*Pooecetes gramineus*	NA
—Lark Sparrow	*Chondestes grammacus*	NA
—Black-throated Sparrow	*Amphispiza bilineata*	NA, MA
—Sage Sparrow	*Amphispiza belli*	NA, MA
—Stripe-headed Sparrow	*Aimophila ruficauda*	MA
—Black-chested Sparrow	*Aimophila humeralis*	MA
—Bridled Sparrow	*Aimophila mystacalis*	MA
—Cinnamon-tailed Sparrow	*Aimophila sumichrasti*	MA
—Tumbes Sparrow	*Aimophila stolzmanni*	SA
—Stripe-capped Sparrow	*Aimophila strigiceps*	SA
—Rufous-winged Sparrow	*Aimophila carpalis*	NA, MA

INTERNATIONAL ENGLISH NAME	SCIENTIFIC NAME	REGION(S)
—Cassin's Sparrow	*Aimophila cassinii*	NA, MA
—Bachman's Sparrow	*Aimophila aestivalis*	NA
—Botteri's Sparrow	*Aimophila botterii*	NA, MA
—Rufous-crowned Sparrow	*Aimophila ruficeps*	NA, MA
—Rusty Sparrow	*Aimophila rufescens*	MA
—Oaxaca Sparrow	*Aimophila notosticta*	MA
—Five-striped Sparrow	*Aimophila quinquestriata*	MA
—Zapata Sparrow	*Torreornis inexpectata*	NA
—Striped Sparrow	*Oriturus superciliosus*	MA
—Blue Finch	*Porphyrospiza caerulescens*	SA
—Green-tailed Towhee	*Pipilo chlorurus*	NA
—Collared Towhee	*Pipilo ocai*	MA
—Spotted Towhee	*Pipilo maculatus*	NA, MA
—Eastern Towhee	*Pipilo erythrophthalmus*	NA
—White-throated Towhee	*Pipilo albicollis*	MA
—Canyon Towhee	*Pipilo fuscus*	NA, MA
—California Towhee	*Pipilo crissalis*	NA
—Abert's Towhee	*Pipilo aberti*	NA, MA
—Rusty-crowned Ground Sparrow	*Melozone kieneri*	MA
—Prevost's Ground Sparrow	*Melozone biarcuata*	MA
—Cabanis's Ground Sparrow	*Melozone cabanisi*	MA
—White-eared Ground Sparrow	*Melozone leucotis*	MA
—Olive Sparrow	*Arremonops rufivirgatus*	NA, MA
—Tocuyo Sparrow	*Arremonops tocuyensis*	SA
—Green-backed Sparrow	*Arremonops chloronotus*	MA
—Black-striped Sparrow	*Arremonops conirostris*	LA
—Pectoral Sparrow	*Arremon taciturnus*	SA
—Half-collared Sparrow	*Arremon semitorquatus*	SA
—Sao Francisco Sparrow	*Arremon franciscanus*	SA
—Saffron-billed Sparrow	*Arremon flavirostris*	SA
—Orange-billed Sparrow	*Arremon aurantiirostris*	LA
—Golden-winged Sparrow	*Arremon schlegeli*	SA
—Black-capped Sparrow	*Arremon abeillei*	SA
—Chestnut-capped Brush Finch	*Buarremon brunneinucha*	LA
—Green-striped Brush Finch	*Buarremon virenticeps*	MA
—Stripe-headed Brush Finch	*Buarremon torquatus*	LA
—Black-headed Brush Finch	*Buarremon atricapillus*	LA
—Large-footed Finch	*Pezopetes capitalis*	MA
—Sooty-faced Finch	*Lysurus crassirostris*	MA
—Olive Finch	*Lysurus castaneiceps*	SA
—Rufous-capped Brush Finch	*Atlapetes pileatus*	MA
—Moustached Brush Finch	*Atlapetes albofrenatus*	SA
—Ochre-breasted Brush Finch	*Atlapetes semirufus*	SA
—Tepui Brush Finch	*Atlapetes personatus*	SA
—White-naped Brush Finch	*Atlapetes albinucha*	MA
—Yellow-throated Brush Finch	*Atlapetes gutturalis*	LA
—Santa Marta Brush Finch	*Atlapetes melanocephalus*	SA
—Pale-naped Brush Finch	*Atlapetes pallidinucha*	SA
—Yellow-headed Brush Finch	*Atlapetes flaviceps*	SA
—Dusky-headed Brush Finch	*Atlapetes fuscoolivaceus*	SA
—Choco Brush Finch	*Atlapetes crassus*	SA
—Tricolored Brush Finch	*Atlapetes tricolor*	SA
—White-rimmed Brush Finch	*Atlapetes leucopis*	SA

INTERNATIONAL ENGLISH NAME	SCIENTIFIC NAME	REGION(S)
__Rufous-naped Brush Finch	*Atlapetes latinuchus*	SA
__Rufous-eared Brush Finch	*Atlapetes rufigenis*	SA
__Apurimac Brush Finch	*Atlapetes forbesi*	SA
__Black-spectacled Brush Finch	*Atlapetes melanopsis*	SA
__Slaty Brush Finch	*Atlapetes schistaceus*	SA
__White-winged Brush Finch	*Atlapetes leucopterus*	SA
__White-headed Brush Finch	*Atlapetes albiceps*	SA
__Pale-headed Brush Finch	*Atlapetes pallidiceps*	SA
__Bay-crowned Brush Finch	*Atlapetes seebohmi*	SA
__Rusty-bellied Brush Finch	*Atlapetes nationi*	SA
__Cuzco Brush Finch	*Atlapetes canigenis*	SA
__Vilcabamba Brush Finch	*Atlapetes terborghi*	SA
__Grey-eared Brush Finch	*Atlapetes melanolaemus*	SA
__Bolivian Brush Finch	*Atlapetes rufinucha*	SA
__Fulvous-headed Brush Finch	*Atlapetes fulviceps*	SA
__Yellow-striped Brush Finch	*Atlapetes citrinellus*	SA
__Yellow-thighed Finch	*Pselliophorus tibialis*	MA
__Yellow-green Finch	*Pselliophorus luteoviridis*	MA
__Yellow Cardinal	*Gubernatrix cristata*	SA
__Red-crested Cardinal	*Paroaria coronata*	SA
__Red-cowled Cardinal	*Paroaria dominicana*	SA
__Red-capped Cardinal	*Paroaria gularis*	SA
__Crimson-fronted Cardinal	*Paroaria baeri*	SA
__Yellow-billed Cardinal	*Paroaria capitata*	SA
TANAGERS & ALLIES	**Family Thraupidae**	
__Brown Tanager	*Orchesticus abeillei*	SA
__Cinnamon Tanager	*Schistochlamys ruficapillus*	SA
__Black-faced Tanager	*Schistochlamys melanopis*	SA
__Magpie Tanager	*Cissopis leverianus*	SA
__Black-and-white Tanager	*Conothraupis speculigera*	SA
__Cone-billed Tanager	*Conothraupis mesoleuca*	SA
__Red-billed Pied Tanager	*Lamprospiza melanoleuca*	SA
__Scarlet-throated Tanager	*Compsothraupis loricata*	SA
__White-capped Tanager	*Sericossypha albocristata*	SA
__Hooded Tanager	*Nemosia pileata*	SA
__Cherry-throated Tanager	*Nemosia rourei*	SA
__Rufous-crested Tanager	*Creurgops verticalis*	SA
__Slaty Tanager	*Creurgops dentatus*	SA
__Dusky-faced Tanager	*Mitrospingus cassinii*	LA
__Olive-backed Tanager	*Mitrospingus oleagineus*	SA
__Carmioli's Tanager	*Chlorothraupis carmioli*	MA
__Olive Tanager	*Chlorothraupis frenata*	SA
__Lemon-spectacled Tanager	*Chlorothraupis olivacea*	LA
__Ochre-breasted Tanager	*Chlorothraupis stolzmanni*	SA
__Olive-green Tanager	*Orthogonys chloricterus*	SA
__Black-capped Hemispingus	*Hemispingus atropileus*	SA
__White-browed Hemispingus	*Hemispingus auricularis*	SA
__Orange-browed Hemispingus	*Hemispingus calophrys*	SA
__Parodi's Hemispingus	*Hemispingus parodii*	SA
__Superciliaried Hemispingus	*Hemispingus superciliaris*	SA
__Grey-capped Hemispingus	*Hemispingus reyi*	SA
__Oleaginous Hemispingus	*Hemispingus frontalis*	SA

INTERNATIONAL ENGLISH NAME	SCIENTIFIC NAME	REGION(S)
—Black-eared Hemispingus	*Hemispingus melanotis*	SA
—Western Hemispingus	*Hemispingus ochraceus*	SA
—Piura Hemispingus	*Hemispingus piurae*	SA
—Slaty-backed Hemispingus	*Hemispingus goeringi*	SA
—Rufous-browed Hemispingus	*Hemispingus rufosuperciliaris*	SA
—Black-headed Hemispingus	*Hemispingus verticalis*	SA
—Drab Hemispingus	*Hemispingus xanthophthalmus*	SA
—Three-striped Hemispingus	*Hemispingus trifasciatus*	SA
—Grey-hooded Bush Tanager	*Cnemoscopus rubrirostris*	SA
—Fulvous-headed Tanager	*Thlypopsis fulviceps*	SA
—Rufous-chested Tanager	*Thlypopsis ornata*	SA
—Brown-flanked Tanager	*Thlypopsis pectoralis*	SA
—Orange-headed Tanager	*Thlypopsis sordida*	SA
—Buff-bellied Tanager	*Thlypopsis inornata*	SA
—Rust-and-yellow Tanager	*Thlypopsis ruficeps*	SA
—Chestnut-headed Tanager	*Pyrrhocoma ruficeps*	SA
—White-rumped Tanager	*Cypsnagra hirundinacea*	SA
—Pardusco	*Nephelornis oneilli*	SA
—Black-goggled Tanager	*Trichothraupis melanops*	SA
—Grey-headed Tanager	*Eucometis penicillata*	LA
—Flame-crested Tanager	*Tachyphonus cristatus*	SA
—Yellow-crested Tanager	*Tachyphonus rufiventer*	SA
—Fulvous-crested Tanager	*Tachyphonus surinamus*	SA
—White-shouldered Tanager	*Tachyphonus luctuosus*	LA
—Tawny-crested Tanager	*Tachyphonus delatrii*	LA
—Ruby-crowned Tanager	*Tachyphonus coronatus*	SA
—White-lined Tanager	*Tachyphonus rufus*	LA
—Red-shouldered Tanager	*Tachyphonus phoenicius*	SA
—Black-throated Shrike-Tanager	*Lanio aurantius*	MA
—White-throated Shrike-Tanager	*Lanio leucothorax*	MA
—Fulvous Shrike-Tanager	*Lanio fulvus*	SA
—White-winged Shrike-Tanager	*Lanio versicolor*	SA
—Crimson-collared Tanager	*Phlogothraupis sanguinolenta*	MA
—Masked Crimson Tanager	*Ramphocelus nigrogularis*	SA
—Crimson-backed Tanager	*Ramphocelus dimidiatus*	LA
—Huallaga Tanager	*Ramphocelus melanogaster*	SA
—Silver-beaked Tanager	*Ramphocelus carbo*	SA
—Brazilian Tanager	*Ramphocelus bresilius*	SA
—Passerini's Tanager	*Ramphocelus passerinii*	MA
—Cherrie's Tanager	*Ramphocelus costaricensis*	MA
—Flame-rumped Tanager	*Ramphocelus flammigerus*	SA
—Lemon-rumped Tanager	*Ramphocelus icteronotus*	LA
—Blue-grey Tanager	*Thraupis episcopus*	LA
—Sayaca Tanager	*Thraupis sayaca*	SA
—Glaucous Tanager	*Thraupis glaucocolpa*	SA
—Azure-shouldered Tanager	*Thraupis cyanoptera*	SA
—Golden-chevroned Tanager	*Thraupis ornata*	SA
—Yellow-winged Tanager	*Thraupis abbas*	MA
—Palm Tanager	*Thraupis palmarum*	LA
—Blue-capped Tanager	*Thraupis cyanocephala*	SA
—Blue-and-yellow Tanager	*Thraupis bonariensis*	SA
—Vermilion Tanager	*Calochaetes coccineus*	SA
—Blue-backed Tanager	*Cyanicterus cyanicterus*	SA

INTERNATIONAL ENGLISH NAME	SCIENTIFIC NAME	REGION(S)
__Blue-and-gold Tanager	*Bangsia arcaei*	MA
__Black-and-gold Tanager	*Bangsia melanochlamys*	SA
__Golden-chested Tanager	*Bangsia rothschildi*	SA
__Moss-backed Tanager	*Bangsia edwardsi*	SA
__Gold-ringed Tanager	*Bangsia aureocincta*	SA
__Orange-throated Tanager	*Wetmorethraupis sterrhopteron*	SA
__Hooded Mountain Tanager	*Buthraupis montana*	SA
__Black-chested Mountain Tanager	*Buthraupis eximia*	SA
__Golden-backed Mountain Tanager	*Buthraupis aureodorsalis*	SA
__Masked Mountain Tanager	*Buthraupis wetmorei*	SA
__Santa Marta Mountain Tanager	*Anisognathus melanogenys*	SA
__Lacrimose Mountain Tanager	*Anisognathus lacrymosus*	SA
__Scarlet-bellied Mountain Tanager	*Anisognathus igniventris*	SA
__Blue-winged Mountain Tanager	*Anisognathus somptuosus*	SA
__Black-chinned Mountain Tanager	*Anisognathus notabilis*	SA
__Grass-green Tanager	*Chlorornis riefferii*	SA
__Buff-breasted Mountain Tanager	*Dubusia taeniata*	SA
__Chestnut-bellied Mountain Tanager	*Delothraupis castaneoventris*	SA
__Diademed Tanager	*Stephanophorus diadematus*	SA
__Purplish-mantled Tanager	*Iridosornis porphyrocephalus*	SA
__Yellow-throated Tanager	*Iridosornis analis*	SA
__Golden-collared Tanager	*Iridosornis jelskii*	SA
__Golden-crowned Tanager	*Iridosornis rufivertex*	SA
__Yellow-scarfed Tanager	*Iridosornis reinhardti*	SA
__Fawn-breasted Tanager	*Pipraeidea melanonota*	SA
__Shrike-like Tanager	*Neothraupis fasciata*	SA
__Glistening-green Tanager	*Chlorochrysa phoenicotis*	SA
__Orange-eared Tanager	*Chlorochrysa calliparaea*	SA
__Multicolored Tanager	*Chlorochrysa nitidissima*	SA
__Plain-colored Tanager	*Tangara inornata*	LA
__Cabanis's Tanager	*Tangara cabanisi*	MA
__Grey-and-gold Tanager	*Tangara palmeri*	LA
__Turquoise Tanager	*Tangara mexicana*	SA
__White-bellied Tanager	*Tangara brasiliensis*	SA
__Paradise Tanager	*Tangara chilensis*	SA
__Seven-colored Tanager	*Tangara fastuosa*	SA
__Green-headed Tanager	*Tangara seledon*	SA
__Red-necked Tanager	*Tangara cyanocephala*	SA
__Brassy-breasted Tanager	*Tangara desmaresti*	SA
__Gilt-edged Tanager	*Tangara cyanoventris*	SA
__Blue-whiskered Tanager	*Tangara johannae*	SA
__Green-and-gold Tanager	*Tangara schrankii*	SA
__Emerald Tanager	*Tangara florida*	LA
__Golden Tanager	*Tangara arthus*	SA
__Silver-throated Tanager	*Tangara icterocephala*	LA
__Saffron-crowned Tanager	*Tangara xanthocephala*	SA
__Golden-eared Tanager	*Tangara chrysotis*	SA
__Flame-faced Tanager	*Tangara parzudakii*	SA
__Yellow-bellied Tanager	*Tangara xanthogastra*	SA
__Spotted Tanager	*Tangara punctata*	SA
__Speckled Tanager	*Tangara guttata*	MA
__Dotted Tanager	*Tangara varia*	SA
__Rufous-throated Tanager	*Tangara rufigula*	SA

INTERNATIONAL ENGLISH NAME	SCIENTIFIC NAME	REGION(S)
—Bay-headed Tanager	*Tangara gyrola*	LA
—Rufous-winged Tanager	*Tangara lavinia*	LA
—Burnished-buff Tanager	*Tangara cayana*	SA
—Lesser Antillean Tanager	*Tangara cucullata*	NA
—Black-backed Tanager	*Tangara peruviana*	SA
—Chestnut-backed Tanager	*Tangara preciosa*	SA
—Scrub Tanager	*Tangara vitriolina*	SA
—Green-capped Tanager	*Tangara meyerdeschauenseei*	SA
—Rufous-cheeked Tanager	*Tangara rufigenis*	SA
—Golden-naped Tanager	*Tangara ruficervix*	SA
—Metallic-green Tanager	*Tangara labradorides*	SA
—Blue-browed Tanager	*Tangara cyanotis*	SA
—Blue-necked Tanager	*Tangara cyanicollis*	SA
—Golden-hooded Tanager	*Tangara larvata*	LA
—Masked Tanager	*Tangara nigrocincta*	SA
—Spangle-cheeked Tanager	*Tangara dowii*	MA
—Green-naped Tanager	*Tangara fucosa*	MA
—Beryl-spangled Tanager	*Tangara nigroviridis*	SA
—Blue-and-black Tanager	*Tangara vassorii*	SA
—Black-capped Tanager	*Tangara heinei*	SA
—Sira Tanager	*Tangara phillipsi*	SA
—Silver-backed Tanager	*Tangara viridicollis*	SA
—Straw-backed Tanager	*Tangara argyrofenges*	SA
—Black-headed Tanager	*Tangara cyanoptera*	SA
—Opal-rumped Tanager	*Tangara velia*	SA
—Opal-crowned Tanager	*Tangara callophrys*	SA
—Swallow Tanager	*Tersina viridis*	LA
—White-bellied Dacnis	*Dacnis albiventris*	SA
—Black-faced Dacnis	*Dacnis lineata*	SA
—Yellow-tufted Dacnis	*Dacnis egregia*	SA
—Yellow-bellied Dacnis	*Dacnis flaviventer*	SA
—Turquoise Dacnis	*Dacnis hartlaubi*	SA
—Black-legged Dacnis	*Dacnis nigripes*	SA
—Scarlet-thighed Dacnis	*Dacnis venusta*	LA
—Blue Dacnis	*Dacnis cayana*	LA
—Viridian Dacnis	*Dacnis viguieri*	LA
—Scarlet-breasted Dacnis	*Dacnis berlepschi*	SA
—Short-billed Honeycreeper	*Cyanerpes nitidus*	SA
—Shining Honeycreeper	*Cyanerpes lucidus*	LA
—Purple Honeycreeper	*Cyanerpes caeruleus*	SA
—Red-legged Honeycreeper	*Cyanerpes cyaneus*	LA
—Green Honeycreeper	*Chlorophanes spiza*	LA
—Golden-collared Honeycreeper	*Iridophanes pulcherrima*	SA
—Sulphur-rumped Tanager	*Heterospingus rubrifrons*	MA
—Scarlet-browed Tanager	*Heterospingus xanthopygius*	LA
—Guira Tanager	*Hemithraupis guira*	SA
—Rufous-headed Tanager	*Hemithraupis ruficapilla*	SA
—Yellow-backed Tanager	*Hemithraupis flavicollis*	LA
—Black-and-yellow Tanager	*Chrysothlypis chrysomelas*	MA
—Scarlet-and-white Tanager	*Erythrothlypis salmoni*	SA
—Tit-like Dacnis	*Xenodacnis parina*	SA
—Chestnut-vented Conebill	*Conirostrum speciosum*	SA
—White-eared Conebill	*Conirostrum leucogenys*	LA

INTERNATIONAL ENGLISH NAME	SCIENTIFIC NAME	REGION(S)
__Bicolored Conebill	*Conirostrum bicolor*	SA
__Pearly-breasted Conebill	*Conirostrum margaritae*	SA
__Cinereous Conebill	*Conirostrum cinereum*	SA
__Tamarugo Conebill	*Conirostrum tamarugense*	SA
__White-browed Conebill	*Conirostrum ferrugineiventre*	SA
__Rufous-browed Conebill	*Conirostrum rufum*	SA
__Blue-backed Conebill	*Conirostrum sitticolor*	SA
__Capped Conebill	*Conirostrum albifrons*	SA
__Giant Conebill	*Oreomanes fraseri*	SA
__Cinnamon-bellied Flowerpiercer	*Diglossa baritula*	MA
__Slaty Flowerpiercer	*Diglossa plumbea*	MA
__Rusty Flowerpiercer	*Diglossa sittoides*	SA
__Chestnut-bellied Flowerpiercer	*Diglossa gloriosissima*	SA
__Glossy Flowerpiercer	*Diglossa lafresnayii*	SA
__Moustached Flowerpiercer	*Diglossa mystacalis*	SA
__Merida Flowerpiercer	*Diglossa gloriosa*	SA
__Black Flowerpiercer	*Diglossa humeralis*	SA
__Black-throated Flowerpiercer	*Diglossa brunneiventris*	SA
__Grey-bellied Flowerpiercer	*Diglossa carbonaria*	SA
__Venezuelan Flowerpiercer	*Diglossa venezuelensis*	SA
__White-sided Flowerpiercer	*Diglossa albilatera*	SA
__Scaled Flowerpiercer	*Diglossa duidae*	SA
__Greater Flowerpiercer	*Diglossa major*	SA
__Indigo Flowerpiercer	*Diglossopis indigotica*	SA
__Golden-eyed Flowerpiercer	*Diglossopis glauca*	SA
__Bluish Flowerpiercer	*Diglossopis caerulescens*	SA
__Masked Flowerpiercer	*Diglossopis cyanea*	SA
__Black-backed Bush Tanager	*Urothraupis stolzmanni*	SA
__Tanager Finch	*Oreothraupis arremonops*	SA
__Coal-crested Finch	*Charitospiza eucosma*	SA
__Many-colored Chaco Finch	*Saltatricula multicolor*	SA
__Black-masked Finch	*Coryphaspiza melanotis*	SA
__Grey Pileated Finch	*Coryphospingus pileatus*	SA
__Red Pileated Finch	*Coryphospingus cucullatus*	SA
__Crimson-breasted Finch	*Rhodospingus cruentus*	SA
__Black-hooded Sierra Finch	*Phrygilus atriceps*	SA
__Peruvian Sierra Finch	*Phrygilus punensis*	SA
__Grey-hooded Sierra Finch	*Phrygilus gayi*	SA
__Patagonian Sierra Finch	*Phrygilus patagonicus*	SA
__Mourning Sierra Finch	*Phrygilus fruticeti*	SA
__Plumbeous Sierra Finch	*Phrygilus unicolor*	SA
__Red-backed Sierra Finch	*Phrygilus dorsalis*	SA
__White-throated Sierra Finch	*Phrygilus erythronotus*	SA
__Ash-breasted Sierra Finch	*Phrygilus plebejus*	SA
__Carbonated Sierra Finch	*Phrygilus carbonarius*	SA
__Band-tailed Sierra Finch	*Phrygilus alaudinus*	SA
__White-bridled Finch	*Melanodera melanodera*	SA
__Yellow-bridled Finch	*Melanodera xanthogramma*	SA
__Slaty Finch	*Haplospiza rustica*	LA
__Uniform Finch	*Haplospiza unicolor*	SA
__Peg-billed Finch	*Acanthidops bairdii*	MA
__Black-crested Finch	*Lophospingus pusillus*	SA
__Grey-crested Finch	*Lophospingus griseocristatus*	SA

INTERNATIONAL ENGLISH NAME	SCIENTIFIC NAME	REGION(S)
—Long-tailed Reed Finch	*Donacospiza albifrons*	SA
—Gough Finch	*Rowettia goughensis*	AO
—Tristan Finch	*Nesospiza acunhae*	AO
—Wilkins's Finch	*Nesospiza wilkinsi*	AO
—White-winged Diuca Finch	*Diuca speculifera*	SA
—Common Diuca Finch	*Diuca diuca*	SA
—Short-tailed Finch	*Idiopsar brachyurus*	SA
—Cinereous Finch	*Piezorhina cinerea*	SA
—Slender-billed Finch	*Xenospingus concolor*	SA
—Great Inca Finch	*Incaspiza pulchra*	SA
—Rufous-backed Inca Finch	*Incaspiza personata*	SA
—Grey-winged Inca Finch	*Incaspiza ortizi*	SA
—Buff-bridled Inca Finch	*Incaspiza laeta*	SA
—Little Inca Finch	*Incaspiza watkinsi*	SA
—Bay-chested Warbling Finch	*Poospiza thoracica*	SA
—Bolivian Warbling Finch	*Poospiza boliviana*	SA
—Plain-tailed Warbling Finch	*Poospiza alticola*	SA
—Rufous-sided Warbling Finch	*Poospiza hypochondria*	SA
—Rusty-browed Warbling Finch	*Poospiza erythrophrys*	SA
—Cinnamon Warbling Finch	*Poospiza ornata*	SA
—Black-and-rufous Warbling Finch	*Poospiza nigrorufa*	SA
—Black-and-chestnut Warbling Finch	*Poospiza whitii*	SA
—Red-rumped Warbling Finch	*Poospiza lateralis*	SA
—Rufous-breasted Warbling Finch	*Poospiza rubecula*	SA
—Collared Warbling Finch	*Poospiza hispaniolensis*	SA
—Ringed Warbling Finch	*Poospiza torquata*	SA
—Black-capped Warbling Finch	*Poospiza melanoleuca*	SA
—Cinereous Warbling Finch	*Poospiza cinerea*	SA
—Chestnut-breasted Mountain Finch	*Poospizopsis caesar*	SA
—Cochabamba Mountain Finch	*Compsospiza garleppi*	SA
—Tucuman Mountain Finch	*Compsospiza baeri*	SA
—Stripe-tailed Yellow Finch	*Sicalis citrina*	SA
—Puna Yellow Finch	*Sicalis lutea*	SA
—Bright-rumped Yellow Finch	*Sicalis uropygialis*	SA
—Citron-headed Yellow Finch	*Sicalis luteocephala*	SA
—Greater Yellow Finch	*Sicalis auriventris*	SA
—Greenish Yellow Finch	*Sicalis olivascens*	SA
—Patagonian Yellow Finch	*Sicalis lebruni*	SA
—Orange-fronted Yellow Finch	*Sicalis columbiana*	SA
—Saffron Finch	*Sicalis flaveola*	SA
—Grassland Yellow Finch	*Sicalis luteola*	LA
—Raimondi's Yellow Finch	*Sicalis raimondii*	SA
—Sulphur-throated Finch	*Sicalis taczanowskii*	SA
—Wedge-tailed Grass Finch	*Emberizoides herbicola*	LA
—Lesser Grass Finch	*Emberizoides ypiranganus*	SA
—Duida Grass Finch	*Emberizoides duidae*	SA
—Pampa Finch	*Embernagra platensis*	SA
—Serra Finch	*Embernagra longicauda*	SA
—Blue-black Grassquit	*Volatinia jacarina*	LA
—Buffy-fronted Seedeater	*Sporophila frontalis*	SA
—Temminck's Seedeater	*Sporophila falcirostris*	SA
—Slate-colored Seedeater	*Sporophila schistacea*	LA
—Plumbeous Seedeater	*Sporophila plumbea*	SA

INTERNATIONAL ENGLISH NAME	SCIENTIFIC NAME	REGION(S)
__Variable Seedeater	*Sporophila corvina*	LA
__Grey Seedeater	*Sporophila intermedia*	SA
__Wing-barred Seedeater	*Sporophila americana*	SA
__Caqueta Seedeater	*Sporophila murallae*	SA
__Cinnamon-rumped Seedeater	*Sporophila torqueola*	MA
__White-collared Seedeater	*Sporophila morelleti*	NA, MA
__Rusty-collared Seedeater	*Sporophila collaris*	SA
__Lesson's Seedeater	*Sporophila bouvronides*	SA
__Lined Seedeater	*Sporophila lineola*	SA
__Black-and-white Seedeater	*Sporophila luctuosa*	SA
__Yellow-bellied Seedeater	*Sporophila nigricollis*	LA
__Double-collared Seedeater	*Sporophila caerulescens*	SA
__White-throated Seedeater	*Sporophila albogularis*	SA
__White-bellied Seedeater	*Sporophila leucoptera*	SA
__Parrot-billed Seedeater	*Sporophila peruviana*	SA
__Drab Seedeater	*Sporophila simplex*	SA
__Black-and-tawny Seedeater	*Sporophila nigrorufa*	SA
__Capped Seedeater	*Sporophila bouvreuil*	SA
__Ruddy-breasted Seedeater	*Sporophila minuta*	LA
__Tawny-bellied Seedeater	*Sporophila hypoxantha*	SA
__Rufous-rumped Seedeater	*Sporophila hypochroma*	SA
__Dark-throated Seedeater	*Sporophila ruficollis*	SA
__Marsh Seedeater	*Sporophila palustris*	SA
__Chestnut-bellied Seedeater	*Sporophila castaneiventris*	SA
__Chestnut Seedeater	*Sporophila cinnamomea*	SA
__Black-bellied Seedeater	*Sporophila melanogaster*	SA
__Chestnut-throated Seedeater	*Sporophila telasco*	SA
__Entre Rios Seedeater	*Sporophila zelichi*	SA
__Lesser Seed Finch	*Oryzoborus angolensis*	LA
__Nicaraguan Seed Finch	*Oryzoborus nuttingi*	MA
__Large-billed Seed Finch	*Oryzoborus crassirostris*	SA
__Great-billed Seed Finch	*Oryzoborus maximiliani*	SA
__Black-billed Seed Finch	*Oryzoborus atrirostris*	SA
__Blue Seedeater	*Amaurospiza concolor*	LA
__Blackish-blue Seedeater	*Amaurospiza moesta*	SA
__Carrizal Seedeater	*Amaurospiza carrizalensis*	SA
__Cuban Bullfinch	*Melopyrrha nigra*	NA
__White-naped Seedeater	*Dolospingus fringilloides*	SA
__Band-tailed Seedeater	*Catamenia analis*	SA
__Plain-colored Seedeater	*Catamenia inornata*	SA
__Paramo Seedeater	*Catamenia homochroa*	SA
__Cuban Grassquit	*Tiaris canorus*	NA
__Yellow-faced Grassquit	*Tiaris olivaceus*	NA, LA
__Dull-colored Grassquit	*Tiaris obscurus*	SA
__Black-faced Grassquit	*Tiaris bicolor*	NA, SA
__Sooty Grassquit	*Tiaris fuliginosus*	SA
__Yellow-shouldered Grassquit	*Loxipasser anoxanthus*	NA
__Puerto Rican Bullfinch	*Loxigilla portoricensis*	NA
__Greater Antillean Bullfinch	*Loxigilla violacea*	NA
__Lesser Antillean Bullfinch	*Loxigilla noctis*	NA
__Barbados Bullfinch	*Loxigilla barbadensis*	NA
__Orangequit	*Euneornis campestris*	NA
__St. Lucia Black Finch	*Melanospiza richardsoni*	NA

INTERNATIONAL ENGLISH NAME	SCIENTIFIC NAME	REGION(S)
—Large Ground Finch	*Geospiza magnirostris*	SA
—Medium Ground Finch	*Geospiza fortis*	SA
—Small Ground Finch	*Geospiza fuliginosa*	SA
—Sharp-beaked Ground Finch	*Geospiza difficilis*	SA
—Common Cactus Finch	*Geospiza scandens*	SA
—Large Cactus Finch	*Geospiza conirostris*	SA
—Vegetarian Finch	*Camarhynchus crassirostris*	SA
—Large Tree Finch	*Camarhynchus psittacula*	SA
—Medium Tree Finch	*Camarhynchus pauper*	SA
—Small Tree Finch	*Camarhynchus parvulus*	SA
—Woodpecker Finch	*Camarhynchus pallidus*	SA
—Mangrove Finch	*Camarhynchus heliobates*	SA
—Warbler Finch	*Certhidea olivacea*	SA
—Cocos Finch	*Pinaroloxias inornata*	MA
—Common Bush Tanager	*Chlorospingus ophthalmicus*	LA
—Tacarcuna Bush Tanager	*Chlorospingus tacarcunae*	LA
—Pirre Bush Tanager	*Chlorospingus inornatus*	MA
—Dusky Bush Tanager	*Chlorospingus semifuscus*	SA
—Sooty-capped Bush Tanager	*Chlorospingus pileatus*	MA
—Yellow-whiskered Bush Tanager	*Chlorospingus parvirostris*	SA
—Yellow-throated Bush Tanager	*Chlorospingus flavigularis*	LA
—Yellow-green Bush Tanager	*Chlorospingus flavovirens*	SA
—Ashy-throated Bush Tanager	*Chlorospingus canigularis*	LA
—Flame-colored Tanager	*Piranga bidentata*	MA
—Tooth-billed Tanager	*Piranga lutea*	LA
—Red Tanager	*Piranga flava*	SA
—Hepatic Tanager	*Piranga hepatica*	NA, MA
—Summer Tanager	*Piranga rubra*	NA, MA
—Rose-throated Tanager	*Piranga roseogularis*	MA
—Scarlet Tanager	*Piranga olivacea*	NA
—Western Tanager	*Piranga ludoviciana*	NA
—White-winged Tanager	*Piranga leucoptera*	LA
—Red-headed Tanager	*Piranga erythrocephala*	MA
—Red-hooded Tanager	*Piranga rubriceps*	SA
—Red-crowned Ant Tanager	*Habia rubica*	LA
—Red-throated Ant Tanager	*Habia fuscicauda*	LA
—Black-cheeked Ant Tanager	*Habia atrimaxillaris*	MA
—Sooty Ant Tanager	*Habia gutturalis*	SA
—Crested Ant Tanager	*Habia cristata*	SA
—Puerto Rican Tanager	*Nesospingus speculiferus*	NA
—Black-crowned Tanager	*Phaenicophilus palmarum*	NA
—Grey-crowned Tanager	*Phaenicophilus poliocephalus*	NA
—Western Chat-Tanager	*Calyptophilus tertius*	NA
—Eastern Chat-Tanager	*Calyptophilus frugivorus*	NA
—Western Spindalis	*Spindalis zena*	NA
—Hispaniolan Spindalis	*Spindalis dominicensis*	NA
—Puerto Rican Spindalis	*Spindalis portoricensis*	NA
—Jamaican Spindalis	*Spindalis nigricephala*	NA
—Rosy Thrush-Tanager	*Rhodinocichla rosea*	LA
—Plushcap	*Catamblyrhynchus diadema*	SA

INTERNATIONAL ENGLISH NAME	SCIENTIFIC NAME	REGION(S)
GROSBEAKS, SALTATORS & ALLIES	**Family Cardinalidae**	
__Dickcissel	*Spiza americana*	NA, LA
__Mexican Yellow Grosbeak	*Pheucticus chrysopeplus*	MA
__Black-thighed Grosbeak	*Pheucticus tibialis*	MA
__Southern Yellow Grosbeak	*Pheucticus chrysogaster*	SA
__Black-backed Grosbeak	*Pheucticus aureoventris*	SA
__Rose-breasted Grosbeak	*Pheucticus ludovicianus*	NA
__Black-headed Grosbeak	*Pheucticus melanocephalus*	NA
__Northern Cardinal	*Cardinalis cardinalis*	NA, MA
__Vermilion Cardinal	*Cardinalis phoeniceus*	SA
__Pyrrhuloxia	*Cardinalis sinuatus*	NA, MA
__Black-faced Grosbeak	*Caryothraustes poliogaster*	MA
__Yellow-green Grosbeak	*Caryothraustes canadensis*	SA
__Yellow-shouldered Grosbeak	*Parkerthraustes humeralis*	SA
__Crimson-collared Grosbeak	*Rhodothraupis celaeno*	MA
__Red-and-black Grosbeak	*Periporphyrus erythromelas*	SA
__Slate-colored Grosbeak	*Saltator grossus*	LA
__Black-throated Grosbeak	*Saltator fuliginosus*	SA
__Black-headed Saltator	*Saltator atriceps*	MA
__Buff-throated Saltator	*Saltator maximus*	LA
__Black-winged Saltator	*Saltator atripennis*	SA
__Green-winged Saltator	*Saltator similis*	SA
__Greyish Saltator	*Saltator coerulescens*	LA
__Orinoco Saltator	*Saltator orenocensis*	SA
__Thick-billed Saltator	*Saltator maxillosus*	SA
__Black-cowled Saltator	*Saltator nigriceps*	SA
__Golden-billed Saltator	*Saltator aurantiirostris*	SA
__Masked Saltator	*Saltator cinctus*	SA
__Black-throated Saltator	*Saltator atricollis*	SA
__Rufous-bellied Saltator	*Saltator rufiventris*	SA
__Lesser Antillean Saltator	*Saltator albicollis*	NA
__Streaked Saltator	*Saltator striatipectus*	LA
__Glaucous-blue Grosbeak	*Cyanoloxia glaucocaerulea*	SA
__Blue-black Grosbeak	*Cyanocompsa cyanoides*	LA
__Ultramarine Grosbeak	*Cyanocompsa brissonii*	SA
__Blue Bunting	*Cyanocompsa parellina*	MA
__Blue Grosbeak	*Passerina caerulea*	NA, MA
__Indigo Bunting	*Passerina cyanea*	NA
__Lazuli Bunting	*Passerina amoena*	NA
__Varied Bunting	*Passerina versicolor*	NA, MA
__Painted Bunting	*Passerina ciris*	NA
__Rose-bellied Bunting	*Passerina rositae*	MA
__Orange-breasted Bunting	*Passerina leclancherii*	MA

Index